BASIC Programming

A Complete Course Text

3rd Edition

B.J. Holmes, B.Sc., M.Sc., MBCS, Cert. Ed.

DP PUBLICATIONS LTD
Aldine Place, 142-144 Uxbridge Road
Shepherds Bush Green
London W12 8AA
1989

A CIP Catalogue Record for this book is available from the British Library.

First Edition	1982
Reprinted	1983
Second Edition	1985
Reprinted with corrections	1986
Third Edition	1989

ISBN 1 870941 33 0
Copyright B.J. HOLMES ©1989

All rights reserved
No part of this publication may be reproduced, stored in a retrieval system, or transmitted in any form or by any means, electronic, mechanical, photocopying, recording or otherwise, without the prior permission of the copyright owner.

Printed by Guernsey Press Company Ltd
Braye Road, Vale,
Guernsey, Channel Islands.

Contents

Preface

Aim

The aim of the book is to present to the reader the many facets of the BASIC language, in the context of a college-based course on computer programming. The book has already proved to be very popular with those students studying for computing examinations, where BASIC is the preferred language.

In addition, the home-computer enthusiast who wishes to progress beyond the *game-playing* stage, will also find this text invaluable in understanding how to program a computer.

Need

There are many books written on the BASIC language, however, the need as seen by the author, was for a book that offered the following advantages over other books.

BASIC Programming (third edition), forms a complete text on programming.

The text is useful for all computers that use BASIC, however, particular emphasis has been placed on the IBM PC and PC compatible computers, and the BBC model B and Electron computers.

A full coverage of the BASIC language is presented, with example programs being coded in Microsoft and BBC BASIC. The book is packed with 47 documented worked examples and 121 questions complete with answers.

Suitability

The book is equally suitable as a course text or a self-instruction text. The text teaches the *beginner* how to program correctly through designing, coding and testing. The development of programs and the language being taken in easily manageable steps, to enable the reader to build a comprehensive knowledge of the subject.

Within a single book there is enough information to provide a sound basis for any reader who wishes to go further in the subject and eventually develop and implement commercial, industrial and scientific computer systems.

The majority of chapters contain worked examples, used to illustrate the topics of the chapter, sections on keywords, and self-test questions for which the answers are available in Appendix I. The keywords section provides a concise summary of the contents of each chapter and acts as a check-list of topics that should be understood before progressing to the next chapter.

Primer questions (answers not available) are given in Appendix II to stimulate project work for college courses.

Notes on the Third Edition

In writing a new edition of the very popular BASIC Programming, the author has included the following changes to the second edition.

Old dialects of the BASIC language have been removed, and much emphasis has been placed on writing programs for PC compatibles using Microsoft BASIC, and BBC model B computers.

All the answers to the self-test questions are now available in Appendix I.

BJH
Oxford
March 1989

Bibliography

BASIC Programming – first edition, B.J. Holmes, DP Publications, 1982
BASIC Programming – second edition, B.J. Holmes, DP Publications, 1985
IBM Personal Computer BASIC, Microsoft, IBM, 1983
BBC Microcomputer User Guide, John Coll, BBC, 1982
SBAS Structured BASIC, Software Production Associates, Research Machines Ltd, 1984

1 Introduction

1.1 What is Basic?

1.1.1 History and Purpose

BASIC stands for Beginners Allpurpose Symbolic Instruction Code. The language was developed in 1964 at Dartmouth College, U.S.A. by Professors John Kemeny and Thomas Kurtz, as a means of teaching students a simple language for programming a computer.

The language can be used to solve problems covering a wide range of applications on many different types of digital computer.

In recent years many small and inexpensive microcomputers have come on to the market that use BASIC, therefore, it is no longer necessary to have access to a large and expensive computer in order to study the principles of programming. Because the BASIC language has been designed for ease of use and is readily available on most computers, program development can be achieved in the minimum time, with the minimum effort and often with the minimum cost. BASIC is known as a high-level language since it consists of statements written using English words and mathematical notation. The following example illustrates several BASIC statements in a computer program.

```
10  READ X, Y
20  IF X > 10 THEN STOP
30     LET Z = (A*B)/(C*D)
```

In general high-level languages are meant to be independent of any specific make of computer, however, many computer manufacturers tend to enhance languages with statements that are not compatible with other computers. Since BASIC is probably the only language that can be used on many small microcomputers the compatibility of the language between different makes of computer has suffered. The BASIC language has evolved into many different dialects, with each dialect having a common core of statements that resemble the 1960's version of the language, but also include many extra features that tend to be specific to one particular computer.

1.1.2 Dialects

Dialects of the language have evolved through extra features being introduced into the language to support such areas as structured programming, file processing, graphics and the use of sound. **This book has not been written for any one dialect, but deliberately written for use with any computer that uses BASIC.** However, the dialect differences between Microsoft BASIC as used on the IBM PC and PC compatibles and BBC/Electron BASIC are included.

1.2 Programming

Writing a computer program can be likened to writing a recipe for making a food dish. Each statement of a recipe indicates how the ingredients are to be prepared to produce a food dish whereas each statement in a computer program indicates how the data is to be processed in order to produce the results.

Programming can be broken down into three distinct tasks — designing (including testing the design), coding using a computer language and testing the program on a computer using test data. In designing a computer program the programmer will either receive or write a detailed specification of the solution to the problem and represent the detailed logical stages to this solution in the form of a descriptive language known as pseudocode or a diagramatic representation in the form of a flowchart or structure diagram of the procedures to be carried out. The program design is given a desk check to ensure that it is feasible and will produce the results required.

The coding process is a matter of translating each statement of the design into a statement or several statements in the computer language being used and thus building up a computer program. Once a program is coded it must be transferred to the computer and tested using suitable test data. If errors are found in the program they must be corrected (and the design corrected if necessary) and the program re-tested until it is error free.

1.2.1 Design

The majority of books published on the BASIC language tend to concentrate on BASIC coding and pay little attention to the design of programs prior to coding. Such books encourage the composition of programs at the keyboard which generally leads to poorly designed programs that often contain errors and become very difficult to maintain. Throughout this book the emphasis is on structured program design through the use of pseudocode (and in earlier chapters through flowcharts), desk checking designs with test data and finally coding the designs into a computer program. This method produces well designed, reliable and maintainable computer programs.

1.2.2 Coding

A great deal of emphasis has been placed on writing structured programs, the ingredients of structured programming — sequence, selection, repetition and procedures or subroutines have been described in separate chapters so that the importance of these features can be emphasised.

1.2.3 Testing and Implementation

A computer cannot recognise the statements found in the BASIC language without the aid of a translator. The majority of BASIC languages use a program called an *interpreter*, supplied by the computer manufacturer, to allow the computer to understand and obey the BASIC statements in a computer program. For the beginner the use of an interpreter over any other form of translator has distinct advantages. Many interpreters will inform of program errors during the process of obeying the program. This will be helpful during the initial stages of understanding how to program a computer and also at an advanced stage for speeding up the development time of a program. Program statements can be changed and their effects noted without having to re-translate the complete program or re-load the complete program into the computer.

After a program has been coded it must be transferred to a computer. In studying BASIC programming a detailed knowledge of the computer equipment being used is not necessary. The author has chosen to include descriptions of equipment that are common to most microcomputers in order that the reader may begin to understand the relationship between the computer equipment (hardware) and the programs and data (software).

1.3 Keywords

BASIC, high-level, dialect;
design, coding, testing;
interpreter, hardware, software.

2 A Computer Model

2.1 Introduction

This chapter introduces the reader to the major components of a computer and illustrates how data is input, processed and output in a computer system.

2.2 A Computer Model

Figure 2.1 illustrates a simple computer model containing three units. An input unit which allows data and computer programs to be input into the computer model. A central processing unit (C.P.U.) that is used to store programs and data, and obey the instructions contained in a program. An output unit which allows processed information to be output from the computer model.

A computer model, therefore consists not only of the three major units described, but also contains data, programs and information.

2.2.1 Programs, Data and Information

A **program** is a series of coded instructions for the computer to obey and represents a logical solution to a problem.

Data is any representation of a fact that can be communicated or manipulated by some process. For example, in a business the number of hours worked by employees or the level of items of stock. Data is input to a computer, processed under the direction of a program into **information** that is output in the form, for example, of a payslip or a report on out of stock items.

2.2.2 A Digital Computer

A digital computer is an electronic machine capable of storing and obeying the instructions in a program at a very high speed. For example an instruction can be obeyed in one hundred millionth of one second. The term digital implies the manner in which the data and programs are represented and handled within a machine.

The heart of a digital computer is the **central processing unit** (C.P.U) and **main memory**. The C.P.U. contains two sub-units; the **arithmetic and logic unit** (A.L.U) performs the processes of arithmetic and logical operations on data and the **control unit** fetches the program instructions from main memory, interprets and obeys them and coordinates the flow of data about the computer system.

The main memory is used to temporarily store programs and data. A computer can only obey programs that are stored in the main memory.

2.2.3 Input and Output Units

The most popular input unit used in computers is a keyboard. The keyboard is very similar to that of a typewriter keyboard and data is input to the computer by depressing the appropriate keys on the keyboard. A television screen can also be used to display to the user the data that is being typed into the computer. Such a display is meant to provide a means of visually checking that the correct data is being entered.

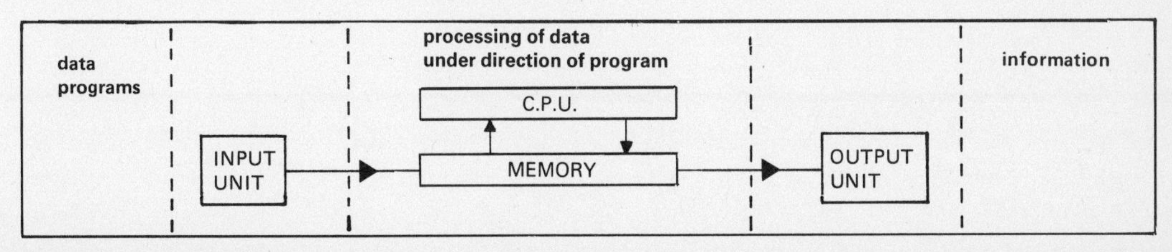

Figure 2.1 A computer model

The television screen has a dual function, as well as displaying data that is typed at a keyboard it is also used as an output unit in its own right. Information that has been processed by the computer can also be displayed on the screen. A single device called a visual display unit (V.D.U.) that combines both a keyboard (and screen) input unit and a screen output unit. Such devices are very common as input/output units on computers other than for the *home* market.

2.3 Data types

Data is classified into two types *numbers* and *character strings*. For example the numbers

+16 −32.47 82 9.1763 −1259

all represent numeric data, whilst the groups of characters

"AVERAGE VALUE" "123 HILL VIEW RD." "FRED WILSON"

all represent character string data.

There is nothing new about numeric data since we all use numbers in the format shown. The numbers are of two different types, integers (whole numbers) +16, 82, −1259 and real numbers (numbers that contain a decimal fraction) −32.47, 9.1763. Both types of numbers can contain a sign + or − however, if the number is positive then the + sign can be omitted. No spaces or commas are permitted in either type of number.

Character string data will probably be new to most readers. A character string is normally written between identical inverted commas " . . . . . ." and can contain a mixture of digits, letters of the alphabet or special characters (e.g. punctuation characters).

A computer is capable of storing both numbers and character strings in its memory.

2.4 Memory

The memory of a computer is made up from many thousands of storage cells called *bytes*. Each byte has a unique address in the memory of a computer.

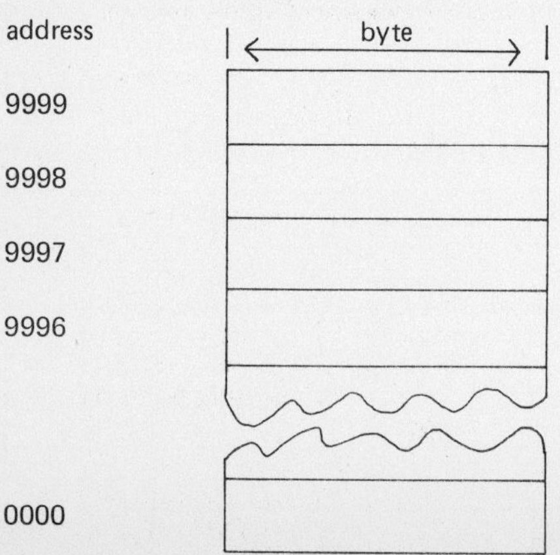

Several bytes of memory are grouped together to store either numbers or character strings.

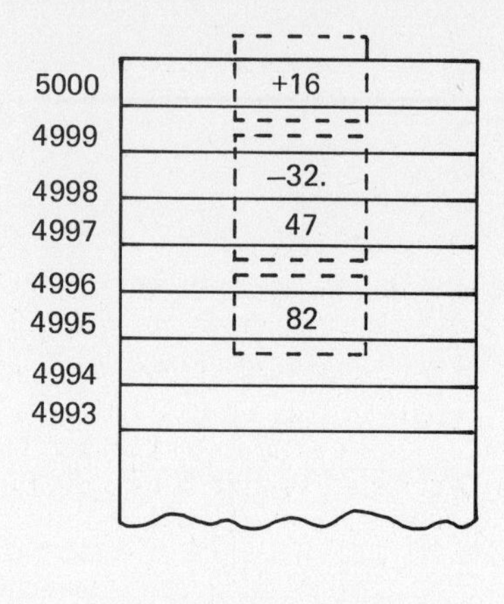

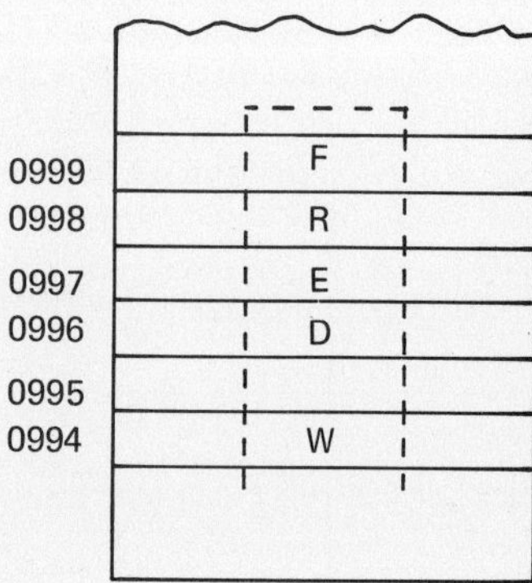

Data can be thought of as occupying areas of the computer's memory in the same way as people occupy houses in a street. To distinguish different families in different houses we could use either the surname of the family or the number of the house. To distinguish data in different areas of memory we could give the data a name (data-name) or use the numeric memory address where the data is stored. In the BASIC language it is much easier to refer to data by a name and let the computer do the work of finding out where in memory the data is stored.

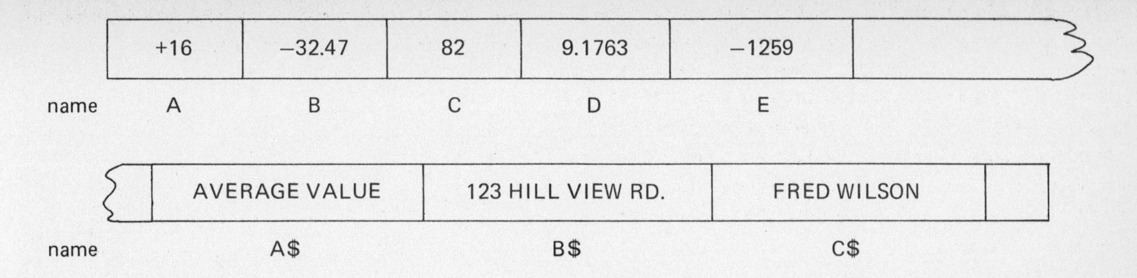

2.5 Input of data

The majority of microcomputers have an inbuilt keyboard to allow a user to type information into the memory of a computer. When data is to be input into the memory of a computer, the computer will wait for the user to type a value, number or character string, at the keyboard and then store that value at the data-name specified. For example the statement

input age

would allow a user to type a number at the keyboard, say 16, and this value would be stored in the memory of the computer under the data-name **age**. Similarly, the statement

input town

would allow a user to type a character string at the keyboard, say "WINCHESTER" and this value would be stored in the main memory of the computer under the data-name **town.**

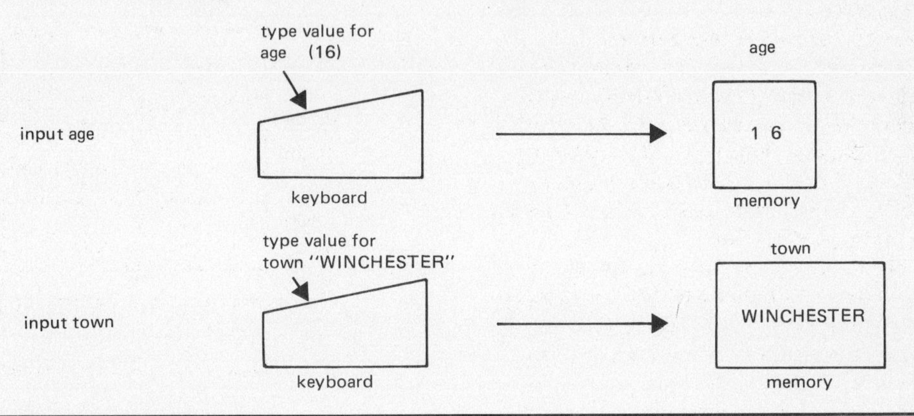

2.6 Output of Information

A method of obtaining information from the computer is to have the computer connected to a monitor (television) and get the computer to print information on a screen. The contents of an area of memory can be printed on a screen by stating which area of memory (data-name) is to be output. For example the statement

print age

would output the contents of the data-name **age**, 16, at the screen of a monitor. Similarly, the statement

print town

would output the contents of the data-name **town**, WINCHESTER, at the screen of the monitor.

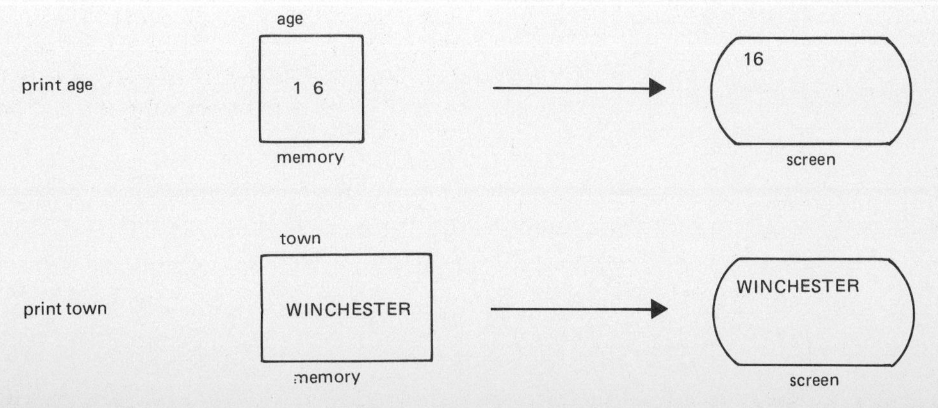

The reader should not be confused that when using a keyboard to input data, the data is also displayed on the screen. This has nothing to do with the output of information from a data-name but merely informs the user of the data that has been entered at the keyboard.

2.7 Calculations on numeric data

Numeric data can be used in arithmetic so that the contents of data-names will change according to the computation being carried out.

For example, the data-names **number-1** and **number-2** contain the values 6 and 13 respectively. The statement number-3 = number-1 + number-2 would cause the contents of **number-1** and **number-2** to be added together and the result, 19, to be stored under data-name **number-3**. The original contents of **number-3** is lost. This operation can be summarised by considering the contents of memory before the addition, then after the addition.

	number-1	number-2	number-3
before	6	13	12
after	6	13	~~12~~ 19

From this example **number-3** contained an arbitrary value of 12, a result from a previous calculation perhaps, however, this value was lost when the computer was instructed that **number-3** was to contain the result of adding **number-1** to **number-2**. The original values of **number-1** and **number-2** remain unchanged after the addition.

The reader must never assume that because a data-name has not been used prior to a calculation, as in the case of **number-3**, that it will either not contain data or that numeric data will initially be set to the value of zero.

Similar before and after situations can be applied to other computations.

2.7 (cont.)

A = B + C + D

	A	B	C	D
before	15	2	3	4
after	~~15~~ 9	2	3	4

X = Y – Z

	X	Y	Z
before	21	16	9
after	~~21~~ 7	16	9

ALPHA = BETA * EPSILON

	ALPHA	BETA	EPSILON
before	20	3	8
after	~~20~~ 24	3	8

mean = sum / count

	mean	sum	count
before	26	360	10
after	~~26~~ 36	360	10

Note: the symbol * means multiplication and the symbol / means division.

count = count + 1

	count
before	9
after	~~9~~ 10

Note: the original value of count is increased by 1 and the result 10 is stored back in count changing the original value from 9 to 10.

Y = 2 * X – 3

	X	Y
before	5	6
after	5	~~6~~ 7

Note: in these examples the data-name that is used to store the result of the calculation must be the only data-name to the left of the = sign.

2.8 Dialect Differences

Table 2.1 compares the differences in the size of numbers, strings, and computer memory between two different computers and hence dialects of BASIC.

A character is stored in 1 byte of memory in a coded format. The coded representation of each character is given in table 2.2, which illustrates the American Standard Code for Information Interchange (ASCII). This is a standard code used for exchanging information among data processing systems and associated equipment. An ASCII file is a text file where the characters are represented in ASCII codes.

computer model	integer range	real range	smallest real	max string length	memory size
IBM PC	+32767 to −32768	$\pm 1.7 \times 10^{38}$	2.9×10^{-39}	255	64Kb
BBC/Electron	+2147483647 −2147483648	$\pm 2 \times 10^{38}$	1.7×10^{-39}	255	64Kb

Note: string length is given in characters and memory size in Kilobytes Kb.

Table 2.1

ASCII CHARACTER CODES.

DECIMAL	CHAR.	DECIMAL	CHAR.	DECIMAL	CHAR.
000	NUL	043	+	086	V
001	SOH	044	'	087	W
002	STX	045	–	088	X
003	ETX	046	.	089	Y
004	EOT	047	/	090	Z
005	ENQ	048	0	091	[
006	ACK	049	1	092	\
007	BEL	050	2	093	]
008	BS	051	3	094	↑
009	HT	052	4	095	↓
010	LF	053	5	096	@
011	VT	054	6	097	a
012	FF	055	7	098	b
013	CR	056	8	099	c
014	SO	057	9	100	d
015	SI	058	:	101	e
016	DLE	059	;	102	f
017	DC1	060	<	103	g
018	DC2	061	=	104	h
019	DC3	062	>	105	i
020	DC4	063	?	106	j
021	NAK	064	'	107	k
022	SYN	065	A	108	l
023	ETB	066	B	109	m
024	CAN	067	C	110	n
025	EM	068	D	111	o
026	SUB	069	E	112	p
027	ESC	070	F	113	q
028	S	071	G	114	r
029	GS	072	H	115	s
030	RS	073	I	116	t
031	US	074	J	117	u
032	SP	075	K	118	v
033	!	076	L	119	w
034	''	077	M	120	x
035	#	078	N	121	y
036	$	079	O	122	z
037	%	080	P	123	(
038	&	081	Q	124	:
039	'	082	R	125	)
040	(	083	S	126	∿
041	)	084	T	127	DEL
042	*	085	U		

Table 2.2

2.9 Keywords

Input unit, output unit, central processing unit;
programs, data, information;
digital computer, main memory, arithmetic and logic unit, control unit;
keyboard, screen, visual display unit;
integer, real, character string;
byte, address, ASCII.

2.10 Questions

1 From your knowledge of computers in every-day life describe three input devices and three output devices not mentioned in this chapter.

2 In booking a holiday through a computerised reservation system describe typical items of data and distinguish these from information.

3 Classify the following data into the types integer, real and character string.

49 36.874 −144.26 "1234" "ZERO"
"123 ST. CLEMENT AVE." 290491

4 Which items of data contain errors and what is the nature of the error?

− 42.760 − 128.21 "AVERAGE "INPUT SURNAME"
0.0147− 9,3238 £761.54

5 What are the values of the following data-names after the execution of the respective instructions (to execute means to obey).

Instruction				
B = A C = A D = A	A 36	B 98	C 45	D 29
D = A + B + C + D	A 10	B 14	C 29	D 36
C = A + B	A 24	B 98	C 23	
Y = X − Y	X 17	Y 32		
X = U − V − W	U 29	V 32	W 84	X 78
B = A − 3	A 16	B 22		
Z = X * Y	X 18	Y 3	Z 27	
B = B / A	A 6	B 42		

6 Using table 2.2 what are the ASCII codes for the following characters?

A M * a m / ? BEL NUL

3 Program Design

3.1 Introduction

This chapter introduces the design of computer programs using a descriptive pseudocode and as an alternative approach the flowchart. The chapter also describes how to choose test data and check the validity of a program design.

3.2 A Computer Program

In order to change the values stored in memory under data-names it is necessary to provide the computer with a list of instructions. These instructions tell the computer what data to input (the names of the memory areas not the actual values), how to calculate the results from the data already stored in the memory and what information to output. A list of such instructions is known as a **computer program.** The computer will obey each instruction in the order that the instructions are written until it is instructed to stop. The computer will start at the first instruction in the program and work through to the last instruction obeying each instruction in turn.

3.3 Program Design

Before a computer program is coded into a computer language, such as BASIC, it should be designed on paper. The purpose of the design is for the programmer to organise into a logical order the necessary stages in the solution to a problem. When the design is complete it is given a *desk check* to see whether it is feasible and will produce the predicted results. **Only when the design is logically correct should the programmer attempt to convert the design into program code.**

In designing a computer program the programmer is providing working documentation relevant to a specific program. After the program has been used over a period of time it may require changes made to it. The changes to the program may have to be made by a different programmer. The program design documents give the person who has to change (maintain) the program a better insight into what various parts of the program are meant to do. Without a program design the maintenance programmer must rely on tracing through the program code to determine what each section of code does, a practice that can be very time consuming.

There are many different methods for designing computer programs, two such methods, the use of pseudocode and flowcharts, will be explained in this chapter and expanded in later chapters.

3.3.1 Pseudocode

A pseudocode provides a means of designing a computer program independently of any make of computer or computer language. The pseudocode statements clearly state what each step on the solution to a problem should be. For example a design for a computer program to input two numbers at a keyboard, calculate the sum of the numbers and output the sum to the screen of a monitor can be expressed in the following pseudocode.

```
input number-1
input number-2
number-3 = number-1 + number -2
print number-3
stop
```

3.3.2 Flowcharts

The older traditional method of designing a computer program is by drawing a flowchart. Flowcharts have become much less popular in recent years with the emergence of methods that are more compatible with the ideas of structured programming. However, many teachers of programming find the flowchart a useful aid in the early stages of teaching programming techniques. Furthermore, many examination boards continue to set questions in Computer Studies papers that require a knowledge of flowcharting techniques. For these reasons the designs to computer programs found in the earlier chapters will consist of both pseudocode and flowchart. However, in later chapters the use of flowcharts will be dropped and only pseudocode will be used at the design stage.

A flowchart is composed of symbols that represent specific activities, for example.

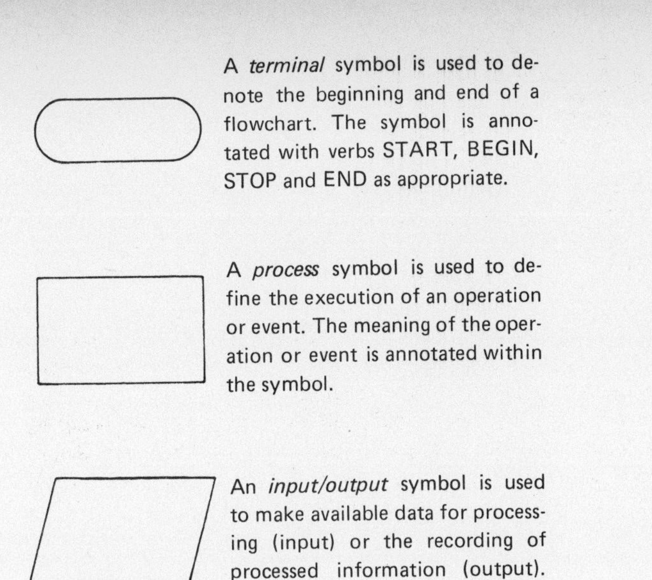

A *terminal* symbol is used to denote the beginning and end of a flowchart. The symbol is annotated with verbs START, BEGIN, STOP and END as appropriate.

A *process* symbol is used to define the execution of an operation or event. The meaning of the operation or event is annotated within the symbol.

An *input/output* symbol is used to make available data for processing (input) or the recording of processed information (output).

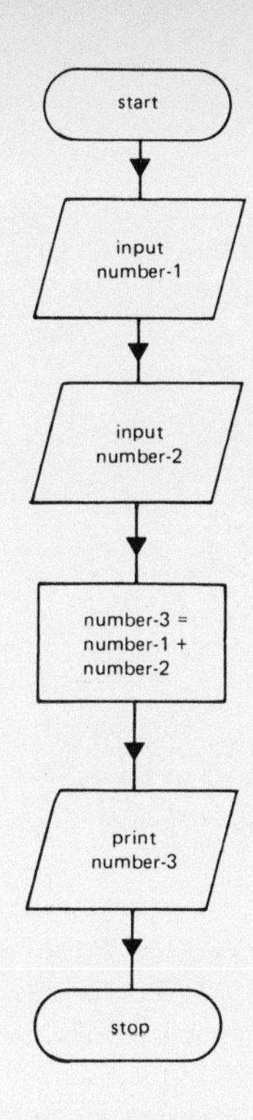

The symbols are connected by arrowed lines indicating the direction of flow. The direction of flow is generally from the top to the bottom of a page. The example used to illustrate pseudocode can be used to illustrate a program design using a flowchart.

3.3.3 Computer Model

If number-1 was chosen to be 9, and number-2 was chosen to be 16 then the program design would have the following meaning in terms of the computer model described in chapter 2.

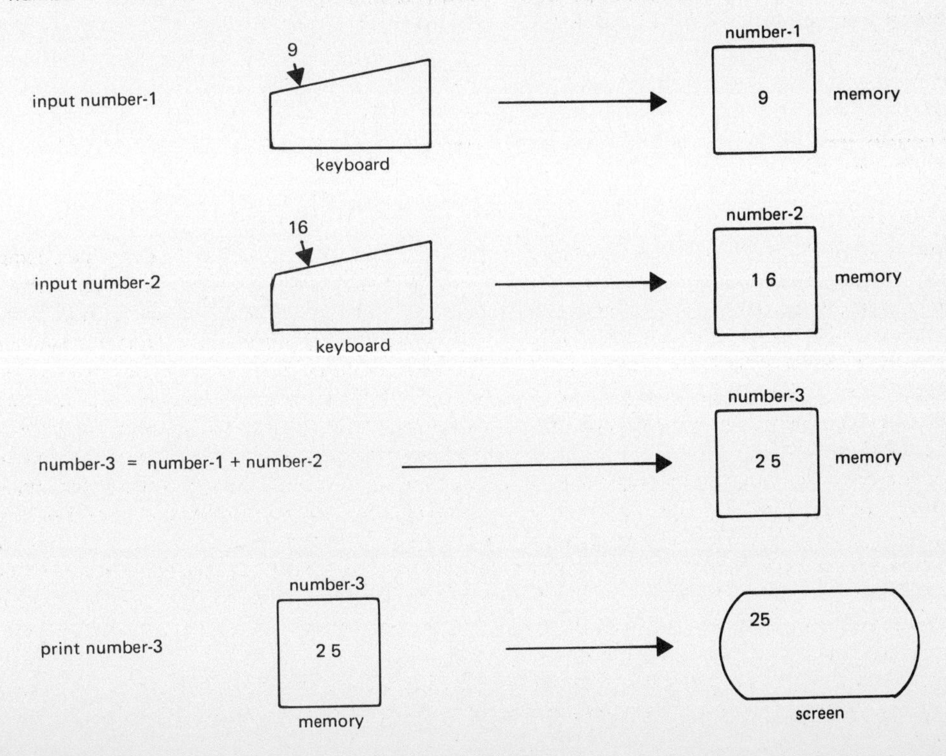

3.4 Test Data and a Desk Check

A programmer having designed a solution to a problem must verify that the design is correct before proceeding with the coding. In order to verify that the design represents a correct solution to a problem it is necessary to follow through the design using suitable test data. The outcome of such a check will be the test data and results summarised in a tabular format.

In the last example the desk check on the design can be summarised as:

Data-names	number-1	number-2	number-3
Contents	9	16	25

When choosing test data the following points should be kept in mind.

The type and nature of the data is representative of the problem.
Numerical data, where applicable, should be chosen for ease of calculation.
Data is meaningful and within well defined ranges. This assumes that the design being tested will always use valid data. However, this is not always the case since some designs will be specifically written to trap bad data. **In such circumstances the data must be chosen to cover all eventualities.**

3.5 Worked Example

Design a program to input three values for the prices of newpapers, calculate the total price and the average (mean) price and output both the total price and the average price.

3.5.1 Pseudocode

```
input price-1
input price-2
input price-3
total = price-1 + price-2 + price-3
average = total / 3
print total
print average
stop
```

3.5.2 Flowchart

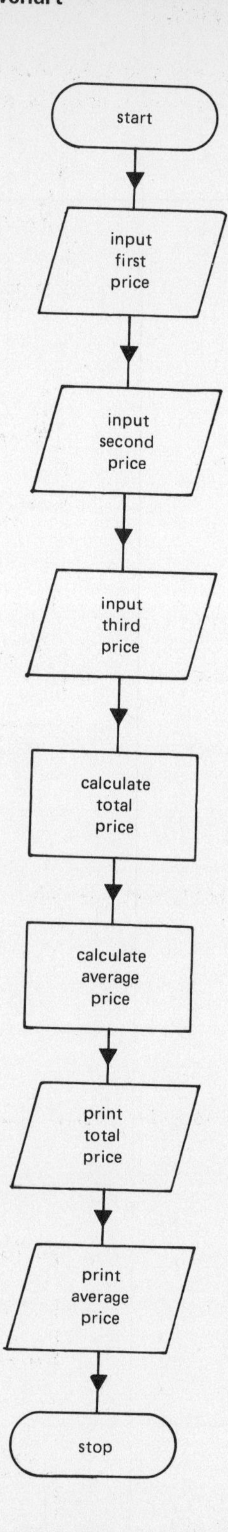

3.5.3 Computer Model

The program design would have the following meaning in terms of the computer model described in chapter 2.

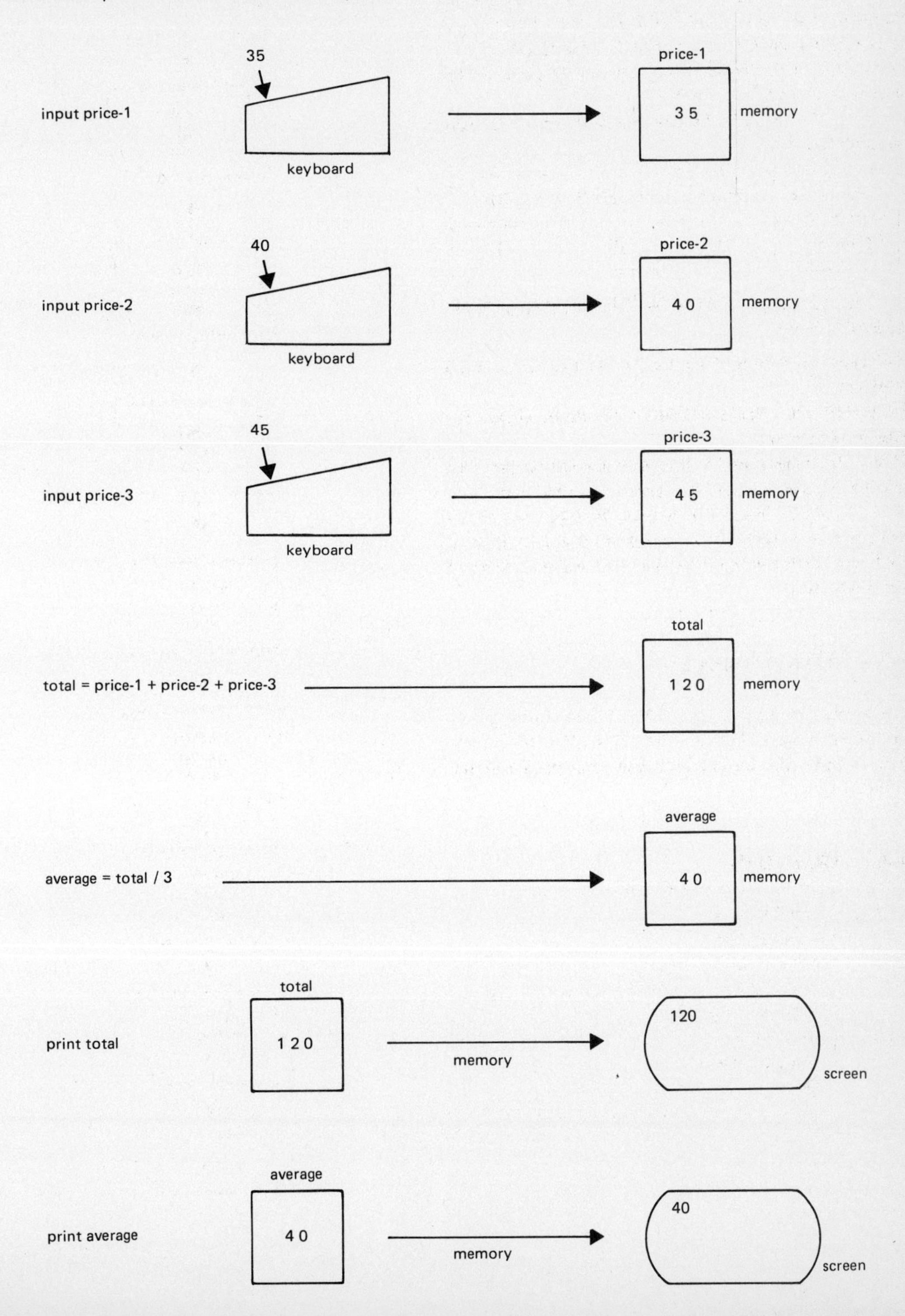

3.5.4 Test Data and Desk Check

Test data: newspaper price-1 35p
newspaper price-2 40p
newspaper price-3 45p

Summary of desk check.

Data-names	price-1	price-2	price-3	total	average
Contents	35	40	45	120	40

3.6 Worked Example

Design a program to input your name, a friend's name and telephone number. Get the computer to print a message to you to phone your friend on the number given. For example the values that are input could be:

your name	JIM
friend's name	SUSIE
telephone number	WATFORD 328

and the message that is output could be:

HI JIM
'PHONE SUSIE
ON WATFORD 328

3.6.1 Pseudocode

```
input your name
input friend's name
input friend's telephone number
print first line of message
print second line of message
print third line of message
stop
```

3.6.2 Flowchart

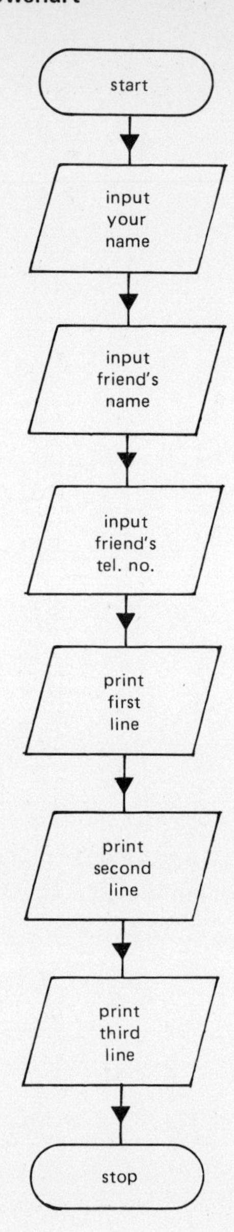

3.6.3 Computer Model

The program would have the following meaning in terms of the computer model described in chapter 2.

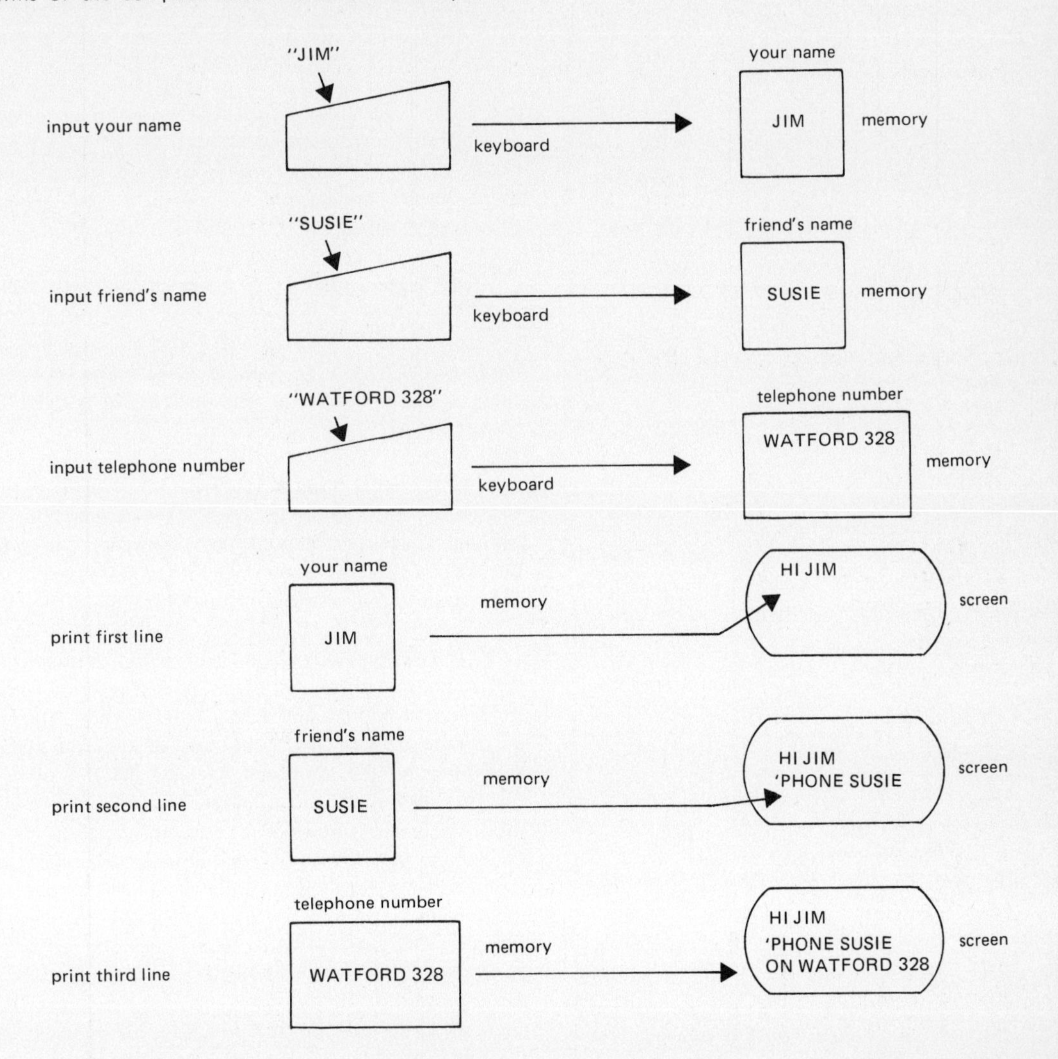

From this example it is clear that the computer can print information that has not been directly stored in the memory of the computer by the programmer. The words HI, 'PHONE and ON appear in the message yet have no data-names. This technique will be explained in chapter 4.

3.6.4 Test Data and Desk Check

Test data: JIM
SUSIE
WATFORD 328

Summary of desk check.

Data-name	your name	friend's name	telephone number
Contents	JIM	SUSIE	WATFORD 328

3.7 Keywords

Program, pseudocode, flowchart;
test data, desk check.

3.8 Questions

In your solutions to the following questions invent test data and complete a desk check table for each of your program designs. If the results of your desk check do not give you expected results then go back and re-design your program.

1 Design a program to print a menu with the following format.

RESTAURANT MENU FOR THURSDAY

STARTER: MELON OR SOUP OR FRUIT JUICE
MAIN COURSE: BEEF AND YORKSHIRE PUDDING WITH VEGETABLES
DESSERT: FRESH FRUIT OR CHEESE AND BISCUITS

THANK YOU FOR YOUR CUSTOM

The program should allow the name of a day in the week, descriptions of starter, main course and dessert to be typed at the keyboard of the computer before the menu is printed.

2 Design a program to input your name, height in inches and weight in stones, convert the height to centimentres and weight to kilogrammes and print the following information.

PERSONAL DETAILS
NAME: JOSEPH JONES
HEIGHT (cm): 180
WEIGHT (Kg): 75

3 Design a program to input at the keyboard of a computer a temperature in degrees Fahrenheit and output to a screen the equivalent temperature in degrees Centigrade. The formula for temperature conversion is:

Centigrade temp = (Fahrenheit temp – 32) * (5 / 9)

4 Design a program to input both the length and width of a garden lawn at the keyboard of a computer, calculate the area of the lawn and cost of turfing the lawn. Assume the cost of turf is £0.50 per m^2. Output the area of the lawn and the cost of turfing this area at the screen of a monitor.

5 Design a program to input the radius of a circle at the keyboard of a computer, calculate the circumference and area of the circle and output these values to the screen of a monitor. Assume the circumference of a circle is 2*PI*R, and the area of a circle is PI*R*R where PI = 3.142.

6 Design a program to input the length, width and depths at the deepest and shallowest ends of a swimming pool at the keyboard of a computer. Calculate the volume of water required to fill the swimming pool and output to the screen of a monitor this value.

7 The dimensions of a living room in a house are 7m length, 5m width and 2.5m height. The room has a window area of $3m^2$ and a door area of $1.5m^2$. Design a program to input at the keyboard of a computer the dimensions of the room and calculate the area of the available wall space. If wallpaper is sold in rolls 0.6m wide and 8m long at a cost of £2.50 per roll, calculate the number of rolls necessary to wallpaper the walls of the room and the total cost of the wallpaper. Output to the screen of a monitor the area of the walls, number of rolls of paper required to cover the walls and the total cost of the wallpaper. (You may assume a cost for a part roll of paper).

Modify your program design to cater for any room of the same shape but having different window and door areas. Also cater for different wallpaper sizes and costs.

4 Elementary BASIC – a sequence

4.1 Introduction

The purpose of this chapter is to introduce the reader to four statements in the BASIC language that will enable the program designs developed in the last chapter to be coded into computer programs.

4.2 Data-names

Throughout the last chapter the names given to data stored in memory were chosen to represent the nature of the data e.g. your name, friend's name, telephone number etc. In the BASIC language there are restrictions on the way in which data-names are composed. The **minimum** requirement for the composition of data-names is:

for numeric data-names:
- a single letter of the alphabet (A – Z), or
- a single letter (A – Z) followed by a single digit (0 – 9),

for character string data-names:
- a single letter (A – Z) followed by a dollar symbol $.

For example A, B, C0, D3, X9, Z1 are all legal numeric data-names, and A$, B$, C$ are all legal character string data-names.

Whenever the programmer is restricted to using data-names that only contain several characters it is advisable to write a glossary of the data-names used in the design of the program and the corresponding data-names used in coding the computer program into BASIC. For example:

Glossary

number-1	N1
number-2	N2
number-3	N3

Many modern dialects of BASIC will permit data-names to contain enough characters for the name to be meaningful. Examples on the extension of the rules for the composition of data-names will be given towards the end of this chapter under the headings of *Dialect Differences.*

4.3 Four Basic Statements

The functions of the BASIC verbs INPUT, PRINT and STOP are identical to the verbs input, print and stop described in the pseudocode in chapter 3. The only minor modification is to the calculation statement. All statements of this nature should be preceded by the verb LET, however, this restriction does not apply to some dialects where the use of LET is optional.

4.3.1 Notation

In the description of the formats of the BASIC statements that follow in this and subsequent chapters the following notation will be used.

All reserved words are printed in uppercase letters.

The use of square brackets [ ] indicates that items within the square brackets can be omitted.

The use of braces { } indicates that a choice must be made between the various contents of the braces. If the braces contain a single entry then no choice is implied.

The use of ellipsis . . . . . . represents the position at which the user elects repetition of a portion of the format. The portion of the format that may be repeated is as follows. Given . . . . . in a format, scanning right to left, determine the] or } delimiter immediately to the left of the . . . . .; continue scanning right to left and determine the logically matching [or { delimiter; the . . . . applies to the portion of the format between the determined pair of delimiters.

4.3.2 Input

The INPUT statement allows a value, numeric or character string, to be typed at the keyboard of a computer and stored in the computer's memory at the data-name specified.

Format: INPUT data-name

Examples: INPUT X — will enable a numeric value for X to be entered at a keyboard and stored in the memory under the data-name X.

INPUT A$ will enable a string value for A$ to be entered at a keyboard and stored in the memory under the data-name A$.

When the computer executes (obeys) an INPUT statement it will output to the screen of a terminal a prompt, either ? or ! depending upon the system being used, and wait for the user to enter a value at the keyboard. Normally the depression of either a RETURN key or ENTER key is a signal to the computer that the data entry is now complete and the computer can continue with the execution of the next instruction in the program.

When several INPUT statements are used in a program to allow values to be assigned to different data-names the computer generated prompt (e.g ? or !) does not convey the nature of the data to be entered. Therefore, to avoid any confusion all INPUT statements should contain programmer designed prompts. The format of the INPUT statement to allow for programmer designed prompts will vary between dialects of the language, however, the following format is common.

Format: INPUT literal, data-name

Examples: INPUT "COST OF NEWSPAPER", N1

will output to the terminal the prompt COST OF NEWSPAPER and enable a numeric value for N1 to be entered at the keyboard and stored under the data-name N1.

INPUT "WHAT IS YOUR NAME?", N$

will output to the terminal the prompt WHAT IS YOUR NAME? and enable a string value for N$ to be entered at a keyboard and stored in the memory under the data-name N$.

4.3.3 Print

The PRINT statement allows a literal or the contents of the data-name specified to be displayed on the screen of a monitor or visual display unit.

Format: PRINT { literal / data-name }

Examples: PRINT "COMPUTING IS FUN"

will display the literal COMPUTING IS FUN on the screen and return the cursor to the left-hand end of the next line. A cursor is a marker on the screen that indicates the position of the next character to be displayed on the screen.

PRINT N

will display a value for N on the screen; if N contains the numeric value 145 then this value will be displayed.

PRINT A$

will display a value for A$ on the screen; if A$ contains the string value JIM then this value will be displayed.

The literal and data-name used in PRINT statements can be combined into one statement. For example:

PRINT "NAME OF PAPER-BOY", N$

would output to a screen:

NAME OF PAPER-BOY JIM

if the value for N$ was JIM.

PRINT without a literal and/or data-name will output a blank line.

4.3.4 Let

The LET statement evaluates an arithmetic expression and stores the result, or assigns either a literal or a data-name to another data-name. Note, structured BASIC uses the symbol := (becomes) in place of = (equal to).

Format: LET data-name-1 = { expression / literal / data-name-2 }

4.3.4 (cont.)

Examples:		
	LET A = B	will assign to A the value of B; if B contains 36, A will contain 36.
	LET M = 3	will assign to M the value 3.
	LET N$ = "TRUE"	will assign to N$ the value TRUE
	LET X = A + B	will evaluate A + B and assign to X the result; if A contains 3 and B contains 7 then X will contain 10.

4.3.5 Stop

The STOP statement is used to terminate the execution of a program.

Format: STOP

4.4 The format of a Basic Program

A computer program is a set of instructions to be obeyed by the computer. The order in which the instructions are written is of vital importance, since the computer will start executing (obeying) a program from the first instruction, then progress to the second instruction and so on, until re-directed by a loop to repeat a sequence of instructions or a selection to change or avoid a sequence of instructions. The most common format for a BASIC program is:

One instruction or statement per line.
Each line must begin with a line-number.
Line-numbers are unsigned positive integers, the allowable range varies between computers, however, 1 through 9999 is common.
Line-numbers should increase in, say, steps of 10 to allow for the insertion of extra lines at a later stage of program development.

4.5 Program Coding

The program design given in 3.3 to input two numbers, calculate and output the sum can be coded into BASIC as follows.

The data-names given in the program design should be converted to BASIC data-names as illustrated in the glossary.

number-1	N1
number-2	N2
number-3	N3

4.5 (cont.)

Program design (pseudocode) → BASIC computer program

```
input number-1                      ——►  10 INPUT "FIRST NUMBER", N1
input number-2                      ——►  20 INPUT "SECOND NUMBER", N2
number-3 = number-1 + number-2      ——►  30 LET N3 = N1 +N2
print number-3                      ——►  40 PRINT "SUM", N3
stop                                ——►  50 STOP
```

The program design given in 3.5 to input three values for the prices of newspapers and calculate and output the total price and average price can now be coded into BASIC in a similar manner. As with the last example the data-names given in the program design should be converted to BASIC data-names as illustrated in the glossary.

price-1	P1
price-2	P2
price-3	P3
total	T
average	A

Program design (pseudocode) → BASIC computer program

```
input price-1                         ——►  10 INPUT "FIRST PRICE", P1
input price-2                         ——►  20 INPUT "SECOND PRICE", P2
input price-3                         ——►  30 INPUT "THIRD PRICE", P3
total = price-1 + price-2 + price-3   ——►  40 LET T = P1 + P2 + P3
average = total / 3                   ——►  50 LET A = T / 3
print total                           ——►  60 PRINT "TOTAL COST", T
print average                         ——►  70 PRINT "AVERAGE COST", A
stop                                  ——►  80 STOP
```

In the following example the flowchart developed for the program design given in 3.6 to input your name, and a friend's name and telephone number, and print a message to you to 'phone your friend on the number given can be coded into BASIC. The glossary is derived from the names used in the flowchart.

your name	N$
friend's name	F$
telephone number	T$

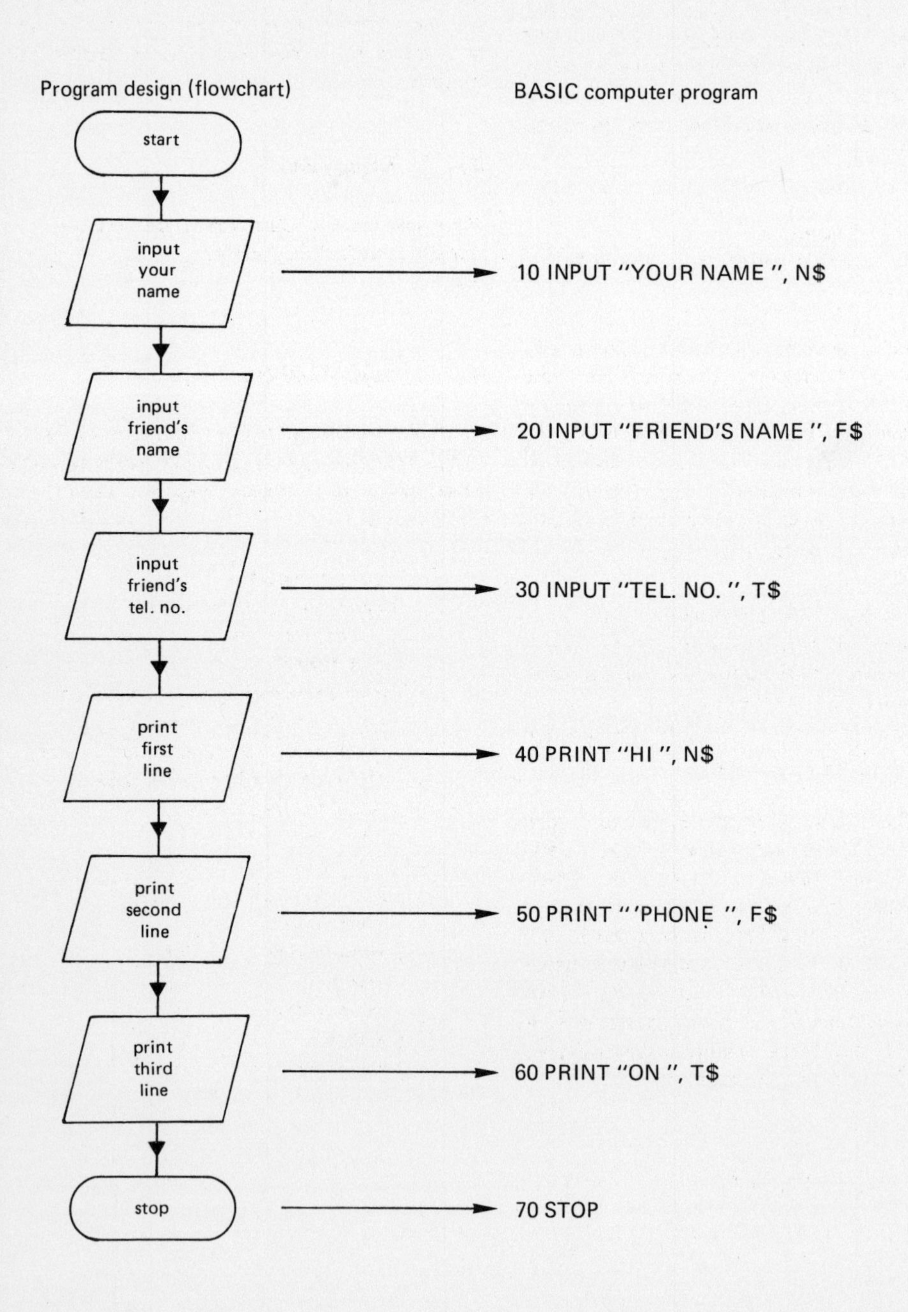

Comments. Some dialects of BASIC will allow string delimiters to be either " or ' however, the left hand delimiter must match the right hand delimiter. If either of these characters are to be used as part of the string literal then the remaining character must be used as the string delimiter. For example in the last example "FRIEND'S NAME" and '"PHONE" are defined in both INPUT and PRINT statements respectively.

Notice from the coding that there is no equivalent BASIC statement for the terminal symbol START. The only command that could equate to this symbol is RUN which would enable a program to start to be executed by the computer. The details of this command are left to the next chapter.

4.6 Dialect Differences

4.6.1 Data-names (also known as variables or identifiers)

Microsoft. BASIC variable names may be of any length. If the name is longer than 40 characters, however, only the first 40 characters are significant. The characters allowed in a variable name are letters and numbers, and a decimal point. The first character must be a letter. A variable name may not be a reserved word (BASIC verbs etc). A variable name ending with one of the following characters implies a type declaration.

- $ – string variable
- % – numeric integer (whole number) variable
- ! – single-precision variable (4 bytes) for storing numbers with a decimal fraction (real numbers)
- # – double-precision variable (8 bytes) for storing real numbers whose decimal fraction can be stored to a greater accuracy.

BBC/Electron. No restriction on the length of a data-name, however, there must be no spaces in the middle of a data-name, all data-names must start with a letter, no punctuation marks must be used in the name and data names must not begin with BASIC reserved words. The character set used in the data-name can be either upper case, lower case or a mixture of both cases. Integer types can be distinguished from real numeric types by the use of the character % after the data-name. String data types are expressed in the conventional manner.

4.6.2 Verbs Input, Print, Let and Stop

Microsoft. Input – as described, however, the comma after the prompt can be replaced by a semi-colon to cause a question mark to be printed after the prompt. An input statement without a prompt will display a question mark.

BBC/Electron. Input – as described, however, leave out the comma between the prompt and the data-name and the question mark will not be printed after the prompt.

4.7 Keywords

Data-name (also variable or identifier), glossary;
INPUT, PRINT, LET and STOP;
coding.

4.8 QUESTIONS

Using the designs for the programs in 3.8 and the glossaries provided, code complete BASIC programs. The program designs have been repeated here for the readers convenience.

1

input name of day
input starter
input main course
input dessert
print first line of menu – name of day
print second line of menu – starter
print third line of menu – main course
print fourth line of menu – dessert
print fifth line of menu
stop

glossary	
name of day	N$
starter	S$
main course	M$
dessert	D$

2
input name
input height
input weight
convert height to centimetres
convert weight to kilogrammes
print first line – personal details
print second line – name
print third line – height in cm
print fourth line – weight in Kg
stop

glossary	
name	N$
height (in)	H
weight (st)	W
height (cm)	H1
weight (Kg)	W1

3
input Fahrenheit temp
calculate Centigrade temp
print Centigrade temp
stop

glossary	
fahrenheit temp	F
Centigrade temp	C

4
input length
input width
calculate area
calculate cost of turf
print area
print cost of turf
stop

glossary	
length	L
width	W
area	A
cost of turf	T

5
input radius
calculate circumference
calculate area
print circumference
print area
stop

glossary	
radius	R
circumference	C
area	A

5 Program Implementation

5.1 Introduction

In the last chapter the reader was shown how to code a computer program from a program design. This chapter takes the development of a computer program one stage further by introducing the ideas of storing, retrieving and running a program on a computer. The reader is also shown how to test and edit computer programs.

5.2 Extended Computer Model

The computer model illustrated in figure 2.1 would allow a program to be stored in the main memory of a computer by, say, typing the program line-by-line at the input unit. The stored program could then be executed by the computer and the results transferred to the output unit.

When another computer program is to be stored in the main memory and executed the previous computer program would be destroyed and it could only be recreated by re-typing the entire program again at the input unit. Clearly there is a need to be able to save computer programs for re-use without having to re-type the program. The computer model must therefore be extended to include a unit for preserving computer programs.

Figure 5.1 illustrates an extra unit, known as a secondary storage unit, that has been added to the original computer model. The extended model also indicates that programs as well as data can be input to the main memory via the input unit, and the secondary storage unit is used to store data as well as programs. However, in this chapter the secondary storage unit will only be used to store computer programs.

5.2.1 Tape Cassette Unit

The cheapest method of preserving programs on a secondary storage unit is to use an audio cassette recorder/ player. Computer programs are stored one after another in a serial manner along a length of audio magnetic tape. Each program is given a name so that it can be distinguised from the other programs on the tape. The storage of a new program from the main memory to the magnetic tape must begin after the last program on the tape. This means that the tape must be wound to this position before recording takes place. Unless this practice is carried out there is the danger of overwriting (destroying) existing programs on the tape. The retrieval of a program from a tape is done by the computer searching through the length of the tape until the program name is found for the program to be loaded into the main memory of the computer.

The disadvantage of using a tape cassette unit as a secondary storage unit is that access to programs on the tape can be slow, of the order of minutes, and that the tape has to be wound on to the next free length of tape before programs can be stored (recorded).

The number of programs that can be stored on a tape depends on the length of the programs and the length of the tape. Obviously a C10 tape has a smaller storage capacity than a C60 tape, however, programs stored on

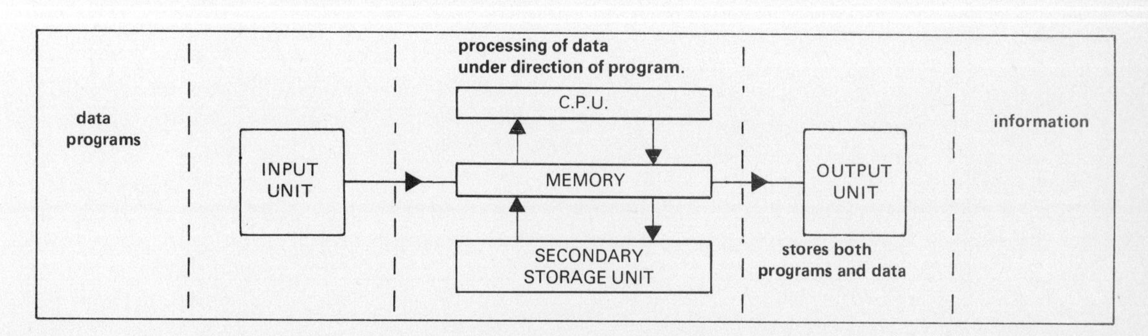

Figure 5.1 An extended computer model

a library of C10 tapes might be quicker to retrieve than many programs stored on one C60 tape.

5.2.2 Floppy Disc Unit

A floppy disc is made from a material similar to magnetic tape but thicker to improve the rigidity of the disc. The magnetic disc is stored in a card envelope for protection; the disc rotates inside the envelope and access to the surface of the disc is gained through slots cut in the envelope. The computer stores in its main memory a map of the surface of the disc which provides information about the position of each program stored on the disc, and the amount of freespace available for storing new programs.

One advantage of using magnetic disc over magnetic tape is that the retrieval of programs is much faster owing to the computers ability to access the program directly without having to search through many of the other programs on the disc. Furthermore, the computer can store new programs directly onto the disc since the map indicates the position on the disc surface of freespace.

Floppy discs vary in size from 3½", 5¼", 8". The storage capacity of these discs varies not only according to their size but also the type of disc unit being used (single sided single density, single sided double density, double sided double density, etc.) Typical storage capacities for the discs will vary from 80,000 characters to 1,000,000 characters. Each character is equivalent to 1 byte of storage. If a typical main memory size for a microcomputer is approximately 32,000 bytes then the reader should appreciate the amount of extra storage space a floppy disc can provide.

5.3 Storing

The most common method of storing a BASIC program is to type the program statements line-by-line at the keyboard of an input device such as a visual display unit, so that the program becomes directly resident in the main memory of the computer.

Before a new program can be entered into the main memory of a computer the main memory should be cleared of any previously stored program. This is achieved by typing the BASIC command NEW at the keyboard of the terminal. Failure to do this will result in part of the old program in the memory being inserted into the new program and will result in an unintelligible program.

The new computer program can be typed at the terminal in the format in which it is written. At the end of typing each BASIC statement or command the *return* or *enter* key must be pressed. The program becomes stored in the main memory of the computer as it is typed at the keyboard. When the complete program has been entered it can be copied from the main memory onto either magnetic tape or magnetic disc secondary storage media. The command for such copying of a program will differ between computers, however, FILE or SAVE are most common. The format of the command being:

FILE "filename" or SAVE "filename"

where filename is a name given to the program so that it can be identified and recalled at a later time.

5.4 Loading

A program that is stored on magnetic tape or disc is permanently recorded. Readers should develop the habit of storing their programs on tape or disc since the main memory of a computer is volatile. That is to say, when you switch the power off from your computer the program stored in the main memory will be destroyed! The command for loading a program into main memory will vary between computers, but LOAD or OLD are common. The format of the command being:

LOAD "filename" or OLD "filename"

The selected program is then copied from the secondary storage medium into main memory.

5.5 Listing

A computer generated copy of a program listing is important because it forms part of the documentation of a program being developed and is necessary when tracing the causes of errors in a program. A program listing can be generated by using the command LIST. When using a visual display unit as a terminal the current program in the main memory will be displayed on the screen as a response to the LIST command.

5.6 Running

When a computer program is in the main memory it can be executed or run. These terms mean that the computer will obey each program statement in the order specified. The command for program execution is RUN, and the computer will execute the program until one of the following occurs.

A STOP statement is executed. This implies that program termination is a natural process as directed by the programmer.

A syntax error. The format of a statement in the program does not conform to the rules of the BASIC language.

An execution error. For example an arithmetic over-

flow error caused by dividing a number by zero.
A hardware error. This is not a fault of the computer program but the machine itself.

5.7 Testing

When a computer program is run it should always be tested using the test data devised for the desk check, since the expected results from this test data will be known in advance of the computer generated results. If the two sets of results do not agree then either an error has occurred in the design of the program or the program coding is wrong. At this stage both the program design and coding should be systematically traced through in an attempt to find the error. When the error or *bug* has been found the computer program may need editing.

5.8 Editing

When a program contains errors the process of finding the causes of the errors or bugs is called *de-bugging.* De-bugging will inevitably mean changing or editing program statements. The changes will involve the insertion of new statements, amendment of existing statements and deletion of statements. The insertion of new statements and amendment of existing statements is possible in BASIC by typing the line number followed by the new or amended BASIC statement. The deletion of a statement is possible by typing the line number only. Every edit is terminated by a return or enter key.

Edited programs can be filed as before using the same or different filenames. Remember if a different filename is used then you will retain a copy of the file as it was before it was edited under the old filename. The techniques discussed for editing programs will only apply if the program has been loaded into the main memory of the computer.

5.9 Worked Example

The following dialogue illustrates a typical session at the computer. The last coded program given in 4.5 is entered into the computer, however, deliberate mistakes have been introduced into the coding in order to represent a beginners attempt at programming. Throughout this dialogue the heavy type indicates the computer's responses that are displayed on the screen and the lighter type the instructions and commands that are entered through the keyboard. Depending upon the model of computer being used either the RETURN or ENTER key must be pressed after each complete instruction or command. The type in italics is used to comment upon the dialogue. In the dialogue READY is a computer generated prompt.

Clear the memory of the last resident program

NEW
READY

Entering a new program into the memory

```
10 INPUT "YOUR NAME ", N$
20 INPUT "FRIEND'S NAME, F$
30 INPUT "TEL. NO. ", T
40 PRINT HI, N$
50 PRINT '"PHONE ",F$
60 PRINT "ON ", T$
70 STOP
```

Attempting to run the program

RUN
YOUR NAME JIM
LINE 20 MISSING DELIMITER

The program has failed at line 20 owing to a syntax error which was caused when typing the program into the computer. The line can be corrected by re-typing the complete line again

20 INPUT "FRIEND'S NAME ", F$

Attempting to run the program

RUN
YOUR NAME JIM
FRIEND'S NAME SUSIE
TEL. NO. WATFORD 328
REDO FROM START

There is a data type mismatch in line 30. The data-name in the program is T, yet the user has typed a string WATFORD 328. Since the computer is now waiting for a numeric value to be entered the program must be aborted by pressing the BREAK key or equivalent. Line 30 can now be edited

READY
30 INPUT "TEL. NO. ", T$

Attempting to run the program

RUN
YOUR NAME JIM
FRIEND'S NAME SUSIE
TEL. NO. WATFORD 328
LINE 40 VARIABLE NOT DECLARED

The computer has taken the string literal HI for a data-name since the string did not contain delimiters. Line 40 should be edited

```
40 PRINT "HI ", N$
```

Attempting to run the program

```
RUN
YOUR NAME        JIM
FRIEND'S NAME    SUSIE
TEL. NO.         WATFORD 328
LINE 50 MISSING DELIMITER
```

The computer cannot match the left apostrophe with a right apostrophe. In several dialects this will not be flagged as an error since the apostrophe is used to control moving the cursor to a new line. Line 50 should be edited

```
50 PRINT " 'PHONE ", F$
```

Attempting to run the program

```
RUN
YOUR NAME        JIM
FRIEND'S NAME    SUSIE
TEL. NO.         WATFORD 328
HI JIM
'PHONE SUSIE
ON WATFORD 328
LINE 70 PROGRAM STOP
READY
```

Success at last! The program has done what was predicted from the desk check at the design stage. Now the program is running correctly it can be permanently stored

```
SAVE "MEMO1"
READY
```

Type and SAVE "MEMO1" on your computer and RUN the program.

Correct the lines of code as illustrated in the example.

Do not be put off by different error messages being output from your computer.

SAVE the corrected program.

If the programmer wanted to change the message printed by the program without having to re-type the entire program, then amendments can be made to the original program as follows.

```
LOAD "MEMO1"
READY
45  PRINT "I HAVE A MESSAGE FOR YOU"
50  PRINT F$, "WOULD LIKE TO HEAR FROM YOU'
60  PRINT "PLEASE RING", T$
65  PRINT "BYE – YOUR FRIENDLY COMPUTER"
```

Type these lines of code into your computer and LIST the complete program. Notice that the new lines have been inserted into the old program. RUN the program using your own test data.

Lines 45 and 65 have been inserted into the original program in numerical sequence, and lines 50 and 60 in the original program have been changed. Despite these amendments the original version of the program can still be obtained by re-loading the program file called MEMO1. If the current program stored in the memory is listed on the screen then it is clear that the changes have been made.

```
LIST
10  INPUT "YOUR NAME ", N$
20  INPUT "FRIEND'S NAME ", F$
30  INPUT "TEL. NO. ", T$
40  PRINT "HI ", N$
45  PRINT " I HAVE A MESSAGE FOR YOU"
50  PRINT F$, "WOULD LIKE TO HEAR FROM YOU"
60  PRINT "PLEASE RING ", T$
65  PRINT "BYE – YOUR FRIENDLY COMPUTER"
70  STOP
READY
```

Attempting to run the program

```
RUN
YOUR NAME        JIM
FRIEND'S NAME    SUSIE
TEL. NO.         WATFORD 328
HI JIM
I HAVE A MESSAGE FOR YOU
SUSIE WOULD LIKE TO HEAR FROM YOU
PLEASE RING WATFORD 328
BYE – YOUR FRIENDLY COMPUTER
```

If the original program is to be preserved then the amended program can be filed under a different filename.

```
SAVE "MEMO2"
READY
```

At the end of this dialogue the user has successfully implemented two programs on the computer and saved the programs under the filenames of MEMO1 and MEMO2 for use at a later date.

Using your computer

Type and SAVE the first two programs given in section 4.5 of chapter 4.

LOAD and RUN both programs using the test data provided in sections 3.4 and 3.5.4 respectively.

Specimen results

```
 LOAD "SUMS"
>LIST
   10 INPUT "FIRST NUMBER ",N1
   20 INPUT "SECOND NUMBER ",N2
   30 LET N3=N1+N2
   40 PRINT "SUM ",N3
   50 STOP
>RUN
FIRST NUMBER ?9
SECOND NUMBER ?16
SUM                  25

STOP at line 50
>LOAD "PAPERS"
>LIST
   10 INPUT "FIRST PRICE ",P1
   20 INPUT "SECOND PRICE ",P2
   30 INPUT "THIRD PRICE ",P3
   40 LET T=P1+P2+P3
   50 LET A=T/3
   60 PRINT "TOTAL COST ",T
   70 PRINT "AVERAGE COST ",A
   80 STOP
>RUN
FIRST PRICE ?35
SECOND PRICE ?40
THIRD PRICE ?45
TOTAL COST                      120
AVERAGE COST                     40

STOP at line 80
>
```

Check the results, are they correct?

5.10 Dialect Differences

5.10.1 Save

Microsoft. Format: SAVE filespec [,A]
SAVE filespec [,P]

where filespec is a string expression of the form device: filename. Storage device names on the IBM PC are CAS1, A, B, C and D. CAS1 implies a cassette tape player, A and B refer to the first and second floppy disc drives and C and D to the first and second fixed disc drives. A filename must conform to the following rules.

For cassette files:

the filename should not be longer than eight characters and must not include colons, 00 or FF.

For floppy disc files:

the name may consist of two parts separated by a period name.extension, where the name should not be longer than eight characters and the extension not longer than three characters.

The A option saves the program in ASCII format, otherwise the program is saved in a compressed binary format to save space. The P option saves the program in an encoded binary format for protection, any attempt to LIST or EDIT the program will result in an error message being output by the computer.

Examples. SAVE "MEMO1" will save the current program in memory on either a cassette or on a floppy disc in the default drive of the system and have .BAS appended to it as an extension.
SAVE "B:PROG", A saves PROG.BAS on drive B in an ASCII format.
SAVE "A:SECRET.BOZ", P saves SECRET. BOZ, on drive A, protected so it may not be altered.

BBC/Electron. Format: SAVE filename

where filename may be up to 10 characters long for a tape file and up to 7 characters long for a disc file. The name may not include spaces or punctuation and must start with a letter. If a specific disc drive and directory is to be specified then the filename can be prefixed with the disc drive number and directory letter.

Examples. SAVE "MEMO2" will save the current program in memory on either a cassette or on a floppy disc in the drive being used and on the current directory.
SAVE ":1.B.LANDER" would save the file on floppy disc in drive 1 directory B.

5.10.2 Load

Microsoft. Format: LOAD filespec [,R]

where filespec has the same meaning as defined for SAVE. If R is included in this command then the file is both loaded and run.

Examples. LOAD "MEMO1" will load the program MEMO1 but does not run it, however,
LOAD "MEMO1",R will load MEMO1 and begin executing the program from the first instruction.
LOAD "B:REPORT.BAS" will load the file REPORT.BAS from the floppy disc in disc drive B.
LOAD "CAS1:MEMO2" will load the program MEMO2 from a cassette tape.
LOAD "CAS1:" will load the next program on the tape.

BBC/Electron. Format: LOAD filename

where filename has the same meaning as defined for SAVE.

Examples. LOAD "MEMO1" will load the program MEMO1 from either cassette tape or disc.
LOAD A$ will load the program whose name is stored in the string data-name A$.
LOAD"" will load the next program to be found.

5.10.3 Directory Access

When programs are stored on magnetic disc the computer system must keep an up-to-date table of what is stored on the disc. Such a table is know as a directory. In a similar manner to a telephone directory providing telephone numbers for names of subscribers so a magnetic disc file directory will enable the computer to find a program on the disc given the name of the program. The format of the BASIC command to inspect the contents of a directory will vary between computers.

Microsoft. Format: FILES [filespec]

Examples. FILES will display all the filenames on the current directory of the default disc drive.
FILES "*.BAS" will display the names of all the files with the postfixed abbreviation .BAS stored on the default disc.
FILES "B:*.*" will display all the files on disc drive B.

BBC/Electron. Format: *CAT
will give a catalogue of the contents of the tape or disc.

5.10.4 List

The LIST command operates in the manner described in the text, however, there are minor enhancements in the four dialects being considered.

Microsoft. Format: LIST [line1] [-[line2]] [,filespec]

Examples.

LIST 10-150	lists lines 10 through to 150 on the screen
LIST 200-	lists all the lines from 200 through to the end of the program
LIST -200	lists all the lines from the start of the program to line 200
LIST 10-300, "CAS1:PROG5"	lists lines 10 through to 300 from a file stored on tape cassette named PROG5
LIST 125	list line 125 only.

BBC/Electron. Format: LIST [line1] [,[line2]]

Examples.

LIST 280	lists a single line
LIST 100,450	lists a range of lines
LIST ,400	will list all the lines up to and including line 400
LIST 500,	will list all the lines beyond line 500

5.10.5 Run

The RUN command operates in the manner described in the text, the only minor modification is that Microsoft, allows the program to be executed from a specific line number. For example RUN 100 would direct the computer to start at line 100.

5.10.6 Line Numbering

If the line numbers in a program increase by a fixed amount then the programmer need not type the line number to each instruction but get the computer to automatically generate the numbers using the AUTO command. The format of this command varies between dialects.

Microsoft. Format: AUTO [number] [,[increment]]

Examples.

AUTO	generates line numbers 10,20,30,40, ...
AUTO 100,50	generates line numbers 100,150,200, 250, ...
AUTO 500,	generates line numbers 500,550,600, 650, ...

(the increment is 50 since this 50 was the increment in the previous AUTO command).

AUTO ,20	generates line numbers 10,20,40, 60, ...

To exit from the AUTO command press the CONTROL and BREAK keys together.

BBC/Electron. This is similar to Microsoft BASIC in as much as the first two examples apply only. Exit from the AUTO command by pressing the ESCAPE key.

Microsoft. Format:

RENUM [newnumber] [,[oldnumber] [,increment]]

newnumber is the first line number to be used in the new sequence (default value 100, oldnumber is the line in the current program where renumbering is to begin (default first line of old program) and increment is the numerical difference between the line numbers in the new sequence.

Examples.

```
RENUM            renumbers 10,20,30,40, . . . . . . .
RENUM 100,10,5   renumbers 100,105,110, . . . . . .
```

BBC/Electron. Format:

RENUMBER [start number [,increment]]

Examples.

```
RENUMBER           renumbers 10,20,30,40, . . . .
RENUMBER 100       renumbers 100,110,120,130, . . . .
RENUMBER 500,5     renumbers 500,505,510,515, . . . .
```

Microsoft. Format: DELETE { [line1] [-line2] / [line1-] }

Examples.

DELETE 40	deletes line 40
DELETE 40-100	deletes lines 40 through to 100 inclusive.
DELETE 40-	deletes lines 40 through to the end of the program.
DELETE -40	deletes all lines up to and including line 40.

BBC/Electron. Format: DELETE line1, line2

Examples.

DELETE 120,340	deletes lines 120 to 340 inclusive
DELETE 0,150	deletes lines from the start of the program to line 150
DELETE 550,32767	deletes all the lines from line 550 to the end of the program. Since line 32767 is the highest line available this can always be used to denote the highest line number in a program.

5.10.7 Deleting Stored Programs

To prevent the build up of program files that are no longer required various dialects of BASIC have commands for erasing program files stored on either disc or cartridge.

Microsoft. Format: KILL filespec

Examples. KILL "TEST.BAS"
KILL "A:PROG1.BAS"

BBC/Electron. Format: *DELETE filename

Example. *DELETE MYPROG

5.11 Keywords

Secondary storage;
cassette, floppy disc, microdrive cartridge;
NEW, SAVE, LOAD, LIST, RUN;
de-bugging, editing, program maintenance;
AUTO, RENUMBER;
DELETE, KILL.

5.12 Questions

Using the coded programs to the questions in sections 3.8 and 4.8 transfer the programs to your computer and carry out the following operations.

LIST the program to the screen of your computer, if you detect any typing or coding errors then correct them by typing the correct version of the line again.
RUN the program using the same test data as you devised in section 3.8. Check to see whether the computed results are the same as the results of your desk check. If the results are different then check the design and the coding for errors. Correct the errors. Re-run the program.
When the program is running correctly SAVE or FILE the program on either magnetic tape or disc.

6 Selection

6.1 Introduction

In chapter 3 the reader was introduced to a simple program design that was based on the input of data, calculations made using the data, and the output of results. The design of that type of program was no more than a *sequence* of instructions. Programs designed in this manner are fine for solutions to simple problems, but are of no use if a decision is to be made in a program design. This chapter incorporates the process of *selection* into the design of computer programs and illustrates the different methods of coding selections in the BASIC language.

6.2 Worked Example

A company pays a car allowance to its employees based on the size of engine in the car. Those employees whose car engines are less than or equal to 1500cc receive 8p per mile, and those employees whose car engines are greater than 1500cc receive an additional 2p per mile. Design a program to input the mileage and engine size, calculate the total mileage allowance and output this figure.

6.2.1 Pseudocode

input mileage
calculate basic mileage allowance at 8p per mile
input size of engine

test for engine size and calculate additional allowance if necessary

print mileage allowance
stop

To test for the engine size, in order to calculate the additional allowance, new pseudocode is necessary. The format of the code is:

IF condition **THEN**
  pseudocode statement(s)
END IF

In this example the pseudocode would be written as:

IF size of engine > 1500 **THEN**
  increase mileage allowance by 2p per mile
END IF

This selection, based on the size of the engine, can be written into the design of the program as part of a sequence of instructions.

input mileage
calculate allowance at 8p per mile
input size of engine
IF size of engine > 1500 **THEN**
  increase mileage allowance by 2p per mile
END IF
print allowance
stop

6.2.2 Flowchart

When constructing a flowchart for the design of a program a decision symbol is used to indicate a selection. The symbol is:

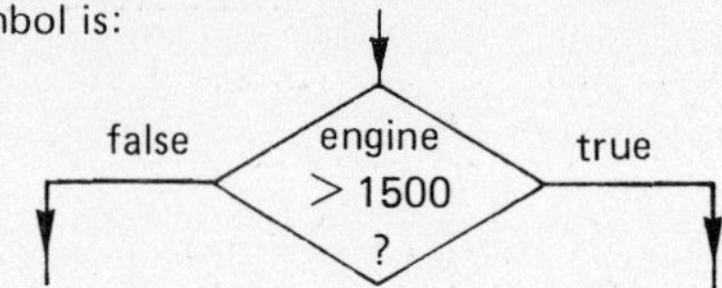

The condition that the selection is based on is written inside the decision symbol, and the outcome, either true or false, is represented by two flow-lines emerging from the symbol. The selection based on the size of the engine can be represented in a flowchart as follows.

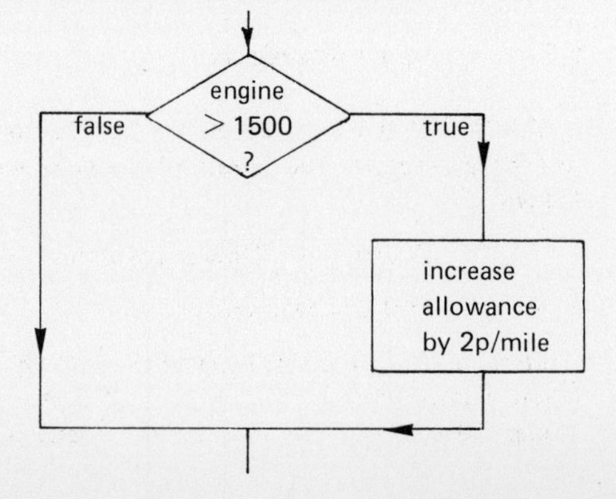

This selection can be incorporated into a flowchart that represents a design for the solution to the problem.

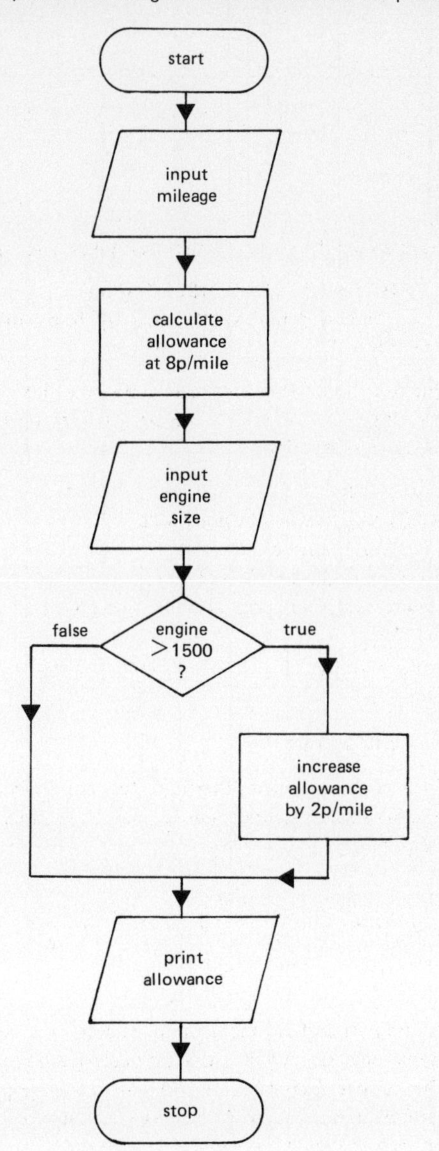

6.3 Coding a Selection

The BASIC language uses an IF...THEN... statement to code a selection. The format of the statement is as follows.

IF condition THEN instruction

where the format of a condition is:

{ literal-1 / data-name-1 / expression-1 } relational operator { literal-2 / data-name-2 / expression-2 }

The relational operators have the following meanings.

Operator	Meaning
>	greater than
<	less than
=	equal to
>=	greater than or equal to
<=	less than or equal to
<>	not equal to

The following examples all represent conditions.

A = 6, B > 15, X < Y, H > = I + J,
A + B > C + D, Y$ > X$, B$ = "ADAMS"

Notes

The latter two cases indicate that strings can be compared alphabetically. For example "A" < "B" since the ASCII code for A is less than for B, similarly, "APPLE" < "BANANA"; "GRAPE" > "FIG"; etc.

Both sides of a conditional operator must be of the same data type.

In a conditional statement if the condition is true the statement following THEN is obeyed, after which the next instruction in the program sequence is obeyed. However, if the condition is false the next instruction in the program sequence is obeyed.

If the following glossary is derived from the design of the solution to the last problem.

Glossary
M – mileage
A – allowance
E – engine size

the selection incorporated into the design can be coded as follows;

```
IF E > 1500 THEN LET A = A + 0.02 * M
```

and implies that if the condition E > 1500 is true then the statement to increase the allowance by 2p per mile will be executed.

The complete program to this design can be coded as:

```
10 INPUT "MILEAGE ",M
20 LET A = 0.08 * M
30 INPUT "ENGINE SIZE ",E
40 IF E > 1500 THEN LET A = A + 0.02 * M
50 PRINT "CAR ALLOWANCE ",A
60 STOP
```

Using your computer

Type and SAVE the last program.

LOAD and RUN the program three times using the following test data

mileage	engine size
10000	1200
10000	2000
12000	1500

Calculate the answers using pencil and paper and check if the computer is correct.

Specimen results

```
>
>LOAD "CARS"
>RUN
MILEAGE ?10000
ENGINE SIZE ?1200
CAR ALLOWANCE                       800

STOP at line 60
>RUN
MILEAGE ?10000
ENGINE SIZE ?2000
CAR ALLOWANCE                      1000

STOP at line 60
>RUN
MILEAGE ?12000
ENGINE SIZE ?1500
CAR ALLOWANCE                       960

STOP at line 60
>
```

6.4 Logical Operators

When a selection is based upon one or more conditions being true it is possible to combine the conditions together using logical operators and the resultant compound condition will either be true or false. The following *truth* tables illustrate the outcome of combining two conditions using the logical operators stated.

6.4.1 Logical And

condition X	condition Y	compound condition X AND Y
false	false	false
false	true	false
true	false	false
true	true	true

X AND Y is true only if X is true AND Y is true.

Example.

condition X A = B
condition Y C = D
IF (A = B) AND (C = D)
THEN LET T = A + B + C + D

The statement following THEN would be executed by the computer only if A = B was true and C = D was true.

6.4.2 Inclusive Or

condition X	condition Y	compound condition X OR Y
false	false	false
false	true	true
true	false	true
true	true	true

X OR Y is true if X is true OR Y is true and including both being true.

Example.

condition X A < B
condition Y C > D
IF (A < B) OR (C > D)
THEN LET P = A*B*C*D

The statement following THEN would be executed by the computer if A < B was true OR C>D was true OR both were true.

6.4.3 Exclusive Or

condition X	condition Y	compound condition X EOR Y
false	false	false
false	true	true
true	false	true
true	true	false

X EOR Y is true if X is true OR Y is true but excluding both being true.

Example.

condition X A = B
condition Y C < D
IF (A = B) EOR (C < D)
THEN M = M + 1

This statement following THEN would be executed if A = B was true OR C < D was true. If however A = B and C<D were both either true or false then the statement following THEN would **not** be executed.

6.4.4 Not

The logical operator NOT negates or reverses a condition, so true becomes false and false becomes true.

condition X	NOT condition X
false	true
true	false

Example. condition X A < B
IF NOT (A < B) THEN LET P = S*T

This implies that if A < B was false then NOT (A < B) would be true and the statement after THEN would be executed by the computer.

Note. In the last four examples parenthesis () has been used to clarify the conditions X and Y. The BASIC language will accept parenthesis in selection statements in this context.

6.4.5 Worked Example

Witnesses at the scene of a crime gave descriptions about two suspects who were seen leaving in a hurry. The first suspect was described as being short and very overweight (height < 165cm and weight > 90Kg), and the second suspect was described as being tall and very thin (height > 190cm and weight < 60Kg). Write a computer program to input the name, height and weight of known criminals in the area and to print out a list of all possible suspects.

Note. The program will be re-run for each criminal.

Glossary
Name – N$
Height – H
Weight – W

6.4.5 (cont.)

Program coding

```
10 INPUT "NAME",N$
20 INPUT "HEIGHT ", H
30 INPUT "WEIGHT ", W
40 IF (H < 165 AND W > 90) EOR (H > 190 AND W < 60) THEN PRINT N$
50 STOP
```

Using your computer

Type and SAVE the last program.

LOAD and RUN the program using the following test data

Name	Height	Weight
BLOGGS	170	85
JONES	163	92
DAVIES	165	90
SMITH	190	55
WILSON	192	59

The suspects should be JONES and WILSON.

Specimen results

```
>LOAD "SUSPECT"
>RUN
NAME ?BLOGGS
HEIGHT ?170
WEIGHT ?85

STOP at line 50
>RUN
NAME ?JONES
HEIGHT ?163
WEIGHT ?92
JONES

STOP at line 50
>RUN
NAME ?DAVIES
HEIGHT ?165
WEIGHT ?90

STOP at line 50
>RUN
NAME ?SMITH
HEIGHT ?190
WEIGHT ?55

STOP at line 50
>RUN
NAME ?WILSON
HEIGHT ?192
WEIGHT ?59
WILSON

STOP at line 50
>
```

6.5 Binary Selection

The manager of a newsagent pays two different rates for the delivery of newspapers. A boy can earn £1.50 on a morning delivery, but only £1.20 on an evening delivery. Boys are employed for either a morning paper-round or an evening paper-round but not both morning and evening paper-rounds.

Design a program to input at the keyboard of a computer the description of a round (e.g. AM or PM) and the number of complete paper-rounds in a week made by a boy. Calculate the gross weekly earnings and output this value to the screen of a monitor.

This problem can be solved in an identical manner to problem 6.2, or alternatively, the solution can be redesigned using a *binary selection.*

6.5.1 Pseudocode

In this problem the calculation of earnings depends on the question "which paper-round – morning (AM) or evening (PM)?".

If the answer is morning (AM) the earnings are:

£1.50 x number of rounds

else (if the answer is evening (PM)) the earnings are:

£1.20 x number of rounds.

This statement can be built into the design of a computer program by using the structure:

```
IF round = "AM" THEN
   earnings = 1.5 * number-of-rounds
ELSE
   earnings = 1.2 * number-of-rounds
END IF
```

If the condition round = "AM" is *true* then the statement earnings = 1.5 * number-of-rounds will be obeyed by the computer. However, if the condition round = "AM" is *false* this implies that round = "PM" and the statement following **ELSE**, earnings = 1.2 * number-of-rounds will be obeyed by the computer. **IF** marks the beginning of the selection, and **END IF** marks the end of the selection. Every **IF** must be paired with an **END IF**. The statement that follows **THEN** will be obeyed if the condition is true, otherwise, the statement that follows **ELSE** will be obeyed if the condition is false. This selection can now be built into the following sequence of instructions to complete the program design.

Program design.

```
input round
input number-of-rounds
IF round = "AM" THEN
   earnings = 1.5 * number-of-rounds
ELSE
   earnings = 1.2 * number-of-rounds
END IF
print earnings
stop
```

6.5.2 Flowchart

There are no new symbols necessary in the representation of a binary selection in a flowchart. The two different calculations based on whether the round is in the morning or evening can be shown as follows.

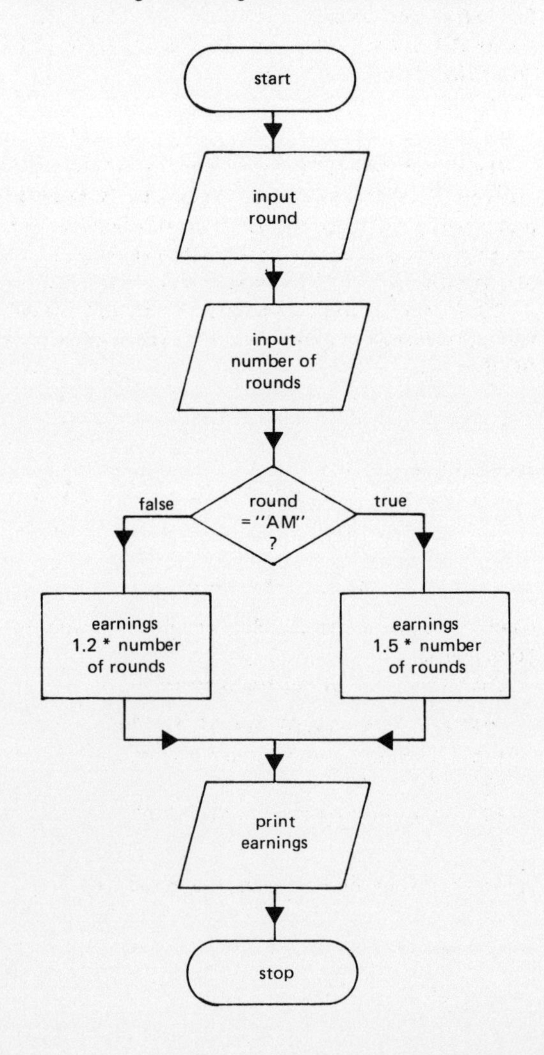

6.5.3 Coding a binary selection

The method of coding a binary selection in BASIC has not been standardised. Several dialects of BASIC use IF...THEN...ELSE... which is equivalent in meaning to the pseudocode. However, many dialects only provide for IF...THEN... and the implementation of a binary selection has to be supplemented by the use of GOTO.

The format of the IF...THEN...ELSE... statement in BASIC is:

IF condition THEN instruction corresponding to **true**
ELSE instruction corresponding to **false**

Using the program design described in the last section the following glossary can be constructed and program coded.

Glossary

R$	–	round AM or PM
N	–	number of rounds
E	–	earnings

6.5.3 (cont.)

Program

```
10  INPUT "AM OR PM", R$
20  INPUT "ROUNDS", N
30  IF R$ = "AM" THEN LET E = 1.5 * N ELSE LET E = 1.2 * N
40  PRINT "EARNINGS", E
50  STOP
```

The use of the GOTO instruction has received considerable criticism since its use can lead to unstructured programming. The use of GOTO in this book will be confined, unless otherwise stated, to the implementation of *control structures* of which selection is one structure.

GOTO will allow unconditional branching from one line in a program to another line. The format of a GOTO statement is:

GOTO linenumber

For example

```
10
20  GOTO 50  ──┐
30             │
40             │
50  ◄──────────┘
```

directs the computer to branch unconditionally from line 20 to line 50.

The binary selection can be implemented as:

100 IF **not** condition THEN GOTO 130
110   statement corresponding to **true**
120 GOTO 140
130   statement corresponding to **false**
140

An alternative form of coding the program is:

```
10  INPUT "AM OR PM", R$
20  INPUT "ROUNDS", N
30  IF R$ <> "AM" THEN GOTO 60
40    LET E = 1.5 * N
50  GOTO 70
60    LET E = 1.2 * N
70  PRINT "EARNINGS", E
80  STOP
```

Using your computer

Type and SAVE the last program.
LOAD and RUN twice using the following test data.

round	number
AM	4
PM	5

Check if the computer is correct.

Specimen results

```
>LOAD "ROUND"
>RUN
AM OR PM ?AM
ROUNDS ?4
EARNINGS              6

STOP at line 80
>RUN
AM OR PM ?PM
ROUNDS ?5
EARNINGS              6

STOP at line 80
>
```

6.6 Multiple Selection

A program is to be designed to use a computer as a calculator. The user inputs a code; 1 for addition, 2 for subtraction, 3 for multiplication and 4 for division; and then inputs the two numbers that are to be computed. The computer calculates the answer and then outputs the result.

6.6.1 Pseudocode

```
input code
input first number
input second number
```

test value of code and perform appropriate arithmetic

```
print answer
stop
```

A pseudocode statement that represents a multiple selection is the *case* statement. The multiple selection in this problem can be expressed in the following manner.

```
CASE code OF
WHEN 1
  add numbers
WHEN 2
  subtract numbers
WHEN 3
  multiply numbers
OTHERWISE
  divide numbers
END CASE
```

Alternatively, if the program design was to cater for an invalid code being entered by the user the *case* statement represented here could be modified as follows.

```
CASE code OF
WHEN 1
  add numbers
WHEN 2
  subtract numbers
WHEN 3
  multiply numbers
WHEN 4
  divide numbers
OTHERWISE
  report error
END CASE
```

6.6.2 Flowchart

In designing this program using a flowchart the multiple selection could be represented as *nested* binary selections or alternatively represented by one decision symbol having one flow line emerging from it which then divides into multiple flow lines each annotated with the appropriate condition.

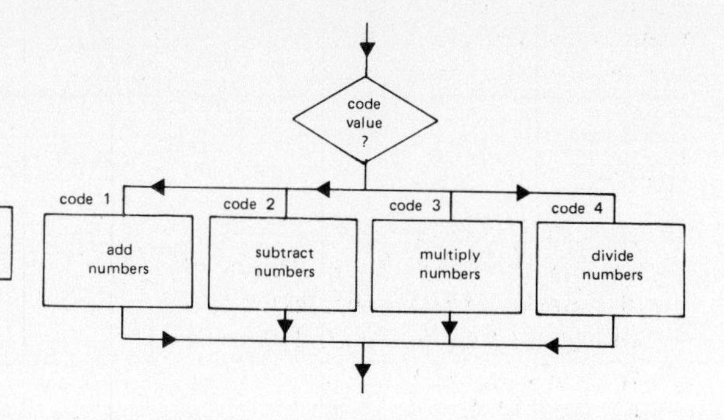

This diagramatic representation of a multiple selection can be regarded as the equivalent in flowcharting of a *CASE* structure.

6.6.3 Implementation

The following programs illustrate three different methods of coding the multiple selection found in the design to the last problem.

Glossary

C — code
N1 — first number
N2 — second number
A — answer

Program 1

```
 10  INPUT "CODE 1–4", C
 20  INPUT "FIRST NUMBER", N1
 30  INPUT "SECOND NUMBER", N2
 40  ON C GOTO 50, 70, 90, 110
 50    LET A = N1 + N2
 60  GOTO 120
 70    LET A = N1 – N2
 80  GOTO 120
 90    LET A = N1 * N2
100  GOTO 120
110    LET A = N1 / N2
120  PRINT "ANSWER", A
130  STOP
```

In this first program a new statement has been introduced. The ON....GOTO.... statement in line 40 will permit multiple selection depending on the value of C. If C = 1 then the computer will branch to line 50, if C = 2 the branch will be to line 70, if C = 3 the branch will be to line 90 and finally if C = 4 the branch will be to line 110. The format of the ON....GOTO.... statement is:

$$\textbf{ON} \left\{ \begin{array}{l} \text{numeric data-name} \\ \text{arithmetic expression} \end{array} \right\} \textbf{GOTO} \text{ line-1, line-2, ...}$$

where the data-name or evaluated arithmetic expression should represent a positive integer; the value of this integer must not exceed the number of line numbers present after the GOTO.

Note. If the value of the integer lies outside the permissible range then depending upon the BASIC dialect being used one of two actions will take place. The computer will inform the user of the error or the computer will execute the next statement in sequence after the ON....GOTO.... statement.

Very few dialects of BASIC support the *CASE* structure. The ON....GOTO.... statement is not general enough since branching is dependent upon the expression evaluating to a positive integer. The *CASE* structure, however, will cause branching on any specified value, numeric or string. The second program in this section illustrates how the *CASE* structure can be implemented using IF....THEN.... and GOTO statements.

Program 2

```
 10  INPUT "CODE 1–4", C
 20  INPUT "FIRST NUMBER", N1
 30  INPUT "SECOND NUMBER", N2
 40  IF C<>1 THEN GOTO 70
 50    LET A = N1 + N2
 60  GOTO 140
 70  IF C<>2 THEN GOTO 100
 80    LET A = N1 – N2
 90  GOTO 140
100  IF C<>3 THEN GOTO 130
110    LET A = N1 * N2
120  GOTO 140
130    LET A = N1 / N2
140  PRINT "ANSWER", A
150  STOP
```

Using your computer

Type and SAVE the last program.
LOAD and RUN using the following test data

code	first number	second number
1	10	15
2	150	65
3	9	8
4	250	50
5	10	20

Check your answers for codes 1, 2, 3 and 4. What has happened when the code was 5?

Specimen results

```
>LOAD "ARITH"
>RUN
CODE 1-4?1
FIRST NUMBER?10
SECOND NUMBER?15
ANSWER                25

STOP at line 150
>RUN
CODE 1-4?2
FIRST NUMBER?150
SECOND NUMBER?65
ANSWER                85

STOP at line 150
>RUN
CODE 1-4?3
FIRST NUMBER?9
SECOND NUMBER?8
ANSWER                72

STOP at line 150
>RUN
CODE 1-4?4
FIRST NUMBER?250
SECOND NUMBER?50
ANSWER                 5

STOP at line 150
>RUN
CODE 1-4?5
FIRST NUMBER?10
SECOND NUMBER?20
ANSWER               0.5

STOP at line 150
>
```

A third method of implementing multiple selection is by using *nested* IF...ELSE... statements. The pseudocode to the last problem could have been expressed as follows.

```
input code
input first number
input second number
IF code = 1 THEN
  add numbers
ELSE
  IF code = 2 THEN
    subtract numbers
  ELSE
    IF code = 3 THEN
      multiply numbers
    ELSE
      divide numbers
    END IF
  END IF
END IF
print answer
stop
```

To indicate the nesting of one selection within another the pseudocode of the next level selection is always indented to the right. For example:

```
IF ..... THEN
  .....
ELSE
  IF ..... THEN
    .....
  ELSE
    .....
  END IF
END IF
```

and

```
IF ..... THEN
  IF ..... THEN
    .....
  ELSE
    .....
  END IF
ELSE
  .....
END IF
```

both represent nested selection statements.

Program 3

```
10 INPUT "CODE 1–4", C
20 INPUT "FIRST NUMBER", N1
30 INPUT "SECOND NUMBER", N2
40 IF C = 1 THEN LET A = N1 + N2
   ELSE IF C = 2 THEN LET A = N1 – N2
   ELSE IF C = 3 THEN LET A = N1 * N2
   ELSE LET A = N1 / N2
50 PRINT "ANSWER", A
60 STOP
```

Note: many popular dialects of BASIC will only allow *nested* IF...THEN...ELSE to be on one BASIC line as illustrated in line 40.

6.7 Worked Example

A man has found that the following rules enable him to travel to work comfortably in all weathers.

If the barometer indicates *stormy* he takes his umbrella and wears his overcoat;
if *rainy* is indicated then he takes his umbrella and wears his raincoat;
if *change* is indicated, he behaves as for *dry* if it rained yesterday and as for *rainy* if it did not;
if *dry* is indicated he simply takes his umbrella;
if *very dry* is indicated then he takes neither coat nor umbrella.

Design and write a program to input the barometer reading and print the type of clothing to take.

6.7.1 Pseudocode

```
input barometer reading
CASE barometer reading OF
  WHEN stormy
    print overcoat and umbrella
  WHEN rainy
    print raincoat and umbrella
  WHEN change
    input if rain fell yesterday
    IF rained yesterday THEN
      print umbrella
    ELSE
      print raincoat and umbrella
    END IF
  WHEN dry
    print umbrella
  OTHERWISE
    (do nothing)
END CASE
stop
```

6.7.2 Flowchart showing the nested IF structure

The flowchart is used here to illustrate an alternative design technique only.

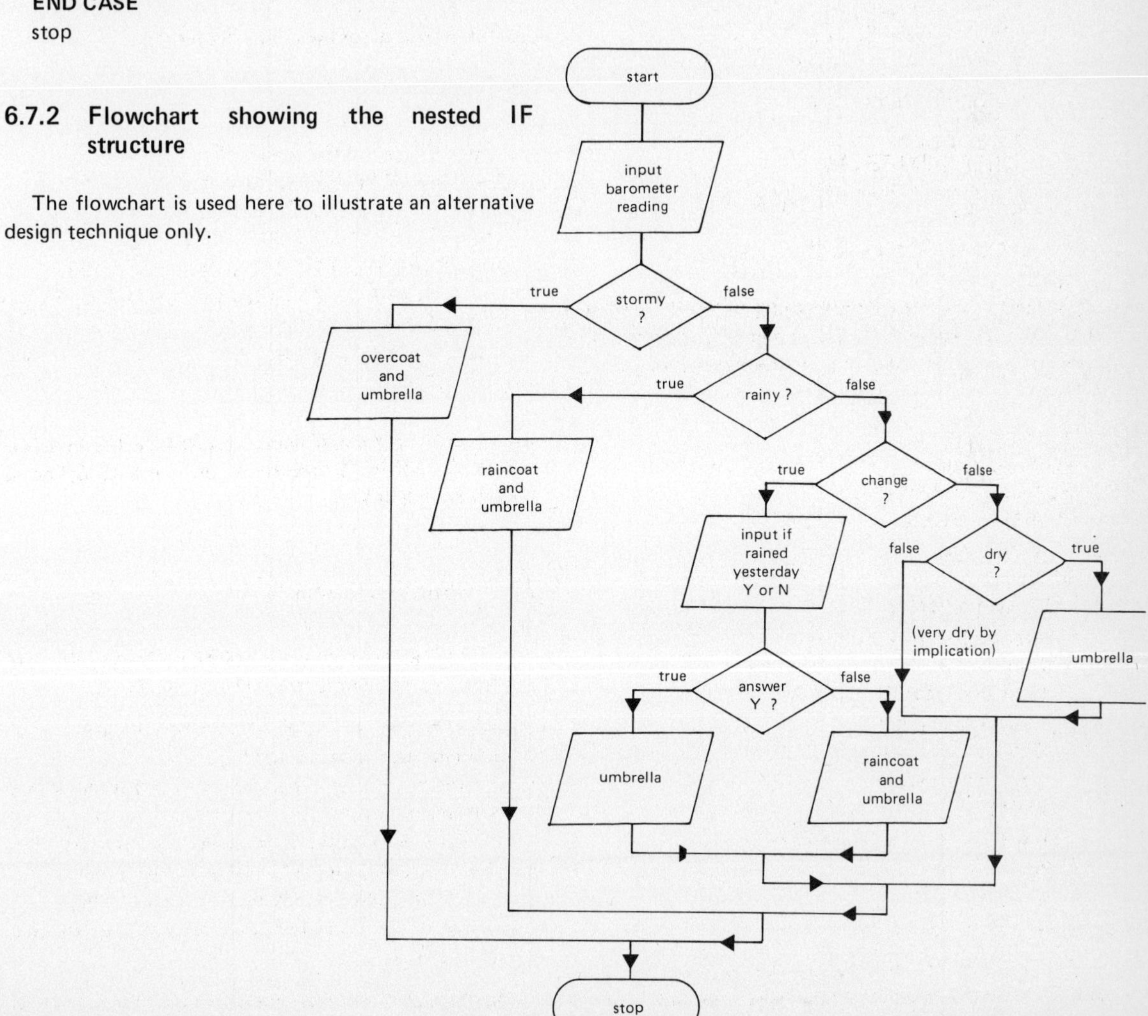

6.7.3 Desk Check

Test data: rainy; change, yes; very dry; stormy; change, no.

Data-names	barometer	answer	(printed output)
	rainy	–	raincoat and umbrella
	change	yes	umbrella
	very dry	–	(no output)
	stormy	–	overcoat and umbrella
	change	no	raincoat and umbrella

6.7.4 Coding

Glossary

barometer reading	B$
answer to rain yesterday	A$

Two methods of coding the multiple selection, the first uses Microsoft BASIC, the second uses a form of structured BASIC.

Method 1 Microsoft

```
 10 INPUT "BAROMETER READING", B$
 20 IF B$ <> "STORMY" THEN 50
 30   PRINT "OVERCOAT AND UMBRELLA"
 40 GOTO 160
 50 IF B$ <> "RAINY" THEN 80
 60   PRINT "RAINCOAT AND UMBRELLA"
 70 GOTO 160
 80 IF B$ <> "CHANGE" THEN 150
 90   INPUT "DID IT RAIN YESTERDAY Y OR N", A$
100   IF A$ = "N" THEN 130
110     PRINT "UMBRELLA"
120   GOTO 160
130     PRINT "RAINCOAT AND UMBRELLA"
140   GOTO 160
150 IF B$ = "DRY" THEN PRINT "UMBRELLA"
160 STOP
```

Method 2 Structured BASIC

```
 10 INPUT "barometer reading", barometer$
 20 CASE barometer$ OF
 30   WHEN "stormy"
 40     PRINT "overcoat and umbrella"
 50   WHEN "rainy"
 60     PRINT "raincoat and umbrella"
 70   WHEN "change"
 80     INPUT "did it rain yesterday y or n", answer$
 90     IF answer$ = "y" THEN
100       PRINT "umbrella"
110     ELSE
120       PRINT "raincoat and umbrella"
130     END IF
140   WHEN "dry"
150     PRINT "umbrella"
160   OTHERWISE
170     PRINT
180 END CASE
190 STOP
```

Using your computer

Type and SAVE the last program using a dialect applicable to your computer.

LOAD and RUN using the test data given in 6.7.3.

Are the results consistent with the desk check?

Specimen results

```
>LOAD "WEATHER"
>RUN
BAROMETER READING?RAINY
RAINCOAT AND UMBRELLA

STOP at line 160
>RUN
BAROMETER READING?CHANGE
DID IT RAIN YESTERDAY Y OR N?Y
UMBRELLA

STOP at line 160
>RUN
BAROMETER READING?VERY DRY

STOP at line 160
>RUN
BAROMETER READING?STORMY
OVERCOAT AND UMBRELLA

STOP at line 160
>RUN
BAROMETER READING?CHANGE
DID IT RAIN YESTERDAY Y OR N?N
RAINCOAT AND UMBRELLA

STOP at line 160
>
```

6.8 Dialect Differences

Both dialects support the statements IF...THEN...; IF...THEN...ELSE...; GOTO and ON...GOTO... and the logical operators AND, inclusive OR, exclusive XOR (EOR on the BBC/Electron) and NOT.

6.8.1 If...then...else...

Microsoft and BBC/Electron. The binary selection statement can only occupy one line of BASIC code. In practice this means several lines on the screen of a monitor. The splitting up of IF and ELSE on separate BASIC lines is prohibited. Statements can be nested but the depth is governed by the length of a BASIC line (this is **not** the width of a screen).

If more than one BASIC statement is required on either the true or false branch then multiple statements must be separated by colons.

Example.

```
100  IF A>B THEN X=2:Y=3 ELSE X=5:Y=6
```

6.8.2 Multiple Selection

ON..GOTO.. In the **BBC/Electron** implementation an error message is printed if the integer variable does not correspond with the number of line numbers in the statement. However, with **Microsoft** if the integer variable does not correspond with the number of lines then the computer will continue with the next executable statement after the ON...GOTO... This last sentence is only true if the integer variable lies within defined range, otherwise an error message will be output. The ranges are 0–255 for **Microsoft**.

6.9 Keywords

Selection, IF...THEN...
condition, relational operator;
logical operators, AND, OR, EOR, NOT;
Binary selection, IF...THEN...ELSE
GOTO;
Mutliple selection, case;
ON...GOTO..., nested IF's...

6.10 Questions

1 If A = 1, B = –2, C = 3, D = 4, E$ = "SMITH" and F$ = "JONES" then state whether the following conditions are true or false.

```
A=B          A>B              (A<C) AND (B<D)
(A<C) AND (B>D)               (A>B) OR (C<D)
(A>B) EOR (C>D)               E$>F$
((A+C)>(B–D)) AND ((B+C)<(D–A))
```

2 How would you code the following conditions in BASIC?

X is equal to Y
X is not equal to Y
A is not less than or equal to B
Q is not greater than T
X is greater than or equal to Y
X is less than or equal to Y and A is not equal to B
A is greater than 18 and H is greater than 68 and W is greater than 75
G is less than 100 and greater than 50
H is less than 50 or greater than 100

3 Comment upon the errors in the following pseudocode.

```
IF A>B THEN          IF A>B THEN
ELSE                    X=Y
   X=Y                  IF C>D THEN
                           P=Q
                        END IF
                        ELSE
                           Z=X
                     ELSE
                        A=B
                     END IF
```

4 Trace through the following segment of code for each new value of A, B and C given in the table, and state the output in each case.

```
IF A>0 THEN
  IF B<0 THEN
    PRINT "X"
  ELSE
    IF C>20 THEN
      PRINT "Y"
    END IF
  END IF
  PRINT "Z"
END IF
```

A	B	C
16	16	32
16	−18	32
−2	−4	16

5 The cost of a standard size trophy is determined by the type of material from which it is made. The following table gives a list of costs.

material	cost of trophy
gold	£5000
silver	£2100
stainless steel	£1000
bronze	£300
pewter	£200

Design and write a program to input the type of material and print the cost of the trophy.

6 A salesman earns a commission on the value of his sales. The following table shows the scale of the commission.

Value of Sales (Inclusive)	Percentage Commission on Sale Value
£1 – £999	1
£1000 – £9999	5
£10000 – £99999	10

Design and write a program to input a figure for the value of his sales (in whole pounds only), and calculate and print his commission.

7 The following table shows that the product code of an article indicates the percentage commission a salesman can earn from the value of a sale.

Product Code	Commission %
1	0.5
2	1
3	2
4	2.5
5	3.5

Design and write a program to input the product code (1 – 5) and the value of a sale, calculate and print the commission on that product.

8 The difference in gas meter readings taken over two consecutive quarters of a year will give the amount of gas used in cubic feet.

Domestic gas is charged for on a sliding scale.
The first 50 therms 24p per therm.
Remainder 21p per therm.

If the difference in gas readings is multiplied by a factor of 1.040 this will give the number of therms used.

Design and write a program to input meter readings from two consecutive quarters, calculate the cost (in pence) of gas used and print the result.

9 A man is paid at the hourly rate of £8 per hour for the first 35 hours worked.

Thereafter overtime is paid at 1½ times the hourly rate for the next 25 hours and 2 times the hourly rate for further hours worked.

Design and write a program to input the number of hours worked per week, calculate and print his gross weekly wage.

10 A student studying Computer Science at a college is examined by coursework and written examination. Both components of the assessment carry a maximum of 50 marks.

The following rules are used by the examiners in order to pass or fail students.

A student must score a total of 40% or more in order to pass.

A total mark of 39% is moderated to 40%.

However, each component must be passed with a minimum mark of 15.

If a student scores 40% or more but does not achieve the minimum mark in one component he is given a technical fail of 39% (This mark is **not** moderated to 40%).

Design and write a program to input the marks for each component and print the final mark.

7 Repetition

7.1 Introduction

In designing computer programs it is often necessary to repeat part of a program a number of times. One way of achieving this would be to write out that part of the program as many times as it was needed. This, however, is a very impractical method since it would produce a very lengthy computer program and the number of times part of the program was to be repeated is not always known in advance. The purpose of this chapter is to introduce the reader to three methods for repetition that overcome the disadvantages just mentioned. These methods are based on the control structures known as **REPEAT....UNTIL**; **WHILE....DO**; and **FOR....NEXT**.

7.2 Loops controlled by counters

The following flowchart illustrates a program design to calculate the gross weekly wage of an hourly paid employee.

7.2 (cont.)

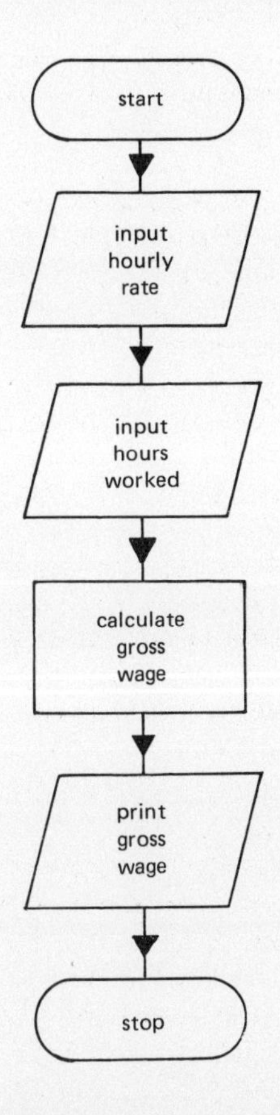

This sequence of instructions can be repeated to process the gross weekly wages for say, ten employees all paid at the same hourly rate, by introducing a *loop*. A loop enables part of a program to be repeated over and over again. However, in setting up a loop it is vital to be able to control the number of times the loop will be executed. Failure to do this would result in the part program being repeated forever and the programmer would have set up what is known as an infinite loop.

In this problem the number of employees gross wages to be processed is known in advance, therefore, it is a simple matter of using a counter to control the number of times the loop is executed. The counter is initially set to zero, and every time an employees wage is processed the counter is increased by 1. Clearly when the counter reaches the value 10 (the number of employees) the computer will exit from the loop.

The following flowchart illustrates the introduction of a loop controlled by a counter.

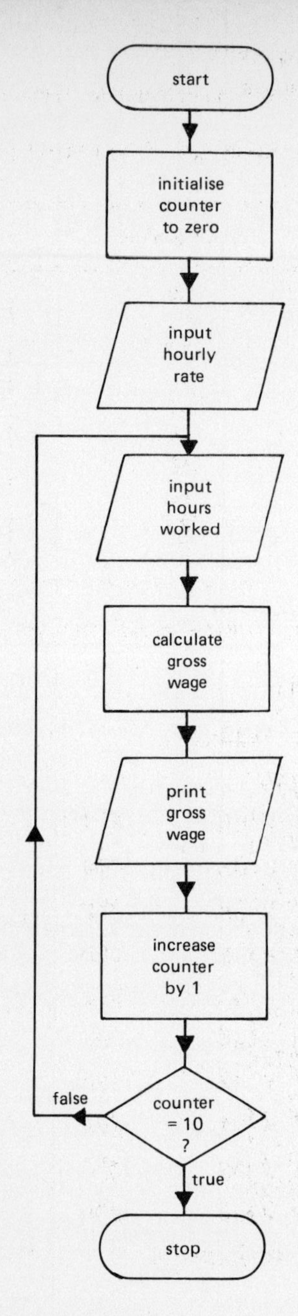

The method used to code this type of loop uses a combination of IF...THEN... and GOTO statements as the following program illustrates.

Glossary
C — counter
R — hourly rate of pay
H — hours worked
G — gross wage

Program

```
10  LET C = 0
20  INPUT "RATE", R
30   INPUT "HOURS", H
40   LET G = H * R
50   PRINT "GROSS WAGE", G
60   LET C = C + 1
70  IF C = 10 THEN STOP
80  GOTO 30
```

Note. If the condition to exit from the loop is changed to *counter* < *10* and the true and false answers swapped over

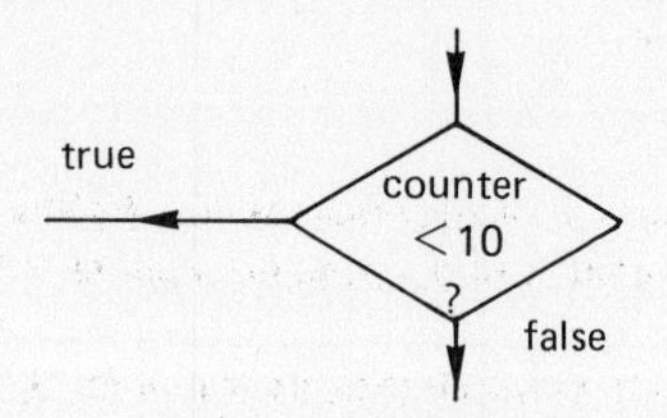

then lines 70 and 80 in this program can be changed to:

```
.
.
70 IF C < 10 THEN GOTO 30
80 STOP
```

Furthermore, the majority of the dialects of BASIC will permit the GOTO statement after the THEN in the IF...THEN... statement to be omitted giving:

```
70 IF C < 10 THEN 30
```

7.3 Repeat...Until...

The last program could have been designed using pseudocode. New pseudocode is necessary to represent testing for the exit condition at the **end** of the loop. By comparing a skeletal form of the last flowchart with the new pseudocode it will be clear to see the function of the **REPEAT....UNTIL....** construct.

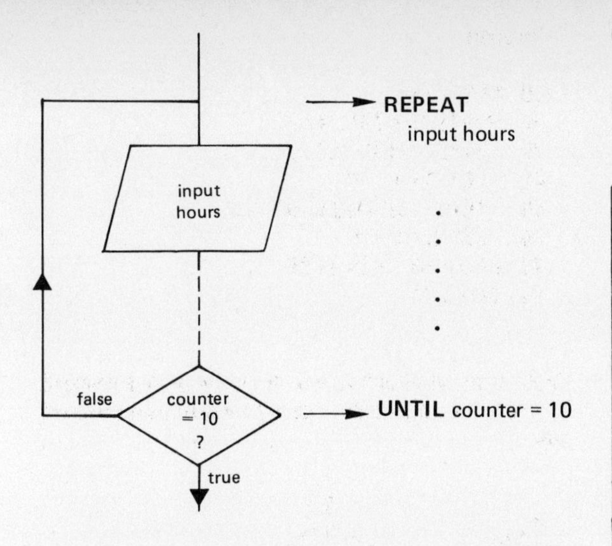

All the statements that appear between the **REPEAT** and **UNTIL** are executed until the condition *counter = 10* becomes true.

With this type of loop the statements within the loop must be executed by the computer at least once.

The full program design using pseudocode for this problem can be documented as follows.

```
initialise counter to zero
input hourly rate
REPEAT
   input hours worked
   calculate gross wage
   print gross wage
   increase counter by 1
UNTIL counter = 10
stop
```

Many dialects of BASIC now support the **REPEAT... UNTIL...** construct. The design to the last problem could be coded as follows.

```
10  LET counter = 0
20  INPUT "RATE", rate
30  REPEAT
40    INPUT "HOURS", hours
50    LET wage = hours * rate
60    PRINT "GROSS WAGE", wage
70    LET counter = counter + 1
80  UNTIL counter = 10
90  STOP
```

Using your computer

Type and SAVE an appropriate version of the last program.

LOAD and RUN using the following test data.

rate	hours worked
10	40
	55
	35
	10
	55
	60
	45
	25
	35
	20

Check that the gross wages, for each employee are correct.

Specimen results

```
>LOAD "WAGE1"
>RUN
RATE?10
HOURS?40
GROSS WAGE        400
HOURS?55
GROSS WAGE        550
HOURS?35
GROSS WAGE        350
HOURS?10
GROSS WAGE        100
HOURS?55
GROSS WAGE        550
HOURS?60
GROSS WAGE        600
HOURS?45
GROSS WAGE        450
HOURS?25
GROSS WAGE        250
HOURS?35
GROSS WAGE        350
HOURS?20
GROSS WAGE        200

STOP at line 90
>
```

7.4 Loops controlled by rogue values

In the last example the number of employees was known in advance to be ten. How could such a program be designed if this figure was not known in advance?

The answer is to use the input data as a *trigger* to exit from the loop. In the employee wages example if the number of hours worked was a negative value this would signify the end of the data to be processed. This change in exit from the loop can be demonstrated in the following flowchart.

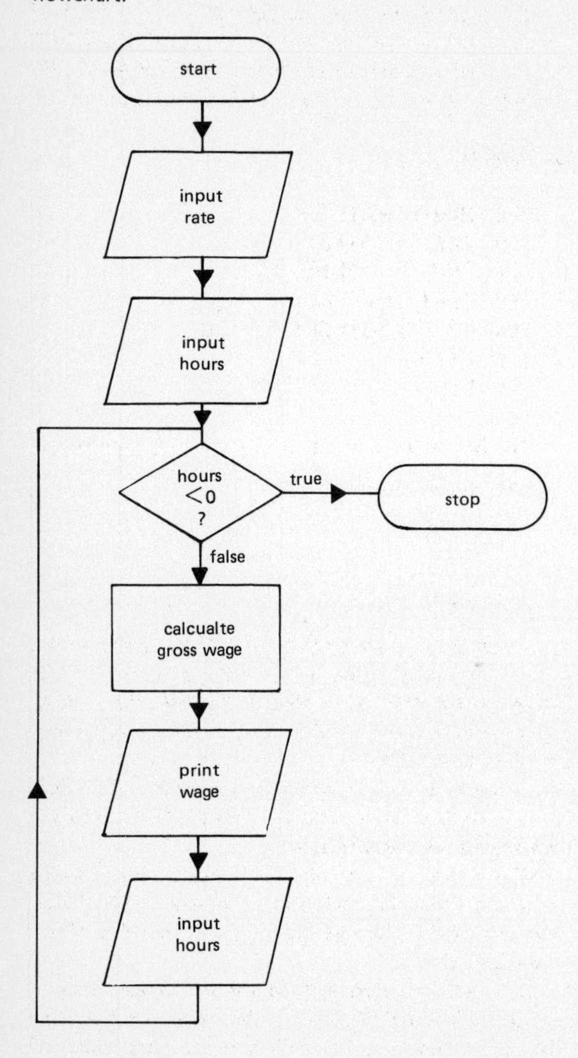

The reader may question the use of *input hours* twice in the flowchart. The reason for this is to preserve the structure of the loop. As can be seen from the flowchart the method of testing for the exit condition is through the **first** statement in the loop which conforms to a standard control structure. If the second *input hours* was re-drawn to loop-back to the first *input hours* then the first statement in the loop no longer becomes the test for the exit condition.

The coding of this design uses a combination of IF... THEN... and GOTO statements.

Program

```
10 INPUT "RATE", R
20 INPUT "HOURS", H
30 IF H < 0 THEN STOP
40   LET G = H * R
50   PRINT "GROSS WAGE", G
60   INPUT "HOURS", H
70 GOTO 30
```

7.5 While... Do...

If this last program had been designed using pseudocode then another new pseudocode instruction would be necessary to represent testing for the exit condition at the **beginning** of the loop. By comparing a skeletal form of the last flowchart with the new pseudocode it will be clear to see the function of the WHILE... DO construct.

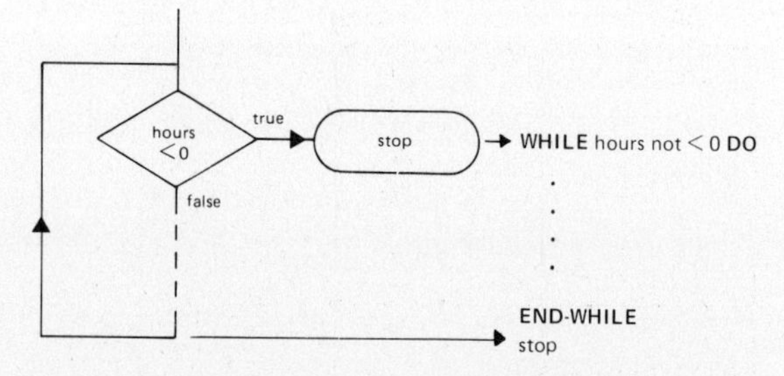

All the statements that appear between the WHILE... DO and END WHILE are executed until the condition *hours not < 0* becomes false. There has been a need to negate the condition given in the flowchart.

With this type of loop the statements within the loop may be executed zero or more times. In other words since the test for the exit condition comes at the beginning of the loop the statements within the body of the loop may never be executed if the condition to execute the loop body is false.

The full program design using pseudocode for this problem can be documented as follows.

```
input hourly rate
input hours worked
WHILE hours worked not < 0 DO
  calculate wage
  print wage
  input hours worked
END WHILE
stop
```

Some dialects of BASIC support the **WHILE...DO** construct. The design to the last problem could be coded as follows, using Microsoft BASIC.

Program

```
10  INPUT "RATE", rate
20  INPUT "HOURS", hours
30  WHILE hours NOT < 0
40    LET wage = hours * rate
50    PRINT "GROSS WAGE", wage
60    INPUT "HOURS", hours
70  WEND
80  STOP
```

Using your computer

Type and SAVE an appropriate version of the last program.

LOAD and RUN using the following test data.

rate	hours worked
10	35
	40
	20
	60
	0
	−1

Check the results.
Why did 0 not stop the computer?

Specimen results

```
>LOAD "WAGE2"
>RUN
RATE?10
HOURS?35
GROSS WAGE          350
HOURS?40
GROSS WAGE          400
HOURS?20
GROSS WAGE          200
HOURS?60
GROSS WAGE          600
HOURS?0
GROSS WAGE            0
HOURS?-1

STOP at line 30
>
```

7.6 For...Next

From the example of controlling a loop by a counter given in section 7.2 it is evident that the coding involves

setting up a loop counter to an initial value;
increasing the value of the loop counter each time a program segment within the loop has been executed;
testing the loop counter to determine whether its value has reached in order to exit from the loop.

The process of coding the loop control in a computer program can be simplified by the use of the FOR...NEXT ... statements. Using these statements the example program given in section 7.2 could be re-coded as follows.

Program

```
10  INPUT "RATE", R
20  FOR C = 0 TO 9
30    INPUT "HOURS", H
40    LET G = H * R
50    PRINT "GROSS WAGE", G
60  NEXT C
70  STOP
```

The two statements that provide the loop control are:

```
20  FOR C = 0 TO 9
      .
      .
      .
60  NEXT C
```

When the statement FOR C = 0 TO 9 is executed C is set to the initial value 0. Upon the execution of the NEXT C statement the computer increases the value of C by 1 and tests whether the new value for C has exceeded the final value of 9.

If the value of C is still within the range of the values from 0 to 9 the statements between the FOR...NEXT... statements are executed again.

The re-execution of these statements will continue until C exceeds the final value of 9, when the computer will exit from the loop by executing the statement following NEXT C.

The recommended method for the implementation of the FOR...NEXT...loop is shown in the following flowchart. However, this method is not always followed by writers of the various dialects of BASIC and it is common for the statements between the FOR and NEXT to be executed at least once regardless of the initial and final values of the controlling variable.

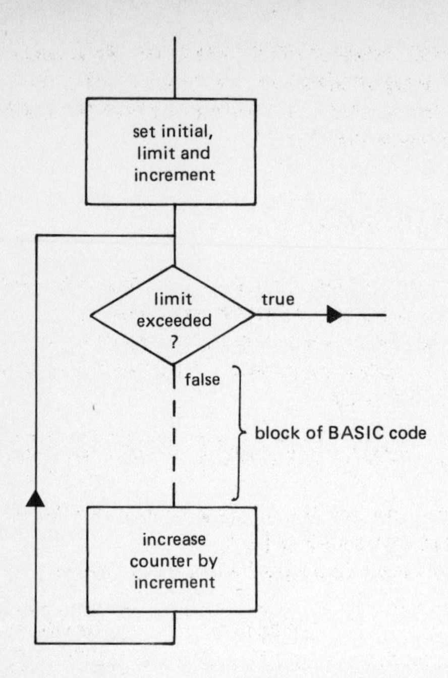

The reader should note that the loop is terminated when the counter limit is exceeded rather than when it is reached. For this reason it is not advisable to use the counter for arithmetic when the loop has been exited unless the counter is re-initialised.

7.6.1 Format of For...Next

The syntax of this statement is as follows.

FOR data-name = initial **TO** final [**STEP** increment]
.
.
NEXT data-name.

Note. **STEP** is optional and when omitted an incremental value of +1 is assumed. Initial, final and increment values can be numeric literals, numeric data-names or arithmetic expressions.

Examples.

```
FOR K = 1 TO 9 STEP 2
.
.
NEXT K
```

K will be assigned the values 1, 3, 5, 7, 9 for each iteration of the program statements.

```
FOR L = I to J STEP K
.
.
NEXT L
```

L will be assigned the values I, I + K, I + 2K, I + 3K, ...J for each iteration of the program statements. If I + nK will never become equal to J then iteration will continue until I + nK is greater than the final value J.

```
FOR X = A TO A * B
.
.
NEXT X

FOR Z = 16 TO 4 STEP -4
.
.
NEXT Z
```

If the increment value is negative then the initial value should be numerically higher than the final value.

7.6.2 Rules for Using For...Next Loops

Loops may be nested (embedded one inside the other).

Example.

```
10 FOR I = 1 TO 2
20   PRINT I
30   FOR J = 1 TO 3
40     PRINT J
50   NEXT J
60 NEXT I
70 STOP
```

The depth to which loops may be nested depends upon the computer system being used, however, in practice nesting rarely exceeds 3 or 4 loops in depth.

Loops must never cross each other. This following program segment is **wrong.**

Example.

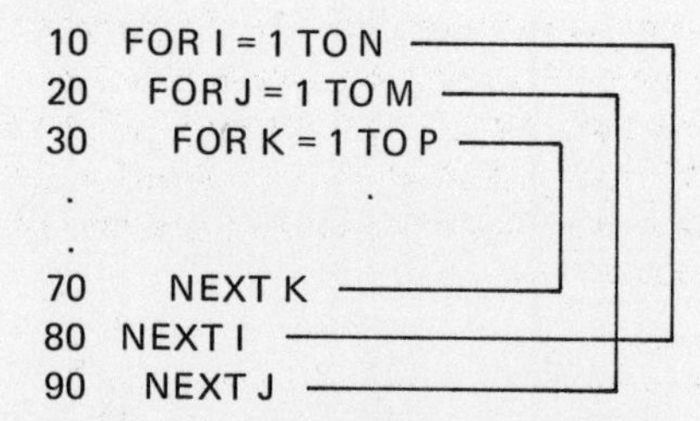

```
10 FOR I = 1 TO N
20   FOR J = 1 TO M
30     FOR K = 1 TO P
.
.
70     NEXT K
80 NEXT I
90   NEXT J
```

If pairs of FOR...NEXT... statements are indented then the starting and ending positions of loops in a program can easily be identified. The indentation of the NEXT statements in this last example has clearly gone wrong and serves as an indication that two loops have crossed over. The segment of code should have been written as follows.

```
10  FOR I = 1 TO N
20    FOR J = 1 TO M
30      FOR K = 1 TO P
 .
 .
70      NEXT K
80    NEXT J
90  NEXT I
```

The numeric data-name given to a loop variable should never be re-assigned with a different value within the loop.

Example.

```
10  FOR I = 1 TO N
20    LET I = I + 1
 .
 .
50  NEXT I
```

It is permissible to branch outside a FOR...NEXT... loop (as indeed it is for REPEAT...UNTIL... and WHILE...DO loops) provided the parameters of the loop are not changed and transfer is back into the loop.

Example.

```
10  FOR I = 1 TO N
20    GOTO 100
30
 .
 .
60  NEXT I
 .
 .
 .
100 LET X = I * I
110 PRINT X
120 GOTO 30
```

Note. Branching out of a loop using GOTO statements in this example is not recommended for the reader who wishes to use structured programming methods correctly.

The following diagrams illustrate the ranges of several FOR...NEXT... loops. Diagram i shows branches that are permissible and diagram ii shows those branches that are not permissible.

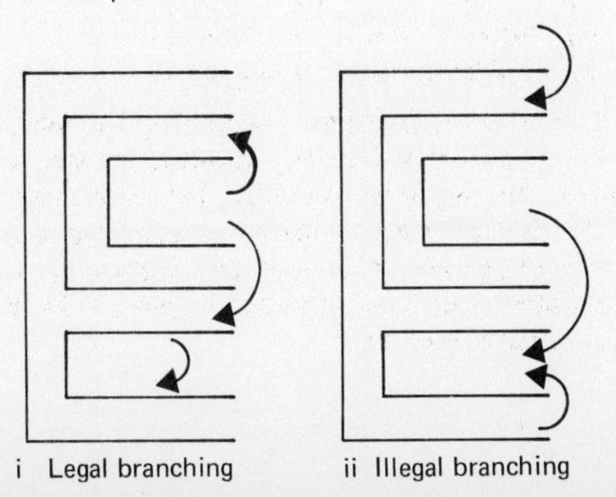

i Legal branching   ii Illegal branching

Avoid fractional STEP values since these could lead to rounding problems. In long loops the values generated may not be exact representations inside the computer of the values intended.

7.6.3 Example

Consider having a number of childrens' wooden building bricks each of a different colour.

If two bricks are placed side by side they will form a pattern, change the position of one brick and another pattern is formed.

e.g. [RED] [YELLOW]   [YELLOW] [RED]

Thus the number of patterns that can be formed using two bricks is 2 or 1 x 2.

If three bricks are used the patterns become:

RED	YELLOW	GREEN
YELLOW	RED	GREEN
YELLOW	GREEN	RED
RED	GREEN	YELLOW
GREEN	RED	YELLOW
GREEN	YELLOW	RED

Thus with three bricks the number of patterns is 6 or 1 x 2 x 3. Similarly with:

4 bricks number of patterns is 1 x 2 x 3 x 4
5 bricks number of patterns is 1 x 2 x 3 x 4 x 5
6 bricks number of patterns is 1 x 2 x 3 x 4 x 5 x 6
etc.

From these results the reader should deduce that the number of patterns is always the product of the integers from 1 to the number of bricks.

Write a computer program to output the number of patterns formed as the number of different coloured building bricks increases from 3 to 9.

```
design
FOR bricks = 3 TO 9
  initialise number of patterns to 1
  FOR brick counter = 2 TO bricks
    calculate number of patterns
  NEXT brick counter
  print bricks
  print numbers of patterns
NEXT brick
stop
```

glossary	
bricks	B
brick counter	C
number of patterns	P

```
program
 10  FOR B = 3 TO 9
 20    LET P = 1
 30    FOR C = 2 TO B
 40      LET P = P*C
 50    NEXT C
 60    PRINT "NUMBER OF BRICKS", B
 70    PRINT "NUMBER OF PATTERNS", P
 80    PRINT
 90  NEXT B
100  STOP
```

Using your computer

Type and SAVE the last program.

LOAD and RUN the program.

Which loop is executed the most by the computer B or C?

Specimen results

```
>LOAD "BRICKS"
>RUN
NUMBER OF BRICKS              3
NUMBER OF PATTERNS            6

NUMBER OF BRICKS              4
NUMBER OF PATTERNS           24

NUMBER OF BRICKS              5
NUMBER OF PATTERNS          120

NUMBER OF BRICKS              6
NUMBER OF PATTERNS          720

NUMBER OF BRICKS              7
NUMBER OF PATTERNS         5040

NUMBER OF BRICKS              8
NUMBER OF PATTERNS        40320

NUMBER OF BRICKS              9
NUMBER OF PATTERNS       362880

STOP at line 100
>
```

7.7 Worked Example

7.7.1 Problem

In an examination four pass grades and one fail grade is awarded:

A for marks between 70 and 100 inclusive,
B for marks between 60 and 69 inclusive,
C for marks between 50 and 59 inclusive,
D for marks between 40 and 49 inclusive,
F for marks below 40.

Design and write a program to input an examination mark for a student and print the grade. Repeat the procedure until the examination mark is 999, then print the total number of students in each of the five grades.

7.7.2 Design

Pseudocode

```
initialise the total number in each grade to zero
input mark
WHILE mark not = 999 DO
  CASE mark OF
  WHEN 70 TO 100
    increase grade A count by 1
    print grade A
  WHEN 60 TO 69
    increase grade B count by 1
    print grade B
  WHEN 50 TO 59
    increase grade C count by 1
    print grade C
  WHEN 40 TO 49
    increase grade D count by 1
    print grade D
  OTHERWISE
    increase grade F count by 1
    print grade F
  END CASE
  input mark
END WHILE
print grade counts for A,B,C,D,F
stop
```

Flowchart (as alternative)

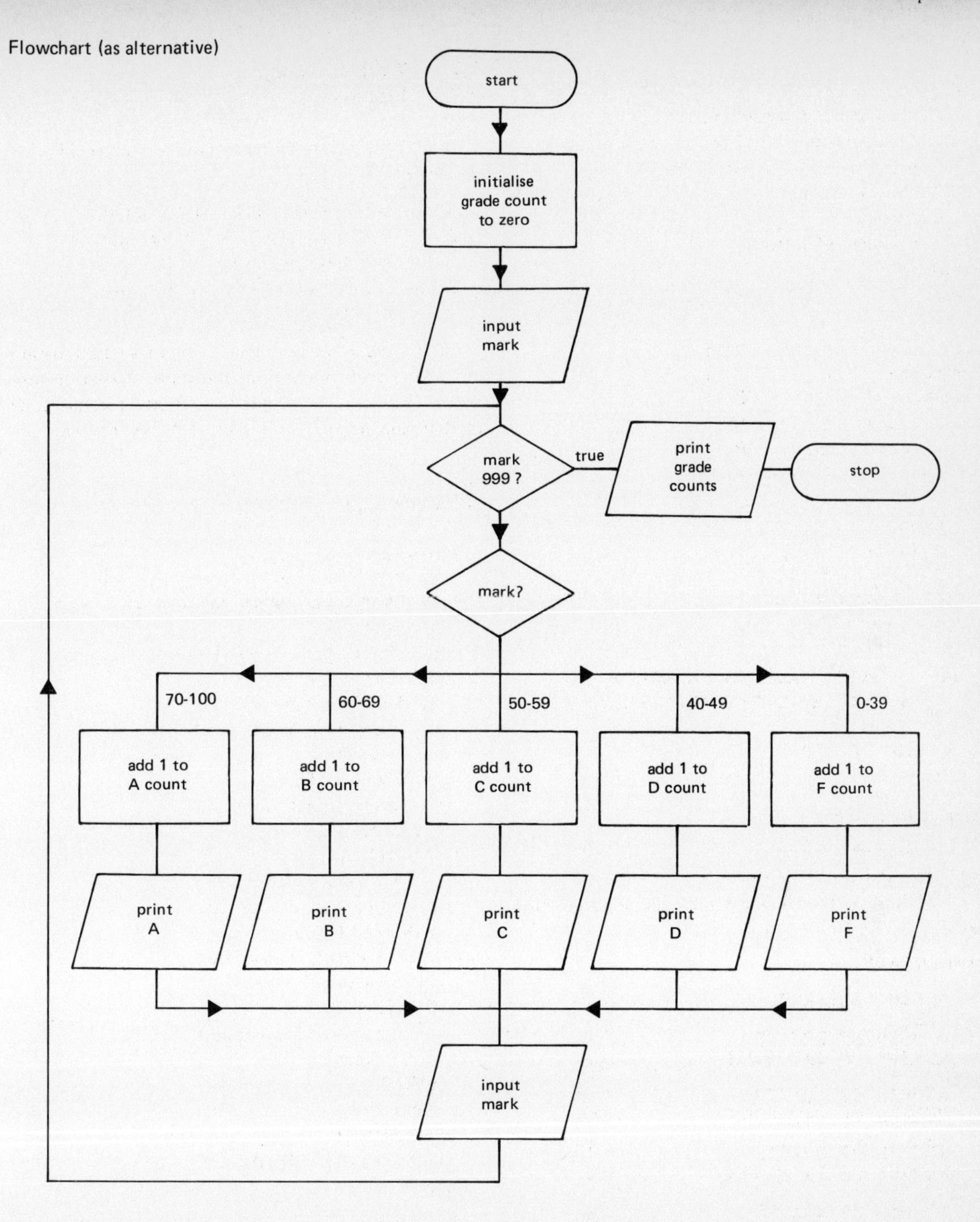

7.7.3 Desk Check

Test data: 95,60,71,20,50,62,54,999

mark	count A	count B	count C	count D	count F	(printed output)
	0	0	0	0	0	
95	1					A
60		1				B
71	2					A
20					1	F
50			1			C
62		2				B
54			2			C
999						2,2,2,0,1

7.7.4 Coding

Glossary	
count A	A
count B	B
count C	C
count D	D
count F	F
mark	M

Note: if a WHILE loop is not available in your dialect then substitute

```
 70 IF M = 999 THEN 280
270 GOTO 70
```

Method 1 **Microsoft**

```
 10 LET A = 0
 20 LET B = 0
 30 LET C = 0
 40 LET D = 0
 50 LET F = 0
 60 INPUT "MARK", M
 70 WHILE M <> 999
 80   IF M < 70 THEN 120
 90     LET A = A + 1
100     PRINT "GRADE A"
110   GOTO 260
120   IF M < 60 THEN 160
130     LET B = B + 1
140     PRINT "GRADE B"
150   GOTO 260
160   IF M < 50 THEN 200
170     LET C = C + 1
180     PRINT "GRADE C"
190   GOTO 260
200   IF M < 40 THEN 240
210     LET D = D + 1
220     PRINT "GRADE D"
230   GOTO 260
240     LET F = F + 1
250     PRINT "GRADE F"
260   INPUT "MARK", M
270 WEND
280 PRINT "A", A
290 PRINT "B", B
300 PRINT "C", C
310 PRINT "D", D
320 PRINT "F", F
330 STOP
```

Method 2 Structured BASIC

```
 10 A: = 0: B: = 0: C: = 0: D: = 0: F: = 0
 20 INPUT "mark", mark
 30 WHILE mark <> 999 DO
 40   CASE mark OF
 50     WHEN 70 to 100
 60       A: = A + 1: PRINT "grade A"
 70     WHEN 60 TO 69
 80       B: = B + 1: PRINT "grade B"
 90     WHEN 50 TO 59
100       C: = C + 1: PRINT "grade C"
110     WHEN 40 TO 49
120       D: = D + 1: PRINT "grade D"
130     OTHERWISE
140       F: = F + 1: PRINT "grade F"
150   ENDCASE
160   INPUT "mark", mark
170 ENDWHILE
180 PRINT "grade A", A
190 PRINT "grade B", B
200 PRINT "grade C", C
210 PRINT "grade D", D
220 PRINT "grade F", F
230 STOP
```

Using your computer

Type and SAVE the last program using an appropriate dialect.

LOAD and RUN using the test data in 7.7.3.

Are the results consistent with the desk check?

Specimen results

```
>LOAD "GRADES"
>RUN
MARK?95
GRADE A
MARK?60
GRADE B
MARK?71
GRADE A
MARK?20
GRADE F
MARK?50
GRADE C
MARK?62
GRADE B
MARK?54
GRADE C
MARK?999
A                    2
B                    2
C                    2
D                    0
F                    1

STOP at line 330
>
```

7.8 Dialect Differences

7.8.1 Repeat . . . Until

Microsoft does not support the structure.

BBC/Electron BASIC supports this loop structure. The format is identical to that shown in 7.3.

7.8.2 While . . . Do

Microsoft BASIC supports this loop structure. The format of the structure in Microsoft BASIC is illustrated in section 7.5.

7.8.3 For . . . Next

This loop structure is implemented in both dialects.

Microsoft. The format of the statement is:

```
FOR variable = x TO y STEP z
 —
 —
NEXT variable ,variable . . . .
```

The body of the loop is skipped over if $x > y$ when $z > 0$ or if $x < y$ when $z < 0$. If $z = 0$ an infinite loop is created. When using nested loops NEXT K,J,I is the same as:

```
    NEXT K
  NEXT J
NEXT I
```

If the variables in the NEXT statement are omitted the most recent FOR is matched with the NEXT (although this is bad programming practice the program will run faster). Use integer variables in FOR . . . NEXT loops to also improve program performance times.

BBC/Electron. The format is the same as described in section 7.6. However, regardless of the values of the parameters (x,y,z) the loop always executes at least once.

7.9 Keywords

Loop, counter, REPEAT. . .UNTIL;
rogue value, WHILE. . .DO;
FOR. . .NEXT, nested loops;

7.10 Questions

1 Comment upon the errors in the following segments of code.

a)
```
10  FOR I = 10 TO 1
20  –
30  –
40  NEXT
```

b)
```
10  FOR I = 1, 3
20    FOR J = 1, 4
30  –
40  –
50    NEXT I
60  NEXT J
```

c)
```
10  FOR I = 1 TO 5
20  LET I = 3*I ↑ 2 + 4*I – 7
30  –
40  –
50  NEXT I
```

2 Comment upon the errors in the following segments of code.

a)
```
100  WHILE I = 1 TO 4
     –
     –
200  END WHILE
```

b)
```
100  REPEAT UNTIL J > 3
     –
     –
200  END REPEAT
```

c)
```
100  I = 3
110  WHILE I > 0
      –
      –
190   I = I + 1
200  END WHILE
```

3 Write a program to calculate and output the overtime pay for ten employees. Overtime is paid at £12.00 per hour for every hour worked over 40 hours per week. Assume that employees **do not** work for fractional parts of an hour.

4 Write a program to output.

a. The odd integers between 1 and 49.
b. The squares of even integers between 2 and 50.
c. The sum of the cubes of odd integers between 11 and 19.

5 Write a program to output the first twenty terms of the Fibonacci series (1 1 2 3 5 8 · · · ·).

Note: The next value in the series is the sum of the previous two values.

6 Design and write a procedure to find the arithmetic mean of a list of positive numbers, and print the arithmetic mean. The number of numbers is not known in advance. Terminate the procedure with zero.

7 Design and write a procedure to find the largest number from a list of ten numbers. Print the largest number.

8 Design and write a procedure to input an amount of money as a whole number of Pounds Sterling and produce a breakdown of the number of notes required to make up the sum of money using the minimum number of notes. Only £10, £5 and £1 notes are used.

8 Worked Examples

8.1 Introduction

This chapter serves as a milestone in the book since it brings together all the work of the previous chapters and illustrates to readers the design, coding and testing of complete programs that incorporate the fundamental constructs of structured programming – sequence, selection and repetition. The design of computer programs is documented through pseudocode and as an alternative design technique through flowcharts. The flowchart has been retained as far as this chapter since many examination boards for Computer Studies still have algorithm design by flowchart in their syllabuses. The use of the flowchart as a method of design will be abandoned in favour of pseudocode in the chapters that follow. Program coding is illustrated using the two dialects of BASIC considered in this book, and in addition through a Structured BASIC.

8.2 Problem One

A schoolteacher keeps the names and addresses of his class of pupils on record cards. Pupils travel to school from many different villages in the rural region. The schoolteacher wants to design a computer program to count those pupils in his class who fall into the following categories.

Distance to school	Category
0 to less than 1 mile	A
1 to less than 5 miles	B
5 to less than 10 miles	C
10 miles or further	D

The schoolteacher has for reference a map of the region with circles drawn from the school as centre having radii representing 1 mile, 5 miles and 10 miles. From a pupils record card he knows the village where a pupil lives, therefore, the distance from the school in a straight line can be obtained from the map.

For a class of pupils the input to the computer will be the number of pupils in a class followed by the distance each pupil lives away from school. When data input is complete the computer will output the number of pupils in each of the four categories A–D.

8.2.1 Program design

Pseudocode.

```
initialise contents of categories A–D to zero
input class size
FOR pupil = 1 TO class size
 input distance
 IF distance < 1 THEN
  category A = category A + 1
 ELSE
  IF distance < 5 THEN
   category B = category B + 1
  ELSE
   IF distance < 10 THEN
    category C = category C + 1
   ELSE
    category D = category D + 1
   END IF
  END IF
 END IF
NEXT pupil
print category A
print category B
print category C
print category D
stop
```

Flowchart

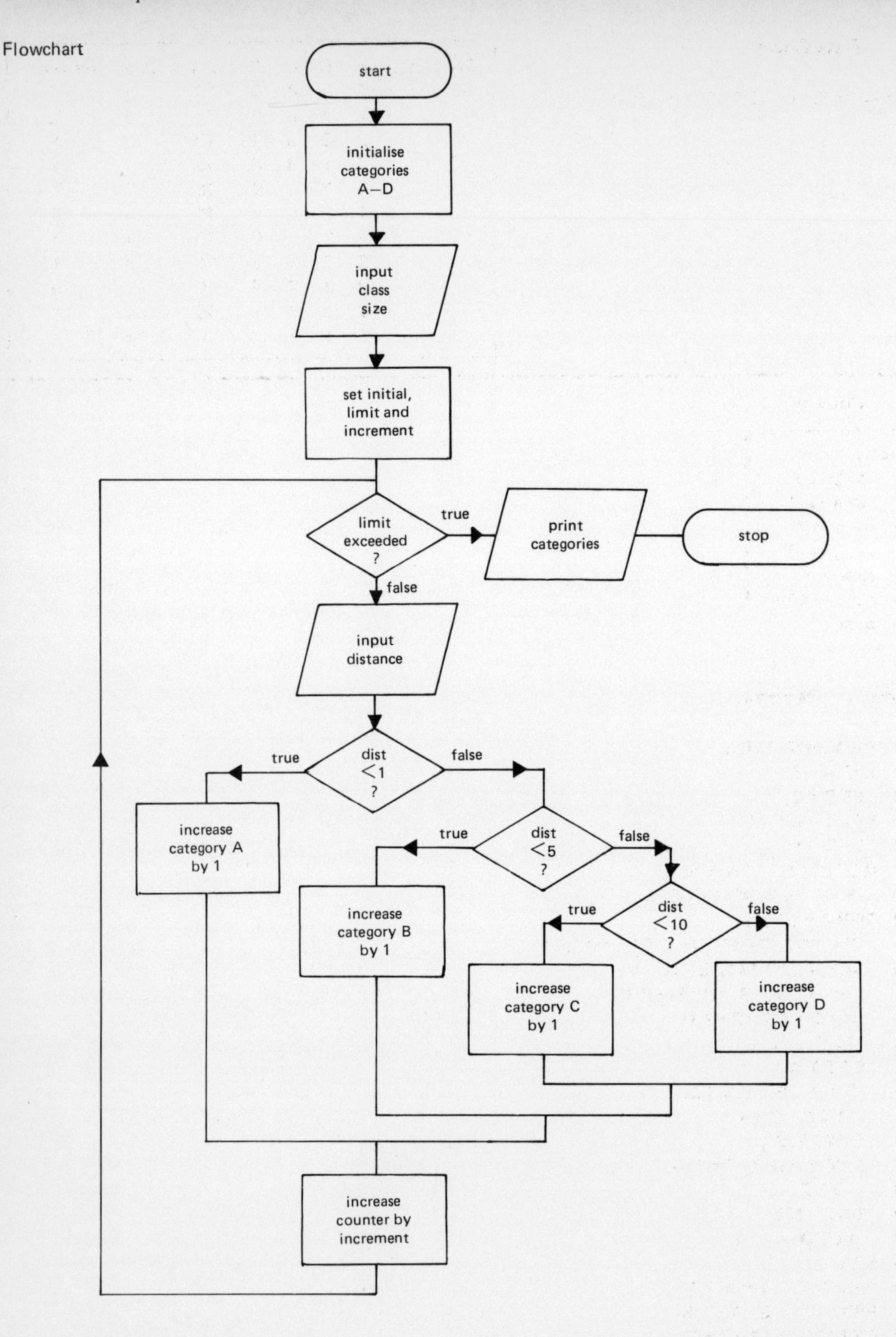
start
initialise categories A–D
input class size
set initial, limit and increment
limit exceeded ?
true
print categories
stop
false
input distance
dist <1 ?
true
false
increase category A by 1
dist <5 ?
true
false
increase category B by 1
dist <10 ?
true
false
increase category C by 1
increase category D by 1
increase counter by increment

8.2.2 Desk Check

Test data: 10 ½ ¾ 1 2 ½ 5 7 4 15 3

Data-names	A	B	C	D	class size	pupil	distance
Contents	0	0	0	0	10	1	½
	1	0	0	0	10	2	¾
	2	0	0	0	10	3	1
	2	1	0	0	10	4	2
	2	2	0	0	10	5	½
	3	2	0	0	10	6	5
	3	2	1	0	10	7	7
	3	2	2	0	10	8	4
	3	3	2	0	10	9	15
	3	3	2	1	10	10	3
	3	4	2	1	10	11	

8.2.3 Coding

Glossary
A – category A
B – category B
C – category C
D – category D
S – class size
P – pupil number
X – distance

Method 1 Microsoft

```
 10 REM..INITIALISE
 20 LET A = 0
 30 LET B = 0
 40 LET C = 0
 50 LET D = 0
 60 REM..INPUT CLASS SIZE
 70 INPUT "SIZE OF CLASS", S
 80 FOR P = 1 TO S
 90   REM..INPUT DISTANCE TRAVELLED
100   INPUT "DISTANCE", X
110   REM..PROCESS CATEGORY
120   IF X >= 1 THEN 150
130     LET A = A + 1
140   GOTO 220
150   IF X >= 5 THEN 180
160     LET B = B + 1
170   GOTO 220
180   IF X >= 10 THEN 210
190     LET C = C + 1
200   GOTO 220
210     LET D = D + 1
220 NEXT P
230 PRINT "0 – 1 mile", A
240 PRINT "1 – 5 miles", B
250 PRINT "5 – 10 miles", C
260 PRINT "10 miles or further", D
270 STOP
```

Method 2 Structured BASIC

```
 10  a: = 0: b: = 0: c: = 0: d: = 0     'initialise
 20  INPUT "size of class?", class_size
 30  FOR pupil: = 1 TO class_size
 40    INPUT "distance?", distance
 50    IF distance < 1 THEN       'categorise distances
 60      a: = a + 1
 70    ELSE
 80      IF distance < 5 THEN
 90        b: = b + 1
100      ELSE
110        IF distance < 10 THEN
120          c: = c + 1
130        ELSE
140          d: = d + 1
150        ENDIF
160      ENDIF
170    ENDIF
180  NEXT pupil
190  PRINT "0 – 1 mile", a     'print categories
200  PRINT "1 – 5 miles", b
210  PRINT "5 – 10 miles", c
220  PRINT "10 miles or further", d
230  STOP
```

Using structured BASIC the nested IF's could have been re-coded as follows, however, this method does not correspond exactly with the pseudocode. Lines 140 to 170 would need to be deleted.

```
 50  IF distance < 1 THEN
 60    a: = a + 1
 70    ELIF distance < 5 THEN
 80      b: = b + 1
 90    ELIF distance < 10 THEN
100      c: = c + 1
110    ELSE
120      d: = d + 1
130  ENDIF
```

Using your computer

Type and SAVE the last program using an appropr-ate dialect.

LOAD and RUN using the test data in 8.2.2.

Are the results consistent with the desk check?

Specimen results

```
>LOAD "SCHOOL"
>RUN
SIZE OF CLASS?10
DISTANCE?0.5
DISTANCE?0.75
DISTANCE?1
DISTANCE?2
DISTANCE?0.5
DISTANCE?5
DISTANCE?7
DISTANCE?4
DISTANCE?15
DISTANCE?3
0 - 1 mile                      3
1 - 5 miles                     4
5 - 10 miles                    2
10 miles or further             1

STOP at line 270
>
```

8.2.4 Documenting Code

If the reader looks back at the presentation of the first program in the last section it is evident that a new BASIC statement has been introduced. The statement is REM, short for REMark, and will allow a programmer to document parts of a program. The format of the REM statement is as follows.

REM string of characters

A REM statement can be followed by any combination of ASCII characters. A REM statement is used to include narrative in a program and is **not** obeyed by the computer.

In method 2 an alternative symbol to the REM statement has been used, this is an apostrophe (') on the same line as the BASIC code. All characters after the apostrophe are ignored by the computer and therefore, serves the same purpose as a REM statement.

When using a microcomputer with a small main memory REM statements will soon use up valuable program space and you will run out of memory quickly. However, it is good practice to include as many comments in a program as necessary. If memory space is at a premium you can always selectively remove REM statements from your program. Start with the principle of using plenty of REM statements.

8.2.5 Multiple Statements on one line

Many dialects of BASIC will permit more than one statement on a line. In method 1 the initialisation of A, B, C and D was carried out over four lines, however, as method 2 shows these statements could have been written on one line as:

```
10  a: = 0: b: = 0: c: = 0: d: = 0    'initialise
```

Each statement must be separated from the next statement by a colon (:).

This technique can be useful if more than one statement is to be executed if a condition is either true or false in a binary selection. An example of such a selection would be:

```
100 IF A<B THEN X=2*Y:P=Q:U=3*T:GOTO 120
110   X = Y: P = --Q: U = 2*T
120
```

This technique can also be extended to a multiple selection.

8.3 Problem Two

The lengths of four sides of a quadrilateral and one internal angle, are input to a computer. Design a computer program to categorise the shape of the quadrilateral as a square, rhombus, rectangle, parallelogram or irregular quadrilateral. Include a loop in the design so that the shape of more than one quadrilateral can be determined. Only exit from the loop when the angle is zero degrees.

To help the reader the following table summarises the shapes.

8.3 (cont.)

Name	Shape	All Sides Equal	Opposite Sides Equal	Angle 90°
Square		Yes	Yes	Yes
Rectangle		No	Yes	Yes
Rhombus		Yes	Yes	No
Parallelogram		No	Yes	No
Irreg. Quad		No	No	–

A quadrilateral can be labelled according to the following diagram.

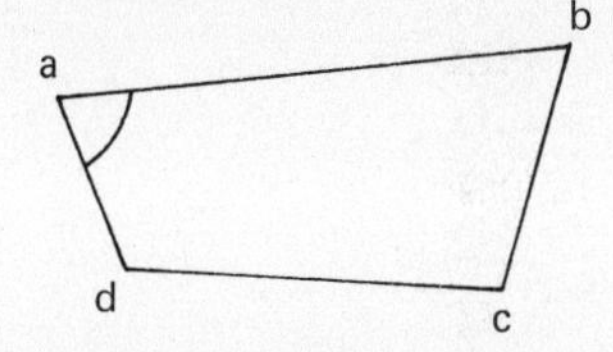

side ab = A
bc = B
cd = C
da = D
angle a = X

8.3.1 Program Design

Pseudocode.

```
input angle-a
WHILE angle-a NOT = 0 DO
  input side-ab
  input side-bc
  input side-cd
  input side-da
  IF side-ab = side-bc AND side-bc = side-cd AND side-cd = side-da THEN
    IF angle-a = 90 THEN
      print square
    ELSE
      print rhombus
    END IF
  ELSE
    IF side-ab = side-cd AND side-bc = side-da THEN
      IF angle-a = 90 THEN
        print rectangle
      ELSE
        print parallelogram
      END IF
    ELSE
      print irregular
    END IF
  END IF
    input angle-a
END WHILE
stop
```

Flowchart

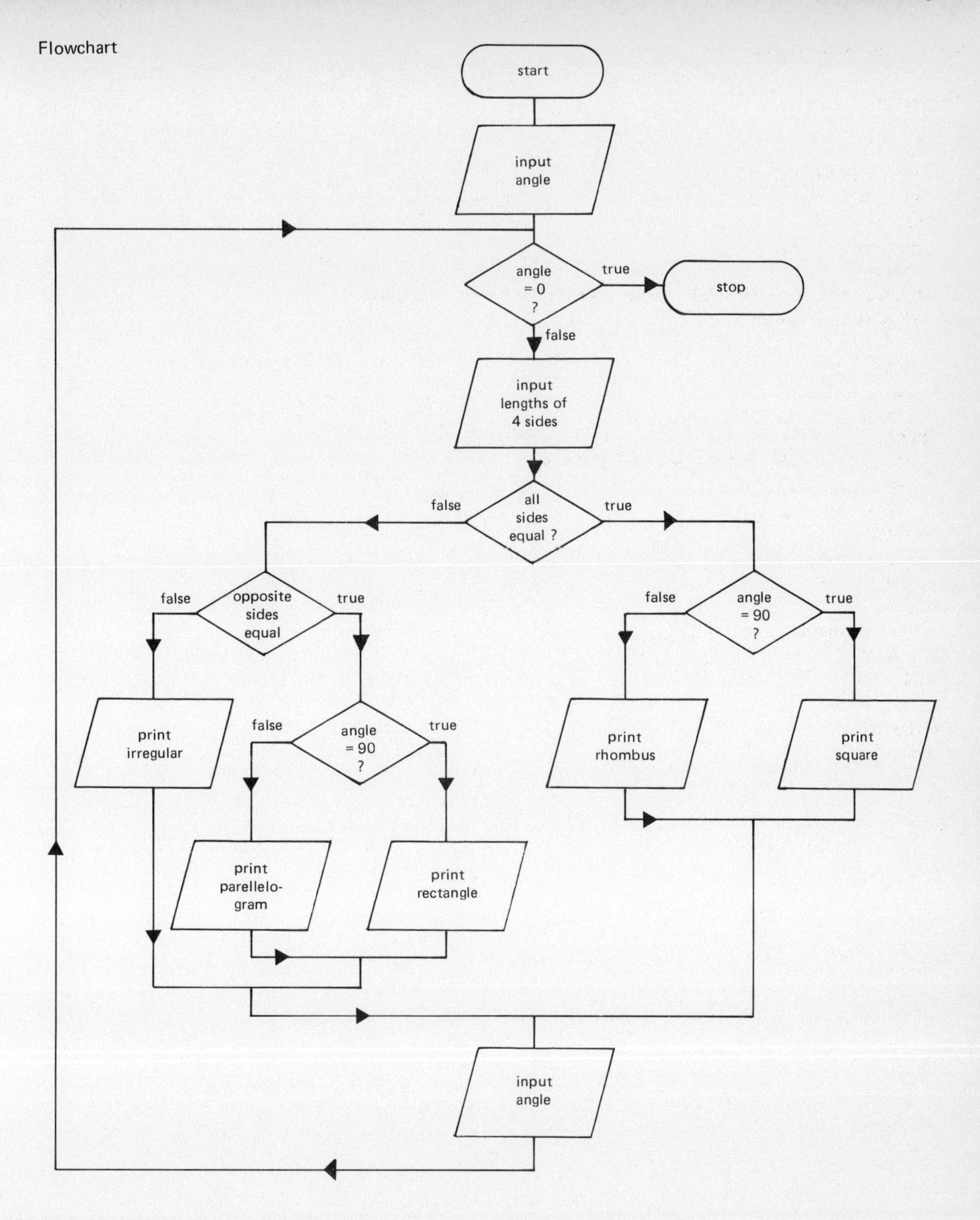
start
input angle
angle = 0 ?
true
stop
false
input lengths of 4 sides
all sides equal ?
false
true
opposite sides equal
false
true
angle = 90 ?
false
true
print irregular
angle = 90 ?
false
true
print rhombus
print square
print parellelo-gram
print rectangle
input angle

8.3.2 Desk Check

Test data:

```
 90  1  2  1  2
 90  1  1  1  1
 75  1  3  2  2½
 80  1  2  1  2
120  1  1  1  1
  0
```

side-ab	side-bc	side-cd	side-da	angle-a	output to screen
1	2	1	2	90	RECTANGLE
1	1	1	1	90	SQUARE
1	3	2	2½	75	IRREGULAR
1	2	1	2	80	PARALLELOGRAM
1	1	1	1	120	RHOMBUS
				0	

8.3.3 Coding

Glossary
X – angle
A – side ab
B – side bc
C – side cd
D – side da

Method 1 Microsoft

```
 10  REM..INPUT ANGLE
 20  INPUT "ANGLE?", X
 30  WHILE X<>0
 40    REM..INPUT LENGTHS OF SIDES
 50    INPUT "SIDE A", A
 60    INPUT "SIDE B", B
 70    INPUT "SIDE C", C
 80    INPUT "SIDE D", D
 90    REM..ANALYSE SHAPE
100    IF A<>B AND B<>C AND C<>D THEN 160
110      IF X<>90 THEN 140
120        PRINT "SQUARE"
130      GOTO 230
140        PRINT "RHOMBUS"
150      GOTO 230
160      IF A<>C AND B<>D THEN 220
170        IF X<>90 THEN 200
180          PRINT "RECTANGLE"
190        GOTO 230
200          PRINT "PARALLELOGRAM"
210        GOTO 230
220        PRINT "IRREGULAR"
230      INPUT "ANGLE?", X
240  WEND
250  STOP
```

If your computer has not got the WHILE....WEND structure then replace the code with:

```
 30  IF X = 0 THEN 250
240  GOTO 30
```

Method 2 Structured BASIC

```
10  INPUT "angle?", angle
20  WHILE angle <> 0 DO
30    INPUT "input lengths of sides a,b,c,d", a,b,c,d
40    IF a = b AND b = c AND c = d THEN
50      IF angle = 90 THEN
60        PRINT "square"
70      ELSE
80        PRINT "rhombus"
90      ENDIF
100   ELSE
110     IF a = c AND b = d THEN
120       IF angle = 90 THEN
130         PRINT "rectangle"
140       ELSE
150         PRINT "parallelogram"
160       ENDIF
170     ELSE
180       PRINT "irregular"
190     ENDIF
200   ENDIF
210   INPUT "angle?", angle
220 ENDWHILE
230 STOP
```

Using your computer

Type and SAVE the last program using an appropriate dialect.

LOAD and RUN with the test data in 8.3.2.

Are the results consistent with the desk check?

Specimen results

```
>LOAD "SHAPES"
>RUN
ANGLE?90
SIDE A?1
SIDE B?2
SIDE C?1
SIDE D?2
RECTANGLE
ANGLE?90
SIDE A?1
SIDE B?1
SIDE C?1
SIDE D?1
SQUARE
ANGLE?75
SIDE A?1
SIDE B?3
SIDE C?2
SIDE D?2.5
IRREGULAR
ANGLE?80
SIDE A?1
SIDE B?2
SIDE C?1
SIDE D?2
PARALLELOGRAM
ANGLE?120
SIDE A?1
SIDE B?1
SIDE C?1
SIDE D?1
RHOMBUS
ANGLE?0

STOP at line 250
>
```

8.3.4 Modified Input Statement

As can be seen from the programs in the last section there is no need to write separate INPUT statements for each data-name to be assigned a value. For example:

```
50  INPUT "SIDE A", A
60  INPUT "SIDE B", B
70  INPUT "SIDE C", C
80  INPUT "SIDE D", D
```

given in the first program (method 1) can be shortened to:

```
30 INPUT "input lengths of sides a,b,c,d", a,b,c,d
```

as given in the second program (method 2). Notice that in this method the data-names in the INPUT statement are separate by commas.

8.4 Problem Three

A bicycle shop in Oxford hires bicycles by the day at different rates throughout the year. The following table illustrates how the hire charge varies throughout the year.

Season	Charge £
Spring (Mar–May)	1.00
Summer (June–Aug)	1.50
Autumn (Sept–Nov)	0.75
Winter (Dec–Feb)	0.50

The proprietor also gives a discount on the number of days a bicycle is hired for. If the hire period is greater than 7 days then a reduction of 25% is made. For every bicycle hired a deposit of £5.00 must be paid. Design and code a program to input the season and number of days the bicycle is required for and output the hire charge including the deposit.

8.4.1 Program Design

Pseudocode.

```
 REPEAT
  input season
  input number of days for hire
  CASE season OF
  WHEN spring
   hire charge = number of days
  WHEN summer
   hire charge = number of days * 1.5
  WHEN autumn
   hire charge = number of days * 0.75
  OTHERWISE
   hire charge = number of days * 0.5
  END-CASE
  IF number of days > 7 THEN
   hire charge = 0.75 * hire charge
  END IF
  hire charge = hire charge + 5
  print hire charge
  print "another customer?"
  input answer
 UNTIL answer = "NO"
stop
```

Flowchart (as an alternative)

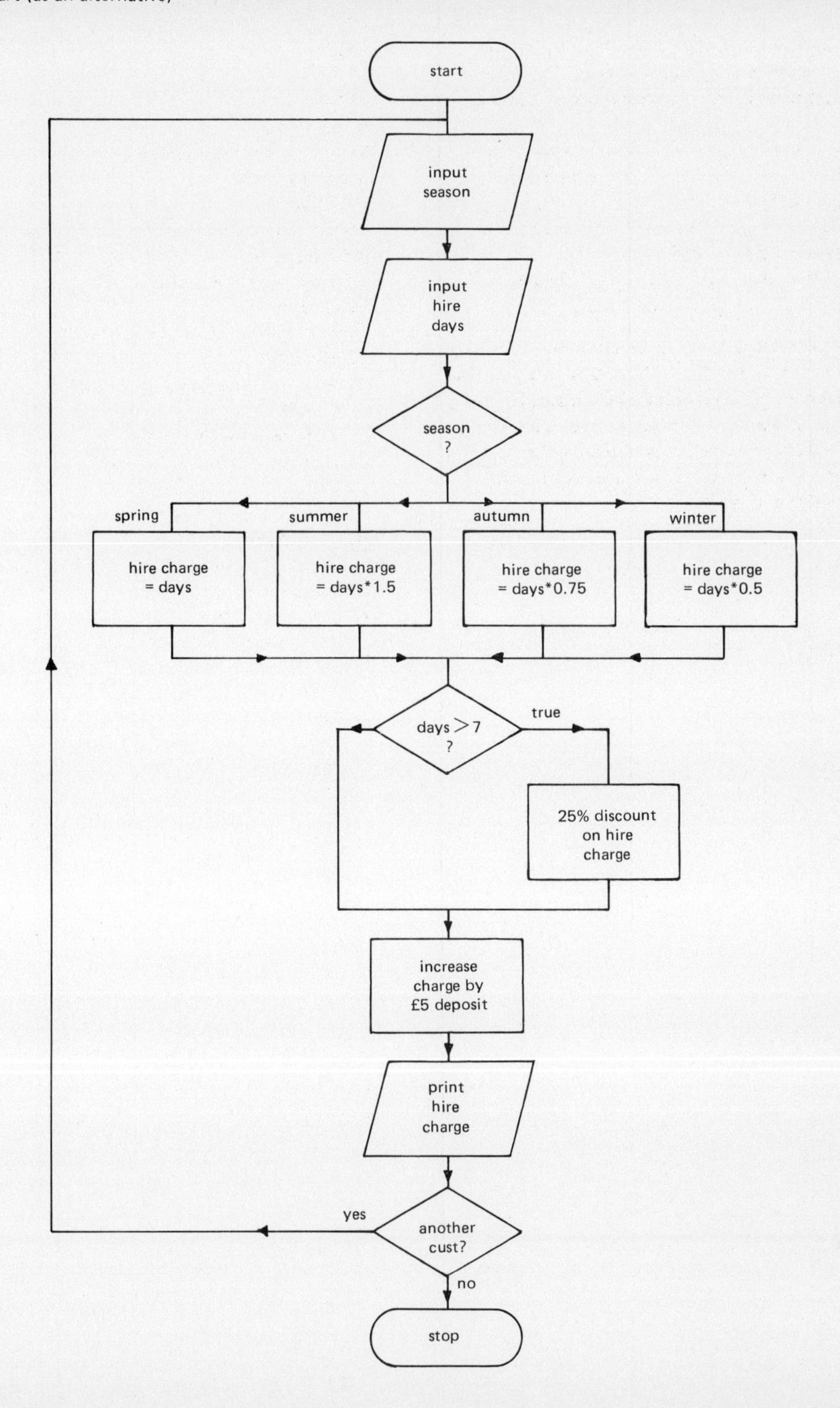

8.4.2 Desk Check

Test data: summer 4 yes
summer 8 yes
autumn 5 yes
spring 2 no

Data-names	season	days hire	hire charge	answer
contents	summer	4	6.00	
			11.00	yes
	summer	8	12.00	
			9.00	
			14.00	yes
	autumn	5	3.75	
			8.75	yes
	spring	2	2.00	
			7.00	no

8.4.3 Coding

Glossary
S$ – season
D – days hire
H – hire charge
A$ – answer (yes or no)

Method 1 BBC/Electron

```
 10  REPEAT
 20    REM..INPUT NAME OF SEASON
 30    INPUT "SEASON?", S$
 40    REM..INPUT NUMBER OF DAYS FOR HIRE
 50    INPUT "HIRE PERIOD?", D
 60    REM..HIRE CHARGE DEPENDS UPON SEASON
 70    IF S$ <> "SPRING" THEN 100
 80      LET H = D
 90    GOTO 190
100    IF S$ <> "SUMMER" THEN 130
110      LET H = D*1.5
120    GOTO 190
130    IF S$ <> "AUTUMN" THEN 160
140      LET H = D*0.75
150    GOTO 190
160      LET H = D*0.5
170    REM..CALCULATE REDUCTION IF HIRE MORE
180    REM..THAN 7 DAYS
190    IF D > 7 THEN LET H = H*0.75
200    REM..INCREASE HIRE CHARGE BY DEPOSIT
210    LET H = H + 5
220    PRINT "CHARGE FOR HIRING BICYCLE IS £", H
230    REM..ASK IF THERE IS ANOTHER CUSTOMER
240    INPUT "ANOTHER CUSTOMER – YES OR NO", A$
250  UNTIL A$ = "NO"
260  STOP
```

If your computer does not have the REPEAT...UNTIL structure then change line 250 to:

```
250  IF A$ = "YES" THEN 30
```
and delete line 10.

Method 2 Structured BASIC

```
10  REPEAT
20    INPUT "season?", season$
30    INPUT "hire period?", days
40    CASE season$ OF
50    WHEN "spring"
60      hire_charge : = days
70    WHEN "summer"
80      hire_charge : = 1.5 * days
90    WHEN "autumn"
100     hire_charge : = 0.75 * days
110   OTHERWISE
120     hire_charge : = 0.5 * days
130   ENDCASE
140   IF days > 7 THEN hire_charge : = hire_charge * 0.75
150   hire_charge : = hire_charge + 5            'include deposit
160   PRINT "charge for hiring a bicycle is £", hire_charge
170   INPUT "another customer – yes or no?", answer$
180 UNTIL answer$ = "no"
190 STOP
```

Using your computer

Type and SAVE the last program using an appropriate dialect.

LOAD and RUN using the test data in 8.4.2.

Are the results consistent with the desk check?

Specimen results

```
>LOAD "HIRE"
>RUN
SEASON?SUMMER
HIRE PERIOD?4
CHARGE FOR HIRING BICYCLE IS £          11
ANOTHER CUSTOMER - YES OR NO?YES
SEASON?SUMMER
HIRE PERIOD?8
CHARGE FOR HIRING BICYCLE IS £          14
ANOTHER CUSTOMER - YES OR NO?YES
SEASON?AUTUMN
HIRE PERIOD?5
CHARGE FOR HIRING BICYCLE IS £        8.75
ANOTHER CUSTOMER - YES OR NO?YES
SEASON?SPRING
HIRE PERIOD?2
CHARGE FOR HIRING BICYCLE IS £           7
ANOTHER CUSTOMER - YES OR NO?NO

STOP at line 260
>
```

8.5 Dialect Differences

The only new statements that have been introduced in this chapter are REM, multiple statements on one BASIC line and multiple INPUT of variables on one BASIC line. Both dialects Microsoft and BBC/Electron, support these features in the manner illustrated in the text.

8.6 Keywords

REM, multiple statements and multiple INPUT on one line.

8.7 Questions

Design and write computer programs to solve the following problems. Your answers should include the following documentation.

A complete design using either pseudocode or flowchart;

test data;

a desk check of the design with specimen results;

a fully annotated (using REM statements or equivalent) program listing;

a glossary (if necessary);

the results from a program run using the test data previously invented.

1 A butcher has recently received joints of meat. He wishes to calculate the total number of joints in each of the following weight-classes:

Those weighing up to 1kg (inclusive) TOTAL A; those weighing more than 1kg and up to 2kg TOTAL B; those weighing more than 2kg and up to 4kg TOTAL C; those weighing more than 4kg TOTAL D.

Most of the joints are large, and likely to weigh more than 4kg.

Each joint is to be weighed individually.

Design a procedure to input each weight, categorise the weight, and at the end of all the weighings print the total number of joints in each category.

2 A survey is being made of passengers using a particular train route.

On each train using the route during the survey period, each passenger is asked his/her ticket type: first or second class; single, day or period return. This data is encoded for input to a computer.

Design a procedure for the analysis of the above information.

Print the total number of passengers using the route during the survey period.

Print the number of passengers with each ticket type.

Print the average number of passengers, per day, with day return tickets.

3 The following rules enable an insurance company to determine the type of motor-insurance to issue, and the cost of the premium with any excesses to its clients.

If the age of the driver is 25 years or more, the car is manufactured in the U.K. and the accident record is good, the premium charged is 6% of the declared value of the car and a comprehensive policy is issued. If the accident record is not good, the premium is raised to 7%, the policy holder pays the first £10 of a claim and a comprehensive policy is issued.

If the age of the driver is 25 years or more, the car is **not** of U.K. manufacture and the accident record is good, the policy holder pays the first £10 of any claim and a comprehensive policy of 6% is issued. If the above conditions apply except that the accident record is **not** good, the premium is raised to 7% and a third party only policy is issued.

If the age of the driver is less than 25 years, the car is manufactured in the U.K. and the accident record is good the premium charged is 6% and a comprehensive policy is issued with the holder paying the first £10 of a claim.

If the age of the driver is less than 25 years, the car is **not** manufactured in the U.K. and the accident record is good, the premium charged is 8%, the policy holder pays the first £10 of any claim and a comprehensive policy is issued. If the accident record is not good and all other conditions apply then the risk is declined.

Assume that if a person has **not** had an accident within the last three years then the accident record is good.

Write a computer program to output

a. The type of motor insurance policy.
b. The amount of the premium.
c. Excess payable on any claim if applicable.

when the following information is input to the system.

i. Age of driver.
ii. U.K. or foreign car.
iii. Number of years since last accident.
iv. Insured value of car.

4 Consider the following rules for calculating income tax in Utopia.

Personal allowances are £1,200 for a single person and £2,300 for a married man.

A child allowance is £100 per child.

Taxable Income is the amount remaining after deducting the personal allowance and total child allowance from the Gross Income.

Income Tax is calculated from Taxable Income according to the following table.

Taxable Income on	Percentage tax on Taxable Income
First £1,000	no tax
Next £1,000	20%
Next £2,000	30%
Above £4,000	40%

If gross salary, personal status (married or single) and number of children are input to a computer, design a procedure to calculate and print the income tax to be paid.

Assume that married women are classified as single for tax purposes.

5 A simple method for finding the area under a curve y = f(x) by computer is to find the area between the plotted function y = f(x), the x axis and the limits x = a, x = b, using Simpson's rule.

An approximation to the area becomes

$$\tfrac{1}{3} h (y_0 + 4y_1, + y_2)$$

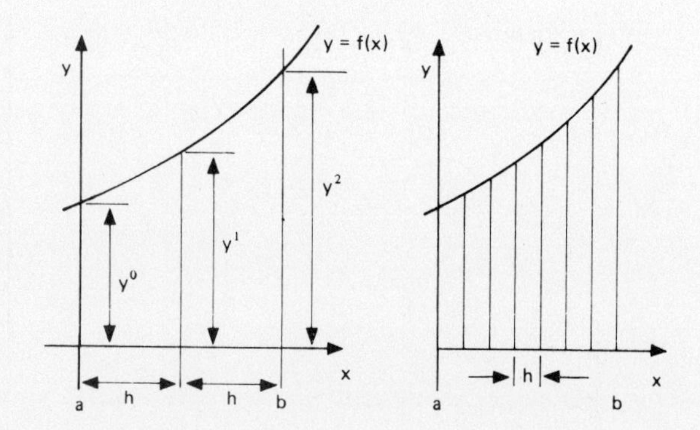

If the area under the curve is divided into strips, and Simpson's rule is applied to each strip between the limits $x = a$ and $x = b$ then clearly the more strips there are the more accurate will be the estimation of the area. Also the more strips there are the smaller h becomes.

Write a program to evaluate the area under a curve using Simpson's rule, and apply the program to find the area under the function $y = x^2$ the x axis and the limits $x = 1$ to $x = 4$.

6 A picture-framer has a supply of picture mouldings of various lengths. He wants to cut from them as many 0.5m lengths as possible and where a 0.5m length cannot be cut he will cut 0.2m lengths. Design a program to input at the keyboard of a computer the length of a strip of moulding, calculate the number of 0.5m lengths, 0.2m lengths and the amount of wasted moulding. Repeat the procedure for different lengths of moulding and keep a running total of the number of 0.5m lengths and 0.2m lengths. Terminate the procedure for a length of 0 (zero). Output to the screen of a monitor the number of 0.5m, 0.2m and waste lengths for each length input and at the end of the procedure the total number of 0.5m and 0.2m lengths.

7 A computer is used to control certain operations in a house. The following schedule illustrates the computer controlled events that happen over a 2 hour period.

6.00 switch on central heating
6.45 switch on automatic bedside tea-maker
6.55 switch off automatic bedside tea-maker
7.00 switch on radio in bedroom
7.01 switch on lights in bedroom
7.05 switch on bath-taps
7.07 switch off bath-taps
7.08 switch on bathroom and landing lights
7.30 switch on hall lights
7.45 switch off central heating
7.55 switch off radio in bedroom
7.59 switch off all the lights in the house

Design and write a program using a loop to simulate the passing of time and at the appropriate time print the time and function that is to be performed.

8 In choosing a new car a prospective customer specifies to a car-salesman the type of car and number of doors required. The car-salesman uses a computer to print the price, engine-size and model of car. Design and write a computer program to perform this procedure given the following information.

type	doors	price (£)	engine size	model
hatchback	3	4,000	1400	A
hatchback	5	4,500	1400	B
saloon	2	8,000	2100	C
saloon	4	8,750	2100	D
estate	5	9,950	2300	E

Repeat the procedure for different customers assuming that they all specify the type and number of doors.

9 Further Input/Output

9.1 Introduction

When using the INPUT statement in a program it becomes both laborious and time consuming if the same data has to be entered through a keyboard each time the same computer program is run. Under such circumstances it would be far better to have the data written into the program and in this chapter the use of the statements READ, DATA and RESTORE are explained for this purpose. The layout of printed information from the computer is also very important. This chapter illustrates how the PRINT statement can be used in various formats to improve printed output.

9.2 Read/Data

READ/DATA statements should be used in a program when the volume of data is large enough to preclude the use of INPUT and the data to be stored is of a permanent nature (i.e. a set of constants). The format of the READ/DATA statements are as follows.

```
READ data-name-1  [,data-name-2] ........
DATA literal-1   [,literal-2] ........
```

Example.

```
10 READ A,B,C
20 DATA 5,3,2
```

The data-names in the READ statement are associated with the literals in the DATA statement when both statements are scanned from left to right by the computer. In the example when the READ statement is executed the following assignments take place.

A = 5   B = 3   C = 2

DATA statements cannot be executed by the computer, they are only used in conjunction with the READ statements, therefore, DATA statements can be placed anywhere in a program. However, it is advisable to group associated READ and DATA statements together since it will make desk checking and de-bugging a program much easier, especially if the program contains a proliferation of READ/DATA statements.

If there are fewer literals in a DATA statement than variable names in a READ statement then the next DATA statement in sequence will be scanned so that any outstanding data-names can be assigned values.

Example.

```
10 READ A,B,C,D
20 DATA 10,9
30 READ E,F
40 DATA 8,7,6
50 DATA 5
```

When the READ statements are executed in this example the data-names will contain the following values.

A = 10   B = 9   C = 8   D = 7   E = 6   F = 5

In this example the reader may wonder why one READ/DATA statement was not used. Well it could have been written as:

```
10 READ A,B,C,D,E,F
20 DATA 10,9,8,7,6,5
```

and the assignments would have been the same. However, there will come a time when the data to be assigned to data-names will be physically too large to fit on to one BASIC line, and it will be necessary to divide the data into two or more DATA statements even though there might only be one READ statement. It is worth noting that the length of a line in a BASIC program is governed by several factors. These are the type of system being used and the input device the programmer is using to input the program. Line widths can typically vary between 80-255 characters or more depending upon the system being used.

The literals found in a DATA statement must be consistent with their associated data names. For example:

```
10 READ A$,B$,C$
20 DATA "FORD", "B.L.", "VOLVO"
```

In this example string variables are used, however, it is possible to mix both string variables and numeric variables in the same READ statement provided they are consistent with the literals in the DATA statement. In the example:

```
10 READ A$,S1,B$,S2
20 DATA "ENGLAND",13,"WALES",12
```

A$ = ENGLAND   S1 = 13   B$ = WALES   and S2 = 12

when the READ statement was executed.

9.3 Restore

If it is necessary to re-read part or all of the same set of data then a RESTORE statement should be used. This will alleviate the need to duplicate the same set of data in a program. For example:

```
10 READ A,B,C,D
20 DATA 5,7,4,2
30 RESTORE
40 READ E,F,G,H
```

When the READ statements are executed the following assignments will take place.

A = 5 B = 7 C = 4 D = 2 E = 5 F = 7 G = 4 H = 2

Thus the RESTORE statement causes the computer to re-scan the DATA statement(s) starting at the DATA statement with the lowest line-number. In the example if RESTORE had not been used the computer would inform the user that it was *out of data in line 40* when the program segment was executed.

If however the RESTORE statement is followed by a line-number then the computer will re-scan the DATA statement(s) starting at the DATA statement with the line-number specified. For example:

```
10 READ A,B,C,D
20 DATA 6,8
30 DATA 5,9
40 RESTORE 30
50 READ X,Y
```

When the READ statements are executed the following assignments will take place.

A = 6 B = 8 C = 5 D = 9 X = 5 Y = 9

9.4 Zone Printing

The output of information can be divided into zones across a screen or page by using commas between variable names and/or literals. The width of each zone is the same across the screen or page, however, zone widths vary according to the dialect of BASIC being used. Between 8 and 21 character positions are common widths giving between 4 and 5 print zones depending upon the width of the output medium being used. For example a BASIC dialect having a zone width of 10 characters using a screen of 40 characters in width will give 4 print zones, whereas a zone width of 15 characters using a screen width of 80 characters will give 6 print zones — the last zone having a width of 5 characters.

The format of the PRINT statement to allow zone printing is:

PRINT { literal-1 | data-name-1 } [, { literal-2 | data-name-2 }] .....

For example if a zone width of 14 characters is assumed then on running the next program segment the following output is obtained.

```
10 READ A,B,C
20 DATA 4.6, –8.1,7.9
30 PRINT A,B,C
```

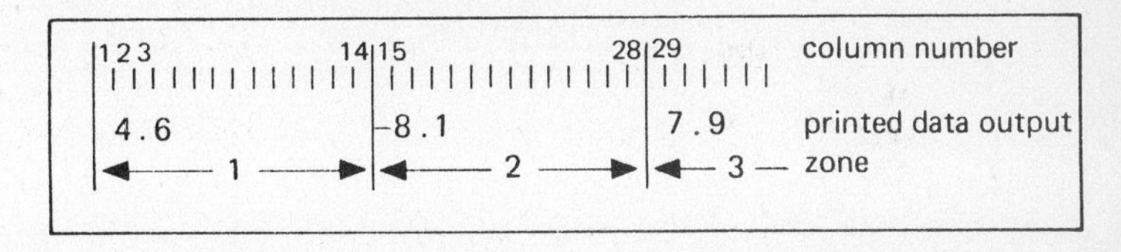

9.4 (cont.)

Note: Many dialects of BASIC stipulate that printed numbers have a leading space if the number is positive, a leading minus sign if the number is negative and both positive and negative numbers have a trailing space printed. However, the output of leading and trailing spaces does not apply to printing literals as the following example illustrates.

```
10 READ A$,B$
20 DATA "SALARY", "TAX"
30 PRINT A$, B$
```

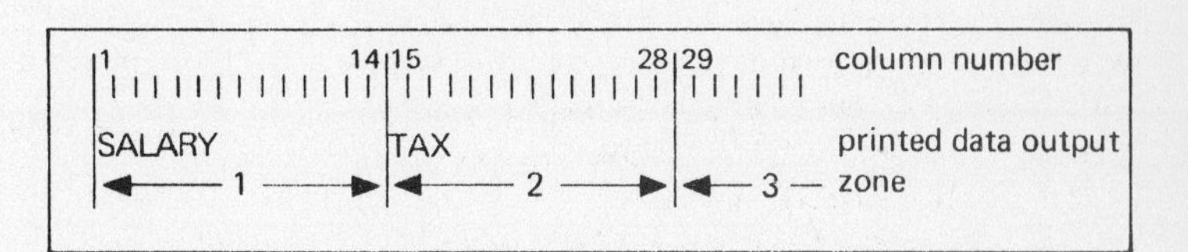

From the next example it is clear that both literals and variables can be used in zone printing.

```
10 READ R
20 DATA 10
30 LET C = 2*3.14*R
40 LET A = 3.14*R *R
50 PRINT "CIRCUMFERENCE", C
60 PRINT "AREA", A
```

Output from program segment being run.

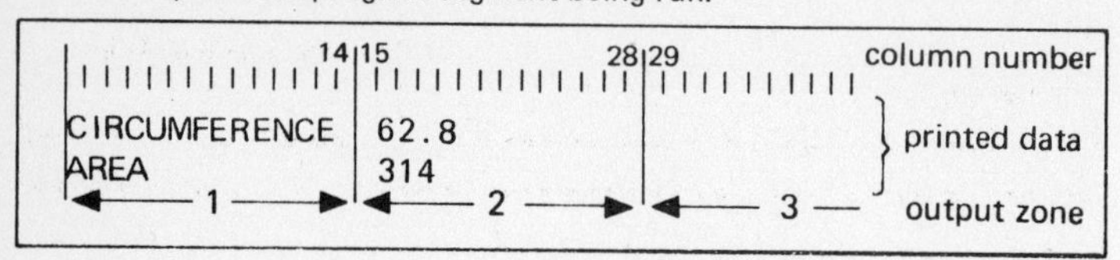

It is possible to suppress zone printing if the comma, used for zone separation, in a PRINT statement is replaced by a semi-colon (;) then the variables and/or literals listed in a PRINT statement will be printed one after another.

```
10 READ N$, A, H
20 DATA "JONES", 26,177.8
30 PRINT "NAME ";N$
40 PRINT "AGE (YEARS) ";A;"HEIGHT (CM) ";H
```

Output from program segment being run.

```
1         11        21        31          column number
NAME JONES                               } printed data
AGE (YEARS)  26 HEIGHT (CM)   177.8      } output
```

Note: In line 30 if a space had not been deliberately introduced after NAME, i.e. "NAME" then the printed result would be NAMEJONES. Although this technique has been used for printing AGE(YEARS) and HEIGHT(CM), whenever a number is printed many dialects of BASIC will output a leading space for positive numbers and a hyphen (minus sign) for negative numbers.

9.5 Tabulation

If a programmer does not want to use zoned output then a facility is available for a programmer to specify the position and spacing of printed output on screen or page. The use of TAB(n) will permit printing to start n columns from the left-hand margin of the screen or page – n can be a numeric constant, numeric variable or the result of an arithmetic expression. In this text the range of n is $1 \leqslant n \leqslant$ line-width, however, some dialects of BASIC use $0 \leqslant n \leqslant$ line-width. The format for a combined PRINT and TAB statement is:

$$\text{PRINT TAB(n1)} \left[; \begin{Bmatrix} \text{data-name-1} \\ \text{literal-1} \end{Bmatrix} \right] \text{[; TAB(n2)]} \left[; \begin{Bmatrix} \text{data-name-2} \\ \text{literal-2} \end{Bmatrix} \right] \cdots\cdots$$

Note: Each item of the PRINT statement is separated by a semi-colon. This ensures that each value is printed in the specified TAB position and departs from zone spacing.

The following examples illustrate the use of the PRINT statement including TAB.

Example.

```
10 PRINT TAB (3); "GROSS"; TAB (18); "NETT"
20 READ A,B
30 DATA 1400, 1100
40 PRINT TAB (2); A; TAB(17); B
```

Output from program segment being run.

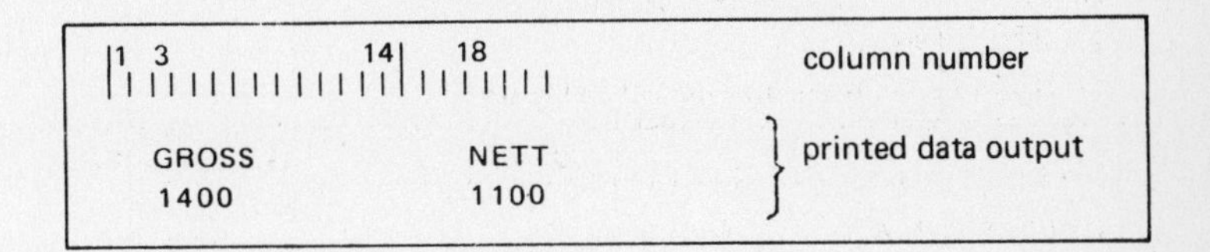

9.5 (cont.)

Note: Since a leading space is printed with the values for A and B they become lined up under the headings GROSS and NETT.

Example.

```
10 READ F
20 IF F = 0 THEN STOP
30   PRINT TAB(F); "*"
40   READ F
50 GOTO 20
60 DATA 5,9,15,6,1,0
```

Output from program being run.

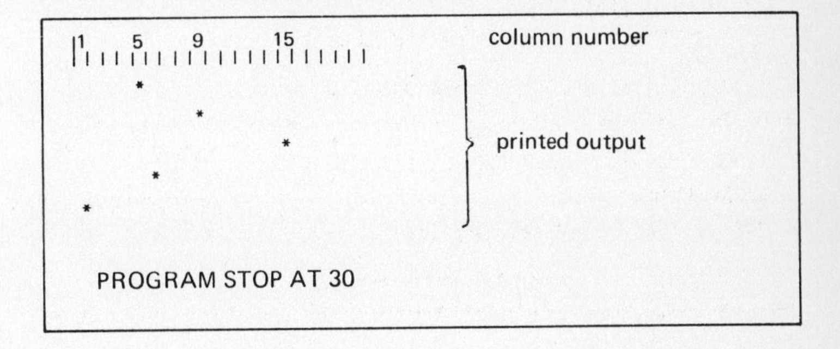

9.5.1 Zone Spacing and Tabulation

Both zone spacing and tabulation can be mixed within a single PRINT statement.

```
10 READ T, S
20 DATA 1400, 6050
30 PRINT TAB (5); "TAX", T; TAB (25); "SALARY", S
```

Output from program segment being run.

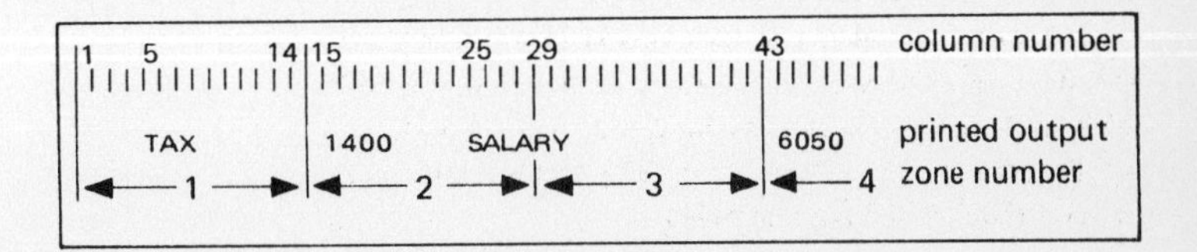

Note: If printed output continues across a zone then the next item to be printed will appear in the next zone if comma separation between the two items in a PRINT statement exists.

9.5.2 Suppression of Line Feeds

Generally the contents of each PRINT statement will be printed on a new line, however, this can be overcome by using either a comma or semi-colon at the end of the PRINT statement.

```
10  READ N$,R$,T$,P$
20  DATA "F.SMITH", "2 BOW WALK", "FREETOWN", "BX4 9JG"
30  PRINT "NAME",
40  PRINT N$
50  PRINT "ADDRESS ";
60  PRINT R$,T$,P$
70  STOP
```

Output from program segment when run.

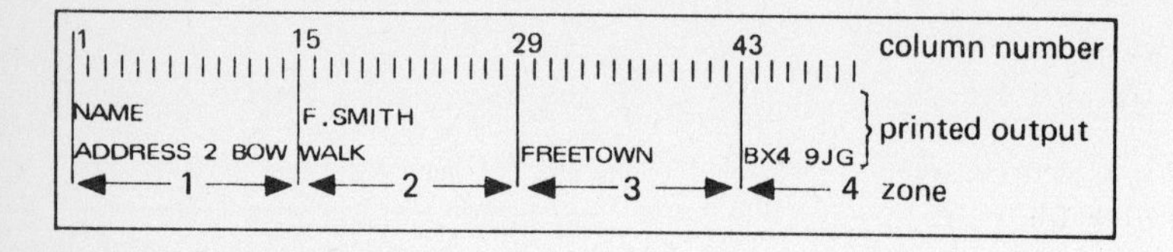

9.6 Worked Example

Problem. Design and write a computer program to print a single electricity bill from the following layout.

```
                              ELECTRICITY BILL
                              ----------- ----

MR. P.L. SMITH                                    REF.NO. 1793 8462 1961
16 CORN STREET                                    DATE 21 AUG 1981
WATFORD

PREVIOUS    PRESENT     TARIFF      UNITS       PRICE       AMOUNT
READING     READING                             PER UNIT    (PENCE)

 681           1165     DOMESTIC    484         4.5            2178

QUARTERLY CHARGE                                                600

                                                TOTAL          2778
```

9.6.1 Design

read electricity details (price per unit and quarterly charge) and date

read details of consumer (name, address, reference number, previous and present meter readings)

calculate charges

print electricity bill using the layout shown

stop

Glossary	
Price per unit of electricity	U
Quarterly charge	Q
Today's date	D$
Name of customer	N$
Address – Street	S$
Town	T$
Reference number	R$
Previous meter reading	P1
Present meter reading	P2
Amount	A
Total	T

9.6.2 Program

```
 10 REM..READ ELECTRICITY DETAILS AND DATE OF ACCOUNT
 20 READ U,Q,D$
 30 DATA 4.5,600,"21 AUGUST 1981"
 40 REM..READ DETAILS OF CONSUMER
 50 READ N$,S$,T$,R$,P1,P2
 60 DATA "MR. P.L.SMITH", "16 CORN STREET", "WATFORD", "1793 8462 1961"
 70 DATA 681,1165
 80 REM..CALCULATE CHARGES
 90 LET A = U * (P2-P1)
100 LET T = Q + A
120 REM..PRINT ELECTRICITY BILL
130 PRINT TAB(20); "ELECTRICITY BILL"
140 PRINT TAB(20); "----------- ----"
150 PRINT
160 PRINT N$; TAB(35); "REF.NO.";R$
170 PRINT S$; TAB(35); "DATE "; D$
180 PRINT T$
190 PRINT
200 PRINT "PREVIOUS   PRESENT   TARIFF         UNITS   PRICE        AMOUNT"
210 PRINT "READING    READING                          PER UNIT     (PENCE)"
220 PRINT
230 PRINT TAB(1);P1;TAB(11);P2;TAB(19);"DOMESTIC";TAB(30);P2-P1;TAB(38);U;TAB(49);A
240 PRINT
250 PRINT "QUARTERLY CHARGE";TAB(50); Q
260 PRINT
270 PRINT TAB(39); "TOTAL"; TAB(49); T
280 STOP
```

Using your computer

Type and SAVE the last program.

LOAD and RUN the program. The results should be similar to the designed output on the layout form.

Specimen results

```
>LOAD "BILL"
>RUN
                    ELECTRICITY BILL
                    ----------- ----

MR. P.L.SMITH                         REF.NO.1793 8462 1961
16 CORN STREET                        DATE 21 AUGUST 1981
WATFORD

PREVIOUS  PRESENT  TARIFF      UNITS   PRICE     AMOUNT
READING   READING                      PER UNIT  (PENCE)

 681       1165    DOMESTIC    484     4.5         2178

QUARTERLY CHARGE                                    600

                                        TOTAL      2778

STOP at line 280
>
```

Note: in the production of electricity bills the details that are required to print a bill are not read from statements in a program but read from records in a computer file. The use of READ/DATA in this example simulates the reading of data from a file. An introduction to the use of data files is covered in chapters 16 and 17.

9.7 Screen and Page Design

The only contact many computer users have with a computer is through either a visual display unit or printed output on a page. When developing a computer program that contains many instructions for the user to follow the following points should be kept in mind.

The information displayed on a screen or printed on a page takes the user through the input/output phase of the system, and provides the user with adequate information so that the system can be operated without having to resort to reading a manual. Data entry should be clearly defined regarding the sequence in which data is *keyed in* and the format of the data, and error messages to the user should be informative.

The programmer's job of coding an input/output phase to a program is made easier if every item of information that is conveyed to the user is first written on a design document. Notice in the last example how simple the coding of each line of the electricity bill was once the design of the bill was known.

Figure 9.1 illustrates the design of one screen of information taken from a medical package requiring data to be input on a patient who belongs to a *risk group* category.

The reader should develop the habit of designing all complex input and output on squared paper before attempting to code such information into a computer program.

```
PATIENT: X XXXXXXXXXXXXXXXXXXXXX                        NHS NUMBER XX XXXXX

AT RISK GROUPS ARE CATEGORISED AS:

A = DRUG SENSITIVITY               E = HYPERTENSION
B = DIABETES                       F = LONG TERM THERAPY
C = EPILEPSY                       G = ATTEMPTED SUICIDE
D = TUBERCULOSIS                   H = MEASLES

INPUT UP TO FOUR CODES IN ONE LINE (E.G. ACF) THEN PRESS RETURN KEY

IF NO CODES APPLY PRESS RETURN KEY
--->
```

Figure 9.1

9.7 (cont.)

When designing the layout for input/output information the programmer should **avoid** producing a mass of unrelated facts and figures, computer jargon (remember the people who use the computer system may not be computer specialists) and misleading, irrelevant or incorrect information.

9.8 Print Using Statement

The PRINT USING statement allows a programmer to specify accurately an edited format for printing numeric and string values. This is not possible using only the PRINT statement since the computer will always revert to the default values for the accuracy to which numbers can be printed and will not allow for information to be edited so that it appears in a more presentable format for reading. The format of the PRINT USING statement is:

PRINT USING format string, { literal-1 / data-name-1 } [, { literal-2 / data-name-2 }] ....

where the format string can be a literal, variable or line number.

9.8.1 Output of Numeric Values

There are up to seven characters used in defining a format string for the output of numeric values. Those characters are:

character is used to represent each digit of a number.

. character represents the position of a decimal point.

, character represents the position of a comma between groups of digits. If all digits prior to the comma are zero then the comma is replaced by a space.

↑ or ^ character is used in sets of four to represent the exponent of a number in exponential format — ↑↑↑↑ corresponds to E ± nn.

± character as the first character of a format string causes either a ± or − to be printed, depending on the sign of a number, in front of a number.

− character has a similar effect to a ± character when it is the first character of a format string. However, if the number to be printed is positive a space will price the number, whereas, if the number is negative a − character will precede the number.

$ character represents the position of a dollar sign to be printed.

Examples of the effect of format strings on numerical values to be printed. In all these examples a ∇ symbol represents a space character.

9.8.1 (cont.)

The # character.

Numeric Value	Format String	Printed Result	Comments
25	##	25	Each # represents a digit position.
25	####	∇∇25	Digits become right-hand justified.
1.95	##	∇2	Only integers are printed; the number is rounded.
73468	###	***	Number too large for specified field so * is printed for each # character present.

The . character (decimal point).

Number Value	Format String	Printed Result	Comment
37.24	##.##	37.24	Value represented as specified in format string.
20	####.##	∇∇20.00	An alignment takes place about the decimal point of the number and format string, leading digit positions are replaced by spaces, trailing digit positions by zeros.
29.347	###.##	∇29.35	Number is rounded.
784.21	##.###	**	Number is too large to print using format specified.

The , character.

Numeric Value	Format String	Printed Result	Comments
2000	#,###	2,000	Comma printed in indicated position.
14793.721	##,###.###	14,973.721	
37.9	##,###.##	∇ ∇ ∇ ∇ 37.90	When leading digits are blank the comma is substituted for a space.

The ↑ character.

Numeric Value	Format String	Printed Result	Comments
170.35	##.###↑↑↑↑	17.035E+01	Position of decimal point shifted.
1.2	####↑↑↑↑	1200E−03	
6004.7	#.###↑↑↑↑	6.005E+02	Number rounded.

The + character.

Numeric Value	Format String	Printed Result	Comments
20.5	+##.#	+20.5	Sign appears before number.
7.36	+###.##	+∇∇7.36	Leading digit positions replaced by spaces.
10.40	++##.##	∇+10.40	Plus signs can be used to replace #. The effect is to print sign to immediate left of leading digit.
15.90	++++.##	∇+15.90	

The − character.

Numeric Value	Format String	Printed Result	Comments
−20.5	−##.#	−20.5	Sign appears before number.
20.5	−##.#	∇20.5	If number positive, sign replaced by space.
−7.36	−−−−.##	∇ ∇−7.36	Minus signs can be used to replace #.
0.47	−−−.#	∇ ∇0.5	Leading zero printed, number rounded.

The $ character.

Numeric Value	Format String	Printed Result	Comments
30.512	$###.##	$ ∇ 30.51	Dollar printed in position shown in format.
−30.512	+$###.##	−$ ∇ 30.51	Both sign and dollar printed.
13.20	+$$$$#.##	+ ∇∇ $13.20	Dollar signs can be used to replace #. $ printed immediately to left of leading digit. Some dialects use a £ character.

9.8.2 Output of String Values

Three characters are used to define the format for string output

character is used to represent each character of a string.
< character is used for the left-justification of a string when printed.
> character is used for the right-justification of a string when printed.

Examples of format strings used to output string values.

String Value	Format String	Printed Result	Comments
COMPUTING	####	COMP	Only the left four characters are output.
FROG	<######	FROG ▽ ▽	Left-justified space filled to right.
NO	>######	▽ ▽ ▽ ▽ NO	Right-justified space filled to left.

The PRINT USING statement is used in the same way as illustrated earlier.

e.g. PRINT USING ">##########", N$

If N$ is "UNITED" the output would be ▽ ▽ ▽ ▽UNITED'

9.9 Worked Example

Problem. Design and write a program to print a sales invoice for motor-car spares. The layout of the sales invoice is given as:

QTY	DESCRIPTION	UNIT COST (PENCE)	COST
3	LIGHT BULBS	76	2.28
4	SPARK PLUGS	50	2.00
1	OIL FILTER	325	3.25
1	AIR FILTER	175	1.75
1	CONTACT POINTS	254	2.54
		SUB-TOTAL	11.82
		VAT @ 15%	1.77
		TOTAL	£ 13.59

Read the quantity, description and unit cost of the spares sold from a DATA statement, and assume that V.A.T. is fixed at 15%.

9.9.1 Design

initialise sub-total to zero
print headings of invoice
read quantity, description and unit cost
WHILE quantity not = 0 **DO**
  calculate cost of spare
  increase sub-total by cost of spare
  print line of details on invoice
  read quantity, description and unit cost
END WHILE
calculate VAT and total cost
print sub-total
print VAT
print total cost
stop

glossary	
Quantity Sold	N
Description of spares	Q$
Unit cost	C
Cost	X
Sub-total	S
VAT	V
Total	T

9.9.2 Program

```
 10  REM..INITIALISE SUB-TOTAL TO ZERO
 20  LET S = 0
 30  REM..PRINT HEADINGS OF INVOICE
 40  PRINT "QTY"; TAB(7); "DESCRIPTION"; TAB(29); "UNIT COST"; TAB(43); "COST"
 50  PRINT TAB(29); "(PENCE)"
 60  PRINT
 70  PRINT
 80  REM..READ QUANTITY, DESCRIPTION, UNIT COST
 90  READ N, Q$, C
100  DATA 3, "LIGHT BULBS", 76
110  IF N = 0 THEN 280
120    REM..CALCULATE COST OF SPARE PART
130    LET X=N*C/100
140    REM.. INCREASE SUB-TOTAL
150    LET S = S + X
160    REM..PRINT LINE OF DETAILS OF INVOICE
170    PRINT N; TAB(7); Q$; TAB(29); C; TAB(41);
180    PRINT USING "###.##", X
190    REM..READ QUANTITY,DESCRIPTION,UNIT COST
200    READ N, Q$, C
210    DATA 4, "SPARK PLUGS",50
220    DATA 1, "OIL FILTER",325
230    DATA 1, "AIR FILTER",175
240    DATA 1, "CONTACT POINTS",254
250    DATA 0, "X",0
260  GOTO 110
270  REM..CALCULATE V.A.T AND TOTAL
280  LET V = 0.15 * S
290  LET T = S + V
300  REM..PRINT SUB-TOTAL, V.A.T, AND TOTAL
310  PRINT
320  PRINT TAB(29); "SUB-TOTAL"; TAB(41);
330  PRINT USING "###.##",S
340  PRINT
350  PRINT TAB(29); "VAT @ 15%"; TAB(41);
360  PRINT USING "###.##",V
370  PRINT
380  PRINT TAB(29); "TOTAL"; TAB(40); "£";
390  PRINT USING "###.##",T
400  STOP
```

Using your computer

Type and SAVE the last program.

LOAD and RUN the program. The result should be similar to the designed output on the layout form.

Specimen results

```
   OLD INVOICE.BAS
   RUN
  INVOICE.BAS       MON, APR 01 1985            15:16:40


  QTY   DESCRIPTION           UNIT COST      COST
                              (PENCE)


  3     LIGHT BULBS           76              2.28
  4     SPARK PLUGS           50              2.00
  1     OIL FILTER            325             3.25
  1     AIR FILTER            175             1.75
  1     CONTACT POINTS        254             2.54

                              SUB-TOTAL      11.82

                              VAT @ 15%       1.77

                              TOTAL        £ 13.59
  STOP AT LINE 400
```

Notes: The use of the READ/DATA statements in this example are to simulate the data either being read from a computer file or input at a keyboard.

PRINT USING and PRINT should not be mixed on the same line.

A PRINT USING statement normally generates a carriage-return line feed after the value has been printed, suppression is not usually possible by including a semi-colon after the PRINT USING statement.

From this example it is clear that the same format string has been used in four areas of the program (lines 180,330,360,390). Some dialects will permit the format string to be defined on a separate line, and the format string in the PRINT USING statement is replaced by a line number.

Example.

```
  5   "###.##"
180   PRINT USING 5,X
330   PRINT USING 5,S
360   PRINT USING 5,V
390   PRINT USING 5,T
```

This can also be expressed as:

```
  5   LET A$ "###.## "
180   PRINT USING A$,X
330   PRINT USING A$,S
360   PRINT USING A$,V
390   PRINT USING A$,T
```

In the example the use of a dollar sign for currency was not desirable, therefore, a £ sign was printed separately (line 380) from the format string of line 390.

9.10 Dialect Differences

READ, DATA and RESTORE as described in the chapter are identical in the two dialects.

9.10.1 Print and Tab

Microsoft. The width of a zone is 14 characters. All numbers printed are followed by a space. Positive numbers are preceded by a space and negative numbers are preceded by a minus sign.

BBC/Electron. The width of a zone is 10 characters. Numbers are not followed by a space, positive numbers are not preceded by a space, however, negative numbers are preceded by a minus sign.

9.10.2 Print Using

Microsoft. For numeric fields this is similar to the explanation in the chapter, however, there are several minor enhancements.

A plus sign at the beginning or end of a format string causes the sign of the number (plus or minus) to be printed before or after the number.

A minus sign at the end of the format field causes negative numbers to be printed with a trailing minus sign.

A double asterisk at the beginning of the format string causes leading spaces in the numeric field to be filled with asterisks. The double asterisk ** also specifies the position of two digits in a number.

A double dollar sign causes a dollar sign to be printed to the left of the most significant digit. The double dollar $$ also specifies two more digit positions, one of which is the dollar sign. If negative numbers are to be used then the minus sign must be specified as being trailing if the $$ format is used.

The double asterisk and dollar can be combined **$ to provide a combined function for inserting asterisks in place of leading spaces and a dollar sign to the left of the most significant non-zero digit.

There are three characters that control the output for string fields.

A ! specifies that only the first character in the given string is to be printed.

n spaces specifies that 2+n characters from the string will be printed.

If the string is longer than the field the extra characters are truncated.

If the field is longer than the string the string is justified to the left of the field and space filled to the right.

A & will output a string in the same format as it is input. For example:

```
10  A$ = "ABCD": B$ = "WXYZ"
20  PRINT USING "!";A$;B$
30  PRINT USING "\▽ ▽ ▽ ▽\";A$;B$
40  PRINT USING "!";A$;
50  PRINT USING "&";B$
```

when run on a computer will output

```
AW
ABCD▽▽WXYZ
AWXYZ
```

An underscore in a format string causes the next character in the string to be output as a literal.

If numeric items are two large to be output using the string format given, a % sign will be output preceding the number.

BBC/Electron. This dialect does not support the PRINT USING statement. However, it is possible to control the overall field width, the total number of digits printed and the number of decimal places printed by referencing one variable @%. This variable can be considered as a number that occupies four bytes of memory, where each byte controls one aspect of the print format.

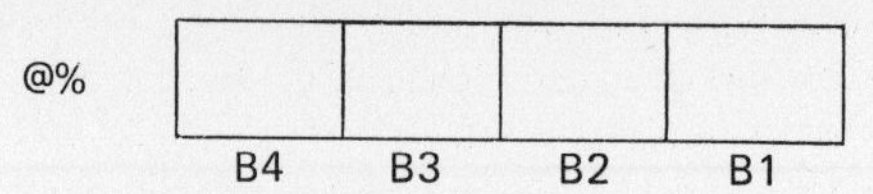

B4 – initially set at 0; only when set at 1 will numbers be formatted as required.

B3 – is used to select the format for printing numbers; set at 0 the general format will be used, set at 1 the exponential format will be used and set at 2 the fixed format will be used.

B2 – controls the total number of digits printed in the selected format.

B1 – sets the overall print field width.

For example if a fixed point format was required having 2 decimal places and a field width of 9 characters then @% would be set to the following value:

B4 = 00 B3 = 02 B2 = 02 B1 = 09

9.10.3 Use of Printers

The reader may well find that by now the use of a screen to display information is rather limited. If a program is longer than the depth of a screen it becomes very tedious to have to list segments of a program in order to correct lines of code. Information that is output from a program may be too long to fit into one screen and furthermore it may be necessary to give that information to someone who does not have access to a terminal (television or monitor). The answer is to be able to obtain a printed listing on paper of programs and information. The computer model described in chapters 2 and 5 needs a further output device in the form of a printer.

BASIC commands that direct output to a printer can be classified into three types – (LLIST) will LIST a program on a printer, (LPRINT) will output specific information from a program and (WIDTH) to control the length of an output line. These commands will of course differ between dialects.

Microsoft. LLIST, LPRINT and LPRINT USING all direct output to a printer and have the same meaning as LIST, PRINT and PRINT USING.

To change the width of a line the format of the WIDTH command is:

WIDTH device, size

where device is a mnemonic (e.g. LPT1 for a printer) and size is the width in characters of the printed line.

BBC/Electron. To enable information to be sent to a printer that is connected to the computer type CONTROL B. This will duplicate all information on the screen to the printer. LIST and PRINT are then used in their normal way. To inhibit the printing of information on the printer type CONTROL C. In a BASIC program the commands VDU2 and VDU3 will enable and disable respectively the use of the printer for output.

9.11 Keywords

READ, DATA, RESTORE;
Zone printing, TAB,
Input/Output design, PRINT USING

9.12 Questions

1 Comment upon the syntax errors in the following BASIC statements.

a) INPUT A;B;C
b) INPUT A,B,C!
c) READ X;Y,Z
d) DATA –6 : 14, 32;
e) RESTORE DATA
f) PRINT "FLIGHT NUMBER;
g) PRINT "NAME OF ACCOUNT" N$
h) PRINT TAB (32); X; TAB (16); Y
i) PRINT;PRINT;PRINT
j) PRINT X / TAB (18); Y; TAB (36): Z

2 Desk-check the following program segment with the data provided. What are the values of the data-names?

```
10  READ A,B,C
20  DATA 8, 16, 32, "EIGHT", "SIXTEEN"
25  DATA "THIRTY-TWO"
30  READ D$, E$, F$
40  RESTORE
50  READ X, Y, Z
```

3 Give the following program segment a desk-check and comment upon the errors.

```
10  READ A,B
20  DATA "SALARY", "TAX"
30  RESTORE
40  READ X$, Y$, Z$
```

4 Comment upon the figure that will be output when the following program segment is run.

```
 10  LET R = 1
 20    PRINT TAB (20); "I"
 30    LET R = R + 1
 40  IF R<4 THEN 20
 50  LET C = 17
 60    PRINT TAB (C); "–";
 70    LET C = C + 1
 80  IF C<24 THEN 60
 90  PRINT "   "
100    PRINT TAB (20); "I"
110    LET R = R + 1
120  IF R<7 THEN 100
130  STOP
```

5 Design and write a computer program to print a currency conversion table from Pounds Sterling to French Francs, German Marks and Italian Lire.

The table should contain a title and each column should have the name of the currency printed.

Use as data a value for Pounds Sterling in the range from £5 to £50 in steps of £5.

You can obtain the current conversion rates from your local bank.

6 Design and write a computer program to print a simple telephone bill. Your program should input:

a. Name of customer.
b. Address.
c. Telephone number.
d. Previous meter reading.
e. Current meter reading.

The number of units used in a quarter year is the difference between the current and previous meter readings. Assume the cost of a unit is 5p. The program should calculate the cost of using the telephone and include a fixed rental charge of £12 per quarter to give a sub-total. Value added tax is charged at 15% on the sub-total. The sum of the sub-total and value added tax gives the total amount due.

The bill should be printed or displayed in the following format.

```
                         TELEPHONE BILL
                         --------- ----

NAME: MR.F.SMYTHE                     ADDRESS: 28 FIELD WAY
                                               OXFORD
TELEPHONE NUMBER: OXFORD 715                   OX1 6QT

PREVIOUS METER READING: 21794
CURRENT METER READING:  21936

CHARGES
-------

CALLS @ 5P PER UNIT ON 142 UNITS                 7.10
RENTAL                                          12.00

SUB-TOTAL                                       19.10
VAT @ 15%                                        2.86

TOTAL AMOUNT DUE                              £ 21.96
```

10 Subroutines and Procedures

10.1 Introduction

The purpose of this chapter is to inform the reader of further program design practices that enhance structured programming. The topic of modular programming is introduced and implemented through the BASIC statements GOSUB/RETURN and defined procedures.

10.2 Modular Programming

Modular programming is a term used to describe dividing a program into areas of code or modules that perform specific tasks.

The programmer designs the program in **levels,** where a level consists of one or more **modules.** The first level is a complete main program, and modules at successive levels consist of submodules referenced, in the prior levels. Figure 10.1 illustrates a typical *top-down* structure for a program.

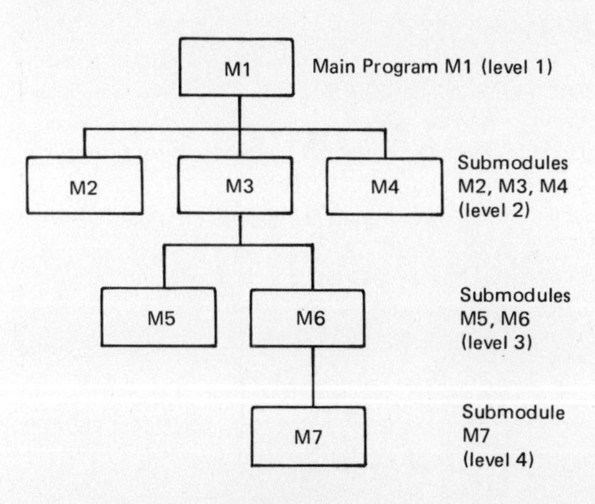

Figure 10.1

A **module** is a set of program statements which, when acting together, complete a specific task, and must have only one entrance and one exit point. In practice a module can be a subroutine, and the main program can consist of a sequence of calls to the subroutines that represent the modules at the next level down.

The order in which the modules are executed by the computer is controlled by the main program. This describes fully the procedures required in the solution to a problem. The procedures being written in the order of machine execution.

Modules should be structured within themselves by incorporating the constructs of sequencing, selection and repetition. This should ensure that each module has only one entry and one exit point. However, it is possible for modules to call other modules since the control of program flow will always return to the *calling* module.

Modular programming offers the following advantages over *monolithic* programming.

By dividing the solution to a problem into many parts it is possible to obtain a better insight into the solution of the problem as a whole.

Because it is often far easier and quicker to document specific tasks related to subroutines than document a complete unstructured program, standards of documentation must improve.

Program maintenance (inserting new modules, amending code and deleting code from existing modules) is simpler for individual modules than for an entire program.

10.2.1 Basic Statements that support modularity

Two BASIC statements enable a program to be divided into modules.

The first statement is **GOSUB,** however, there are limitations associated with subroutines in BASIC.

BASIC uses **global** variable names. Thus a data-name in one subroutine will have the same value as the same data-name in a **different** subroutine.

Since variable names are global there is no separate list of parameters to define, that communicate between the *calling* program module and the *called* program module. Although this can be an advantage it somewhat hinders the development of subroutines in isolation of other modules.

The second statement is **CHAIN**. This loads another program into the memory of a computer, overwriting the original program that was stored in the main memory, and runs the *chained* program usually from a line-number stated by the programmer in the CHAIN instruction.

The format of the **CHAIN** statement will vary between the dialects of BASIC. However, a common format is:

CHAIN filename [line-number]

where filename is the name given to a program stored on disc, and line-number (optional) is the position in the chained program from which program execution is to start.

Example. Three program modules called **INDATA, SORTDATA** and **PRINTDATA** are used to solve a problem. The **CHAIN** statement would be used in the following context.

```
10  ________
    ________
    ________
    ________

500 CHAIN SORTDATA
```

PROGRAM INDATA

The program **INDATA** is loaded and run, since it contains **CHAIN SORTDATA;** the computer upon reaching line 500 will load and run **SORTDATA**

PROGRAM SORTDATA

When line 750 of **SORTDATA** is executed, **PRINTDATA** will be loaded and run from line 300.

PROGRAM PRINTDATA

Notes on the use of CHAIN.

With many dialects of BASIC chaining a program will cause all the variables in the *chained* program to be initialised.

The initialisation of variables in a chained program causes a parameter passing problem between related modules. This can be overcome by storing values associated with variable names on a *datafile,* in which case chaining becomes useful in modular programming.

Chaining would normally only be used if a program was too large to fit into the memory of a computer.

10.3 Subroutines

There is often a need when writing a computer program to write a program segment to perform a specific task, and use that segment at difference places within the program. The program segment should be written once, and branched to from different parts of a program. Such a program segment should provide the facility of returning the computer to the next executable statement after the one which caused the branch to the program segment.

Such a program segment is known as a **subroutine.**

Subroutines have the following advantages in program construction:

The same subroutine can be used anywhere in the program without re-writing it.

Subroutines can be written to perform specific tasks which are needed in a number of places in a program.

The de-bugging of a program is faster since it is easier to trace through subroutines than it is through one large program.

Altering parts of a program would be confined to inserting, deleting or amending subroutines.

The documentation of a large program is much simplified by the documentation of individual subroutines.

The creation of subroutines is possible by the use of the verbs **GOSUB** and **RETURN.** The following illustration shows that the statement **GOSUB 500** causes a branch to line 500, followed by the sequential execution of statements until the **RETURN** is executed. **RETURN** will cause a branch back to the next executable statement after **GOSUB 500.**

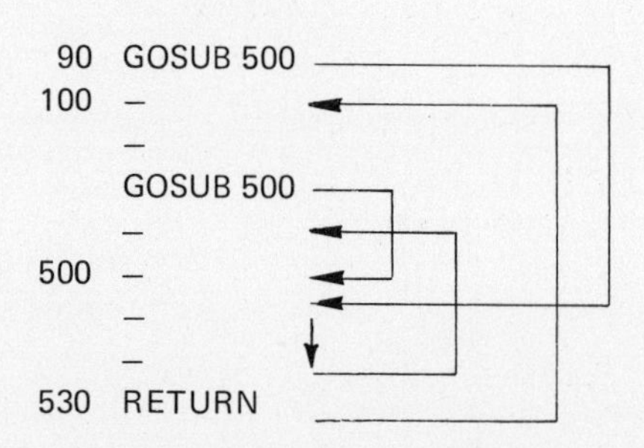

It is possible to *nest* subroutines, that is to have one subroutine branching to or *calling* another subroutine. The called subroutine then calls another subroutine, and so on. There is a limitation to the depth of nesting subroutines, however, this is sufficiently large as not to be a problem to the reader.

The following illustration shows three subroutines nested.

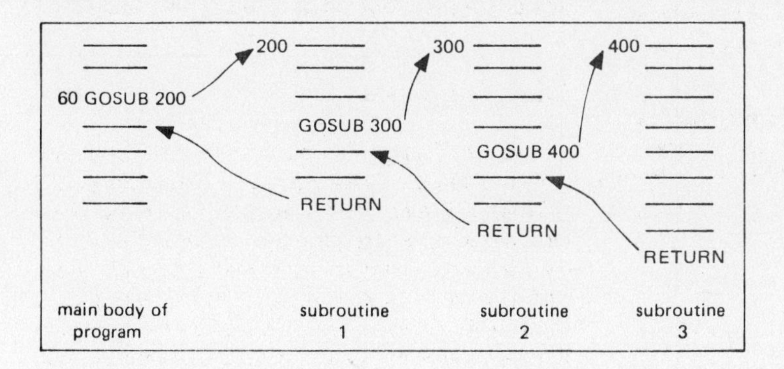

10.3.1 On . . . Gosub

This statement functions in a similar manner to ON . . . GOTO, however, instead of branching to a line number for monolithic code the branch is to a line number representing the start of a subroutine. The return from the subroutine will be to the next executable statement after the ON . . . GOSUB statement.

Example.

```
 100  INPUT X
 110  IF X = 0 THEN STOP
 120   ON X GOSUB 1000, 2000, 3000
 130   INPUT X
 140  GOTO 110

1000  REM . . SUBROUTINE FOR X = 1
      –
      –
      –
1999  RETURN
2000  REM . . SUBROUTINE FOR X = 2
      –
      –
      –
2999  RETURN
3000  REM . . SUBROUTINE FOR X = 3
      –
      –
      –
3999  RETURN
```

ON . . . GOSUB can be very useful in branching to subroutines under the direction of a menu.

Example.

```
 10  PRINT "WHICH OPERATION DO YOU REQUIRE"
 20  PRINT "1  ADDITION"
 30  PRINT "2  SUBTRACTION"
 40  PRINT "3  MULTIPLICATION"
 50  PRINT "4  DIVISION"
 60  PRINT "5  NONE"
 70  INPUT "TYPE CODE 1 – 5", C
 80  ON C GOSUB 100, 150, 200, 250, 300
 90  –
100  –
```

10.4 Worked Example

Problem. Write a computer program to use the computer as a teaching machine for computer aided learning. The subject is the dates of historical events.

The strategy used in this program is as follows.

Ten questions will be asked relating to events in history. The student is invited to type at the keyboard of a terminal a date associated with an event.

If the date is wrong, the question is repeated and the student is given a second chance to give the correct answer.

If the date is wrong after the second attempt the student is given the right answer.

For every correct answer the student scores 1 point.

10.4.1 Modules

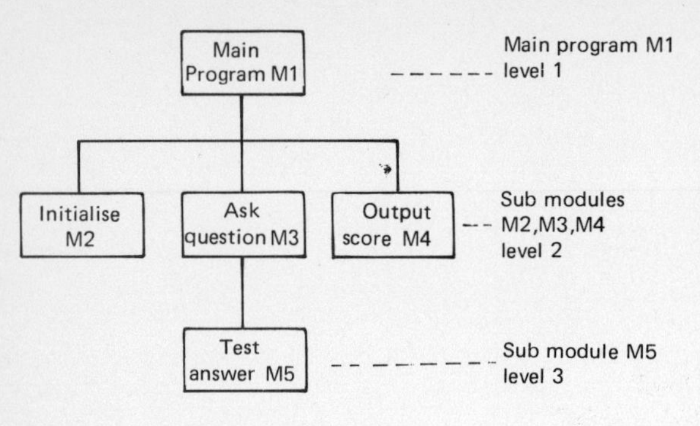

10.4.2 Design of each module

New pseudocode is required for defining and calling either subroutines or procedures.

```
PROC name
        pseudocode statements
END PROC
```

is used to define either a subroutine or procedure.

```
call PROC name
```

is used to invoke either the subroutine or procedure.

```
call PROC initialise
call PROC ask question
call PROC output score
stop
```

Main program M1

```
PROC initialise
  initialise score to zero
  store data
END PROC
```

Sub module M2

```
PROC ask question
  FOR question number = 1 TO 10
    read question and correct answer
    print question
    input answer
    call PROC test answer
    IF answer not correct THEN
      input answer
      call PROC test answer
      IF answer not correct THEN
        print correct answer
      END IF
    END IF
  NEXT question number
END PROC
```

Sub module M3

```
PROC test answer
  set answer flag to zero
  IF answer correct THEN
    print answer is correct
    increase score by 1
    set answer flag to 1
  ELSE
    print answer is wrong
  END IF
END PROC
```

Sub module M5

```
PROC output score
  print score out of 10
END PROC
```

Sub module M4

Glossary	
question	Q$
correct answer	C$
user's answer	A$
question number	N
score	S
answer flag	F

10.4.3 Program

```
  10  REM . . MAIN PROGRAM
  30  GOSUB 1000
  40  GOSUB 2000
  50  GOSUB 4000
  60  STOP

1000  REM . . INITIALISE
1040  LET S = 0
1050  DATA "BATTLE OF HASTINGS", "1066"
1060  DATA "MAGNA CARTA SIGNED", "1215"
1070  DATA "START OF THE BLACK DEATH", "1348"
1080  DATA "DEFEAT OF THE SPANISH ARMADA", "1588"
1090  DATA "CIVIL WAR IN BRITAIN", "1642"
1100  DATA "GREAT FIRE OF LONDON", "1666"
1110  DATA "START OF THE FRENCH REVOLUTION", "1789"
1120  DATA "START OF THE BOER WAR", "1899"
1130  DATA "ACCESSION OF QUEEN ELIZABETH II", "1952"
1140  DATA "FIRST MAN SENT INTO SPACE", "1961"
1150  RETURN

2000  REM . . ASK QUESTION
2010  FOR N = 1 TO 10
2015    READ Q$, C$
2020    PRINT "WHAT DATE WAS THE ";Q$
2030    INPUT A$
2040    GOSUB 3000
2050    IF F = 1 THEN 2090
2060      INPUT "TRY AGAIN ",A$
2070      GOSUB 3000
2080      IF F = 0 THEN PRINT "CORRECT ANSWER IS ";C$
2090  NEXT N
2100  RETURN

3000  REM . . TEST ANSWER
3010  LET F = 0
3020  IF A$ <> C$ THEN 3070
3030    PRINT "CORRECT"
3040    LET S = S + 1
3050    LET F = 1
3060  GOTO 3080
3070    PRINT "WRONG"
3080  RETURN

4000  REM . . OUTPUT SCORE
4010  PRINT "YOU HAVE SCORED ";S;" OUT OF 10"
4020  RETURN
```

Using your computer

Type and SAVE the last program.

LOAD and RUN the program.

Without looking at the answers how many questions can you answer correctly?

Specimen results

```
>LOAD "LESSON"
>RUN
WHAT DATE WAS THE BATTLE OF HASTINGS
?1066
CORRECT
WHAT DATE WAS THE MAGNA CARTA SIGNED
?1215
CORRECT
WHAT DATE WAS THE START OF THE BLACK DEATH
?1346
WRONG
TRY AGAIN ?1348
CORRECT
WHAT DATE WAS THE DEFEAT OF THE SPANISH ARMADA
?1586
WRONG
TRY AGAIN ?1589
WRONG
CORRECT ANSWER IS 1588
WHAT DATE WAS THE CIVIL WAR IN BRITAIN
?1642
CORRECT
WHAT DATE WAS THE GREAT FIRE OF LONDON
?1666
CORRECT
WHAT DATE WAS THE START OF THE FRENCH REVOLUTION
?1788
WRONG
TRY AGAIN ?1789
CORRECT
WHAT DATE WAS THE START OF THE BOER WAR
?1899
CORRECT
WHAT DATE WAS THE ACCESSION OF QUEEN ELIZABETH II
?1952
CORRECT
WHAT DATE WAS THE FIRST MAN SENT INTO SPACE
?1961
CORRECT
YOU HAVE SCORED 9 OUT OF 10

STOP at line 60
>
```

10.5 Procedures

The function of a procedure is similar to that of a subroutine, however, the method of defining a procedure is quite different. All procedures should be defined in the following manner.

DEFine PROCedure name (list of parameters)
REMark to state what the procedure does
LOCAL list of variables applying to procedure only

BASIC program code

END PROCedure

The REM statement is optional, however, its inclusion is a valuable aid to documentation.

The LOCAL list of variables is also optional. When used the values of those variables defined as being local to that procedure will not corrupt (change the value of) variables external to the procedure (to be found in other procedures) having the same variable name.

DEFine PROCedure name and END PROCedure mark the start and finish of the procedure.

10.5.1 Local Variables

In the following example a program is written to calculate the circumference and area of a circle from a known radius. Separate procedures have been written to input a radius, calculate a circumference or an area and print a circumference or an area respectively. The variables that are used in both procedures are local to those procedures even though they may have the same name (R and P). Any attempts to print the values for R,P,C and A in the calling routine (main program) would result in zeroes probably being output for each of the four variables.

10.5.1 (cont.)

```
10  REM . . MAIN PROGRAM (CALLING ROUTINE)
20  CIRCUMFERENCE
30  AREA
40  STOP

100 DEFINE PROCEDURE CIRCUMFERENCE
110 REM . . PROCEDURE TO INPUT RADIUS, CALCULATE AND PRINT CIRCUMFERENCE
120 LOCAL R,P,C
130 LET P = 3.14159
140 INPUT "RADIUS ",R
150 LET C = 2*P*R
160 PRINT "CIRCUMFERENCE ";C
170 END PROCEDURE

200 DEFINE PROCEDURE AREA
210 REM . . PROCEDURE TO INPUT RADIUS, CALCULATE AND PRINT AREA
220 LOCAL R,P,A
230 LET P = 3.14159
240 INPUT "RADIUS ",R
250 LET A = P*R*R
260 PRINT "AREA ";A
270 END PROCEDURE
```

These three routines can be represented diagrammatically to illustrate that the variables are local to each routine and **not** global.

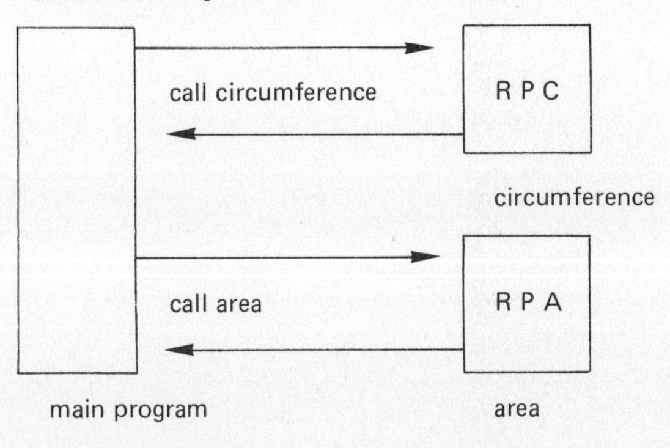

10.5.2 Parameters

In this example the radius and value for π are assigned twice (once in both procedures). These two variables can be treated as *parameters*, defined in the main program and passed across to each procedure in turn. R and P no longer become local variables and the same values can be used in as many procedures as needed provided they are passed as *parameters*.

A parameter is a variable that is defined in one procedure (or main program) and passed across to another procedure (or main program).

```
10  REM . . MAIN PROGRAM
20  LET P = 3.14159
30  INPUT "RADIUS ",R
40  CIRCUMFERENCE (P,R)
50  AREA (P,R)
60  STOP

100 DEFINE PROCEDURE CIRCUMFERENCE (P,R)
110 LOCAL C
120 LET C = 2*P*R
130 PRINT "CIRCUMFERENCE ";C
140 END PROCEDURE

200 DEFINE PROCEDURE AREA (P,R)
210 LOCAL A
220 LET A = P*R*R
230 PRINT "AREA ";A
240 END PROCEDURE
```

The following diagram illustrates that R and P are passed into the two procedures from the main program and are no longer local to their respective procedures.

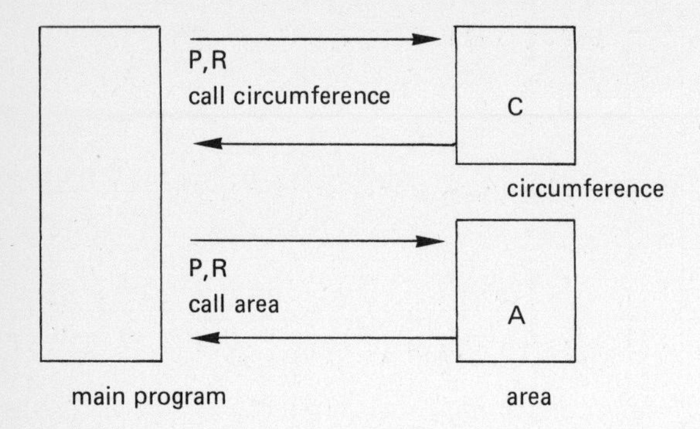

10.5.3 Further Worked Example

Write a program to calculate the number of ways of selecting a team of R players from N players and print the result.

The mathematical solution to this problem is found by using the expression N! / (R! * (N-R)!) where ! means factorial (e.g. 4! = 4x3x2x1).

Since three factorial values for N, R and N-R have to be calculated one procedure for calculating the factorial value of a number should be incorporated into the program.

Design

input team size (R) and number of players (N)
call **PROC** factorial (N,X)
call **PROC** factorial (R,Y)
call **PROC** factorial (N-R,Z)
calculate combinations
print combinations
stop

PROC factorial (F,V)
  initialise factorial value to 1
  FOR count = F **TO** 2 **STEP** −1
    calculate product of F and count
  NEXT count
END PROC

Glossary

main program	
size of team	R
number of players	N
N!	X
R!	Y
(N - R)!	Z
combinations	A
procedure factorial	
count	I
number whose factorial value is to be calculated	F
F!	V

10.5.3 (cont.)

Program

```
 10 INPUT "SIZE OF TEAM ", R
 20 INPUT "NUMBER OF PLAYERS ", N
 30 FACTORIAL N,X
 40 FACTORIAL R,Y
 50 FACTORIAL N-R,Z
 60 LET A = X/(Y*Z)
 70 PRINT "NUMBER OF WAYS OF SELECTING A TEAM ";
 80 PRINT "OF ";R;" PLAYERS FROM ";N;" PLAYERS IS ";A
 90 STOP
100 DEFINE PROCEDURE FACTORIAL (F, V)
110 REM . . PROCEDURE TO CALCULATE FACTORIALS
120 LOCAL I
130 LET V = 1
140 FOR I = F TO 1 STEP − 1
150   LET V = V*I
160 NEXT I
170 END PROCEDURE
```

Using your computer

Type, SAVE, LOAD and RUN the last program.

The following diagram represents the parameters being passed between the main program and the procedure and vice-versa. Parameters being input to the procedure are N,R and N-R, and are represented by the variable F in the procedure. The parameter being output from the procedure is V and is represented by X,Y and Z in the main program.

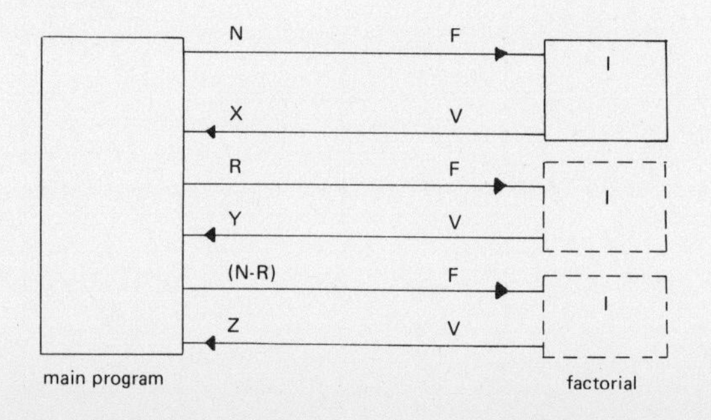

Specimen results

```
 LOAD "TEAMS"
>RUN
SIZE OF TEAM ?5
NUMBER OF PLAYERS ?8
NUMBER OF WAYS OF SELECTING A TEAM OF 5 PLAYERS FROM 8 PLAYERS IS 56

STOP at line 90
>RUN
SIZE OF TEAM ?6
NUMBER OF PLAYERS ?8
NUMBER OF WAYS OF SELECTING A TEAM OF 6 PLAYERS FROM 8 PLAYERS IS 28

STOP at line 90
>RUN
SIZE OF TEAM ?7
NUMBER OF PLAYERS ?8
NUMBER OF WAYS OF SELECTING A TEAM OF 7 PLAYERS FROM 8 PLAYERS IS 8

STOP at line 90
>
```

10.6 Recursion

A recursive procedure is a procedure that can call itself. The following program illustrates how recursion operates.

```
100  LET I = 1
110  RECURSE I
120  STOP
130  DEFINE PROCEDURE RECURSE (I)
140  PRINT I
150  LET I = I + 1
160  If I < 5 THEN RECURSE I
170  LET I = I – 1
180  PRINT I
190  END PROCEDURE
```

The output from this program is:

1 printed on the first entry into RECURSE
2 printed on the second entry into RECURSE
3 printed on the third entry into RECURSE
4 } printed on the fourth entry into RECURSE
4 }
3 printed on the re-entry into the third entry of RECURS
2 printed on the re-entry into the second entry of RECUF
1 printed on the re-entry into the first entry of RECURSE

The following diagram illustrates the recursion of the procedure.

---➤-- broken line represents sequential execution of instructions

—◄— solid line represents either a branch to, or a return from a procedure.

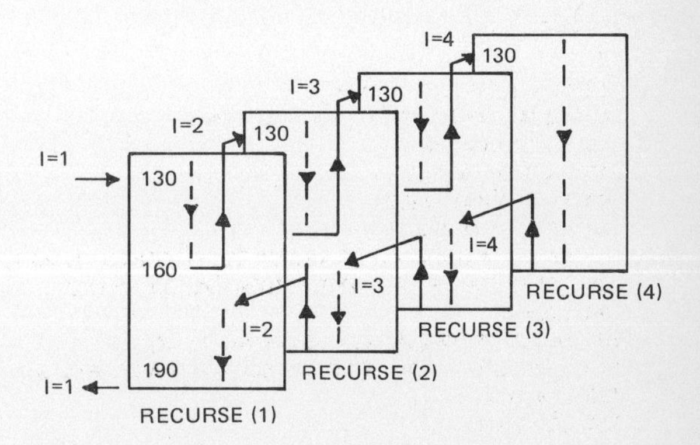

A recursive procedure can be thought of as the same procedure nested as many times as it calls itself.

10.7 Dialect Differences

The two dialects considered in this book all support the GOSUB, ON . . . GOSUB and RETURN statements.

10.7.1 Chain

Microsoft. Format: CHAIN [MERGE] filespec [,[line] [,[ALL] [,DELETE range]]]

where filespec follows the rules for naming Microsoft files in chapter 5; line represents a line-number, it may be in the form of an integer, literal or expression that evaluates to an integer literal.

Examples.

CHAIN "A:PROG1"	chain program PROG1 from drive A and start execution at the first line in the program.
CHAIN "A:PROG1",1000	start execution at line 1000
CHAIN "A:PROG1",1000,ALL	the ALL specifies that every variable in the current program is to be passed to the chained program.
CHAIN MERGE "A: PROG1",1000	the chained program is merged with the current program and execution starts at line 1000
CHAIN MERGE "A:PROG2",1000,DELETE 1000–2000	lines 1000 to 2000 in the current program are deleted **before** PROG2 is chained and merged with the remainder of the current program.

10.7.1 (cont.)

Warning. If a RENUM command is used then be sure to amend the line numbers in a CHAIN command.

Notes. The CHAIN statement leaves files open. The CHAIN statement with MERGE option preserves the current OPTION BASE setting. The CHAIN statement does a RESTORE before running a chained program.

If ALL is not used then variables may be passed from a current program to a chained program by including a COMMON statement in the current program. The purpose of COMMON is to declare all the parameters to be passed to the chained program.

Example. 100 COMMON A,B,C( ),D$

C( ) implies a table that does not need dimensioning in the chained program.

BBC/Electron. Format: CHAIN filename

where filename specifies the name of a program. The various options that are applicable in Microsoft BASIC are **not** applicable here.

10.7.2 Procedures

Microsoft. Basic on the IBM PC does **not** support procedures.

BBC/Electron.

Format:

```
DEF PROCname(parameters)
LOCAL variables
–
–
–
ENDPROC
```

The call to the procedure is made by specifying the procedure name and a parenthesised list of parameters – PROCname(parameters)

The parameters are INPUT parameters only. BBC/Electron procedures **do not** allow output parameters.

10.8 Keywords

modular programming, monolithic programming;
GOSUB, RETURN, ON . . GOSUB, CHAIN;
subroutines, nesting;
procedures, parameters, local variables, global variables;
recursion.

10.9 Questions

1 Detect the errors in the following statements.

a) (main program)

```
________
________
60   GOSUB 1000
________
________
```

(subroutine)

```
100   ________
      ________
      ________
      ________

      RTN
```

b) (main program ALPHA)

```
________
________
60   CHAIN ALPHA 60
________
________
```

c) (main program)

```
________
________
60   GOSUB CALC(X,Y)
________
________
```

(procedure)

```
1000   PROC CALC(X,Y)
       ________
       ________
       ________

       RETURN
```

d) (main program)

```
________
________

60   GOSUB 70
65   REM . . SUBROUTINE
70   ________
     ________
     ________
     ________
     RETURN
```

e) (main program)

```
________
________
60   CALC(X,Y)

________
________
```

(procedure)

```
1000   DEF PROC CALC(X,Y)
1010   LOCAL X,Y
       ________
       ________
       ________
       END PROC
```

2 Discuss the undesirable nature of the following statements.

a) (main program)

```
      ______
      ______
60  GOSUB 1000
70  ______
    ______
```

(subroutine 1)

```
1000  ______
      ______
      ______
1050  GOSUB 2000
1060  ______
      ______
      ______
      RETURN
```

(subroutine 2)

```
2000  ______
      ______
      ______
      GOTO 70
      ______
      RETURN
```

b) (main program)

```
      ______
      ______
60  GOTO 1000
70  ______
    ______
```

(subroutine 1)

```
1000  ______
      ______
      ______
1050  GOTO 2000
      ______
      ______
      RETURN
```

(subroutine 2)

```
2000  ______
      ______
      ______
      RETURN
```

3 Using the test data 2, –3, 2.5, 3, 0, 1, 4 re-run the following program on your computer and determine what happens if X is not 1,2 or 3.

```
 10  INPUT X
 20  ON X GOSUB 100,200,300
 30  STOP
100  PRINT "X = 1"
110  RETURN
200  PRINT "X = 2"
210  RETURN
300  PRINT "X = 3"
310  RETURN
```

4 Desk check the following segments of code. What are the final values of A,B and C in the main program and in the procedure ALPHA?

a) (main program)

```
100  A = 1: B = 2: C = 3
110  ALPHA
120  STOP
```

(procedure ALPHA)

```
1000  DEF PROC ALPHA
1010  LOCAL A,B,C
1020  A = 15: B = 30: C = 45
1030  END PROC
```

b) (main program)

```
100  A = 6: B = 7: C = 8
110  ALPHA A,B,C
120  STOP
```

(procedure ALPHA)

```
1000  DEF PROC ALPHA (A,B,C)
1010  A = B + C: B = C + A: C = A + B
1020  END PROC
```

c) (main program)

```
100  A = 2: B = 7: C = 12
110  ALPHA A,B,C
120  STOP
```

(procedure ALPHA)

```
1000  DEF PROC ALPHA (X,Y,C)
1010  LOCAL A,B
1020  A = X + Y: B = X – Y
1030  C = A + B
1040  END PROC
```

5 Trace through the following code and determine the values of Y and I at each stage of the recursion.

(main program)

```
100  X = 2
110  BETA(X)
120  STOP
```

(procedure BETA)

```
500  DEF PROC BETA(Y)
510  LOCAL I
520  I = Y: Y = I*I
530  PRINT Y,I
540  IF Y-I < 20 THEN BETA(Y)
550  Y = 2*I
560  PRINT Y,I
570  END PROC
```

If statement 510 LOCAL I is deleted, re-trace through the code and determine the values of Y and I at each stage of the recursion.

11 Tables

11.1 Introduction

A table is a data structure that enables data to be stored in the main memory of the computer. By specifying a unique location within the structure it is possible to access the data in a direct manner without having to search through the structure. There are advantages in storing data in tables as follows.

Each item of data does not have a unique variable name (useful if many hundreds of items of data are stored).

The homogeneous nature of data can be classified under one name, for example the heights of a population sample.

Direct access to a single item of data is possible.

Program coding is reduced.

Within this chapter the methods of defining tables, and storing and accessing data within tables are explained. **The term table is also known as** *array.*

11.2 One-dimensional table
11.2.1 Concept

The smallest component of a table is called a *cell* or *element* and contains either a number or a string literal.

143 a *cell* containing an item of data.

The cells are grouped together to form a one-dimensional table.

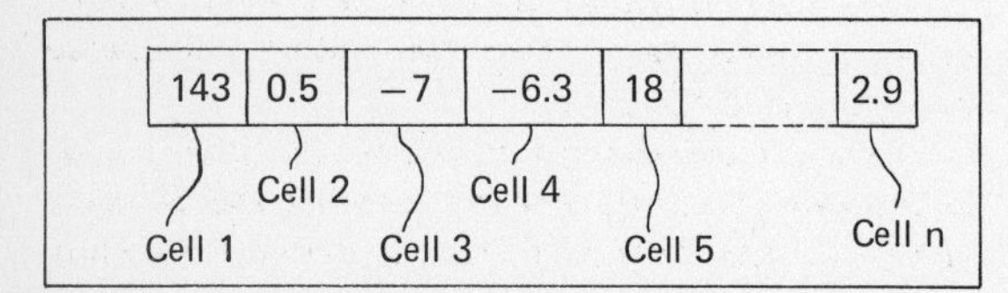

Note: The maximum number of cells is dependent upon the BASIC system being used. In practice it can range from a few cells to several thousand cells.

A table can be given **one** data name, depending upon the type of data to be stored in the table using the same rules of composition as for data names.

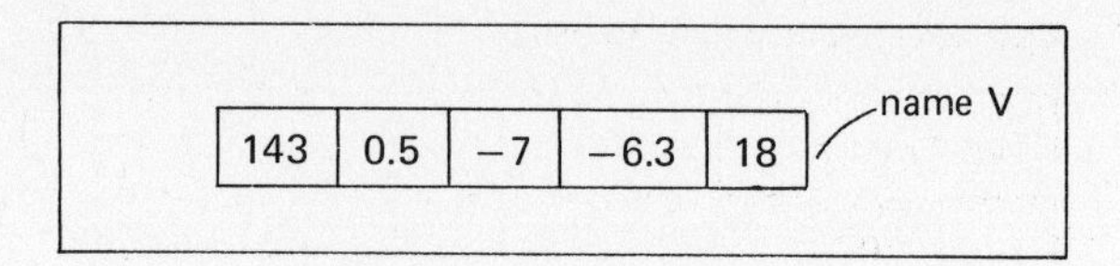

Each cell is given an address called a **subscript,** that defines the position of a cell within a table.

Contents of cells	143	0.5	−7	−6.3	18
Subscripts	1	2	3	4	5

The **contents** of each cell is accessed by the **name** given to the table followed in parenthesis by the **subscript** of the cell.

Thus the notation V (1) = 143 implies that V is the name of the table, 1 is the subscript denoting the position of the cell, and 143 is the contents of the cell.

From the last diagram it is clear that
V (2) = 0.5, V (3) = −7, V (4) = −6.3, V (5) = 18

11.2.2 Declaration

Before a table can be used in a program the name and number of cells that the structure contains must be declared at the **beginning** of a program, in order that the computer knows how much space to allocate for storing data.

The declaration of the name and size of the table is made using a **DIM** statement (short for DIMension)

The declaration of array V would be:

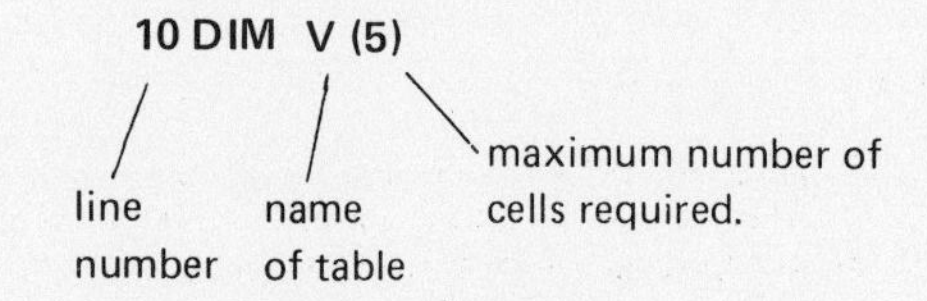

11.2.3 Storing Numbers

The following program segments show the three possible ways of allocating numbers to the cells of a table. The examples relate to table V previously described.

READ/DATA

```
10  DIM V (5)
20  REM · · THE VALUE OF I REPRESENTS THE SUBSCRIPT
30  REM · · WHICH CHANGES AFTER EACH DATUM
40  REM · · HAS BEEN READ INTO ITS APPROPRIATE CELL
50  FOR I = 1 TO 5
60    READ V (I)
70  NEXT I
80  DATA 143, 0.5, −7, −6.3, 18
```

Desk check of program segment.

Line number	I	V (I)
50	1	0
60	1	143
70	1	143
50	2	0
60	2	0.5
70	2	0.5
50	3	0
60	3	−7
70	3	−7
50	4	0
60	4	−6.3
70	4	−6.3
50	5	0
60	5	18
70	5	18

Notes. The zeros in the column headed V (I) indicate that BASIC initialises the contents of each cell to zero after the declaration of the table.

After running the program I has changed from 1 to 5 and the contents of each cell are as shown in the diagram of table V.

INPUT.

```
10  REM · · THIS IS A SIMILAR TECHNIQUE TO THE LAST
20  REM · · PROGRAM SEGMENT
30  DIM V (5)
40  FOR I = 1 TO 5
50    REM · · DATA IS ENTERED AT A KEYBOARD DURING
60    REM · · RUN TIME, AND IS STORED IN THE
70    REM · · RESPECTIVE CELLS OF THE TABLE
80    INPUT V (I)
90  NEXT I
```

LET

```
10  REM · · THIS TECHNIQUE WOULD NORMALLY BE
20  REM · · CONFINED TO ASSIGNING SMALL QUANTITIES
30  REM · · OF DATA AND IS APPLICABLE IF THE
40  REM · · TABLE IS TO CONTAIN THE RESULTS OF
50  REM · · ARITHMETIC ASSIGNMENTS
60  DIM V (5)
70  REM · · NOTE THE SUBSCRIPTS ARE NUMERIC LITERALS
80  REM · · AND NOT DATA NAMES
90  LET V (1) = 143
100 LET V (2) = 0.5
110 LET V (3) = −7
120 LET V (4) = −6.3
130 LET V (5) = 18
```

11.2.4 Storing string literals

The techniques of **READ/DATA, INPUT** and **LET** previously described for storing numbers also apply to storing alphanumeric strings in a table.

However, the names of tables must conform to string variable names. (Use of $ postscript).

The contents of the table must be alphanumeric.

The maximum size of a string in each cell will depend upon the BASIC system being used.

BASIC will initialise the contents of a string table with a **null** character in each cell ie. empty

Example. To store the names of six motor car manufacturers in a table such as:

FORD	B.L.	VAUXHALL	VOLVO	SAAB	AUDI

the coding would be:

```
10  REM · · DECLARE THE NAME AND SIZE OF THE TABLE
20  DIM C$ (6)
30  REM · · USE THE READ/DATA TECHNIQUE
40  REM · · DESCRIBED EARLIER TO STORE STRINGS
50  FOR I = 1 TO 6
60    READ C$ (I)
70  NEXT I
80  REM · · NOTE THE STRINGS USED AS DATA ARE
90  REM · · ENCLOSED BETWEEN QUOTATION MARKS
100 DATA "FORD", "B.L.", "VAUXHALL"
110 DATA "VOLVO", "SAAB", "AUDI"
```

11.3 Worked Example

The prices of five different articles are stored in a one-dimensional table as shown.

PRICE	20	15	16	18	14
PRODUCT-CODE	1	2	3	4	5

Each article is give an product-code from 1 to 5. To reference a price for an article the product code is used as a subscript to the table.

Design and write a program to input the product code and quantity sold for an article, calculate and print the cost of the sale. Terminate the procedure when the product code is out of range.

11.3.1 Design

FOR product code = 1 **TO** 5
  read price of product into table
NEXT product code
input product code
WHILE product code > 0 AND product code < 6 **DO**
  input quantity sold
  calculate value of sale
  print value of sale
  input product code
END WHILE
stop

glossary	
Product code	C
Price	P(C)
Quantity sold	Q
Value of sale	S

11.3.2 Program

```
 10 DIM P(5)
 20 FOR C = 1 TO 5
 30   READ P(C)
 40 NEXT C
 50 DATA 20,15,16,18,14
 60 INPUT "PRODUCT CODE", C
 70 IF C<1 OR C>5 THEN STOP
 80   INPUT "QUANTITY SOLD", Q
 90   LET S = Q * P(C)
100   PRINT "COST OF SALE ",S
110   INPUT "PRODUCT CODE",C
120 GOTO 70
```

Using your computer

Type and SAVE the last program.

LOAD and RUN the program. Use the following test data in the execution of the program.

3 10 5 20 2 100 0

Specimen results

```
>LOAD "SALES1"
>RUN
PRODUCT CODE ?3
QUANTITY SOLD?10
COST OF SALE                160
PRODUCT CODE ?5
QUANTITY SOLD?20
COST OF SALE                280
PRODUCT CODE ?2
QUANTITY SOLD?100
COST OF SALE               1500
PRODUCT CODE ?0

STOP at line 70
>
```

11.4 Two-dimensional table

11.4.1 Concept

A two-dimensional table is formed by placing one-dimensional tables together in **rows**, and allowing the respective cells of each one-dimensional table to form **columns**.

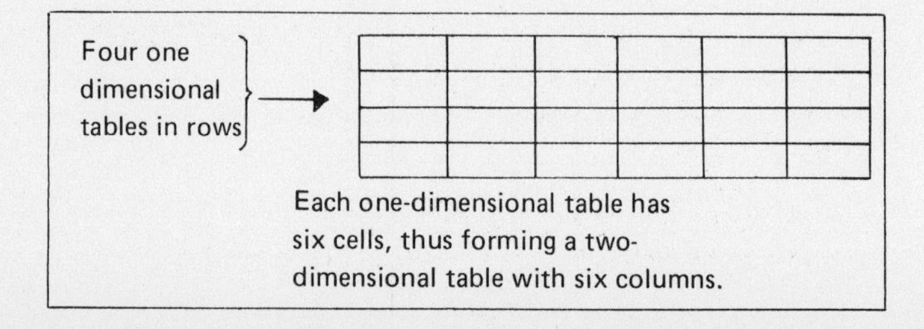

A two-dimensional table is given a name in the same way as a one-dimensional table is named.

Each **row** and **column** are given subscripts to denote the unique position of a cell.

The smallest element of the structure is still a **cell,** and can contain either a number or an alphabetic string as before.

Column Subscripts

name T

Row Subscripts	1	2	3	4	5	6
1		92				
2				16		
3		–8				
4					(34)	

a cell

Access to any cell of the table will be through

The name of the two-dimensional table.
The **row** subscript that the cell is found in.
The **column** subscript that the cell is found in.

The subscripts follow the name of the table and are parenthesised.

The row subscript is written **before** the column subscript and separated by a comma.

With reference to the last diagram T (1, 2) = 92 implies that T is the name of the table, 1 is the ROW value for the cell, 2 is the COLUMN value for the cell, and 92 is the contents of the cell.

From table T
T (2, 4) = 16, T (3, 2) = –8 and T (4, 5) = 34.

11.4.2 Declaration

Two-dimensional tables are declared in a similar manner to one-dimensional tables.

The declaration of table T would be:

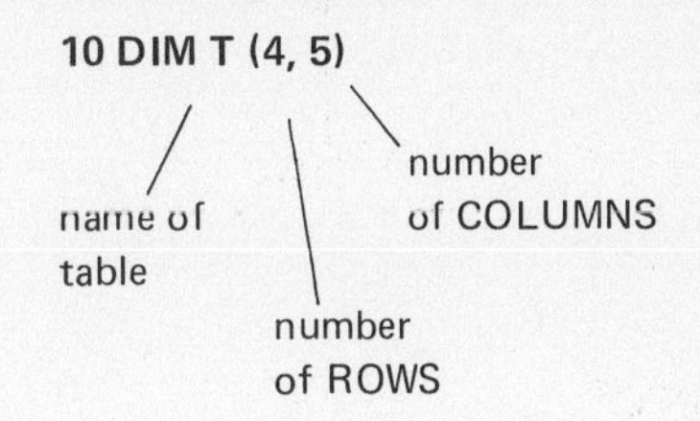

11.4.3 Storing data

The techniques of using **READ/DATA, INPUT** and **LET** for storing numbers and strings as described in 11.2.3, 11.2.4 apply also to two-dimensional tables.

A double loop is used to accommodate the two subscripts when either **reading** or **inputting** data.

Example. The data in the two-dimensional table illustrated could be stored using the following coding.

ALLAN	ANNE	ANDY
BRUCE	BARRY	BERT

11.4.3 (cont.)

```
 10 REM · · DECLARE THE NAME AND SIZE OF THE TABLE
 20 DIM N$ (2, 3)
 30 REM · · SET UP AN OUTER LOOP TO CONTROL THE ROW SUBSCRIPT
 40 FOR I = 1 TO 2
 50   REM · · SET UP AN INNER LOOP TO CONTROL THE COLUMN SUBSCRIPT
 60   FOR J = 1 TO 3
 70     REM · · USE A READ/DATA STATEMENT TO STORE DATA
 80     REM · · SHOWN IN DIAGRAM
 90     READ N$ (I, J)
100   NEXT J
110 NEXT I
120 DATA "ALLAN", "ANNE", "ANDY"
130 DATA "BRUCE", "BARRY", "BERT"
```

11.5 Worked Examples

Problem. The prices of five different articles vary according to the quantities sold. The price bands are up to and including 100 articles (high price), greater than 100 articles but less than and including 500 articles (medium price) and greater than 500 articles (low price). The sale price for each article in the appropriate price band can be stored in a two dimensional table as shown.

TABLE P(3, 5)

	1	2	3	4	5
SALES PRICE <= 100	20	15	16	18	14
SALES PRICE > 100	18	14	13	17	13
SALES PRICE > 500	15	11	10	12	9

product code

Design and write a program to input the product code and quantity sold for an article, calculate and print the cost of the sale. Terminate the procedure when the product code is out of range.

11.5.1 Design

```
FOR band = 1 TO 3
  FOR product code = 1 TO 5
    read price of product into table
  NEXT product code
NEXT band
input product code
WHILE product code > 0 AND product code < 6 DO
  input quantity sold
  IF quantity sold > 100 THEN
    IF quantity sold > 500 THEN
      band = 3
    ELSE
      band = 2
    END IF
  ELSE
    band = 1
  END IF
  calculate value of sale
  print value of sale
  input product code
END WHILE
stop
```

glossary	
band	B
product code	C
Price	P(B,C)
Quantity sold	Q
Value of sale	S

11.5.2 Program

```
 10 DIM P(3,5)
 20 FOR B = 1 TO 3
 30   FOR C = 1 TO 5
 40     READ P(B,C)
 50   NEXT C
 60 NEXT B
 70 DATA 20,15,16,18,14
 80 DATA 18,14,13,17,13
 90 DATA 15,11,10,12,9
100 INPUT "PRODUCT CODE ",C
110 IF C<1 OR C>5 THEN STOP
120   INPUT "QUANTITY SOLD ",Q
130   IF Q<=100 THEN 190
140     IF Q<=500 THEN 170
150       LET B = 3
160     GOTO 200
170       LET B = 2
180   GOTO 200
190     LET B = 1
200   LET S = Q * P(B,C)
210   PRINT "COST OF SALE ",S
220   INPUT "PRODUCT CODE ",C
230 GOTO 110
```

Using your computer

Type and SAVE the last program.

LOAD and RUN the program. Use the following test data in the execution of the program.

2 500 4 1000 3 200 1 450 −1

Specimen results

```
>LOAD "SALES2"
>RUN
PRODUCT CODE ?2
QUANTITY SOLD ?500
COST OF SALE                 7000
PRODUCT CODE ?4
QUANTITY SOLD ?1000
COST OF SALE                12000
PRODUCT CODE ?3
QUANTITY SOLD ?200
COST OF SALE                 2600
PRODUCT CODE ?1
QUANTITY SOLD ?450
COST OF SALE                 8100
PRODUCT CODE ?-1

STOP at line 110
>
```

Problem. A sporting league is divided into three divisions and within each division there are five teams. Each team is named after its home town.

Division 1	Division 2	Division 3
Southampton	Portsmouth	Basingstoke
Winchester	Reading	Banbury
Oxford	Bicester	Gloucester
Thame	Swindon	Cirencester
Poole	Bournemouth	Dorchester

Design and write a program to store the names of the teams in a two-dimensional table. Code a menu driven procedure to interrogate the table and display the following information.

Input a division number and print all the teams in that division.

Input a division number and a team position and print the name of that team.

Input a league position and print the names of all the teams in that position in the three divisions.

Glossary	
menu code	M
division number	D
position	P
team	T$(D,P)

11.5.3 Design

```
FOR division number = 1 TO 3
  FOR position = 1 TO 5
    read team name into table
  NEXT position
NEXT division number
call PROC menu
WHILE menu code not = 4 DO
  CASE menu code OF
  WHEN 1
    input division number
    FOR position = 1 TO 5
      print team (division number, position)
    NEXT position
  WHEN 2
    input division number
    input position
    print team (division number, position)
  WHEN 3
    input position
    FOR division number = 1 TO 3
      print team (division number, position)
    NEXT division number
  END CASE
  call PROC menu
END WHILE
stop

PROC menu
  print details of menu
  input menu code
END PROC
```

11.5.4 Program

```
 10 DIM T$(3,5)
 20 FOR D = 1 TO 3
 30   FOR P = 1 TO 5
 40     READ T$(D,P)
 50   NEXT P
 60 NEXT D
 70 DATA "SOUTHAMPTON", "WINCHESTER", "OXFORD", "THAME","POOLE"
 80 DATA "PORTSMOUTH", "READING", "BICESTER", "SWINDON", "BOURNEMOUTH"
 90 DATA "BASINGSTOKE", "BANBURY", "GLOUCESTER", "CIRENCESTER", "DORCHESTER"
100 GOSUB 500
110 IF M = 4 THEN STOP
120   IF M <> 1 THEN 180
130     INPUT "DIVISION ",D
140     FOR P = 1 TO 5
150       PRINT T$(D,P)
160     NEXT P
170   GOTO 270
180   IF M <> 2 THEN 230
190     INPUT "DIVISION ",D
200     INPUT "POSITION ",P
210     PRINT T$(D,P)
220   GOTO 270
230     INPUT "POSITION ",P
240     FOR D = 1 TO 3
250       PRINT T$(D,P)
260     NEXT D
270   GOSUB 500
280 GOTO 110

500 REM . . MENU SUBROUTINE
510 PRINT "DO YOU WANT TO:"
520 PRINT "1   LIST THE TEAMS IN A DIVISION"
530 PRINT "2   LIST A TEAM FROM A DIVISION IN A GIVEN POSITION"
540 PRINT "3   LIST THE TEAMS IN THE SAME POSITION IN THE DIVISIONS"
550 PRINT "4   STOP"
560 INPUT "TYPE CODE 1 – 4",M
570 RETURN
```

Using your computer

Type and SAVE the last program.

LOAD and RUN the program.Use the following test data in the execution of the program.

```
1   3   2   1   5   3   1   4
```

Specimen results

```
>LOAD "TEAM"
>RUN
DO YOU WANT TO:
1  LIST THE TEAMS IN A DIVISION
2  LIST A TEAM FROM A DIVISION IN A GIVEN POSITION
3  LIST THE TEAMS IN THE SAME POSITION IN THE DIVISIONS
4  STOP
TYPE CODE 1-4 ?1
DIVISION ?3
BASINGSTOKE
BANBURY
GLOUCESTER
CIRENCESTER
DORCHESTER
DO YOU WANT TO:
1  LIST THE TEAMS IN A DIVISION
2  LIST A TEAM FROM A DIVISION IN A GIVEN POSITION
3  LIST THE TEAMS IN THE SAME POSITION IN THE DIVISIONS
4  STOP
TYPE CODE 1-4 ?2
DIVISION ?1
POSITION ?5
POOLE
DO YOU WANT TO:
1  LIST THE TEAMS IN A DIVISION
2  LIST A TEAM FROM A DIVISION IN A GIVEN POSITION
3  LIST THE TEAMS IN THE SAME POSITION IN THE DIVISIONS
4  STOP
TYPE CODE 1-4 ?3
POSITION ?1
SOUTHAMPTON
PORTSMOUTH
BASINGSTOKE
DO YOU WANT TO:
1  LIST THE TEAMS IN A DIVISION
2  LIST A TEAM FROM A DIVISION IN A GIVEN POSITION
3  LIST THE TEAMS IN THE SAME POSITION IN THE DIVISIONS
4  STOP
TYPE CODE 1-4 ?4

STOP at line 110
>
```

11.6 Beyond two-dimensions

Many dialects of BASIC will now support table structures that contain more than two dimensions i.e. more than two subscripts are required to access data in a table. For example, a three-dimensional table should be thought of as a number of two-dimensional tables, with each two-dimensional table given a subscript value. Diagrammatically a three-dimensional table could appear as follows, having a DIMension X(2,3,5).

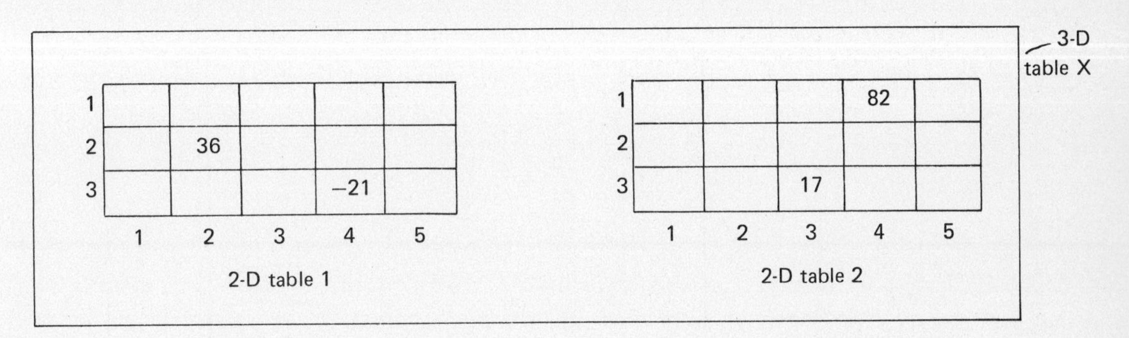

Access to a specific item of data in the three-dimensional table is by a two-dimensional subscript (denoting either table 1 or table 2) and within the appropriate two-dimensional table by row and column subscripts respectively. In the diagram the data value of −21 would be accessed through the subscripts (1,3,4), similarly 36 would be accessed through the subscripts (1,2,2), the value 17 by the subscripts (2,3,3) and the value 82 by the subscripts (2,1,4).

The methods described earlier in the chapter for declaring the size of a table (use of DIM statement), storing information in a table (use of READ/DATA, INPUT and LET) and methods of accessing data in a table will apply to all tables which consist of more than two dimensions.

Table structures of four-dimensions can be regarded as repeated three-dimensional structures, those of five-dimensions can be regarded as repeated four-dimensional structures, and so on.

11.7 Worked Example

A national union of workers is divided into **five** regions. Within each region there are **three** branches. In a national ballot to elect a union president every worker is allowed to vote for one of the **four** candidates. The votes for the candidates are stored by region and by branch within a three-dimensional table as illustrated.

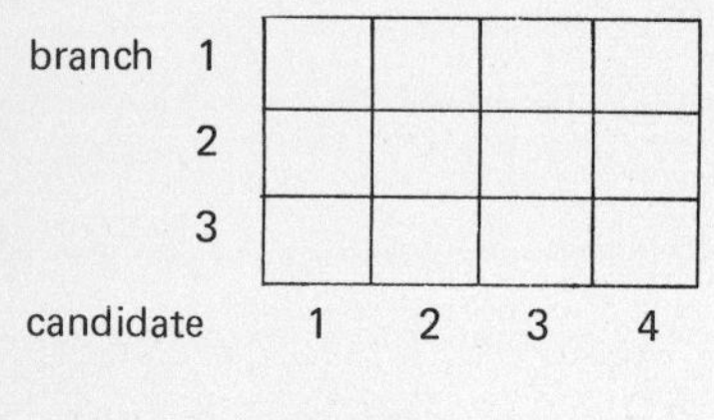

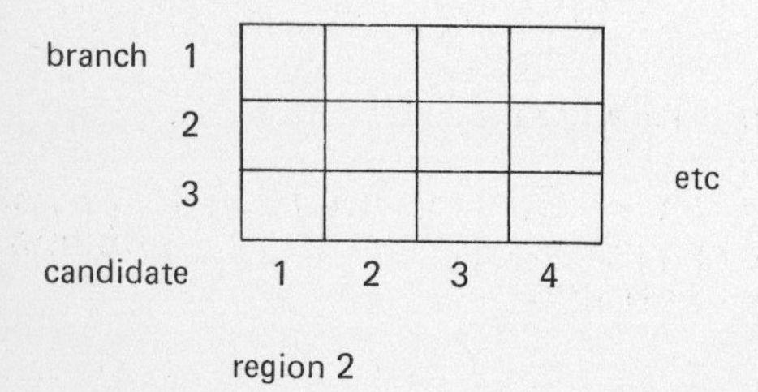

The names of the four candidates are Bloggs, Davies, Jones and Smith and are stored in a separate one-dimensional table which can be accessed by candidate number as subscript.

Design and write a program to execute the following procedures.

Using a READ/DATA statement initialise the three-dimensional table with the votes cast in each region and branch for each candidate. Store in a one-dimensional table the names of the four candidates.

Calculate and print the following information.

The total number of votes cast for all the candidates.

The total number of votes cast for each candidate in each region.

The percentage number of votes cast for each candidate.

The winner of the election. (Assume that there will not be a tie for first place).

11.7.1 Design

Separate procedures or subroutines can be written for the different tasks stated in the problem.

call **PROC** initialise
to store data in both tables and calculate and print the total vote for all candidates.

call **PROC** region votes
this calculates and prints the number of votes cast for each candidate in each region.

call **PROC** percent votes
calculates and prints the percentage vote for each candidate over all the regions — the procedure also stores in a one-dimensional table the total vote for each candidate.

call **PROC** winner
uses the table created in the last procedure to calculate and print the winner.

stop

```
PROC initialise
  initialise total vote to zero
  FOR region = 1 TO 5
    FOR branch = 1 TO 3
      FOR candidate = 1 TO 4
        read number of votes and store in table
        add vote to total vote
      NEXT candidate
    NEXT branch
  NEXT region
  FOR candidate = 1 TO 4
    read name of candidate and store in table
  NEXT candidate
  print total vote
END PROC

PROC region votes
  print headings
  FOR region = 1 TO 5
    print region number
    FOR candidate = 1 TO 4
      initialise region vote to zero
      FOR branch = 1 TO 3
        increase region vote for specific candidate
      NEXT branch
      print candidate and region vote
    NEXT candidate
    print new line
  NEXT region
END PROC

PROC percent votes
  print heading
  FOR candidate = 1 TO 4
    print name of candidate
    initialise vote to zero
    FOR region = 1 TO 5
      FOR branch = 1 TO 3
        increase votes for candidate
      NEXT branch
    NEXT region
    store total votes for candidate in table
    calculate and print percentage vote
  NEXT candidate
END PROC

PROC winner
  initialise winning candidate to 1
  FOR candidate = 2 TO 4
    IF winning candidate votes < candidate votes THEN
      winning candidate = candidate
    END IF
  NEXT candidate
  print name of winning candidate
END PROC
```

glossary	
three dimensional table to store votes	V(5,3,4)
one dimensional table to store total votes for each candidate	T(4)
one dimensional table to store names	N$(4)
total vote for all candidates	X
region	R
branch	B
candidate	C
percentage vote	P
winning candidate (by number not name)	W
votes	V1

11.7.2 Program

```
10   DIM V(5,3,4),T(4),N$(4)
20   GOSUB 1000
30   GOSUB 2000
40   GOSUB 3000
50   GOSUB 4000
60   STOP

1000 REM . . SUBROUTINE INITIALISE
1010 LET X = 0
1020 FOR R = 1 TO 5
1030   FOR B = 1 TO 3
1040     FOR C = 1 TO 4
1050       READ V(R,B,C)
1060       LET X = X + V(R,B,C)
1070     NEXT C
1080   NEXT B
1090 NEXT R
1100 DATA 20,15,8,17,19,11,21,36,32,40,37,18
1110 DATA 15,19,27,14,27,13,13,32,34,18,26,9
1120 DATA 17,25,14,19,21,23,18,16,29,17,12,15
1130 DATA 22,45,17,12,21,37,3,8,36,10,14,7
1140 DATA 26,31,19,20,22,27,8,17,16,36,15,21
1150 FOR C = 1 TO 4
1160   READ N$(C)
1170 NEXT C
1180 DATA "BLOGGS", "DAVIES", "JONES", "SMITH
1190 PRINT "TOTAL VOTE FOR ALL CANDIDATES '
1200 RETURN
```

```
2000 REM . . SUBROUTINE REGION VOTES
2010 PRINT "REGION", "CANDIDATE", "VOTES"
2020 FOR R = 1 TO 5
2030   PRINT R;
2040   FOR C = 1 TO 4
2050   LET V1 = 0
2060     FOR B = 1 TO 3
2070       LET V1 = V1 + V(R,B,C)
2080     NEXT B
2090     PRINT TAB(15);N$(C),V1
2100   NEXT C
2110   PRINT
2120 NEXT R
2130 RETURN

3000 REM . . SUBROUTINE PERCENT VOTE
3010 PRINT "CANDIDATE", "% VOTE"
3020 FOR C = 1 TO 4
3030   PRINT N$(C),
3040   LET V1 = 0
3050   FOR R = 1 TO 5
3060     FOR B = 1 TO 3
3070       LET V1 = V1 + V(R,B,C)
3080     NEXT B
3090   NEXT R
3100   LET T(C) = V1
3110   LET P = V1/X * 100
3120   PRINT P
3130 NEXT C
3140 RETURN

4000 REM . . SUBROUTINE WINNER
4010 LET W = 1
4020 FOR C = 2 TO 4
4030   IF T(W) < T(C) THEN LET W = C
4040 NEXT C
4050 PRINT "WINNER OF ELECTION IS ";N$(W)
4060 RETURN
```

Using your computer

If your dialect of BASIC supports three-dimensional tables type and SAVE the last program.

LOAD and RUN the program.

Specimen results

```
>LOAD "VOTER"
>RUN
TOTAL VOTE FOR ALL CANDIDATES 1237
REGION      CANDIDATE VOTES
 1          BLOGGS     71
            DAVIES     66
            JONES      66
            SMITH      71

 2          BLOGGS     76
            DAVIES     50
            JONES      66
            SMITH      55

 3          BLOGGS     67
            DAVIES     65
            JONES      44
            SMITH      50

 4          BLOGGS     79
            DAVIES     92
            JONES      34
            SMITH      27

 5          BLOGGS     64
            DAVIES     94
            JONES      42
            SMITH      58

CANDIDATE % VOTE
BLOGGS
28.8601455
DAVIES
29.6685529
JONES
20.3718674
SMITH
21.0994341
WINNER OF ELECTION IS DAVIES

STOP at line 60
>
```

11.8 Points to note

Subscripts by definition must be **positive integers.** However, BASIC will allow a subscript of zero.

If a table is **not** declared using a DIM statement then a default value is often assumed by the BASIC system. This value will vary from system to system but a default of eleven cells is common, which implies that a **DIM** statement need not be used for table of eleven or less cells. However, it is bad practice to omit a **DIM** statement.

The programmer is given a choice of whether to use a subscript of zero or a subscript of 1 as the lowest subscript. A choice can be made by using the statement:

OPTION BASE $\left\{ \begin{matrix} 0 \\ 1 \end{matrix} \right\}$

Such a statement must precede the **DIM** statement. If **OPTION BASE** is **not** specified then the minimum value for a subscript is taken to be zero.

11.9 Dialect Differences

The two dialects all support table processing. There are, however, several minor differences between the dialects.

11.9.1 Dim

Both dialects use the DIM statement to dimension a table. Not only does this statement provide the name of the table, number of dimensions and the maximum size of the subscripts but it also initialises all numeric tables to zero and all string tables to the null (or empty string) character.

Microsoft. Without the DIM statement a table can be assigned a maximum of **eleven** cells having the subscripts 0,1,2 . . . . . 10 by default.

The maximum number of dimensions a table may have is 255.

Attempting to dimension the same table twice in a program will lead to an error. If re-dimensioning is required then the table should be deleted by using the ERASE statement before re-defing the table.

BBC/Electron. The name of a table must appear directly after the DIM statement, for example DIMX(4) is legal but DIM   X(4) is illegal.

The only limit on the number of dimensions and maximum size of subscripts is the amount of main memory available in the computer.

The smallest subscript is always 0.

No re-dimensioning of table is allowed.

DIM can be used to reserve main memory space. For example DIM X 24 will reserve (24+1) bytes of memory starting from address (variable name) X.

11.9.2 Option Base

The BBC/Electron dialect does **not** include this statement. Microsoft BASIC uses the format given in section 11.8.

11.10 Keywords

table, cell, element, dimension, DIM, subscripts;
storing numbers, storing strings;
one-dimensions, two-dimensions, three-dimensions
multi-dimensions;
OPTION BASE.

11.11 Questions

1 Comment upon the possible errors in the following program segments.

a)
```
10 DIM A (12)
20 FOR I = 1 TO 50
30   INPUT A (I)
40 NEXT I
```

b)
```
10 DIM X (I)
20 LET X1 = 3.14
30 LET X2 = 14
40 LET X3 = -73.4
```

c)
```
10 DIM B (20,30)
20 INPUT M, N
30 FOR I = 1 TO N
40   FOR J = 1 TO M
50     LET A (I,J) = 2 * B (I + N, J + M)
60   NEXT J
70 NEXT I
```

d)
```
10 DIM V10
20 FOR I = 1 TO N
30   READ V (I)
40 NEXT I
50 DATA BLUE, RED, WHITE, BLACK, YELLOW.
```

e)
```
10 DIM T (5,2)
20 FOR I = 1 TO 2
30   FOR J = 1 TO 5
40     READ T (I,J)
50     DATA FORK, SPADE, SHEARS, TROWEL, RAKE
60     DATA 26,91,108,42,11
70   NEXT J
80 NEXT I
```

Design and write programs as answers to the following questions.

2 A two-dimensional table T, has 6 rows and 9 columns. Devise a procedure to set the contents of every cell to 100.

3 A one-dimensional table X contains 8 numbers sorted into ascending order. Devise a procedure which moves the items in X to another one-dimensional table Y, so that Y contains the 8 numbers sorted into descending order.

4 Devise a procedure to input numbers to two one-dimensional tables A and B having 10 cells each and output:

a) Those numbers that are common between the two tables. The numbers within **each** table are **not** duplicated.

b) The sums of the corresponding elements between A and B.

c) The smallest of the corresponding elements between A and B.

5 Devise a procedure to input letters from a word and store each letter in a cell of a one-dimensional table V, count the number of vowels in the word, and output the value of the count.

6 The Median of a set of numbers is that number which has the same number of values above and below it. In the set

0 3 9 18 7 5 4 the median is 5 since three numbers are larger and three numbers are smaller than 5.

Devise a program to compute the median of a set of numbers input to the computer.

i. For an **odd** number of values (easy).

ii. For an **even** number of values (more difficult).

Note. Clearly for an odd number of values the median will be the central value of an ordered set of numbers. An even number of values will not have one central value, but two central values. The median is taken to be the average of the two central values.

7 Devise a routine to store numbers in a two-dimensional array M having 4 rows and 5 columns and output the highest and lowest values in:

a. Each row.
b. Each column.

8 A selection of towns in three counties in the South of England have the following populations.

county	town	population
Cornwall	Penzance	19,360
	Truro	15,690
	Newquay	13,890
Dorset	Poole	118,922
	Dorchester	13,880
	Shaftesbury	4,180
Hampshire	Southampton	204,406
	Basingstoke	60,910
	Winchester	31,620

Write segments of code to initialise the following tables.

A one-dimensional table containing the names of the counties.

A two-dimensional table containing the names of the towns, where each row represents a different county in the order given in the first table.

A second two-dimensional table containing the population of each town, where each row represents a different county and each column a different town in the order given in the first two-dimensional table.

9 Using the tables defined in the last question write a segment of code to input the name of a county and the name of a town and search the one-dimensional table to match the county and obtain a row subscript, then search the first two-dimensional table to match the town and obtain a column subscript. Using the row and column subscripts access the second two-dimensional table and print a value for the population.

Write a second segment of code to input the name of a county and output the total population for the towns listed in the county. Re-express this figure as a percentage of the population in all the towns defined in the table.

10 When travelling on the M3 motorway westward between junction 1 and junction 6 the towns that are accessible are as follows.

junction	road number	town	distance (miles)
1	A308	Sunbury	
		Kingston	5
	A316	Central London	14
2	M25	The North (M1)	
		Heathrow (M4)	10
		Staines (A30)	4
		Chertsey (A320)	4
3	A322	Guildford	11
		Bracknell	6
4	A325	Farnborough	3
		Farnham	8
	A321	Camberley	3
5	A32	Alton	10
		Reading	14
6	A339	Basingstoke	2
		Newbury	21

Store this information in a two-dimensional table. Write a segment of code to input the name of a town accessible from the motorway and output from the table the junction number of the turn-off, the road number to the town and the distance to the town from the junction where appropriate.

12 String Processing

12.1 Introduction

The purpose of this chapter is to define and demonstrate the string functions and statements that are implemented on the majority of computers using BASIC. There is a need to be able to manipulate string data when processing text and records in a data file.

12.2 String Functions

12.2.1 Ascii

ASC (X$) Returns the numeric decimal value of the ASCII code of a single character within the argument or, in the case of a string, the ASCII value of the first character of the string.

Example.

```
10 LET X$ = "A"
20 PRINT ASC (X$)
```

The ASCII code for character A is 65, so when the program segment is run the value 65 is printed.

```
10 PRINT ASC ("CABLE-CAR")
```

The ASCII code for the first character C is printed, this will result in the value 67 being printed.

12.2.2 Character

CHR$(Y) Returns a single character whose ASCII value is Y. Y is a numeric constant, variable or expression that has a value between the limits of the ASCII code $0 \leqslant Y \leqslant 127$. The function **CHR $** serves the opposite purpose to **ASC**, and is useful in outputting ASCII control characters as part of a **PRINT** statement.

Examples.

```
10 PRINT CHR$ (81)
```

This would result in the character Q being printed since the ASCII code for Q is 81.

```
10 PRINT CHR$ (7)
```

This would result in the warning BELL of the terminal sounding, since the ASCII code for activating the BELL is 7. On some visual display units a *beep* sound is used.

12.2.3 Left

LEFT$ (X$, Y) Returns the leftmost Y characters from the string X$.

Examples.

```
10 LET X$ = "ABCDEFGHIJ"
20 PRINT LEFT$ (X$, 4)
```

This segment when run will output the first four characters of X$; ABCD.

```
10 LET Y = 3
20 PRINT LEFT $ ("ABCDEFGHIJ", Y)
```

The output would be; ABC.

12.2.4 Right

RIGHT$ (X$, Y) Returns the rightmost Y characters from the string X$.

Example.

```
10 LET X$ = "PQRSTUVWXYZ"
20 LET Y = 5
30 PRINT RIGHT$ (X$, Y)
```

Since the last five characters of X$ are VWXYZ these will be printed.

12.2.5 Middle

MID $ (X$, Y, Z) Returns a sub-string of X$, starting at character position Y and containing Z characters.

Example.

```
10  LET X$ = "PQRSTUVWXYZ"
20  LET Y = 4
30  LET Z = 5
40  PRINT MID$ (X$, Y, Z)
```

The fourth character of X$ is S, this is the beginning of the substring which contains five characters, hence the string that is output will be STUVW.

Note. The parameters Y and Z used in the last three functions can be numeric constants, variables or expressions.

12.2.6 Value

VAL (X$) Return a numeric constant equivalent to the value of the number represented by the string X$. The string X$ should consist of all digits, if it does not the consequences will depend on the version of BASIC being used.

Example.

```
10  LET X$ = "12345"
20  LET Y = VAL (X$)
30  PRINT Y
```

The numeric constant 12345 would be output from this program segment. The value of Y can be used in an arithmetic expression since the function VAL has essentially converted the data type from string to numeric.

12.2.7 String

STR$ (Y) This is the reverse operation of **VAL**, the value of Y is converted into a string literal. Y can be either a numeric constant, variable or expression.

Example.

```
10  LET Y = 7384
20  LET X$ = STR$ (Y)
30  PRINT X$
```

The result of running the program segment would be to print the string literal 7384.

12.2.8 Length

LEN (X$) Return the number of characters that are contained within the string X$.

Example.

```
10  LET X$ = "ABCDEFGHIJ"
20  PRINT LEN (X$)
```

Since there are ten characters in the string X$, the numeric constant 10 will be printed.

12.2.9 Inkey

INKEY$ will assign to a string variable any character that is input at the keyboard **without** having to press the return or enter keys. The function can have an argument appended to it. For example, INKEY$(X) where X represents the amount of time the computer must wait for a character to be input at the keyboard. The function returns a null character if no key is pressed in the specified time.

INKEY is a similar function that returns the ASCII code for a key depression.

Example.

```
10  keynumber = INKEY(200)
20  letter$ = INKEY$(200)
30  PRINT keynumber, letter$
```

If this program segment was run and the response to line 10 was to press the key X, and the response to line 20 was to press the key X again then the ASCII code for X would be printed (88) followed by the letter X.

12.3 String Statements

12.3.1 Get

Although the **INPUT** statement can be used to enter a single character at the keyboard of a terminal it has the following disadvantages.

A prompt is displayed or printed at the terminal. The system prompt can be replaced by a user prompt in many dialects of BASIC, however, an application may be such that any kind of prompt is undesirable.

The return key must always be pressed to signal to the computer that input is complete.

The depression of the return key only, can often cause a program to be terminated, or the computer will not recognise the return character as data and require further data to be input.

The **GET** statement (or its equivalent) will allow **any** single ASCII character to be entered through a keyboard **without** having to use the return key to signal that input is complete.

The syntax of the **GET** statement is

GET string variable

Example.

The following program segment will allow any set of characters to be typed at the keyboard of a terminal, and only when a full-stop is entered will the program terminate.

```
10  GET A$
20  IF A$ <> "." THEN 10
30  STOP
```

Some dialects will implement GET as a function using GET$ and GET in a similar way to INKEY$ and INKEY but without the time restriction.

12.3.2 Change

The **CHANGE** statement converts a string literal into the decimal ASCII code for each character and stores these values in a one-dimensional table. The statement can also be used so that the converse is obeyed; the numeric contents of a one-dimensional table is converted to a string of ASCII characters.

The syntax of the **CHANGE** statement is

```
CHANGE { string literal }  TO { numeric table }
       { numeric table  }     { string literal }
```

Example.

Convert the alphabet to twenty-six ASCII codes, and output each character of the alphabet with its respresented code.

```
10  DIM A (26)
20  LET X$ = "ABCDEFGHIJKLMNOPQRSTUVWXYZ"
30  CHANGE X$ TO A
40  PRINT "CHARACTER", "ASCII CODE"
50  FOR I = 1 TO 26
60    PRINT MID$ (X$,I,1), A (I)
70  NEXT I
80  STOP
```

12.4 String Concatenation

String Manipulation. String literals and variables can be manipulated in the following ways.

Alphabetic comparison of strings through the comparison of their ASCII codes. "ALPHA" is less than "BETA" since the ASCII code for A (65) is less than that for B (66). Thus A$ < B$ is true if A$ = "ALPHA" and B$ = "BETA."

Strings can be stored in arrays.

Parts of a string can be made available through the use of string functions.

Strings can be increased in size by *adding* other strings to the *end* of the previous string.

This last item is known as *string concatenation.* A plus sign + is used to denote that two strings are to be joined.

Examples.

```
10  LET A$ = "GRAPE"
20  LET B$ = "FRUIT"
30  LET C$ = A$ + B$
40  PRINT C$
50  LET C$ = B$ + A$
60  PRINT C$
70  STOP
```

If this segment of program was run it would result in two concatenated strings being output.

```
GRAPEFRUIT
FRUITGRAPE
```

The following program segment will allow any character to be typed at the keyboard and saved as part of a concatenated string. The program terminates with a full-stop being input.

```
 10  REM . . INITIALISE STRING USED TO STORE
 20  REM . . CHARACTERS WITH THE NULL CHARACTER
 30  LET X$ = ""
 40    REM . . INPUT ONE CHARACTER
 50    GET A$
 60    REM . . TEST FOR FULL-STOP
 70    IF A$ = "." THEN 120
 80      REM . . CONCATENATE STRING X$
 90      LET X$ = X$ + A$
100      GET A$
110    GOTO 70
120  –
```

12.5 Worked Examples

12.5.1 Design a program to input a sentence terminated by a full stop at the keyboard, count the number of vowels in the sentence and print the results of the vowel count.

Design

input and store ASCII codes of vowels
initialise table to zero for vowel count
input one character
WHILE character not full stop **DO**
  call **PROC** vowel count
  input next character
END WHILE
print contents of vowel count table
stop

```
PROC vowel count
  obtain ASCII code for character
  FOR subscript = 1 TO 5
    IF character code = vowel code THEN
      increase vowel count by 1
    END IF
  NEXT subscript
END PROC
```

Glossary

One dimensional table used to store the ASCII codes for the five vowels AEIOU.	V (5)
One dimensional table used to store the frequency of occurences for each vowel. The first cell holds the number of A's, second cell the number of E's, etc.	C (5)
String of vowels	S$
Subscript of table	I
Single character of sentence	X$
ASCII code of character X$	P

Program

```
  5 DIM V(5), C(5)
 10 REM · · INPUT AND STORE ASCII CODES FOR VOWELS
 20 READ A$
 30 DATA "AEIOU"
 40 CHANGE A$ TO V
 50 REM · · INITIALISE TABLE C
 60 FOR I = 1 TO 5
 70   LET C(I) = 0
 80 NEXT I
 90   REM · · INPUT SINGLE CHARACTER AT KEYBOARD
100   GET X$
110   REM · · TEST FOR END OF SENTENCE
120   IF X$ = "." THEN 190
130     REM · · BRANCH TO SUBROUTINE THAT INSPECTS
140     REM · · CHARACTER FOR VOWEL AND INCREASES
150     REM · · VOWEL COUNT
160     GOSUB 500
165     GET X$
170   GOTO 120
180 REM · · OUTPUT CLASSIFIED VOWEL COUNT
190 PRINT "VOWEL", "COUNT"
200 FOR I = 1 TO 5
210   PRINT MID$ (A$,I,1), C(I)
220 NEXT I
230 STOP
```

```
480 REM · · SUBROUTINE TO CHECK AND COUNT VOWELS
490   REM · · OBTAIN ASCII CODE FOR CHARACTER
500   LET P = ASC (X$)
510   REM · · INSPECT CHARACTER FOR VOWEL
520   FOR I = 1 TO 5
530     IF P = V(I) THEN LET C(I) = C(I) + 1
540   NEXT I
550 RETURN
```

Using your computer

Type and SAVE the last program.
LOAD and RUN the program using the test data:

THE QUICK BROWN FOX JUMPED OVER THE LAZY DOG.

Specimen results

```
 LOAD "VOWEL"
>RUN
THE QUICK BROWN FOX JUMPED OVER THE LAZY DOG.
VOWEL      COUNT
A           1
E           4
I           1
O           4
U           2

STOP at line 230
>
```

Note. This program serves to illustrate the use of **CHANGE, GET, MID$** and **ASC** however, it is not necessary to convert to and from ASCII codes line 530 could have been represented by

```
530 IF X $ = V$(I) THEN LET C(I) = C(I) + 1
```

where V$ is a table containing the strings "A", "E", "I", "O", "U"

Further amendments then necessary for the program to run correctly would be

```
  5 DIM V$(5), C(5)
 10 FOR I = 1 TO 5
 20   READ V$(I)
 30 NEXT I
 40 DATA "A", "E", "I", "O", "U"
160 GOSUB 520
210 PRINT V$(I), C(I)
490
500
```

12.5.2 Design a program to input at the keyboard an integer written in Roman numerals and print the decimal value of this number.

Note. Assume a **maximum** of 20 Roman Numerals in the representation of a number.

The following table shows the Roman Numerals and their equivalent decimal values.

Roman Numeral	Decimal Value
I	1
V	5
X	10
L	50
C	100
D	500
M	1000

Legal representations of 3, 8, 13, 18 etc. are respectively III, VIII, XIII, XVIII and **not** IIV, IIX, XIIV, XIIX.

Similarly legal representations of 4, 9, 14, 19 etc. are respectively IV, IX, XIV, XIX and **not** IIII, VIIII, XIIII, XVIIII.

For the purpose of this exercise assume that only legal representations of numbers are input to the computer.

The data structures used are two arrays.

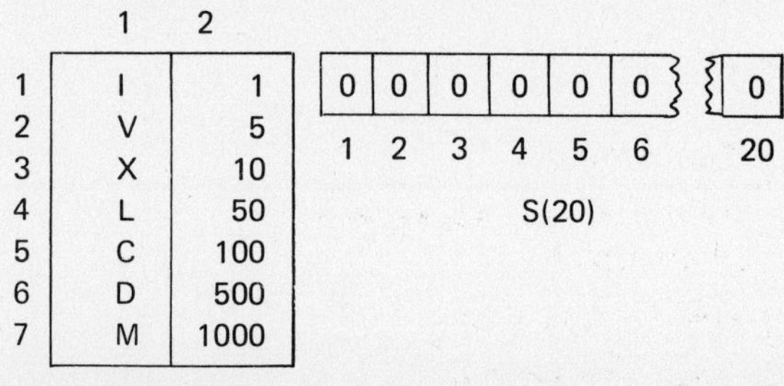

Note. In table R$ the decimal equivalent to the Roman Numerals **must** be stored as strings.

When a Roman number is input at the keyboard it is divided up into single characters, each character is translated into its decimal equivalent; and that decimal equivalent is stored in table S.

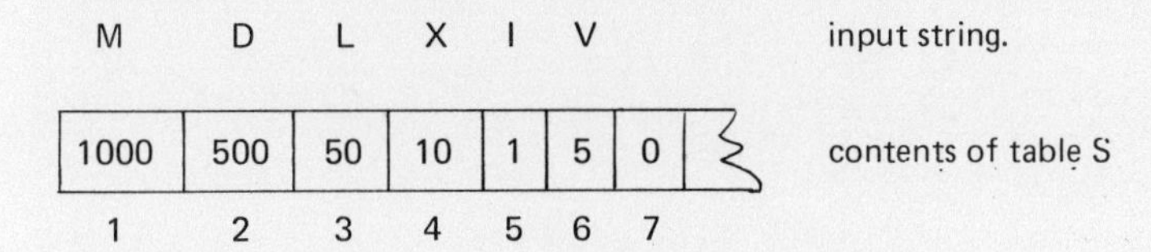

Since IV implies 4 and not 6 the contents of table S must be corrected to reflect this fact.

1000	500	50	10	–1	5	0
1	2	3	4	5	6	7

Hence the sum of S then becomes 1564.

Design

read and store Roman numerals and their decimal equivalent in a two dimensional table
REPEAT
  initialise to zero a table used to store the decimal equivalent of each Roman numeral input
  input Roman number
  represent each Roman numeral in the number by the equivalent decimal value and store the value in a one-dimensional table
  change sign of decimal values to be subtracted
  add together all the decimal values in the one-dimensional table
  print the total
UNTIL no more data
stop

Glossary	
Two-dimensional table to hold Roman Numerals and their equivalent decimal values.	R$ (7, 2)
One-dimensional table used to hold the decimal equivalent of each Roman Numeral from the number input at the keyboard.	S (20)
Table Subscripts.	I J
Roman Number.	N$
Total value of all integers stored in second table S	T
User reply to question	A$
Length of input string.	L

Program

```
 10  DIM R$(7, 2), S(20)
 20  REM · ·
 30  FOR I = 1 TO 7
 40    READ R$(I, 1), R$(I, 2)
 50    DATA "I", "1", "V", "5", "X", "10", "L", "50"
 60    DATA "C", "100", "D", "500", "M", "1000"
 70  NEXT I
 80    REM · · INITIALISE TABLE S TO ZERO
 90    FOR I = 1 TO 20
100      LET S(I) = 0
110    NEXT I
120    REM · · INPUT ROMAN NUMBER
130    INPUT "ROMAN NUMBER", N$
140    REM · · STORE DECIMAL EQUIVALENT OF EACH ROMAN
150    REM · · NUMERAL IN CONSECUTIVE CELLS OF
160    REM · · TABLE S
170    FOR I = 1 TO LEN (N$)
180      FOR J = 1 TO 7
190      REM · · SEARCH TABLE FOR DECIMAL EQUIVALENT OF
200      REM · · ROMAN NUMERAL
210      IF MID $ (N$,I,1) <> R$ (J, 1) THEN 240
220        REM · · STORE DECIMAL VALUE IN TABLE S
230        LET S(I) = VAL (R$ (J, 2))
240      NEXT J
250    REM · · REPEAT PROCEDURE FOR EACH ROMAN NUMERAL
260    REM · · OF THE NUMBER INPUT
270    NEXT I
280    REM · · COMPARE ADJACENT CELLS OF TABLE S
290    REM · · THOSE VALUES TO BE SUBTRACTED ARE
300    REM · · MULTIPLIED BY –1
310    LET L = LEN(N$) –1
320    FOR I = 1 TO L
330      IF S(I) > = S(I + 1) THEN 350
340      LET S(I) = –1 * S(I)
350    NEXT I
360    REM · · FIND THE SUM OF THE CONTENTS OF TABLE S
370    LET T = 0
380    FOR I = 1 TO LEN(N$)
390      LET T = T + S(I)
400    NEXT I
410    REM · · OUTPUT DECIMAL EQUIVALENT OF ROMAN
420    REM · · NUMBER
430    PRINT
440    PRINT "DECIMAL VALUE ="; T
450    REM · · ASK USER IF ANY MORE DATA
460    PRINT "MORE DATA – INPUT Y(YES) N(NO)"
470    INPUT A$
480  IF A$ = "Y" THEN 90
490  STOP
```

Using your computer

Type and SAVE the last program.
LOAD and RUN the program.

Specimen results

```
>LOAD "ROMAN"
>RUN
?MDCLXIV

DECIMAL VALUE=1664
MORE DATA INPUT Y(YES) N(NO)
?Y
?MMMDV

DECIMAL VALUE=3505
MORE DATA INPUT Y(YES) N(NO)
?Y
?IX

DECIMAL VALUE=9
MORE DATA INPUT Y(YES) N(NO)
?Y
?DCCCX

DECIMAL VALUE=810
MORE DATA INPUT Y(YES) N(NO)
?Y
?MVIII

DECIMAL VALUE=1008
MORE DATA INPUT Y(YES) N(NO)
?Y
?MDCVIII

DECIMAL VALUE=1608
MORE DATA INPUT Y(YES) N(NO)
?N

STOP at line 490
>
```

12.5.3 Design a program to translate an integer value input at a keyboard to an amount stated in words. Print the figurative amount.

This routine is used in part of a program to print bank cheques. You can assume that the largest figure input is less than one thousand million, and that cheques for a zero amount are not required.

Two tables are used in the solution to this problem, the first to store the figurative equivalents of the digits, and the second to store the input number in a modified form.

	1	2	3
1	One	Eleven	Ten
2	Two	Twelve	Twenty
3	Three	Thirteen	Thirty
4	Four	Fourteen	Forty
9	Nine	Nineteen	Ninety

X$ (9, 3)

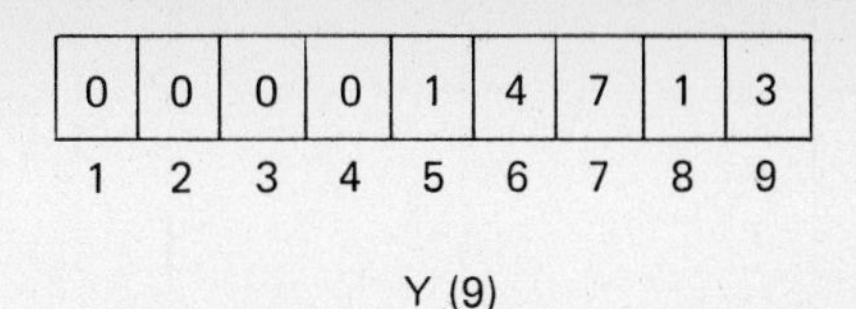

0	0	0	0	1	4	7	1	3
1	2	3	4	5	6	7	8	9

Y (9)

A number would be input without any leading zeros, the purpose of table Y is to isolate the number into digits and introduce leading zeros.

Design

```
read and store figurative constants in
two-dimensional table

REPEAT
  initialise to zero table used to store integer digits
  input integer
  store digits in one-dimensional table
  calculate number of groups of 3 non-zero digits
  call PROC convert
  print figurative number
UNTIL no more data
stop

PROC convert
  IF number of digit groups = 3 THEN
    call PROC evaluate
    build millions string
  END IF
  IF second digit group is non-zero THEN
    IF number of digit groups > 1 THEN
      call PROC evaluate
      build thousands string
    END IF
  END IF
  IF first group is non-zero THEN
    call PROC evaluate
  END IF
END PROC

PROC evaluate
  IF hundreds non-zero THEN
    build hundreds string
  END IF
  IF tens = 1 THEN
    IF units = 0 THEN
      build tens string
    ELSE
      build teens string
    END IF
  ELSE
    IF tens non-zero THEN
      build tens string
    END IF
    build units string
  END IF
END PROC
```

Glossary	
Two dimensional table containing figurative constants.	X$ (9, 3)
One dimensional table containing input number in modified form.	Y (9)
Input number.	N$
Subscripts to tables.	I J
Groups of three digits.	G
Result stored as a string.	T$
User reply to question.	A$

Program

```
 10  DIM X$(9, 3), Y(9)
 20  REM · · INPUT AND STORE FIGURATIVE CONSTANTS
 30  FOR J = 1 TO 3
 40    FOR I = 1 TO 9
 50      READ X$(I, J)
 60    NEXT I
 70  NEXT J
 80  DATA "ONE", "TWO", "THREE", "FOUR", "FIVE", "SIX"
 90  DATA "SEVEN", "EIGHT", "NINE"
100  DATA "ELEVEN", "TWELVE", "THIRTEEN", "FOURTEEN"
110  DATA "FIFTEEN", "SIXTEEN", "SEVENTEEN", "EIGHTEEN"
120  DATA "NINETEEN"
130  DATA "TEN", "TWENTY", "THIRTY", "FORTY", "FIFTY"
140  DATA "SIXTY", "SEVENTY", "EIGHTY", "NINETY"
150    REM · · INITIALISE TABLE FOR STORING NUMBER
160    FOR I = 1 TO 9
170      LET Y (I) = 0
180    NEXT I
190    REM · · INPUT NUMBER IN DIGIT FORM
200    INPUT N$
210    REM · · STORE EACH DIGIT OF NUMBER IN SEPARATE
220    REM · · CELL OF TABLE Y AND FILL WITH LEADING ZEROS
230    LET J = 9
240    FOR I = LEN(N$) TO 1 STEP -1
250      LET Y (J) = VAL (MID$ (N$, I, 1))
260      LET J = J -1
270    NEXT I
280    REM · · CALCULATE NUMBER OF GROUPS OF 3 DIGITS
290    REM · · HAVING NON-ZERO VALUE
300    IF LEN (N$) > 6 THEN 360
310      IF LEN (N$) > 3 THEN 340
320        LET G = 1
330      GOTO 380
340        LET G = 2
350      GOTO 380
360        LET G = 3
370    REM · · PROCESS THE NUMBER ACCORDING TO ITS GROUP
380    LET T$ = ""
```

```
 390    GOSUB 1000
 400    REM · · OUTPUT FIGURATIVE NUMBER
 410    PRINT T$
 420    PRINT
 430    PRINT "MORE DATA ENTER Y(YES) N(NO)"
 440    INPUT A$
 450  IF A$ = "Y" THEN 160
 460  STOP

 999  REM · · SUBROUTINE CONVERT
1000  IF G <> 3 THEN 1040
1010    LET I = 1
1020    GOSUB 2000
1030    LET T$ = T$ + "  MILLION,  "
1040  IF MID$(N$,4,3) = "000" THEN 1090
1050    IF G = 1 THEN 1090
1060      LET I = 4
1070      GOSUB 2000
1080      LET T$ = T$ + "  THOUSAND,  "
1090  IF RIGHT$(N$,3) = "000" THEN 1120
1100    LET I = 7
1110    GOSUB 2000
1120  RETURN

1999  REM · · SUBROUTINE EVALUATE
2000  IF Y(I) = 0 THEN 2020
2010    LET T$ = T$ + X$ (Y(I), 1) + "  HUNDRED  "
2020  IF Y(I + 1) <> 1 THEN 2080
2030    IF Y(I + 2) <> 0 THEN 2060
2040      LET T$ = T$ + X$ (Y(I + 1), 3)
2050    GOTO 2100
2060      LET T$ = T$ + X$ (Y(I + 2), 2) + "  "
2070    GOTO 2100
2080    IF Y (I + 1) <> 0 THEN LET T$ = T$ + X$ (Y(I + 1), 3) + "  "
2090    LET T$ = T$ + X$ (Y(I + 2), 1)
2100  RETURN
```

Using your computer

Type and SAVE the last program.
LOAD and RUN the program.

Specimen results

```
>LOAD "CHEQUE"
>RUN
?1234
ONE THOUSAND, TWO HUNDRED THIRTY FOUR

MORE DATA ENTER Y(YES) N(NO)
?Y
?45
FORTY FIVE

MORE DATA ENTER Y(YES) N(NO)
?Y
?156
ONE HUNDRED FIFTY SIX

MORE DATA ENTER Y(YES) N(NO)
?Y
?78653760
SEVENTY EIGHT MILLION, SIX HUNDRED FIFTY THREE THOUSAND, SEVEN HUNDRED SIXTY

MORE DATA ENTER Y(YES) N(NO)
?Y
?13
THIRTEEN

MORE DATA ENTER Y(YES) N(NO)
?Y
?4001
FOUR THOUSAND, ONE

MORE DATA ENTER Y(YES) N(NO)
?N

STOP at line 460
>
```

12.6 Dialect Differences

The following table illustrates which of the two dialects supports the string functions and statements described in the chapter.

	Microsoft	BBC/Electron
ASC	yes	yes
CHR$	yes	yes
LEFT$	yes	yes
RIGHT$	yes	yes
MID$	yes	yes
VAL	yes	yes
STR$	yes	yes
LEN	yes	yes
GET$	no	yes
INKEY$	yes	yes
CHANGE	no	no
concatenation (+)	yes	yes

12.6.1 Instring

Microsoft. Format: v = INSTR ([n,] X$,Y$)

where n is a numeric expression in the range 1 to 255 and X$, Y$ may be string variables, string expressions or string constants. The function searches for the first occurrence of string Y$ in X$ and returns the position at which the match is found. The optional offset n sets the position for starting the search in X$.

Example.
```
10 A$ = "ABCDEFGFEDCBA"
20 B$ = "F"
30 PRINT INSTR (A$,B$);
40 PRINT INSTR (7, A$, B$)
```

The result of running this program segment is 6 and 8. When the string is searched from the beginning "F" is found at position 6, however, when the search starts from position 7, "F" is found at position 8.

BBC/Electron. Format: v = INSTR (X$,Y$[,n])

with the same meaning as Microsoft BASIC.

12.6.2 String$

Microsoft. Format: v$ = STRING$(n,m)
v$ = STRING$(n,X$)

where n,m are in the range 0 to 255 and X$ is any string expression. The function returns a string of length n whose characters all have ASCII code m or the first character of X$.

Examples.
```
10 X$ = STRING$ (10,65)
20 PRINT X$
```

This program segment would print AAAAAAAAAA.

```
10 A$ = STRING$(5, "ZERO")
20 PRINT A$
```

This program segment would print ZZZZZ.

BBC/Electron. The format of the function is identical to the second format described under Microsoft.

12.6.3 Miscellaneous Functions

Microsoft. The functions CVI, CVS and CVD convert string variables to numeric variables stored as integers, single precision real numbers and double precision real numbers respectively. The string functions MKIS, MKSS and MKDS convert a number, integer, single precision real or double precision real respectively, to a string.

The function SPACES(n) returns a string consisting of n spaces, where n is in the range 0 to 255.

12.7 Keywords

ASC, CHR$, LEFT$, RIGHT$, MID$, VAL, STR$, LEN;
GET, INKEY, CHANGE;
string concatenation.

12.8 Questions

1 Detect the errors in the following statements.

a. LET K$ = ASC (X$)	b. LET K = CHR$ (X$)
c. PRINT RIGHT $ (X$, 3, 4)	d. PRINT MID ("X$", 3, 1
e. LET Y$ = VAL (X)	f. PRINT VAL ("ABCD")
g. PRINT LEN $ (X$)	h. GET Z
i. CHANGE X$ TO Y$	j. Y$ = Y$ – X$

2 Write a program to READ from a DATA statement the alphabet. Your program should then print

a. the entire alphabet
b. the first six characters of the alphabet
c. the last ten characters of the alphabet
d. the tenth character of the alphabet

sections b, c and d require you to use the correct string function.

3 Write a program to create a string from every other letter in the alphabet starting at letter A (eg. ACEG . . . . .) and print

a. the length of the string
b. the position of the substring "QSU", as the number of the character position from the beginning of the string.

4 Write a program to input a short poem and analyse the number of occurrences of each letter. Output a table showing the frequency of use for each letter in the alphabet.

5 Extend the program of 12.5.3 to cater for decimal fractions e.g. change 37.642 into words THIRTY SEVEN POINT SIX FOUR TWO.

6 Write a program to input a sentence, count the number of words in the sentence and output the result.

7 Most dialects of BASIC will not store, say, a 20 digit integer without converting the number to a floating point form. Clearly this will lead to truncation errors and subsequent arithmetic calculations cannot be based on the original values of the integers.

Write a program to store two twenty digit integers as characters of a string, and perform the operations of addition and subtraction on the two integers. Output the answer as a string of digits.

8 The following table illustrates the Morse Code.

A	.–	N	–.
B	–...	O	–––
C	–.–.	P	.––.
D	–..	Q	––.–
E	.	R	.–.
F	..–.	S	...
G	––.	T	–
H	....	U	..–
I	..	V	...–
J	.–––	W	.––
K	–.–	X	–..–
L	.–..	Y	–.––
M	––	Z	––..

Design and write a program to input a sentence to a computer and output the sentence in Morse Code. Extend the program to input a Morse coded sentence and translate and output the sentence in English.

13 Mathematics

13.1 Introduction

Within this chapter the topics of number representation, common mathematical functions, user defined functions and matrix functions are covered with illustrations of their use through worked examples.

13.2 Number Representation

There are three formats for representing numbers in the Basic language, they are integer, fixed-point real and floating-point real.

13.2.1 Integer

Integer numbers (whole numbers with no decimal fraction) are stored within a fixed number of memory bytes using a pure binary representation of the number. Because the number of bytes is fixed an integer, to be represented in this form, must lie within a defined range. From table 2.1 in chapter 2 it was clear that this range differs between computers, however, a range of +32767 to −32768 is common. If a number does not fit into the integer category either because it lies outside the range or contains a decimal fraction then the number will be represented in one of the two formats that follow.

13.2.2 Fixed-Point Real

Real numbers contain decimal fractions (or at least contain a decimal point) and can be represented only to a defined accuracy. Such accuracy will vary between computers but a maximum of 8 digits in a real number is a typical example. In using such a format 136.73294 could be represented accurately, however, 136.732943 would only be stored as 1.3673294×10^2. The least significant digit (3) has been truncated from the number since there is no room in the fixed allocation of bytes to represent a number to this accuracy. If however, the least significant digit had been greater than or equal to 5 then the last digit of the stored number would normally be rounded. For example 136.732947 would be stored as 1.3673295×10^2.

13.2.3 Floating-Point Real

In BASIC the number 1.3673295×10^2 would be represented as 1.3673295E+2 where 1.3673295 is known as the mantissa and 2 as the exponent. The base 10 has been replaced by the letter E. This notation is known as exponential format or scientific notation.

The syntax of a number written in exponential format is:

$\pm$ mantissa E $\mp$ exponent

The + sign is optional for both the mantissa and the exponent.

The exponent must be an integer.

The type of computer and dialect of BASIC being used will determine the accuracy to which the mantissa is represented and the largest positive and negative values of the exponent.

13.2.4 Double Precision

A few dialects of BASIC will permit the accuracy to which numbers are represented to be increased. This is achieved by doubling the number of bytes used to represent the number. Variable names are usually appended with a special symbol (e.g. #) to denote the number is to be stored using twice as many bytes as normal.

13.2.5 Examples

Consider the following representations of numbers in a computer that will store a mantissa to an accuracy of 9 significant figures, and a signed 2 digit exponent in the range 0 to 38.

	Number	BASIC representation
i.	3.7948×10^{16}	3.7948E+16
ii.	−0.00037948	−3.7948E−4
iii.	26394782	26394782
iv.	−2.6394782	−2.6394782

Note: In iii. and iv. the numbers can be represented within 9 significant figures, therefore, BASIC would not convert the numbers to exponential format.

v. 739.4621348 7.39462135E+2

Note: In v. the last digit cannot be represented and is therefore truncated from the mantissa, and 4 rounded to 5.

vi. −17694.327 x 10^{35} overflow

Note: In vi. when the number is adjusted to standard form notation the exponent becomes 39; the largest exponent permissible is 38; the number is too large to be represented and is said to have overflowed.

vii. 0.000000471 x 10^{-34} underflow

Note: In vii. when the number is adjusted to standard form notation the exponent becomes −41; the largest negative exponent permissible is −38; the number is too small to be represented and is said to have underflowed.

13.3 Common Mathematical Functions

The BASIC language will allow the following functions to be used within arithmetic expressions.

The argument of the function has been denoted by the letter X.

Arguments can be: { numeric literals, numeric variables, arithmetic expressions }

13.3.1 Absolute

ABS (X) returns the absolute value or modulus X.
eg. ABS (−3.7) = 3.7

13.3.2 Arctangent

ATN (X) returns the arctangent of X in radians — ie. the angle whose tangent is X. The range of the function is
$-\pi / 2 <$ ATN (X) $< \pi / 2$
eg. ATN (1) = 0.7854 · · · ·
since the tangent of $\pi / 4$ (0.7854 · · · ·)
= 1.

13.3.3 Cosine

COS (X) returns the cosine of X, where X is in radians.
eg. COS (1.0472) = 0.5

Note: $\pi / 3 \triangleq 1.0472$ radians.

13.3.4 Exponential

EXP (X) returns the exponential of X.
ie. The value of the base of natural logarithms raised to the power X. (e^x).
eg. EXP (1) = 2.71828 · · · ·

13.3.5 Integer

INT (X) returns the largest integer not greater than X.
eg. INT (1.3) = 1
INT (−1.3) = −2

13.3.6 Logarithm

LOG (X) returns the natural logarithm of X; **X must be greater than zero.**
eg. LOG (2.71828) = 1
LOG (1) = 0

13.3.7 Random Number

RND returns the next pseudo-random number in a uniformly distributed set of numbers in the range.
0 < = RND (X) < 1.

Note: Many dialects of BASIC permit the function RND (X), the parameter X determining the sequence of random numbers to be generated.

The BASIC statement **RANDOMIZE** when executed will allow the **RND** function to produce different sequences of random numbers.

13.3.8 Sign

SGN (X) returns 1 if the argument is positive, 0 if the argument is zero, and −1 if the argument is negative.
eg. SGN (+4.79) = 1
SGN (0) = 0
SGN (−79) = −1

13.3.9 Sine

SIN (X) returns the sine of X, where X is in radians.
eg. SIN (0.5236) = 0.5

Note: $\pi / 6 \triangleq 0.5236$ radians.

13.3.10 Square Root

SQR (X) returns the square-root of X; **X must not be negative.**

eg. SQR (5) = 2.236 · · · ·

13.3.11 Tangent

TAN (X) returns the tangent of X, where X is in radians.

eg. TAN (0.7854) = 1

Note: $\pi / 4 = 0.7854$ radians.

13.4 User Defined Functions

In addition to the supplied functions the programmer can define new functions within a program.

The syntax of a user defined function would be:

DEF FN α = arithmetic expression.
or **DEF FN** α (β) = arithmetic expression.
where α is a single letter A – Z, and β is a numeric variable that is also used in the arithmetic expression.

Examples.
```
DEF    FNF (X) = X ↑ 4 – 1
DEF    FNA (X) = A * X + B
DEF    FNP = 3.14159
```

The following rules apply to defined functions.

A function is defined as a program statement at the beginning of a program before it is used.

The definition of a function is limited to one program line.

The definition of a function can use supplied functions and other defined functions.

The definition is not recursive ie. it must not appear on both sides of the equation.

A function is used by making reference to its name in context within a program.

13.5 Worked Examples

13.5.1 Write a program to print a table showing the values of EXP (X) and LOG (X) for X varying between 1 and 10 in steps of 0.5.

Design.
```
print headings
FOR X = 1 TO 10 STEP 0.5
  calculate values for EXP(X) and LOG(X)
  print calculated values
NEXT X
stop
```

Glossary	
X function argument	X
Calculated EXP (X)	Y
Calculated LOG (X)	Z

Program
```
 10  REM. . OUTPUT HEADINGS
 20  PRINT "X", "EXP (X)", "LOG (X)"
 30  REM. .SET UP LOOP
 40  FOR X = 1 TO 10 STEP 0.5
 50    REM. .CALCULATE EXP (X) & LOG (X)
 60    LET Y = EXP (X)
 70    LET Z = LOG (X)
 80    REM. .OUTPUT CALCULATED RESULTS
 90    PRINT X,Y,Z
100  NEXT X
110  STOP
```

Using your computer

Type, SAVE, LOAD and RUN the last program.

Specimen results

```
>LOAD "LOGEXP"
>RUN
X      EXP(X)              LOG(X)
1      2.71828183          0
1.5    4.48168907          0.405465108
2      7.3890561           0.693147181
2.5    12.182494           0.916290732
3      20.0855369          1.09861229
3.5    33.1154519          1.25276297
4      54.59815            1.38629436
4.5    90.0171312          1.5040774
5      148.413159          1.60943791
5.5    244.691932          1.70474809
6      403.428793          1.79175947
6.5    665.141632          1.87180218
7      1096.63316          1.94591015
7.5    1808.04241          2.01490302
8      2980.95798          2.07944154
8.5    4914.76883          2.14006616
9      8103.08391          2.19722458
9.5    13359.7268          2.2512918
10     22026.4657          2.30258509

STOP at line 110
>
```

13.5.2 Test the accuracy of your computer by writing a program to evaluate.

$\sin^2 x + \cos^2 x - 1$

and $\tan^2 x - \sec^2 x + 1$

for values of x between 0 and 1 in steps of 0.1 radians.

Design.

```
print headings
FOR X = 0 TO 1 STEP 0.1
  calculate value for Y and Z
  print value for X, Y and Z
NEXT X
stop
```

Glossary	
X function argument	X
$\sin^2 x + \cos^2 x - 1$	Y
$\tan^2 x - \sec^2 x + 1$	Z

Program

```
 10 REM. .OUTPUT HEADINGS
 20 PRINT "X", "Y", "Z"
 30 REM. .SET UP LOOP
 40 FOR X = 0 TO 1 STEP 0.1
 50   REM. .CALCULATE Y & Z
 60   LET Y = SIN (X) ↑ 2 + COS (X) ↑ 2 –1
 70   LET Z = TAN (X) ↑ 2 – (1 / (COS (X) ↑ 2)) + 1
 80   REM. .OUTPUT CALCULATED RESULTS
 90   PRINT X, Y, Z
100 NEXT X
110 STOP
```

Using your computer

Type, SAVE, LOAD and RUN the last program.

Specimen results

```
 LOAD "TRIG"
>RUN
X    Y                 Z
0    0                 0
0.1  -2.32830644E-10   0
0.2  -2.32830644E-10   -4.65661287E-10
0.3  -2.32830644E-10   -4.65661287E-10
0.4  0                 2.32830644E-10
0.5  0                 0
0.6  -2.32830644E-10   -4.65661287E-10
0.7  4.65661287E-10    4.65661287E-10
0.8  -2.32830644E-10   -9.31322575E-10
0.9  0                 9.31322575E-10
1    -2.32830644E-10   0

STOP at line 110
>
```

13.5.3 If a value is to represent a financial amount then its decimal fraction should be represented to no more than two places. However, BASIC will return a number to the accuracy of the machine, therefore, there is a need for a function to truncate a number to two decimal places and another to round to two decimal places.

If **FNT (X) = INT (100 * ABS (X)) / 100**
then for X = 36.9713467 FNT (X) = 36.97
Since 100 * ABS (X) = 3697.13467
INT (100 * ABS (X)) = 3697
INT (100 * ABS (X)) / 100 = 36.97

The function defined as **FNT (X)** can be used to truncate a number to two decimal places.

If **FNR (X) = INT (100 * ABS (X) + 0.5) / 100**
then for X = 4279.74581 FNR (X) = 4279.75
Since 100 * ABS (X) = 427974.581
100 * ABS (X) + 0.5 = 427975.081
INT (100 * ABS (X) + 0.5) = 427975
INT (100 * ABS (X) + 0.5) / 100 = 4279.75

Thus the function **FNR (X)** can be used to round a number to two decimal places.

The function **FNT (X)** is used in the following program to calculate and print the compound interest on a principal (P) borrowed over (N) years at a rate of (R) %.

The amount (A) owing at the end of the term is given by:

$$A = P\left(1 + \frac{R}{100}\right)^N$$

```
 10  REM. .DEFINE FUNCTION TO TRUNCATE  NUMBER
 20  DEF FNT (X) = INT (100 * ABS (X)) / 100
 30  REM. .INPUT VALUES FOR P, R and N.
 40  PRINT "ENTER VALUES FOR PRINCIPAL, RATE AND TERM"
 50  INPUT P, R, N
 60  REM. .CALCULATE AMOUNT (A) OWING
 70  LET A = P * (1 + R / 100) ↑ N
 80  REM. .CALCULATE INTEREST
 90  LET I = A – P
100  REM. .PRINT INTEREST
110  PRINT "COMPOUND INTEREST = £"; FNT (I)
120  STOP
```

Using your computer

Type, SAVE, LOAD and RUN the last program.

Specimen results

```
>LOAD "FNT"
>RUN
ENTER VALUES FOR PRINCIPAL, RATE AND TERM
?2000
?5
?6
COMPOUND INTEREST=£680.19

STOP at line 120
>
```

13.5.4 Write a program to simulate tossing a coin 10 times; 100 times and 1000 times. Use the random number generator function to return a value of 1 to simulate a head appearing face-up, or 0 to simulate a tail appearing face-up. Keep a count of the number of heads and tails for each of the groups.

Note: If the coin is unbiased then theoretically there should be the same number of heads as tails.

If the RND (0) function returns a value X, say, in the range:

$0 <= X < 1$ then for

$X = 0.47135$ $R = INT (0.47135 + 0.5) = INT (0.97135) = 0$

$X = 0.73195$ $R = INT (0.73195 + 0.5) = INT (1.23195) = 1$

Without the +0.5 in the expression for R, R would always be 0.

Design.

```
print headings
read number of trials
WHILE number of trials not = 0 DO
  initialise head and tail totals to zero
  select new random number sequence
  FOR count = 1 TO number of trials
    generate random number
    IF random number = 1 THEN
      increase head total by 1
    ELSE
      increase tail total by 1
    END IF
  NEXT count
  print head and tail totals
  read number of trials
END WHILE
stop
```

Glossary	
Number of trials	N
Head total	H
Tail total	T
Count	C
R. N. (Random Number)	R

Program

```
 10  REM. .OUTPUT HEADINGS
 20  PRINT "TRIALS", "NO.HEADS", "NO.TAILS"
 30  PRINT
 40  REM. .INPUT NUMBER OF TRIALS IN TEST
 50  REM. .IF NUMBER = 0 END OF TRIALS
 60    READ N
 70    DATA 10, 100, 1000, 0
 80    IF N = 0 THEN STOP
 90      REM. .SET HEAD & TAIL TOTALS TO ZERO
100      LET H = 0
110      LET T = 0
120      REM. .SELECT NEW RANDOM NUMBER SEQUENCE
130      RANDOMIZE
140      REM. .SET UP LOOP
150      FOR C = 1 TO N
160        REM. .GENERATE RANDOM NUMBER
170        LET R = INT (RND (0) + 0.5)
180        REM. .TEST FOR HEAD OR TAIL
190        IF R <> 1 THEN 220
200          LET H = H + 1
210        GOTO 230
220          LET T = T + 1
230      NEXT C
240      REM. .OUTPUT RESULTS OF TRIALS
250      PRINT N, H, T
260      READ N
270  GOTO 80
```

Using your computer

Type, SAVE, LOAD and RUN the last program.

Specimen results

```
>LOAD "COINS"
>RUN
TRIALS     NO.HEADS       NO.TAILS

10         5              5
100        54             46
1000       487            513

STOP at line 80
>RUN
TRIALS     NO.HEADS       NO.TAILS

10         4              6
100        54             46
1000       484            516

STOP at line 80
>RUN
TRIALS     NO.HEADS       NO.TAILS

10         5              5
100        46             54
1000       483            517

STOP at line 80
>RUN
TRIALS     NO.HEADS       NO.TAILS

10         8              2
100        52             48
1000       485            515

STOP at line 80
>RUN
TRIALS     NO.HEADS       NO.TAILS

10         3              7
100        55             45
1000       471            529

STOP at line 80
>
```

13.5.5 Write a computer program to plot the value of sine X and cosine X for $15^\circ \leqslant X \leqslant 360^\circ$ in intervals of 15°.

The program should display a horizontal axis to represent the angle X, and a vertical axis to represent the sine and cosine of the angle.

A scale should also be displayed for each axis.

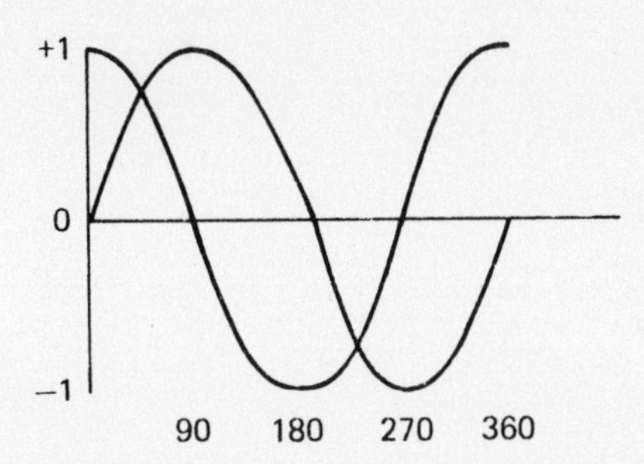

The graph should be stored in a two-dimensional table having 21 rows and 51 columns. Each cell of the table being used to store a single character.

Before the co-ordinates for sine X and cosine X can be stored in the table each cell must be initialised with a space character, then the vertical axis with scale and horizontal axis can be stored.

Using the functions SIN(X) and COS(X) the co-ordinates of the graph can be used as subscripts to the table and an "*" character can be stored to represent the plot of sin (X) and a "+" character stored to represent the plot of cos (X).

When the plotting of characters is completed the contents of the table can be printed row by row, and finally the horizontal scale can be printed at the bottom of the graph.

Since the functions SIN (X) and COS (X) will only produce values in the range −1 to +1 inclusive it is necessary to convert the values to suitable ordinates for plotting. The ordinate values must correspond to row values (1 to 21) inclusive of the table. Thus the ordinate (+1) is transformed to row 1, and the ordinate (−1) is transformed to row 21. Intermediate ordinates must also be transformed to row values. To achieve this transformation it is necessary to define two functions:

FNS (X) = 11 − INT (10 * SIN (X))

When X = 0°, 180°, 360°

FNX (X) = 11 (horizontal axis)

X = 90°

FNS (X) = 1 (first row)

X = 270°

FNS (X) = 21 (last row)

Similarly

FNC (X) = 11 − INT (10 * COS (X))

will transform the ordinates to row values of the table.

Design.

```
call PROC initialise
call PROC store axes
call PROC store plot of functions
call PROC output graph
stop

PROC initialise
FOR row = 1 TO 21
  FOR column = 1 TO 51
    store space in respective element
  NEXT column
NEXT row
END PROC

PROC store axes
FOR row = 1 TO 21
  store "I" in the first column of each row
NEXT row
FOR column = 2 TO 51
  store "–" in each column of the eleventh row
NEXT column
END PROC

PROC store plot of functions
initialise starting position of column coordinate
FOR angle = 15 TO 360 STEP 15
  convert angle to radians
  calculate row coordinate for sine of angle
  calculate row coordinate for cosine of angle
  store symbols (*) for sine point and (+) for cosine point
  in appropriate row and column positions in table
  increase column coordinate
NEXT angle
END PROC

PROC output graph
FOR row = 1 TO 21
CASE row OF
  WHEN 1
    print +1
  WHEN 11
    print 0
  WHEN 21
    print −1
  OTHERWISE
    print space
END CASE
  FOR column = 1 TO 51
    print contents of table element
  NEXT column
NEXT row
print scale for horizontal axis
END PROC
```

Glossary

Table to store characters of graph, having 21 rows and 51 columns.	A$ (21, 51)
Sine and cosine functions, respectively, that represent the ordinate value for a cell.	FNS FNC
Row subscript of table A$	R
Column subscript of table A$	C
Angle represented in degrees	X
Angle represented in radians	X1
Row co-ordinate for sine X	R1
Row co-ordinate for cosine X	R2

program

```
  10 REM · · DECLARE TABLE AND FUNCTIONS
  20 DIM A$ (21, 51)
  30 DEF FNS (X) = 11 – INT (10*SIN(X))
  40 DEF FNC (X) = 11 – INT (10*COS(X))
  50 REM · · CALL SUBROUTINES
  60 GOSUB 1000
  70 GOSUB 2000
  80 GOSUB 3000
  90 GOSUB 4000
 100 STOP

1000 REM · · SUBROUTINE INITIALISE
1010 FOR R = 1 TO 21
1020   FOR C = 1 TO 51
1030     LET A$ (R, C) = "  "
1040   NEXT C
1050 NEXT R
1060 RETURN

2000 REM · · SUBROUTINE STORE AXES
2010 FOR R = 1 TO 21
2020   LET A$(R, 1) = "I"
2030 NEXT R
2040 FOR C = 2 TO 51
2050   LET A$(11, C) = "–"
2060 NEXT C
2070 RETURN
```

```
3000  REM · · SUBROUTINE STORE PLOT OF FUNCTIONS
3010  LET C = 3
3020  FOR X = 15 TO 360 STEP 15
3030    LET X1 = X*3.14159/180
3040    LET R1 = FNS(X1)
3050    LET R2 = FNC(X1)
3060    LET A$(R1, C) = "*"
3070    LET A$ (R2, C) = "+"
3080    LET C = C + 2
3090  NEXT X
3100  RETURN

4000  REM · · SUBROUTINE OUTPUT GRAPH
4010  FOR R = 1 TO 21
4020    IF R <> 1 THEN 4050
4030      PRINT "+1";
4040    GOTO 4120
4050    IF R <> 11 THEN 4080
4060      PRINT " 0";
4070    GOTO 4120
4080    IF R <> 21 THEN 4110
4090      PRINT "–1";
4100    GOTO 4120
4110      PRINT "   ";
4120    FOR C = 1 TO 51
4130      PRINT A$(R,C);
4140    NEXT C
4150    PRINT
4160  NEXT R
4170  PRINT TAB(14);"90";TAB(25);"180";TAB(37);"270";TAB(49);"360"
4180  RETURN
```

Using your computer

Type, SAVE, LOAD and RUN the last program.

Specimen results

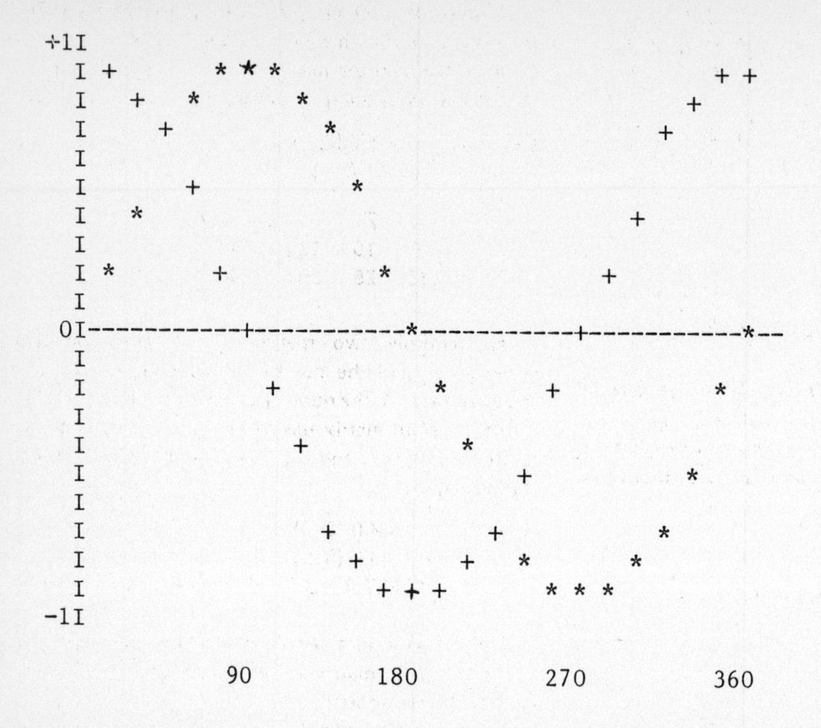

Note:

Sine 75° = 0.9613 · · · ·
Sine 90° = 1.0000 (however, the computer has represented sine 90° = 0.9999 · · · ·)
Thus FNS (75°) = 11 – INT (9.613 · · · ·) = 2
and FNS (90°) = 11 – INT (9.999 · · · ·) = 2

A similar problem also exists for SINE X at 270°, and COSINE X at 180° and 360°.

13.6 Matrices

Supplied functions for matrix processing are normally to be found in dialects of BASIC that run on mini and mainframe computers, for example Honeywell, PR1ME, Data General, ICL. They form an important subset of the supplied mathematical functions in the BASIC language and for this reason will be considered further in this section. Generally a matrix can be thought of as a one or two-dimensional table (or array) containing data. The position of each item of data in the matrix is indicated by **non-zero** row and column subscripts.

Matrices are dimensioned by a DIM statement, as are tables, or are automatically defined when referenced by a MAT (matrix) statement. Such a matrix would be assigned default dimensions of (10,10).

Matrix operations are valid only for that part of a table defined as a matrix, i.e. that portion with non-zero subscripts. Matrix operations include initialization, redimensioning, addition, subtraction, multiplication, inversion and transposition. All matrix operations begin with the keyword MAT. The operations that follow can all be performed on numeric matrices, with the exception of MAT NULL. String matrices can only be initialised to NULL or redimensioned with the DIM option of the MAT statement.

13.6.1 Initialisation

Matrices are assigned initial values by being equated to one of four matrix constants in a MAT statement. These constants, identified by mnemonics are ZER (each element is set at 0), CON (each element is set at 1), IDN (each element not on the leading diagonal is set at 0 and all other elements are set at 1) — this only applies to square matrices, and NULL (each element of a string matrix is set as empty).

Examples. DIM A (3, 4)

MAT A = ZER $\begin{pmatrix} 0 & 0 & 0 & 0 \\ 0 & 0 & 0 & 0 \\ 0 & 0 & 0 & 0 \end{pmatrix}$

MAT A = CON $\begin{pmatrix} 1 & 1 & 1 & 1 \\ 1 & 1 & 1 & 1 \\ 1 & 1 & 1 & 1 \end{pmatrix}$

DIM B (3, 3)
MAT B = IDN $\begin{pmatrix} 1 & 0 & 0 \\ 0 & 1 & 0 \\ 0 & 0 & 1 \end{pmatrix}$

The constants ZER, CON, IDN and NULL can also be used to change the dimensions of a matrix. By specifying the new size of the matrix after the constant the matrix is redimensioned and each element is set to that value indicated by the constant.

Examples. DIM A (4, 5)
MAT A = CON (3, 3) $\begin{pmatrix} 1 & 1 & 1 \\ 1 & 1 & 1 \\ 1 & 1 & 1 \end{pmatrix}$

DIM B (3, 3)
MAT B = ZER (4, 2) $\begin{pmatrix} 0 & 0 \\ 0 & 0 \\ 0 & 0 \\ 0 & 0 \end{pmatrix}$

The dimensions of a matrix can also be changed by assigning to it a matrix of other dimensions.

Example. DIM X (6, 6)
DIM Y (5, 4)
MAT X = Y X becomes a 5x4 matrix

13.6.2 Arithmetic

The elements of two numeric matrices may be added or subtracted and the values assigned to a third matrix.

MAT A = B + C or MAT A = B – C

The source matrices B and C must have the same dimensions and the target matrix A is converted to the same dimensions as B and C.

Example. MAT C = A – B

$$C = \begin{pmatrix} 06 & -11 \\ 17 & 08 \end{pmatrix} \quad A = \begin{pmatrix} 15 & 03 \\ 21 & 10 \end{pmatrix} \quad B = \begin{pmatrix} 09 & 14 \\ 04 & 02 \end{pmatrix}$$

A matrix can be multipled by a scalar numeric expression or by a second matrix. In multiplying a matrix by a scalar value each element of the matrix is multiplied by this value and the result of each product stored in a second matrix of the same dimensions as the first matrix.

Example. DIM Y (2, 3)
MAT Z = 5 * Y

$$Z = \begin{pmatrix} 5 & 10 & 15 \\ 20 & 25 & 30 \end{pmatrix} \quad Y = \begin{pmatrix} 1 & 2 & 3 \\ 4 & 5 & 6 \end{pmatrix}$$

To multiply two matrices, both must be two-dimensional and the number of columns of the first must be equal to the number of rows of the second. The result is a third matrix having the same number of rows as the first matrix and the same number of columns as the second matrix.

Example. DIM B (2, 3)
DIM C (3, 2)
MAT A = B * C the result is a 2x2 matrix.

Each element in matrix A is the result of multiplying the elements of matrix B times the elements of matrix C in the following way.

Multiply each element in row 1 of B, by each element in column 1 of C.

Add the results to obtain the value of the element in the matrix A row 1 column 1.

Continue the pattern multiplying row 1 and column 2 to produce element A(1, 2); row 2 and column 1 to produce A(2, 1) and row 2 column 2 to produce A(2, 2).

$$A = \begin{pmatrix} 35 & 48 \\ 42 & 56 \end{pmatrix} \quad B = \begin{pmatrix} 1 & 3 & 5 \\ 2 & 4 & 6 \end{pmatrix} \quad C = \begin{pmatrix} 1 & 2 \\ 3 & 4 \\ 5 & 6 \end{pmatrix}$$

13.6.3 Inverting and Transposing Matrices

In matrix algebra the function of division is changed to that of inversion. The inverse (or reciprocal) of a matrix has the same property as the inverse of a number. For example the inverse of 4 is ¼ so that 4 x ¼ = 1 and ¼ x 4 = 1.

In matrix algebra the inverse of matrix A would be A^{-1} and A x A^{-1} = 1 and A^{-1} x A = I. Note only square matrices can have inverses, but not every square matrix has an inverse. Note a square matrix has the same number of rows as columns. I represents the unity matrix which has a leading diagonal of all 1's and all other elements are 0.

A matrix can be inverted by using the function INV thus:

```
MAT C = INV (A)
```

will compute a matrix C such that C * A = I, where C has the same dimensions as A.

A square matrix does not have an inverse if the value of its determinant is zero. A function that calculates the value of the determinant of a square matrix is DET. Thus if the determinant of matrix A is to be found then

```
D = DET (A)
```

will calculate the value. The correct code to invert a matrix should also include a test on the determinant of that matrix thus:

```
10  LET D = DET (A)
20  IF D <> 0 THEN MAT C = INV (A)
```

It is often necessary to transpose a matrix (change rows for columns and columns for rows) so that it may be multiplied by another matrix, since two matrices can only be multiplied together if the number of columns of the first matrix is the same as the number of rows of the second matrix. The function TRN will transpose a matrix. For example if matrix A has dimensions 2x3 then

```
MAT B = TRN (A)
```

will transpose the rows and columns of A and put the result into B, thus the dimensions of B become 3x2.

13.6.4 Matrix Input and Output

If the following data is to be stored in a 3x3 matrix then either a MAT READ or MAT INPUT statement should be used.

matrix X			
	12	15	17
	87	34	76
	21	45	19

```
10  DIM X(3, 3)
20  MAT READ X
30  DATA 12,15,17,87,34,76,21,45,19
```

alternatively line 20 could be replaced by MAT INPUT X and the data would be entered via a keyboard. Notice there is no need to use nested FOR . . . NEXT loops when using a matrix read or input.

If more than one matrix is to be read or input then the names of the matrices can appear in one statement, MAT READ X,Y,Z or MAT INPUT X,Y,Z and matrix X will be read or input in its entirety, row by row; then matrix Y, row by row; and finally, matrix Z, row by row.

To output the data to a screen of a terminal a MAT PRINT statement is used. This will output one row at a time, printing each item of data in a zone; if the number of items of data in a row exceeds the number of print zones across the screen then printing continues on a new line. Each row will be printed on a new line. Therefore, to print the data stored in matrix X on three different lines the only BASIC statement that is required is:

```
40 MAT PRINT X
```

13.7 Worked Examples

13.7.1 A fast food chain employs cashiers, waitors/waitresses, chefs and porters throughout its retail outlets according to the size of the outlet as follows.

	size of outlet		
	large	medium	small
cashiers	2	1	1
waitors/ waitresses	12	6	3
chefs	4	2	1
porters	6	3	2

(matrix A)

The number of fast food outlets throughout the U.K. are as follows:

	region		
	North	Central	South
large	20	15	25
medium	10	25	12
small	5	16	18

(matrix B)

Write a program to store the data for matrix A and matrix B, calculate the number of various types of staff that are employed in the three regions, and output this information.

program

```
10  DIM A (4, 3), B (3, 3), C (4, 3)
20  MAT READ A,B
30  DATA 2,1,1,12,6,3,4,2,1,6,3,2
40  DATA 20,15,25,10,25,12,5,16,18
50  MAT C = A * B
60  PRINT "NORTH", "CENTRAL", "SOUTH"
70  MAT PRINT C
80  STOP
```

Results

```
NORTH        CENTRAL      SOUTH
55           71           80
315          378          426
105          126          142
160          197          222

STOP AT LINE 80
```

13.7.2 Two simultaneous equations are represented by:

a1x + b1y = c1
a2x + b2y = c2

If Dx = DET $\begin{vmatrix} c1 & b1 \\ c2 & b2 \end{vmatrix}$, Dy = DET $\begin{vmatrix} a1 & c1 \\ a2 & c2 \end{vmatrix}$

Dz = DET $\begin{vmatrix} a1 & b1 \\ a2 & b2 \end{vmatrix}$

then the solution to the equation is:

x = Dx/ Dz and y = Dy/ Dz

Write a program to solve the simultaneous equations

3x + 4y = 10
2x + 7y = 11

program

```
10 DIM X (2,2), Y (2,2), Z (2,2)
20 MAT READ X,Y,Z
30 DATA 10,4,11,7
40 DATA 3,10,2,11
50 DATA 3,4,2,7
60 LET X = DET (X)/DET(Z)
70 LET Y = DET(Y)/DET(Z)
80 PRINT "X=";X, "Y=";Y
90 STOP
```

Results.

```
X=2                      Y=1
STOP AT LINE 90
```

13.8 Dialect Differences

13.8.1 Number Representation

Table 2.1 in chapter 2 gives a clear comparison of the integer range, real range and smallest real numbers between the two machines being studied in this book. The following table shows the accuracy to which real numbers are stored on the two machines.

computer model	single precision accuracy	double precision accuracy
IBM PC	7 digits	17 digits
BBC/Electron	9 sig. fig	–

13.8.2 Mathematical Functions

Both dialects support the common mathematical functions listed in section 13.3. However, these dialects also offer additional functions as follows.

Microsoft.

CDBL(X) – converts X to a double precision number
CINT(X) – converts X to an integer by rounding
CSNG(X) – converts X to a single precision number
FIX(X) – truncates X to an integer

BBC/Electron.

ACS (X) – arc-cosine, used to calculate an angle whose cosine X is known
ASN(X) – arc-sine, used to calculate an angle whose sine X is known
DEG(X) – converts angles in X radians into degrees
DIV – an operator which gives the integer part of a division (e.g. 11 DIV 4 would give a result of 2)
MOD – gives the remainder after a division (e.g. 11 MOD 4 would give a result of 3)
PI – has the value 3.14159265
RAD(X) – converts an angle in X degrees to radians
LOG(X) – calculates common logarithm to base 10
LN(X) – calculates natural logarithm

Despite each dialect having a random number generator function RND(X) the manner in which this function operates differs between dialects as the following table indicates.

Dialect	X	Comment
Microsoft	>0 or not included	function generates next random number
	=0	repeats last random number
	<0	generates a different sequence of random numbers for a different value of X
BBC/Electron	not included	generates a number in the range −2147483648 to 2147483647.
	<0	returns a value of −X and resets the random number generator
	=0	repeats the last random number given by RND(1)
	=1	generates a random number between 0 and 0.999999
	=N	generates a random number in the range 1 to N (integers only)

13.8.3 User Defined Functions

The definition of a user defined function given in 13.4 is the absolute minimum for most dialects of BASIC. Microsoft and BBC/Electron will all allow single-line user defined functions to have more than one argument. For example:

```
100 DEF FNMEAN (A,B,C) = (A + B + C)/3
```

contains three arguments A,B,C. Note also that the name of the function MEAN is not limited to a single letter in these three dialects.

Normally any user defined function must occur before any reference to the function, however, in the BBC/Electron dialect the definition of a function **must** be coded as a non-executable program statement. In practice this implies that the statement should not be found in a main program before the STOP statement or in a procedure before an ENDPROC statement.

In these dialects the function that is being defined may appear on the right-hand side of the expression. Therefore, a function can call itself and it is said to be *recursive*.

In addition to the single line function definition, BBC/Electron, BASIC will allow multiple-line user defined functions. Such functions appear to be similar to procedures, however, a function returns a value a procedure does not.

Example. Write a multiple-line function that will receive a string as a parameter and reverse the characters in the string assigning the new string to an output parameter.

BBC/Electron.

```
1000 DEF FNREVERSE(A$)
1010 LOCAL D%,B$
1020 FOR D% = 1 TO LEN(A$)
1030   B$ = MID$(A$,D%,1) + B$
1040 NEXT D%
1050 = B$
```

Note: the end of a multi-line function is indicated by a statement that starts with an = sign. The function is given the value of the expression to the right of the = sign.

13.9 Keywords

Integer, fixed-point real, floating-point real, mantissa, exponent, double precision, truncation, rounding, overflow, underflow;
ABS, ATN, COS, EXP, INT, LOG, RND, SGN, SIN, SQR, TAN;
DEF FN, multiple arguments, multiple line functions;
Matrices, ZER, CON, IDN, NULL, MAT, INV, DET, TRN, matrix input and output;

13.10 Questions

1 Show how the following numbers would be expressed in the BASIC langauge if a computer represents numbers to an accuracy of 9 significant figures and a signed exponent in the range 0 to 38.

a. 4817.395
b. −0.0001942
c. 178431.8×10^{32}
d. + 129.74
e. 183796219
f. −0.0000002684715
g. 14937.86×10^{-19}
h. $274647941.3768 \times 10^{26}$
i. 938.24×10^{37}
j. $+79.27194 \times 10^{-38}$

2 What are the values of the following functions?

a. ABS (−4.29)
b. INT (−4.29)
c. SGN (−4.29)
d. ATN (3.7321)
e. TAN (30°)
f. LOG (5.0)
g. EXP (2)
h. SQR (−49)
i. SIN (−270°)
j. SGN (0.001)

Note: To obtain the answers to these questions if your computer can be used in an interactive mode then type PRINT followed by the function. The computer will return an answer to you. This is known as using BASIC in a *calculator mode* or direct mode.

e.g. PRINT ABS (−4.29)

The calculator mode will apply to all arithmetic expressions.

e.g. PRINT 3 ↑ 2 + 4 ↑ 2

3 If $\log_b x = \dfrac{\text{Log}_a x}{\log_a b}$ then derive a user defined function to calculate the logarithm of a number of any valid given base.

Use this function in writing a computer program to find the logarithms of the numbers from 2 to 10 in steps of 0.5 to the bases 2 to 10 in steps of 2.

Your output should be presented in the form of a table having the numbers down the page and the bases across the page.

4 Write a program to calculate the roots of a quadratic equation

$ax^2 + bx + c = 0$ from the formula $x = \dfrac{-b \pm \sqrt{b^2 - 4ac}}{2a}$.

The values of a, b and c being input at the beginning of the program. Consider the implications within your program of $b^2 < 4ac$.

5 Write programs to print graphs for:

a. $y = \tan(x)$ $\quad 0^\circ \leqslant x \leqslant 360^\circ$
b. $y = \log_{10}(x)$ $\quad 0 < x \leqslant 5$
c. $y = \ell^{x}$ $\quad -10 \leqslant x \leqslant 10$

6 Write programs to test the accuracy of your computer by evaluating:

a. $(x^{½})^2 - x$ $\quad 0 \leqslant x \leqslant 1$ step of 0.05
b. $\ell^{\log(x)} - x$ $\quad 1 \leqslant x \leqslant 10$ step of 1
c. $\tan(\arctan(x)) - x$ $\quad -100 \leqslant x \leqslant +100$ step 10

7 Write a program to convert kilometres to miles, yards, feet and inches. Print a table of conversion for the range 1 to 51 kilometres in steps of 5 kilometres.

8 The line Y = 2X + 3 divides the X, Y plane into the two regions. Write a program to input ordered pairs of numbers that represent co-ordinates in the X, Y plane. Compute whether the point indicated by the co-ordinates lies above, below or on the line. Print the co-ordinates indicating the position of the point relative to the line.

9 Write a program to simulate the rolling of two dice and determine the number of doubles that appear for the digits 1 to 6 inclusive, when the dice are rolled.

a. 10 times, b. 100 times, c. 1000 times.

10 Write a program to simulate the game of dice for two players described as follows.

In a game for two players, each player throws two dice in turn and scores 3 points for each of the following occurrences:
Either dice shows a 6
both the dice show the same number,
the total of the two dice adds up to 9.

Note: It is possible to score more than 3 points on one throw.

The winner is the first person to score a total of 51 points exactly.

The players are indentified as 1 and 2 and the total score of any player is shown as s(n), where n equals the player's number.

11 Write procedures to simulate the MAT READ and MAT PRINT statements.

12 Write procedures to simulate the matrix functions ZER, CON, IDN, and TRN for square matrices having N rows and N columns, where $N < 10$.

13 Write procedures to simulate matrix addition, subtraction and multiplication between two matrices having dimensions NxN where $N < 10$.

14 Using similar rules to those for the solution to the simultaneous equations in section 13.7.2 solve the following equations.

$$\begin{aligned} x + 2y + 5z &= 20 \\ 2x + y + z &= 7 \\ 5x - 3y + 2z &= 5 \end{aligned}$$

14 Sorting and Searching

14.1 Introduction

The reader should be well aware of the need to present information in a usable form. Consider the organisation of a telephone directory, entries are ordered into strict alphabetical sequence by name. To find a telephone number knowing the name of the person you wish to call is simply a matter of locating the appropriate section of the directory from the first few letters of the surname, and then searching several pages until a match is found for the surname. The address and telephone number of the person will be listed against the surname.

Another example of the organisation of information is that of a bus timetable from a central station. The destinations of buses are ordered alphabetically by town or village, and for each destination a chronological listing of bus departure times from the central station, with arrival times at places on route are given. If the time of departure of a bus from the station is to be found the page containing the destination can quickly be found because of the alphabetical ordering of towns on respective pages of the timetable. Departure times are also listed in a defined sequence (chronologically) making reference to a specific part of a day simple. Bus departure and arrival times can then be selected from that part of the timetable.

Both examples require the information to be ordered or **sorted** on a part of the information. Telephone directories sorted on names, bus timetables on destinations and times of day. Such information is said to have been sorted on a **key**. Names of people, town or village destination names and times of the day being examples of keys to information.

Computers are capable of storing very large amounts of information, and it is of paramount importance that the information is kept in an ordered format for the following reasons.

To provide fast access to the information given an appropriate key.

To allow for an orderly presentation of information when producing reports.

To simplify changes to the information — insertions, amendments and deletions — without destroying the key order of the remaining information.

The purpose of this chapter is to provide an insight into methods used to organise information. Such methods must provide for:

a means of sorting information using a defined key, so that information is represented in an ordered format;

a means of searching through the information efficiently using a particular key such that the access time to information is fast.

14.2 Classification of Sorting Methods

Sorting methods used in computing can be classified into two areas, *internal* sorting and *external* sorting. Internal sorting involves the storage in main memory of all the data to be sorted. However, when the amount of data is too large to be stored and sorted in the main memory it is stored on an external storage medium, such as tape or disc, and successive parts of the data are sorted in the main memory. Such a technique is known as external sorting. The type of sorting method that is used will depend upon at least one of the following factors.

The amount of information to be sorted. Clearly it would be very time consuming to use a relatively inefficient sorting method on a large quantity of data.

The computer configuration being used — the size of main memory and the number of tape/disc units.

The nature of the application and urgency of the results.

The BASIC programming environment is not always the most suitable environment for sorting data since BASIC is often an interpreted language which can result in the slow execution of programs. A large volume of data will therefore take a long time to sort. Furthermore, because of its simplicity, BASIC has grown in popularity with the new generation of microcomputers that can often lack the storage facilities for sorting large volumes of data.

For these reasons the reader is recommended to investigate the availability of a sorting package for their computer system if a large volume of data is to be sorted.

14.3 Internal Sorting Methods

This section illustrates three methods for sorting data in the main memory of a computer. The first method is the *bubble sort* which is a popular method for sorting a small amount of data (less than 50 items). The second method is the *Shell sort* named after D. L. Shell and is considerably faster than the *bubble sort*. The third method of internal sorting is the *Quicksort* by Hoare and demonstrates the use of recursion. The last two methods can be used to sort a much larger volume of data than the first method.

Consider the results of the following experiment. The computer generated 1000 random numbers in the range 0 to 99 and stored these numbers in a one-dimensional table. The time was recorded before and after entering each of the three sorting methods to be described. The random numbers used were the same set for each sorting method. The following table illustrates the time taken to sort 1000 numbers using the three methods in turn.

Method	Time to completion
Bubble sort	156min 4sec
Shell sort	4min 37sec
Quicksort	2min 56sec

14.3.1 Bubble Sort

The following table illustrates five values of keys and their respective positions when sorted in a one-dimensional table. The position of a key can be taken as a subscript to the table.

Key Position	Key Value
1	17
2	13
3	9
4	5
5	1

We shall assume that the keys are to be sorted into ascending order, such that key position 1 will contain the lowest key value (1) and key position 5 will contain the highest key value (17). The final positions of the keys must appear in reverse order to their original positions.

Starting at key position 1 adjacent pairs of keys are compared, if the first key is greater than the second key of the pair, the keys swap positions. Moving to the next key position this procedure is repeated until eventually the last pair of keys in the table have been compared. The highest value of all the keys will then be at the bottom of the table. The keys are not yet sorted, and only one pass has been made through the table comparing pairs of adjacent keys.

The entire procedure is repeated again starting at key position 1. At the end of this pass through the keys in the table the next highest key value will be stored in position 4 in the table.

Further passes are then made through the table of keys until all the keys have been sorted into ascending order.

Figure 14.1 illustrates the movement of the keys in the table as the sort progresses. A comparision is shown as] and a swap is shown as ↑ for a key moving up the table and ↓ for a key moving down the table.

```
KEY POSITION   KEY VALUE                PASS 1                        PASS 2                       PASS 3                       PASS 4

1  (TOP)       17         17]  13↑  13                13    13]  9↑                 9    9]   5↑                5    5]   1↑                1
2              13         13   17↓] 9↑                9     9    13↓] 5↑            5    5    9↓]  1↑           1    1    5↓]  5           5
3               9              9    17↓] 5↑           5          5    13↓] 1↑       1         1    9↓]          9         9    9]           9
4               5                   5    17↓] 1↑      1               1    13↓] 13            13   13]  13               13   13]  13
5  (BOTTOM)     1                        1    17↓     17                   17   17                 17   17                    17   17
```

Note. The keys are required to be sorted into **ascending** order. Since the values of the keys appear initially in descending order it is necessary to pass through the list of keys (N – 1) times. In this example N = 5 (number of keys) and therefore a maximum of 4 passes through the list of keys is necessary before the keys are sorted into ascending order.

Figure 14.1

Note: Since the method of sorting the keys is described in a subroutine it can be assumed that the keys are already stored in a one dimensional table.

Glossary	
One dimensional table used to store keys	V
Pass value	P
Pointer to key	K
Temporary store	T

Program

```
 999   REM · · SUBROUTINE TO BUBBLE SORT KEYS
1000   FOR P = 1 TO 4
1010     FOR K = 1 TO 4
1020       REM · · COMPARE ADJACENT KEYS
1030       IF V(K) < V(K + 1) THEN 1080
1040         REM · · SWAP KEYS
1050         LET T = V(K)
1060         LET V(K) = V(K + 1)
1070         LET V(K + 1) = T
1080     NEXT K
1090   NEXT P
1100 RETURN
```

This program can be extended to cater for 100 keys and the following minor refinements made to make the subprogram more efficient.

The introduction of a flag will ensure that on a pass through the list of keys if no swap is made, the keys are sorted and an exit can be made from the subroutine.

On the first pass through the list of keys the largest key will be moved to the bottom of the list; on the second pass the second largest key will be moved to the penultimate end position, etc. Thus the number of comparisons on each pass is reduced by using the BASIC statement 1030 for K = 1 TO 100 – P.

Therefore on pass 1, 99 comparisons are made; pass 2, 98 comparisons; pass 3, 97 comparisons; etc.

Program refinement

```
 999   REM · · IMPROVED BUBBLE SORT SUBROUTINE
1000   FOR P = 1 TO 99
1010     REM · · RESET FLAG (F) TO SHOW KEYS NOT SWAPPED
1020     LET F = 0
1030     FOR K = 1 TO 100 – P
1040       REM · · COMPARE ADJACENT KEYS
1050       IF V(K) < V(K + 1) THEN 1110
1060         REM · · SET FLAG TO SHOW SWAP
1070         LET F = 1
1080         LET T = V(K)
1090         LET V(K) = V(K + 1)
1100         LET V(K + 1) = T
1110     NEXT K
1120     REM · · TEST FLAG FOR SWAP – NO SWAP EXIT
1130     IF F = 0 THEN 1150
1140   NEXT P
1150 RETURN
```

Using your computer

Type, SAVE, LOAD and RUN the last program. Remember to set up table V to be sorted first!

Specimen results

```
 LOAD "BUBBLE"
>LIST
   10 DIM V(100)
   15 REM..STORE 100 RANDOM NUMBERS IN THE ORDER GENERATED
   20 FOR I=1 TO 100
   30   LET V(I)=RND(100)
   40 NEXT I
   49 PRINT "CONTENTS OF TABLE BEFORE SORTING"
   50 GOSUB 500
   60 GOSUB 1000
   69 PRINT "CONTENTS OF TABLE AFTER SORTING"
   70 GOSUB 500
   80 STOP
  499 REM.. SUBROUTINE TO PRINT CONTENTS OF TABLE
  500 FOR I=1 TO 100 STEP 4
  510   PRINT V(I),V(I+1),V(I+2),V(I+3)
  520 NEXT I
  530 PRINT
  540 RETURN
  999 REM..SUBROUTINE TO SORT TABLE
 1000 FOR P=1 TO 99
 1020 LET F=0
 1030 FOR K=1 TO 100-P
 1050 IF V(K)<V(K+1) THEN 1110
 1070  LET F=1
 1080  LET T=V(K)
 1090  LET V(K)=V(K+1)
 1100  LET V(K+1)=T
 1110 NEXT K
 1130 IF F=0 THEN 1150
 1140 NEXT P
 1150 RETURN
>
```

```
>LOAD "BUBBLE"
>RUN
CONTENTS OF TABLE BEFORE SORTING              CONTENTS OF TABLE AFTER SORTING
        13        64        38        61           1         2         4         4
        98        89        29        10           5         5         7         8
        79        64        33        91           9         9        10        10
        37       100         1        54          10        10        10        12
        51       100        20        79          12        13        13        13
         7        10        80        19          16        19        20        21
        35        87        63         4          26        28        29        30
        84        88        92        53          30        32        33        33
        61        88        63        84          33        35        35        37
        10         2        83        51          37        37        38        38
        10        88        42        39          39        39        40        42
        70        52        38         4          42        42        44        47
        37        37         9        71          50        51        51        51
        33        94        72        12          52        53        54        54
        16        33         5        13          54        56        59        60
        13         5        71        54          61        61        63        63
        21        10        75        67          63        64        64        67
        54        28         8        40          70        71        71        72
        83        97        42        47          75        76        76        77
        30        89        56        50          79        79        80        83
         9        35        92        63          83        84        84        84
        51        30        32        12          87        88        88        88
        60        44        26        42          89        89        91        91
        95        91        39        76          92        92        94        95
        77        84        59        76          97        98       100       100

                                              STOP at line 80
                                              >
```

14.3.2 Shell Sort

Key Position	Key Value
1	3
2	11
3	6
4	4
5	9
6	5
7	7
8	8
9	10
10	2
11	1

To sort the keys into ascending order the following method is applied.

The list of keys is divided into groups containing pairs of keys. However, if the number of keys in the list is odd then one group will contain three keys. The **distance** between keys in a group is initially half the size of the list (N/2) where N is the number of keys in the list. If the list contains an odd number of keys then the initial distance is (N−1) / 2.

From the table there are five groups of keys at the following key positions.

(1, 6, 11)
(2, 7)
(3, 8)
(4, 9)
(5, 10)

On the first pass through the list, pairs of keys in each group are compared, if the first key of the pair is greater than the second key of the pair then a swap is made. With the exception of the group containing three keys, the keys of the other groups will be in ascending order for each pair only.

To order the group containing three keys the process of sifting is applied to the keys.

If a swap is made, the smaller key of the pair is then compared with its adjacent predecessor in the list. If the predecessor is larger then the keys swap positions. This process of comparison and swapping continues **up** the list until either a smaller predecessor is encountered or the top of the list is reached. This process is known as *sifting.*

The **distance** between the keys of a group is then **halved**. This effectively changes the keys in each group. A pass is then made through the list of keys comparing keys from each group and swapping where necessary. This will **not** ensure that the keys of each group are in ascending order, therefore, it is necessary to apply the process of sifting during the progression through the list.

This is repeated until the distance between the keys is **one.** The final pass through the list then becomes a simple sift.

Thus the idea of the Shell sort is that in the early stages far-apart keys are compared, instead of adjacent ones. This tends to eliminate large amounts of disorder quickly, so later stages have less work to do.

Figure 14.2 illustrates the movement of the keys in the table as the sort progresses. The same symbols have been used as in the *bubble sort*.

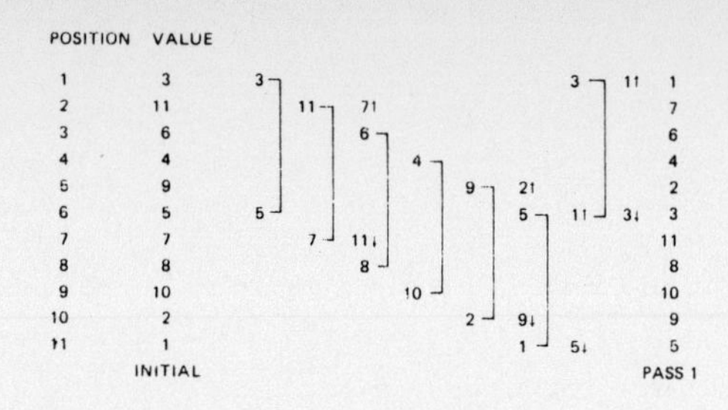

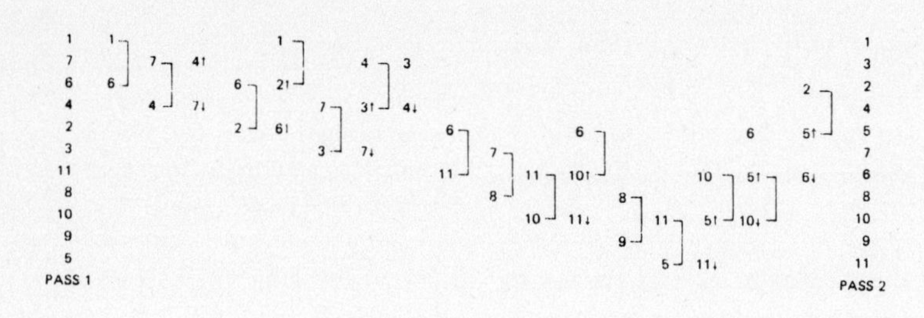

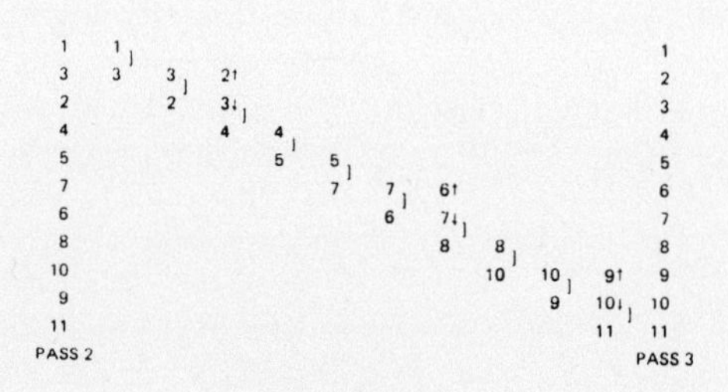

Figure 14.2

Design

PROC shellsort
  REPEAT
    set pointer-1 to top (first) position in table
    calculate distance between keys in a group
    set pointer-2 to second key position of group
    REPEAT
      IF key (pointer-1) > key (pointer-2) **THEN**
        call **PROC** swap
      END IF
      move pointer-1 and pointer-2 down list to next key positions
    UNTIL end of table
  UNTIL distance between keys is 1
END PROC

```
PROC swap
  swap keys
  set pointer-4 to pointer-1
  set pointer-3 to pointer-1 – distance
  WHILE not top of table and key (pointer-3) > key (pointer-4) DO
    swap keys
    decrease pointer-3 and pointer-4 by distance
  END WHILE
END PROC
```

Glossary

Pointer-1	P1
Pointer-2	P2
Pointer-3	P3
Pointer-4	P4
Distance between keys	D
One-dimensional table storing keys	X
Temporary store	T
Number of keys	N

Program

```
1000  REM · · SUBROUTINE SHELLSORT
1010  LET D = N
1020    LET P1 = 1
1030    LET D = INT (D/2)
1040    LET P2 = P1 + D
1050      IF X (P1) > X (P2) THEN GOSUB 2000
1060      LET P1 = P1 + 1: P2 = P2 + 1
1070    IF P2 <= N THEN 1050
1080  IF D > 1 THEN 1020
1090  RETURN

2000  REM · · SUBROUTINE SWAP
2010  LET T = X (P1): X (P1) = X (P2): X (P2) = T
2020  LET P4 = P1
2030  LET P3 = P1 – D
2040  IF P3 <= 0 THEN RETURN
2045  IF X(P3) <= X(P4) THEN RETURN
2050    LET T = X(P3): X(P3) = X(P4): X(P4) = T
2060    LET P3 = P3 – D: P4 = P4 – D
2070  GOTO 2040
```

Using your computer

Type, SAVE, LOAD and RUN the last program. Remember to set up table X first.

Specimen results

```
>LOAD "SHELL"
>LIST
   10 DIM X(30)
   20 REM..GENERATE RANDOM NUMBERS AND STORE IN TABLE
   30 FOR I=1 TO 30
   40   LET X(I)=RND(100)
   50 NEXT I
   60 LET N=30:PASS=0: GOSUB 1000: GOSUB 3000
   70 STOP
 1000 REM..SUBROUTINE SHELLSORT
 1010 LET D=N
 1020 LET P1=1:GOSUB 3000
 1030 LET D=INT(D/2)
 1040 LET P2=P1+D
 1050 IF X(P1)>X(P2) THEN GOSUB 2000
 1060 LET P1=P1+1:P2=P2+1
 1070 IF P2<=N THEN 1050
 1080 IF D>1 THEN 1020
 1090 RETURN
 2000 REM..SUBROUTINE SWAP
 2010 LET T=X(P1):X(P1)=X(P2):X(P2)=T
 2020 LET P4=P1
 2030 LET P3=P1-D
 2040 IF P3<=0 THEN RETURN
 2045 IF X(P3)<=X(P4) THEN RETURN
 2050 LET T=X(P3):X(P3)=X(P4):X(P4)=T
 2060 LET P3=P3-D:P4=P4-D
 2070 GOTO 2040
 3000 REM..SUBROUTINE TO PRINT CONTENTS OF TABLE AT EACH PASS
 3010 PRINT "PASS ";PASS:PASS=PASS+1
 3020 FOR I=1 TO 30 STEP 3
 3030   PRINT X(I),X(I+1),X(I+2)
 3040 NEXT I
 3050 PRINT
 3060 RETURN
>
```

```
LOAD "SHELL"
>RUN
PASS 0
        49        66        51
        70        71        96
        32        83        60
        42        92        86
         5        23         3
        63        28        26
        74        46        18
        27        44        50
        11        78        63
        68        63        75

PASS 1
        49        28        26
        70        46        18
        27        44        50
        11        78        63
         5        23         3
        63        66        51
        74        71        96
        32        83        60
        42        92        86
        68        63        75

PASS 2
         3        28        11
        42        46         5
        23        32        50
        26        51        63
        18        27        44
        63        60        70
        74        71        68
        49        75        66
        78        92        86
        96        63        83

PASS 3
         3        27         5
        18        28        11
        23        32        44
        26        46        50
        42        51        63
        49        60        66
        63        63        68
        74        71        70
        78        75        83
        96        92        86

PASS 4
         3         5        11
        18        23        26
        27        28        32
        42        44        46
        49        50        51
        60        63        63
        63        66        68
        70        71        74
        75        78        83
        86        92        96

STOP at line 70
>
```

14.3.3 Quicksort

In this method the table of data is divided into two partitions. The dividing point is chosen to be the mid-point position in the table. Starting at the lowest position in the table a comparison is made between the datum at this position and the datum at the mid-point position. If the datum is less than the datum at the mid-point position a comparison is made with the next datum in the partition. Comparisons continue until a datum is found to be larger or equal in size to the datum at the mid-point position. Starting at the highest position in the table the process is repeated until a datum is found to be smaller or equal in size to the datum at the mid-point position. The data in each partition that prevented further comparisons being made is then swapped over. Further comparisons and swapping of data will continue until each datum in each partition has been compared.

The method is then applied to each of the partitions recursively until the subpartitions contain only one item of data. Figure 14.3 illustrates how the method is used to sort the eleven numbers given in the last example.

Design

```
PROC quicksort (lower-limit, upper-limit)
  set pointer-1 to lower-limit
  set pointer-2 to upper-limit
  find mid-point key
  WHILE pointer-1 <= pointer-2 DO
    WHILE key (pointer-1) < mid-point key DO
      increase pointer-1 by 1
    END WHILE
    WHILE mid-point key < key (pointer-2) DO
      decrease pointer-2 by 1
    END WHILE
    IF pointer-1 <= pointer-2 THEN
      swap key (pointer-1) with key (pointer-2)
      increase pointer-1 by 1
      decrease pointer-2 by 1
    END IF
  END WHILE
  IF lower-limit < pointer-2 THEN
    call PROC quicksort (lower-limit, pointer-2)
  END IF
  IF pointer-1 < upper-limit THEN
    call PROC quicksort (pointer-1, upper-limit)
  END IF
END PROC
```

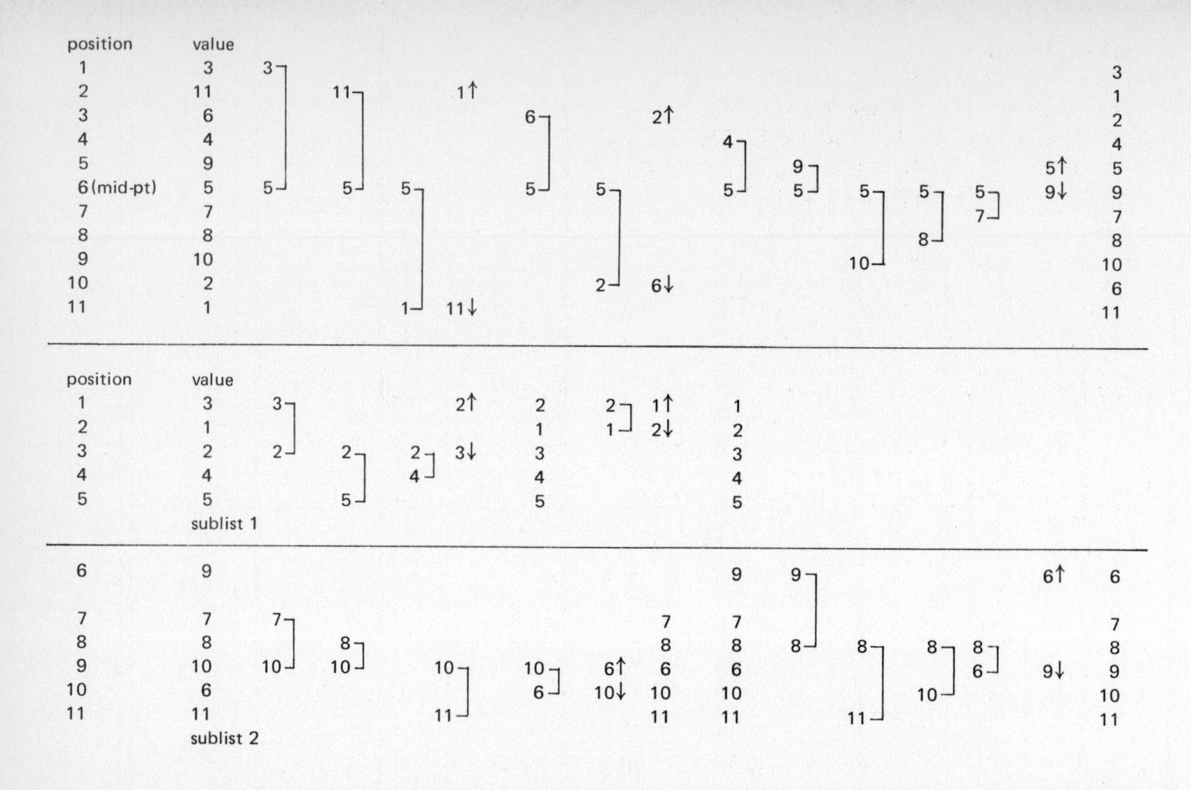

Figure 14.3

Glossary	
lower-limit	L
upper-limit	R
pointer-1	I
pointer-2	J
mid-point	X
table	A
temporary store	W

Program

```
1000  DEFINE PROCEDURE QUICKSORT (L,R,A)
1010  LOCAL I,J
1020    LET I = L
1030    LET J = R
1040    LET X = A (INT(L + R) /2)
1050    IF I > J THEN 1190
1060      IF A (I) > = X THEN 1090
1070        LET I = I + 1
1080      GOTO 1060
1090      IF X > = A (J) THEN 1120
1100        LET J = J – 1
1110      GOTO 1090
1120      IF I > J THEN 1180
1130        LET W = A(I)
1140        LET A(I) = A(J)
1150        LET A(J) = W
1160        LET I = I + 1
1170        LET J = J – 1
1180    GOTO 1050
1190    IF L < J THEN QUICKSORT (L,J,A)
1200    IF I < R THEN QUICKSORT (I,R,A)
1210  END PROCEDURE
```

14.4 Merging

Merging is the process of interleaving keys from sorted lists of keys to provide a single list of sorted keys. Figure 14.4 shows two input lists A and B and the result of a *two way* merge on the lists to produce list C.

INPUT LISTS				OUTPUT LIST	
LIST A		LIST B		LIST C	
Key position	Key value	Key position	Key value	Key position	Key value
1	1	1	3	1	1
2	4	2	6	2	3
3	5	3	7	3	4
4	9	4	10	4	5
5	12	5	13	5	6
				6	7
				7	9
				8	10
				9	12
				10	13

Fig. 14.4 An illustration of a two-way merge

The method of merging two lists consists of comparing individual keys between the lists, the smaller key of the two is written to the output list. The larger key is then compared with the next key from the list whose predecessor was output. The process is repeated until one input list becomes empty in which case the remaining keys of the other input list are output.

Key position	List	Key values		output list C
1	A]	1]	——→	1
1	B	3		
2	A]	4]	——→	3
1	B	3		
2	A]	4]	——→	4
2	B	6		
3	A]	5]	——→	5
2	B	6		
4	A]	9]	——→	6
2	B	6		
4	A]	9]	——→	7
3	B	7		
4	A]	9]	——→	9
4	B	10		
5	A]	12]	——→	10
4	B	10		
5	A]	12]	——→	12
5	B	13		
	A]	empty	——→	13
5	B	13		

Figure 14.5

An implementation of a two-way merge follows. The procedure has been expressed as a subroutine for the sake of generality. However, it is assumed that the keys are stored in two, one-dimensional tables that represent lists A and B respectively. The result of merging the two lists is stored in a third one-dimensional table and represents list C.

Design

```
PROC merge
  set merge flag to 1
  set pointer-A, pointer-B and pointer-C to first
  position in each table
  REPEAT
    IF key (pointer-A) > key (pointer-B) THEN
      move key (pointer-B) to list C
      move pointer-B to next position in list B
    ELSE
      move key (pointer-A) to list C
      move pointer-A to next position in list A
    END IF
    move pointer-C to next position in list C
    IF pointer-A beyond bottom of list A THEN
      IF pointer-B not beyond bottom of list B THEN
        move remainder of list B to list C
      END IF
      reset merge flag to 0
    ELSE
      IF pointer-B beyond bottom of list B THEN
        move remainder of list A to list C
        reset merge flag to 0
      END IF
    END IF
  UNTIL merge flag = 0
END PROC
```

Glossary		
Merge Flag	F	
Pointer-A	P1	
Pointer-B	P2	
Pointer-C	P3	
List A	A	one-dimensional tables
List B	B	
List C	C	
Length of List A	N	Number of keys in each list
Length of List B	M	

Note: The pointers are used as subscripts in each one-dimensional table ie. A(P1); B(P2); C(P3).

Program

```
1000 REM · · SUBROUTINE TO MERGE TWO TABLE
1010 LET F = 1
1020 LET P1 = 1: P2 = 1: P3 = 1
1030   IF A(P1) < B(P2) THEN 1070
1040     LET C(P3) = B(P2)
1050     LET P2 = P2 + 1
1060   GOTO 1090
1070     LET C(P3) = A(P1)
1080     LET P1 = P1 + 1
1090   LET P3 = P3 + 1
1100   IF P1 <= N THEN 1170
1110     IF P2 > M THEN 1160
1120       LET C(P3) = B(P2)
1130       LET P2 = P2 + 1
1140       LET P3 = P3 + 1
1150       IF P2 <= M THEN 1120
1160     LET F = 0
1165   GOTO 1230
1170     IF P2 <= M THEN 1230
1180       LET C(P3) = A(P1)
1190       LET P1 = P1 + 1
1200       LET P3 = P3 + 1
1210       IF P1 <= N THEN 1180
1220     LET F = 0
1230   IF F = 1 THEN 1030
1240 RETURN
```

Using your computer

Type, SAVE, LOAD and RUN the last program. Remember to set up Lists A and B and define List C.

Specimen results

```
>LOAD "TMERGE"
>LIST
   10 DIM A(10),B(10),C(20)
   20 FOR I=1 TO 10
   30  READ A(I),B(I)
   35  DATA 1,2,3,4,5,6,7,8,9,10,11,12,13,14,15,16,17,18,19,20
   40 NEXT I
   50 N=10:M=10:GOSUB 1000
   60 PRINT TAB(4);"TABLE A";TAB(14);"TABLE B"
   70 FOR I=1 TO 10
   80   PRINT A(I),B(I)
   90 NEXT I
  100 PRINT
  110 PRINT "TABLE C FORMED FROM A AND B"
  120 FOR I=1 TO 20
  130   PRINT C(I)
  140 NEXT I
  150 STOP
 1000 REM..SUBROUTINE TO MERGE TWO TABLES
 1010 F=1
 1020 LET P1=1:P2=1:P3=1
 1030 IF A(P1)<B(P2) THEN 1070
 1040 LET C(P3)=B(P2)
 1050 LET P2=P2+1
 1060 GOTO 1090
 1070 LET C(P3)=A(P1)
 1080 LET P1=P1+1
 1090 LET P3=P3+1
 1100 IF P1<=N THEN 1170
 1110 IF P2>M THEN 1160
 1120 LET C(P3)=B(P2)
 1130 LET P2=P2+1
 1140 LET P3=P3+1
 1150 IF P2<=M THEN 1120
 1160 LET F=0
 1165 GOTO 1230
 1170 IF P2<=M THEN 1230
 1180 LET C(P3)=A(P1)
 1190 LET P1=P1+1
 1200 LET P3=P3+1
 1210 IF P1<=N THEN 1180
 1220 LET F=0
 1230 IF F=1 THEN 1030
 1240 RETURN
>
```

```
 RUN
    TABLE A   TABLE B
          1         2
          3         4
          5         6
          7         8
          9        10
         11        12
         13        14
         15        16
         17        18
         19        20
```

```
TABLE C FORMED FROM A AND B
      1
      2
      3
      4
      5
      6
      7
      8
      9
     10
     11
     12
     13
     14
     15
     16
     17
     18
     19
     20

STOP at line 150
>
```

14.5 Searching
14.5.1 Serial Search

There is a requirement to be able to search through a list of keys and be able to match a key in that list. Having matched a key it is a very simple matter to obtain the information associated with that key.

For example, consider the names of personnel to be stored in one table and their switchboard telephone extensions in another table.

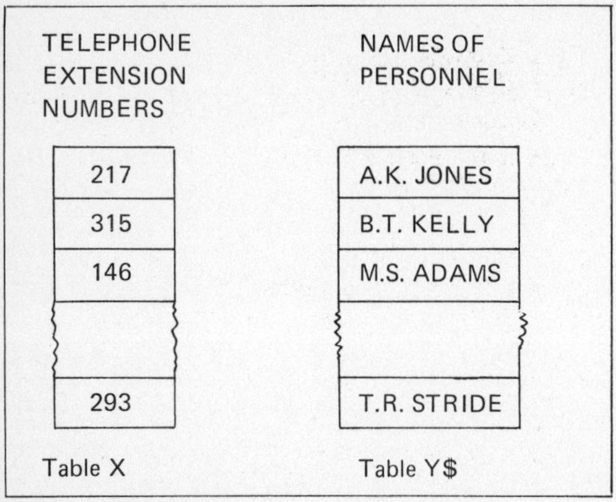

TELEPHONE EXTENSION NUMBERS	NAMES OF PERSONNEL
217	A.K. JONES
315	B.T. KELLY
146	M.S. ADAMS
293	T.R. STRIDE
Table X	Table Y$

If the extension numbers are stored in table X, and the names of respective personnel in Y$ and the maximum number of entries in both tables is N. Then if K represents an extension number and we want to find the name of the person at that extension the following program segment can be used to search table X. P represents the position of a key in both tables.

Program

```
 999   REM . . SUBROUTINE TO DEMONSTRATE SERIAL SEARCH
1000   REM . . SET POINTER AT TOP OF LIST
1010   LET P = 1
1020   REM . . INSPECT KEYS
1030   IF K = X(P) THEN 1120
1040     REM . . MOVE POINTER DOWN LIST OF EXTENSIONS
1050     LET P = P + 1
1060     REM . . CHECK FOR BOTTOM OF LIST
1070     IF P <= N THEN 1030
1080       REM . . KEY NOT MATCHED
1090       PRINT "KEY MATCH NOT FOUND"
1100   RETURN
1110   REM . . OUTPUT INFORMATION RELATING TO KEY
1120   PRINT "NAME OF PERSON"; Y$(P)
1130 RETURN
```

Using your computer

Type, SAVE, LOAD and RUN the last program. Remember to set up the tables X and Y$.

Specimen results

```
 LOAD "SSEARCH"
>LIST
   10 DIM X(10),Y$(10)
   15 N=10
   20 FOR I=1 TO N
   30   READ X(I),Y$(I)
   40 NEXT I
   50 DATA 278,E.ANDREWS,217,J.DAVIES,279,W.FENNEMORE
   60 DATA 207,D.MANSEY,223,P.MARTIN,231,J.MOORE
   70 DATA 286,M.ORMSTON,233,A.PHILLIPS,229,G.THOMAS,285,G.TURNER
   80 INPUT "EXTENSION NUMBER ",K
   90 IF K<=0 THEN STOP
  100 GOSUB 1000
  110 INPUT "EXTENSION NUMBER ",K
  120 GOTO 90
 1000 REM..SUBROUTINE SERIAL SEARCH
 1010 LET P=1
 1030 IF K=X(P) THEN 1120
 1050    LET P=P+1
 1070    IF P<=N THEN 1030
 1090    PRINT "KEY MATCH NOT FOUND"
 1100 RETURN
 1120 PRINT "NAME OF PERSON ";Y$(P)
 1130 RETURN
>
```

```
 LOAD "SSEARCH"
>RUN
EXTENSION NUMBER ?229
NAME OF PERSON G.THOMAS
EXTENSION NUMBER ?207
NAME OF PERSON D.MANSEY
EXTENSION NUMBER ?286
NAME OF PERSON M.ORMSTON
EXTENSION NUMBER ?300
KEY MATCH NOT FOUND
EXTENSION NUMBER ?285
NAME OF PERSON G.TURNER
EXTENSION NUMBER ?278
NAME OF PERSON E.ANDREWS
EXTENSION NUMBER ?0

STOP at line 90
>
```

This method of searching a list has the advantage that the keys in the list do not have to be sorted. The method is suitable for searching a list containing a small number of unordered keys. However, if the number of keys was large, say, 1000 extension numbers in a factory then the average number of key comparisons necessary before a match was found would be 500. Clearly this is unacceptable owing to the increased time factor involved.

If however, the keys were sorted into a list and a serial search was used to find a key match there would not be any need to compare every key in the list if the key was in fact not contained in the list. When the value of the key being compared with a key in the list is **smaller** than the key in the list then clearly a key match cannot be found. This assumes that the keys are arranged in ascending order, if they are in descending order then a key match cannot be found when the key being compared is **larger** than a key in the list.

14.5.2 Binary Search

This method requires that the keys are sorted into ascending or descending order prior to the search. In this example the keys are stored in a one-dimensional table. The key to be matched is compared with keys at the extremities of the list of keys to ensure that it does lie in the list. The list is then divided into two parts, and the relative position of the key with regard to one of the two lists is found. This sub-list is again divided into two lists and the relative position of the key with regard to one of the two new lists is found. The method continues until either a key match is obtained or the size of the sublist is reduced to two keys and neither key matches.

Figure 14.6 illustrates the subdividing of a list until a key match is obtained. When a sub-list contains an even number of keys the mid-value is taken to be the next lowest key from centre. The key to be matched in this illustration is 54. Notice that only three comparisons are necessary compared with ten comparisons in a serial search.

initial list	sub-list 1	sub-list 2
2		
5		
8		
14		
21		
25 → key (54) > mid-value (25)	25	
27	27	
39	39	
53	53 → key (54) > mid-value (53)	53
54	54	54 → key (54) =
60	60	60 mid-value

Figure 14.6

Design

```
PROC search
  initialise status-flag to 0
  set pointer-1 to first position in list
  set pointer-2 to last position in list
  IF key lies outside of list THEN
    set status-flag to 1
  ELSE
    IF key = key (position-1) THEN
      position-match = pointer-1
      set status-flag to 2
    ELSE
      IF key = key (position-2) THEN
        position-match = pointer-2
        set status-flag to 2
      ELSE
        call PROC binary-search
      END IF
    END IF
  END IF
END PROC

PROC binary-search
  REPEAT
    position-match = mid-point of sub-list
    IF no key match THEN
      IF key < key of mid-point THEN
        pointer-2 = position-match
      ELSE
        pointer-1 = position-match
      END IF
      IF sub-list contains two keys THEN
        set status-flag to 1
      END IF
    ELSE
      set status-flag to 2
    END IF
  UNTIL status-flag not zero
END PROC
```

Glossary

status-flag	F
pointer-1	P1
pointer-2	P2
position-match	P3
key	K
table used to store keys	V
number of keys in table	N

Program

```
1000  REM · · SUBROUTINE TO SEARCH TABLE
1010  LET F = 0
1020  LET P1 = 1
1030  LET P2 = N
1040  IF K >= V (P1) AND K <= V (P2) THEN 1070
1050    LET F = 1
1060  GOTO 1140
1070    IF K <> V(P1) THEN 1100
1080      LET P3 = P1
1085      LET F = 2
1090    GOTO 1140
1100      IF K <> V(P2) THEN 1130
1110        LET P3 = P2
1115        LET F = 2
1120      GOTO 1140
1130        GOSUB 2000
1140  RETURN
```

```
2000   REM · · BINARY SEARCH OF TABLE
2010   LET P3 = INT((P1 + P2) /2)
2020   IF K = V (P3) THEN 2090
2030     IF K > V(P3) THEN 2060
2040       LET P2 = P3
2050     GOTO 2070
2060       LET P1 = P3
2070     IF P2 – P1 = 1 THEN LET F = 1
2080   GOTO 2100
2090     LET F = 2
2100   IF F = 0 THEN 2010
2110   RETURN
```

Using your computer

Type, SAVE, LOAD and RUN the last program. Remember to set up table V.

Specimen results

```
>LOAD "BSEARCH"
>LIST
  10 DIM V(10),Y$(10)
  20 N=10
  30 FOR I=1 TO N
  40   READ V(I),Y$(I)
  50 NEXT I
  60 DATA 207,D.MANSEY,217,J.DAVIES,223,P.MARTIN,229,G.THOMAS
  70 DATA 231,J.MOORE,233,A.PHILLIPS,278,E.ANDREWS,279,W.FENNEMORE
  80 DATA 285,G.TURNER,286,M.ORMSTON
  90 INPUT "EXTENSION NUMBER ",K
 100 IF K<=0 THEN STOP
 110 GOSUB 1000
 120 IF F=1 THEN 150
 130   PRINT "NAME OF PERSON ";Y$(P3)
 140 GOTO 160
 150   PRINT "KEY MATCH NOT FOUND"
 160 INPUT "EXTENSION NUMBER ",K
 170 GOTO 100
1000 REM..SUBROUTINE TO SEARCH TABLE
1010 LET F=0
1020 LET P1=1
1030 LET P2=N
1040 IF K>=V(P1) AND K<=V(P2) THEN 1070
1050   LET F=1
1060 GOTO 1140
1070 IF K<>V(P1) THEN 1100
1080   LET P3=P1
1085   LET F=2
1090 GOTO 1140
1100 IF K<>V(P2) THEN 1130
1110 LET P3=P2
1115 LET F=2
1120 GOTO 1140
1130 GOSUB 2000
1140 RETURN
2000 REM..BINARY SEARCH OF TABLE
2010 LET P3=INT((P1+P2)/2)
2020 IF K=V(P3) THEN 2090
2030   IF K>V(P3) THEN 2060
2040       LET P2=P3
2050   GOTO 2070
2060       LET P1=P3
2070   IF P2-P1=1 THEN LET F=1
2080 GOTO 2100
2090   LET F=2
2100 IF F=0 THEN 2010
2110 RETURN
>
```

```
LOAD "BSEARCH"
>RUN
EXTENSION NUMBER ?285
NAME OF PERSON G.TURNER
EXTENSION NUMBER ?229
NAME OF PERSON G.THOMAS
EXTENSION NUMBER ?207
NAME OF PERSON D.MANSEY
EXTENSION NUMBER ?286
NAME OF PERSON M.ORMSTON
EXTENSION NUMBER ?233
NAME OF PERSON A.PHILLIPS
EXTENSION NUMBER ?300
KEY MATCH NOT FOUND
EXTENSION NUMBER ?231
NAME OF PERSON J.MOORE
EXTENSION NUMBER ?0

STOP at line 100
>
```

The parameters that are input to the subroutine to search the table are the number of keys (N) the table V, and the key K.

The parameters that are output from the subroutine are the status-flag (F) and the position of the matched key P3 in the table.

If the status-flag = 1 then no key match was possible and the value of P3 is not used, however, if the status-flag = 2 then a key match did occur and the value of P3 is the position in the table of the matched keys.

14.6 Dialect Differences

Since no features of the BASIC language have been discussed in this chapter a section on dialect differences might seem inappropriate. However, in a study on sorting and searching it is important to consider whether the dialects support any verbs for these and associated activities. Unlike a language such as COBOL that supports SORT and SEARCH verbs, BASIC has no such facility. However, in Microsoft there is a statement to swap the values of two variables.

14.6.1 Swapping

Microsoft. The format of the statement is:

SWAP data-name-1, data-name-2

where data-name-1 and data-name-2 are the names of two variables or table elements.

Example.

```
10 A$ = " TWENTY ": B$ = "ONE"
20 SWAP A$, B$
30 PRINT A$, B$
```

result ONE TWENTY

14.6.2 Timing

From the experiment described in section 14.3 it is clear that recording the time taken to sort or search through data is important in evaluating the most suitable algorithm to use for a particular application. Clearly a stop-watch could be used for this task, however, the internal clock in a computer is far more accurate.

Microsoft. The function TIME$ will either set or retrieve the current time. If the function is used as a variable, V$ = TIME$ then the current time is returned as an eight character string in the format hh:mm:ss. For example PRINT V$ would display 06:30:15 if the time was fifteen seconds past half-past six in the morning.

The current time can be set by using TIME$ = X$ where X$ may be given in one of the following formats.

hh – set the hour 0 to 23, mm and ss are set at 00 by default;
hh:mm – set both the hours and minutes, ss is set at 00;
hh:mm:ss – set all three parameters. For example TIME$ = "12:15:30" implies that the time has been set at thirty seconds past a quarter past twelve in the afternoon.

BBC/Electron. The function TIME can be used to set or read the internal timer. The timer counts in one hundredth of a second intervals and is not a clock that provides a true time of day. However, TIME can be converted to a 24 hour clock by using the following routines.

```
SEC = (TIME DIV 100)MOD 60
MIN = (TIME DIV 6000)MOD 60
HR  = (TIME DIV 360000)MOD 24
```

The time can be set by using:

```
TIME = ((hour*60+mins)*60+secs)*100
```

The time can be accessed by:

```
currenttime = TIME
```

14.7 Keywords

search, sort, key, internal sorting, external sorting;
bubble sort, Shell sort, Quicksort;
merging;
serial search, binary search;
timing.

14.8 Questions

1 A list of integers in the range 1 to 20 are defined in the following DATA statement.

```
DATA 16,18,1,3,20,7,5,2,10,19,17,13,4,6,9,11,8,14,12,15
```

Write a program to read and store these integers in a one-dimensional table containing 20 cells, using the integer value as the subscript to the cell.

What is the result of printing the contents of the table?

2 Write a program to store ten names of people in a one-dimensional table V$ and adapt the Shell sort to sort the names into ascending alphabetical sequence. Print the contents of the sorted table.

3 Write a program to store the names and addresses of twenty people in a two-dimensional table. The names **must** be stored in alphabetical order. If the names are input in alphabetical order there will be **no** need to sort the table on the name.

	name	address
1	ADAMS	2 CEDAR DR. LUTON
2	BAKER	3 PITT PLACE. WIGAN
20	TRUMAN	16 CHURCH ST. YORK

Extend the program to input the name of person; and modify the binary search to search the first column of the table to match a key with the name that was input. If a key match is found output the address of the person, otherwise output the name not found.

4 Write a program to store the sex of a person, the year that person was born and the name of the person. Store these details in a two-dimensional table for twenty people.

	Sex	Year of birth	Name
1	F	1946	J.S. SMITH
2	M	1923	P.T. JACKSON
20	F	1957	F.N. YATES

The sex and year of birth entries must **not** be ordered when the details are initially stored.

The sex is to be taken as the *primary* key, and the year of birth as the *secondary* key.

Pass through the twenty rows of the table sorting the information into **descending** order on the *primary* key. Then pass through the twenty rows of the table again, this time sorting the information into **ascending** order on the *secondary* key, within each primary key group.

The table will then contain information sorted into two groups: males and females. Within each group the people will be ordered by year of birth, hence the oldest people will appear at the top of the group and the youngest at the bottom of the group.

Output the contents of the table.

5 Modify the *telephone extension number* example 14.5.1 such that both number and name are stored in strict ordered sequence in two, one-dimensional tables. Associated with each table is a second one-dimensional table used to store pointers to the details in the other table.

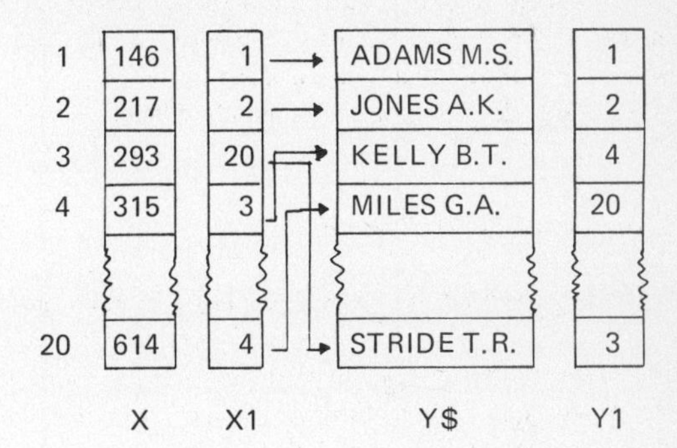

Thus given an extension number (293) say X can be searched until a match is found. The subscript of X (3) can be used to access X1 that contains a pointer (20) to the name of the person in table Y$. The pointer is used as a subscript to Y$.

Alternatively, given the name of a person KELLY B.T. Y$ is searched until a match is found. The subscript of Y$ (3) can be used to access Y1 that contains a pointer (4) to the extension number in table X. The pointer is used as a subscript to X.

Write a program to store twenty extension numbers and names with their respective pointers in table X, X1, Y$ and Y1. Use a binary search to locate a name given an extension number and vice versa.

15 Data Validation

15.1 Introduction

This chapter investigates the meaning of good and error data, the types of errors that can occur in data and the way in which such errors can be detected using statements in the BASIC language.

15.2 Definition of Good and Error Data

In designing a computer program it is vital to cater for both good and error data. There is a clear distinction to be made between valid and invalid data. Valid data is expected data, a program has been designed to process it and the results are predictable. Invalid data is unexpected data, a program has not been designed to process it and, therefore, the results are unpredictable.

Good data is regarded as being correct valid data, whereas error data is incorrect valid data.

A program can be designed to cater for valid data only.

The process of inspecting all valid data that is input to the computer and rejecting data that is unsuitable for use in a program (error data) is known as data validation. A data validation program should ensure that:

all errors present in input data are detected,
the type of errors are notified to the user of the system, and
only good data is passed on for processing.

15.3 Classification of Errors

Data that is input to a computer program could contain one or more of the following errors.

15.3.1 Type Error

The variable name to be assigned a datum is of a different type to the datum being input. For example if the datum "ABCD" was input to a program using the statement **INPUT N**, the BASIC system being used could return this as an error, since there is a conflict of data types. "ABCD" is a **string** literal; **INPUT N** expects a **numeric** literal.

Conflict between the use of real or integer numeric literals exists if an input datum is to be used as, say, a subscript to a table, an error will occur if the datum is real. For example, in a one-dimensional table X, X (3.75) has no meaning.

15.3.2 Format Error

This is the result of the size or arrangement of the data not conforming to what is expected in the program. Such an error can result from an excessive number of characters in a string or areas within a data format that have not been correctly defined. For example, if DD, MM and YY represent three two-digit integers describing a date as day, month and year respectively, then if the format of a date is described within a program as DDMMYY yet input as MMDDYY (031048) then the date will be translated as the 3rd October 1948 and not the 10th March 1948 as input by the user. Similarly if the date was input as 31048 this would not conform to the six digit number that is expected.

15.3.3 Range Error

Such an error results from the value of the data not being within pre-defined limits. For example the numerical value of a month is recognised as being in the range 1 to 12, any value for a month outside these limits would be in error.

15.3.4 Relationship Error

If one item of data is related to another item of data, then a specific value for one item can dictate the range of values for a second item. For example when validating a date in a year, if the month is March, then the maximum value permissible for the number of days would be 31. This maximum value would change for, say, the month of September. However, the maximum value would not only be different for February but dependent upon whether the year was a Leap Year or not.

15.3.5 Feasibility Error

Certain items of data cannot be given exact limits, therefore, in such cases values that are thought of as being reasonable would be chosen for the range limits when performing a range check on the data. For example in validating the weights of humans a maximum weight of 160 Kg would be reasonable, however, weights above this value are likely to be in error.

15.3.6 Data Absent Error

Checks should be made to ensure that all data requested by a program are in fact present. When using the **INPUT** statement if a datum is not entered at the keyboard the system will respond by asking the user to enter more data.

Conversely, if too many items of data are input as a response to an **INPUT** statement then the machine will ignore the extra data, and continue processing.

Example.
```
10 INPUT A,B,C
   RUN
   ? 5, 7, 3, 2, 9
   EXTRA IGNORED
```

However, a situation could arise when an item of data contains a comma such as in an address. In such circumstances it would be undesirable for the *extra* data to be ignored.

Example.
```
10 INPUT N$
   RUN
   ? 23, ST. GEORGE CLOSE
```

BASIC provides a version of INPUT that allows a single string of characters, including commas, to be input. The string is delimited by the *return* character.

Example.
```
10 INPUT LINE N$
   RUN
   ? 23, ST. GEORGE CLOSE
```

would store the entire string.

15.3.7 Transcription Error

It is a very common practice to use a numeric code as a key to access records in a file e.g. bank account number, stock number. Because it is very easy to make a mistake when entering these numbers to a computer each number normally contains a check digit. This digit provides a means for the computer to check that the number has not had any digits transposed when it has been entered into the computer. The check digit method will ensure a detection of all transcription and transposition errors and 91% of random errors.

The modulus 11 check digit for a code number is calculated in the following way.

Using the code number 9118 as an example: multiply each digit by its associated weight, here we have the weights 5,4,3,2, and calculate the sum of the partial products.

i.e. $(5 \times 9) + (4 \times 1) + (3 \times 1) + (2 \times 8) = 68.$

The sum 68 is then divided by 11 and the remainder 2 is then subtracted from 11, the result 9 is the check digit. The code number, including the check digit as the last digit, is 91189. If the value of the check digit is computed to be 10 this is replaced by the letter X.

To check whether a code number has been entered into the computer correctly a similar calculation is carried out. Each digit is multipled by a weight, the check digit has a weight of 1, and the sum of the partial products is calculated.

i.e. $(5 \times 9) + (4 \times 1) + (3 \times 1) + (2 \times 8) + (1 \times 9) = 77.$

The sum 77 is divided by 11 and the remainder is zero. If the remainder was non-zero then a transcription error would have been made when entering the number.

15.4 Type Error Validation

15.4.1 String Input

To avoid the situation described in 15.3.1 it is advisable when using the **INPUT** statement to input **all** data, regardless of type (numeric or string) as string data. Thus numeric data can be input to a program by coding, say, **INPUT N$**, but the converse is **not** true as indicated in 15.3.1. When numeric data is input as a string it **must be converted to the numeric data type** using the **VAL** function before the value can be used in arithmetic expressions, numeric comparisons or subscripts.

Several BASIC systems cause program termination when only the *return* key is depressed as a response to inputting data. Since this is undesirable in an applications system the **INPUT** statement should be substituted by an input subroutine using the **GET** statement or its equivalent.

Example. The following subroutine will allow characters to be input via a terminal keyboard, stored as the string X$, and the routine terminated when the *return* key is depressed.

```
500 REM · · SET STRING TO NULL CHARACTER
510 LET X$ = ""
520   GET Y$
530   REM · · TEST FOR RETURN CHARACTER
540   IF ASC (Y$) = 13 THEN RETURN
550     REM · · BUILD INPUT STRING
560     LET X$ = X$ + Y$
570     GET Y$
580 GOTO 540
```

BEWARE! When inputting a string of characters in this manner it is possible for the comma character to be stored as part of a string. For example, when inputting the number and street of an address.

However, the comma character is used in many BASIC systems as a delimiter between items of data. If a string containing a comma is stored it could lead to the string becoming corrupted.

To remedy this problem all commas can be removed from a string even though they may have been typed at a keyboard. A simple modification to the previous subroutine would be:

```
545   IF ASC (Y$) = 44 THEN 570
```

15.4.2 Alphabetic Type

If an item of data is described as being alphabetic then it consists of letters of the alphabet, upper and lower case, and the space character. The following subroutine can be used to validate an item of data as being alphabetic. The parameters that are passed to and from the subroutine are the string to be validated X$ and an error flag F respectively. If F = 1 then the data is in error.

```
1000  REM · · SUBROUTINE ALPHABETIC VALIDATION
1010  LET F = 0
1020  FOR I = 1 TO LEN (X$)
1030    LET Y = ASC(MID$(X$,I,1))
1040    IF (Y > 64 AND Y < 91) OR (Y > 96 AND Y < 123) OR Y = 32 THEN 1060
1050    LET F = 1: RETURN
1060  NEXT I
1070  RETURN
```

Note. The range of values for Y are taken from the table of ASCII codes. The range 65-90 corresponds to A-Z; 97-122 corresponds to a-z and 32 is the code for the space character.

15.4.3 Numeric Type

An item of data that is described as being numeric will contain a selection of the digits 0-9. The last subroutine can be modified to check for a datum containing only digits by changing line 1040 to:

```
1040  IF Y > 47 AND Y < 58 THEN 1060
```

where the ASCII codes for the digits 0-9 are 48-57 respectively.

An item of numeric data often contains an operational sign + or – and a decimal point. The modification made to the last subroutine would reject numbers that contained such characters, therefore, a new subroutine is required to cope with the validation of signed real or integer numbers.

```
2000  REM · · SUBROUTINE TO VALIDATE A REAL/ INTEGER
2010  REM · · RESET ERROR FLAG AND DECIMAL POINT FLAG
2020  LET F = 0: P = 0
2030  REM · · INSPECT FIRST CHARACTER OF STRING
2040  LET Y = ASC(LEFT$(X$,1))
2050  REM · · TEST FOR SIGN OR DIGIT
2060  IF Y = 43 OR Y = 45 OR (Y > 47 AND Y < 58) THEN 2100
2070  REM · · TEST FOR DECIMAL POINT
2080  IF Y = 46 THEN LET P = 1: GOTO 2100
2090    LET F = 1: RETURN
2100  REM · · INSPECT AND TEST REMAINING CHARACTERS
2110  FOR I = 2 TO LEN(X$)
2120    LET Y = ASC(MID$(X$,I,1))
2130    IF (Y > 47 AND Y < 58) THEN 2160
2140    IF (Y = 46 AND P = 0) THEN P = 1: GOTO 2160
2150      LET F = 1: RETURN
2160  NEXT I
2170  RETURN
```

Notes. If the input string is numeric and contains a leading sign and/or decimal point care must be exercised when using the **VAL** function. Some dialects demand that the first character should be a digit in the range 0-9, and that the string used as an argument in the **VAL** function must either consist of numeric characters or at least start with numeric characters. In the latter case only the numeric characters at the start of the string will be converted to a numeric value.

Other dialects state that if the first non-space character of the string is not a "+", "–", "." or digit then a zero will be returned when the VAL function is used.

The following test can be used to determine whether a numeric quantity is integer or real. X represents a numeric value.

DEF FNT(X) = X – INT(X)
IF FNT(X) = 0 then X is INTEGER, otherwise X is REAL.

15.5 Format and Data absent Validation

Format Validation. If the length of a string representing data is restricted to a fixed number of characters a check can be made on the length of a string by using one of the following techniques.

Use the **LEN** function to determine if the length of the input string is within a permissible limit. If the string is too long then truncate it using the **LEFT$** function, or report the error to the user and re-input the string.

Count the number of characters being input under a **GET** statement and terminate the input routine when either the *return* key is depressed or the number of characters exceeds the stated limit.

When areas within a string representing different items of data are **not** input in an order specified, validation can be difficult. For example if a date is input using the format DDMMYY and the user enters a date as 120122 we assume that the user did mean 12th January 1922, and did not intend the date to be 1st December 1922. A method of detecting the transposition of digits within a datum is possible by using a check digit validation, however, the check digit is calculated in advance and is appended as part of the datum. Such a scheme would be impractical when inputting, say, dates of birth at a terminal.

Data absent validation. If a **GET** statement is being used to input data, then should the user depress the *return* key only as a response to data being input, the length of the input string would be zero. Thus using the **LEN** function to check the length of the string will determine whether data has been entered or not. This function can also be used in determining whether areas within the input string are of the correct length. For example if a date was input as 12011922 using the format DDMMYY then a length check would reveal that the date consisted of too many digits and the user would be invited to re-enter the date.

15.6 Range Validation

The validation technique simply involves testing whether a datum lies between or outside of pre-defined limits.

Program coding for range testing can be simplified if the dialect of BASIC that you are using incorporates the logical operations **AND** and **OR**.

If α and β are defined limits the coding used to determine whether X was valid would be:

IF (X => α) **AND** (X <= β) **THEN** .....
for X to lie **inside** the range $\alpha - \beta$ or,
IF (X < α) **OR** (X > β) **THEN** .....
for X to lie **outside** the range $\alpha - \beta$.

15.6.1 Feasible Data Validation

The program coding technique is identical to that of range error validation, the only difference being in the manner in which the limits for the range are obtained.

If a programmer is required to code a date validation routine the ranges for the number of days in each month are fixed quantities that are well defined.

But what if the programmer is to code a validation routine to input a person's height, weight and age; what limits should be used then? Clearly the programmer should research what would be reasonable ranges for these three attributes, then data input to the computer could be checked as being feasible or not.

15.6.2 Relationship Validation

When two or more data items are related, then the range of legal values for a datum is dependent upon the values of the related data items.

For example, February 29th is a Legal date if the year is a Leap year. A person whose height is only 1 m is **not** likely to weigh more than 50 kg, yet a person whose height is 1.7 m is quite likely to weigh more than 50 kg.

The following subroutine is used to validate a date in the twentieth century. The date has been input using the format DDMMYY and has **already** been validated for format and date type and has been divided into day, month and year.

design

```
PROC date
 reset error flag
 IF month legal THEN
  IF month February THEN
   IF leap year THEN
    IF day illegal THEN
     set error flag
    END IF
   ELSE
    IF day illegal THEN
     set error flag
    END IF
   END IF
  ELSE
   IF day illegal THEN
    set error flag
   END IF
  END IF
 ELSE
  set error flag
 END IF
END PROC
```

Glossary	
Day	D
Month	M
Year	Y
Table containing number of days in each month	V
Error Flag	F
Leap Year Indicator	L

Program

```
 10  REM · · SET UP A ONE DIMENSIONAL TABLE IN
 20  REM · · THE MAIN PROGRAM TO CONTAIN THE
 30  REM · · MAXIMUM NUMBER OF DAYS IN EACH
 40  REM · · MONTH FOR A NON LEAP YEAR
 50  DIM V(12)
 60  FOR I = 1 TO 12
 70    READ V(I)
 80  NEXT I
 90  DATA 31,28,31,30,31,30,31,31,30,31,30,31
     –
     –
     –

500  REM · · SUBROUTINE TO VALIDATE DATE
510  LET F = 0
520  IF M < 1 OR M > 12 THEN LET F = 1: RETURN
530    IF M <> 2 THEN 600
540      LET L = Y – 4*INT(Y/4)
550      IF L <> 0 THEN 580
560        IF D < 1 OR D > 29 THEN LET F = 1: RETURN
570      RETURN
580        IF D < 1 OR D > 28 THEN LET F = 1: RETURN
590      RETURN
600    IF D < 1 OR D > V(M) THEN LET F = 1: RETURN
610  RETURN
```

15.7 Check Digit Validation

Data that relates to, say, a code number for an item of stock could pass the valid format test despite having two digits transposed when the data was input. If the code number contains a check digit then the order in which digits have been input becomes self checking.

The check digit method will ensure a detection of all transcription and transposition errors and 91% of random errors.

Section 15.3.7 gave an explanation of how a check digit is calculated and how a code number can be checked for a transcription error.

The following subroutine is used to check whether a code number using a modulus-11 check digit has been input to the computer without error. The code number contains five digits, the least significant digit being 0 to 9 or X (X represents a check digit of 10). The code number has already been validated for string size (format) and type.

Glossary	
Error Flag	F
Sum	S
Subscript	I
Weight	J
Remainder	R
Input string	X$
Single character of string	C$

```
499 REM · · SUBROUTINE TO CHECK MODULUS – 11 CODE
500   REM · · RESET ERROR FLAG, SET SUM TO ZERO
510   LET F = 0
520   LET S = 0
530   REM · · SET UP LOOP TO INSPECT EACH CHARACTER
540   FOR I = 1 TO 4
550     REM · · OBTAIN WEIGHT FOR THAT CHARACTER
560     LET J = 6 – I
570     REM · · OBTAIN I TH CHARACTER
580     LET C$ = MID$ (X$,I,1)
590     REM · · CALCULATE PARTIAL SUM
600     LET S = S + J * VAL (C$)
610   NEXT I
620   REM · · INSPECT LAST CHARACTER
630   LET C$ = RIGHT$ (X$, 1)
640   REM · · TEST C$ AND CALCULATE SUM
650     IF C$ = "X" THEN S = S + 10
660     IF C$ <> "X" THEN S = S + VAL (C$)
670   REM · · CALCULATE REMAINDER
680   LET R = S – 11 * INT (S / 11)
690   REM · · TEST REMAINDER
700   IF R = 0 THEN 740
710     REM · · OUTPUT ERROR MESSAGE AND SET ERROR FLAG
720     PRINT "ERROR – CHECK DIGIT CALCULATION"
730     LET F = 1
740 RETURN
```

15.8 Worked Example

15.8.1 Problem

Data entries to a computer specify details of stock held in warehouses throughout the United Kingdom. Each entry has the following format.

Field 1 stock number:
5 characters including a check digit as the least significant digit.

Field 2 quantity:
3 digits.

Field 3 location:
4 characters indicating the location of a warehouse in the U.K. Legal warehouse codes are GLAS, LIVE, BIRM, COVE, LOND and SOUT.

Design and write a program to read each data entry and validate each field according to the following criteria.

Field 1: numeric stock number with the exception of the check digit that could be X; check for transcription errors.

Field 2: unsigned integer including zero.

Field 3: legal warehouse code.

Display those records that are in error on the screen using the following format for the report.

```
      ENTRY                          ERROR FIELDS
1543X    12A    POOL              1      2      3
1544X    500    POOL                            3
15411    750    MANC              1             3
```

Two one-dimensional tables are used in the solution to this problem. The first table is used to store the warehouse codes:

W$	GLAS	LIVE	BIRM	COVE	LOND	SOUT

and the second table stores the number of the field that is in error:

E$	1bb	bbb	3bb

The program is to be terminated by using a rogue value for the stock number e.g. "XXXXX".

15.8.2 Design

```
read and store location codes
print headings on screen
read first entry
WHILE stock number not "XXXXX" DO
  reset field error flags
  initialise table for error codes
  call PROC stock-number
  call PROC quantity
  call PROC location
  IF error in entry THEN
    print entry and error codes on screen
  END IF
  read next entry
END WHILE
stop

PROC stock-number
  obtain substring of first four characters
  call PROC numeric
  obtain last character of stock number
  IF error flag (F) set OR (last character invalid) THEN
    set error flag (F1)
  END IF
  IF error flag (F1) not set THEN
    call PROC modulus
  END IF
  IF error flag (F1) set THEN
    store error code 1 in table
  END IF
END PROC

PROC quantity
  IF length of quantity string > 3 THEN
    set error flag (F2)
    store error code 2 in table
    EXIT PROC
  END IF
  call PROC numeric
  IF error flag (F) set THEN
    set error flag (F2)
    store error code 2 in table
  END IF
END PROC

PROC location
  FOR I = 1 TO 6
    IF field 3 = stored location THEN
      EXIT PROC
    END IF
  NEXT I
  set error flag (F3)
  store error code 3 in table
END PROC

PROC numeric
  reset error flag (F)
  FOR I = 1 TO length of substring
    IF I th character not a digit THEN
      set error flag (F)
      EXIT PROC
    END IF
  NEXT I
END PROC

PROC modulus
  initialise sum of products to zero
  FOR I = 1 TO 4
    calculate partial sum
  NEXT I
  IF last character = "X" THEN
    increase sum by 10
  ELSE
    increase sum by value of last digit
  END IF
  calculate remainder
  IF remainder non-zero THEN
    set error flag (F1)
  END IF
END PROC
```

Glossary

table to store warehouse codes	W$
table to store error codes	E$
stock-number	S$
quantity	Q$
location	L$
field 1 error flag	F1
field 2 error flag	F2
field 3 error flag	F3
numeric error flag	F
substring	X$
single character	T$
sum of partial products	S
subscript	I
remainder	R

15.8.3 Program

```
  10  DIM W$ (6), E$ (3)
  20  FOR I = 1 TO 6
  30    READ W$ (I)
  40  NEXT I
  50  DATA "GLAS", "LIVE", "BIRM", "COVE", "LOND", "SOUT"
  70  PRINT "              ENTRY                   ERROR FIELD"
  80  READ S$, Q$, L$
  90  IF S$ = "XXXXX" THEN STOP
 100    F1 = 0: F2 = 0: F3 = 0
 105      LET E$ (1) ="       ": E$ (2) ="       ": E$ (3) ="       "
 110    GOSUB 1000
 120    GOSUB 2000
 130    GOSUB 3000
 140    IF F1 = 0 AND F2 = 0 AND F3 = 0 THEN 160
 150      PRINT S$, Q$, L$;"       "E$ (1) ; E$ (2) ; E$ (3)
 160    READ S$, Q$, L$
 170  GOTO 90

1000  REM . . SUBROUTINE STOCK-NUMBER
1010  LET X$ = LEFT$ (S$, 4)
1020  GOSUB 4000
1030  LET X$ = RIGHT$ (S$, 1)
1040  IF F = 1 OR ((X$ < "0" OR X$ > "9") AND X$ <> "X") THEN LET F1 = 1
1050  IF F1 = 0 THEN GOSUB 5000
1060  IF F1 = 1 THEN E$ (1) = "1    "
1070  RETURN

2000  REM . . SUBROUTINE QUANTITY
2005  IF LEN (Q$) > 3 THEN LET F2 = 1: E$ (2) = "2    ": RETURN
2010  LET X$ = Q$: GOSUB 4000
2020  IF F = 1 THEN LET F2 = 1: E$ (2) = "2    "
2030  RETURN

3000  REM . . SUBROUTINE LOCATION
3010  FOR I = 1 TO 6
3020    IF L$ = W$ (I) THEN RETURN
3030  NEXT I
3040  LET F3 = 1: E$ (3) = "3    "
3050  RETURN

4000  REM . . SUBROUTINE NUMERIC
4010  LET F = 0
4020  FOR I = 1 TO LEN (X$)
4030    LET T$ = MID$ (X$, I, 1)
4040    IF T$ < "0" OR T$ > "9" THEN LET F = 1: RETURN
4050  NEXT I
4060  RETURN
```

```
5000 REM · · SUBROUTINE MODULUS
5010 LET S = 0
5020 FOR I = 1 TO 4
5030   LET S = S+ (6 – I) *VAL (MID$ (S$, I, 1))
5040 NEXT I
5050 IF RIGHT$ (S$, 1) <> "X" THEN 5080
5060   LET S = S + 10
5070 GOTO 5090
5080   LET S = S+VAL (RIGHT$ (S$, 1))
5090 LET R = S – 11*INT (S/11)
5100 IF R <> 0 THEN LET F1 = 1
5110 RETURN

6000 DATA "4345X", "138", "GLAS"
6010 DATA "10732", "A45", "POOL"
6020 DATA "91855", "14I", "OUTH"
6030 DATA "91189", "125", "LIVE"
6040 DATA "80317", "12345", "SOUT"
6050 DATA "XXXXX", "Ø", "X"
```

Using your computer

Type, SAVE, LOAD and RUN the last program.

Specimen results

```
>LOAD "ERROR"
>RUN
               ENTRY                  ERROR FIELD
4345X          138          GLAS       1
10732          A45          POOL       1  2  3
91855          14I          OUTH          2  3
80317          12345        SOUT       1  2

STOP at line 90
>
```

15.9 Keywords

Good, error, valid and invalid data;
type, format, range, relationship, feasible, data absent and transcription errors;
Modulus-11 check-digit;
alphabetic and numeric data types.

15.10 Questions

1 Write a validation procedure for the time of day input as a four digit number using the 24-hour clock representation, e.g. 1436.

2 Write a validation procedure for the date in a non-leap year input as a five character string e.g. MAR18. The year is not input. Your routine should allow for dates being input as MAR1 or MAR 1 to represent the 1st March.

3 A table is used to store the following information about bona fide users of a computer system.

User account number: 6 digits proceded by either TP or PS.
Password: 10 characters composed from digits or letters of the alphabet. The first character must be alphabetic.
Time of last log-out: 6 digit integer representing hours, minutes and seconds on a 24-hour clock format.

When a user logs on to the computer system he must type his account number and password. These two entries are fully validated by the system and if either entry proved to be wrong or the time of the last log-out was less than 30 minutes ago, the user will be denied access to the system.

Design and write a complete validation procedure.

16 Introduction to File Processing

16.1 Introduction

16.1.1 Contents

The purpose of this chapter is to introduce the reader to the fundamental concepts of file processing. The chapter is divided into three parts.

The first part deals with a description of computer files and describes the language statements that are required to process files.

The second part involves the creation of serial files and the production of a report from a file.

The final part investigates the production of a sequential file from a serial file using different techniques of sorting.

16.1.2 An Overview

The only methods described up to now for inputting data to a computer program are through the verbs **INPUT, GET** and **READ/DATA**. These three forms, although useful, are **not** adequate for coping with large volumes of data. Their use has the following disadvantages.

INPUT and **GET** rely on the user entering data through a keyboard device such as a visual display unit. The advantage of using a high-speed computer to process work becomes redundant since the speed of the computer system becomes dependent upon the typing speed of the user at the terminal.

Data that is input via a keyboard to the main memory of a computer is **not** permanently stored. Switch the power off from the computer and the data stored in the main memory is destroyed. Switch the power on again and the user must re-load and run the program before entering all the data again!

Data that is represented in a program through a **READ/DATA** statement uses valuable memory space and causes the program to be larger than is necessary for its processing power. This is critical if you are using a small microcomputer.

Data that is represented in a program cannot be amended, increased in volume or deleted without having to change part of the program.

To avoid these disadvantages data should be stored on magnetic tape or disc in the form of a data file. Such storage has the following advantages.

Peripheral devices such as magnetic tape and disc units can transfer data from the medium on which it is stored to the main memory of a computer at a very fast speed (hundreds of thousands of characters per second). Thus the speed of data input/output becomes more realistic in terms of the power of the computer.

Data can be permanently stored on both magnetic tape and disc. Switch the power off and the data remains on the magnetic medium. Magnetic tapes and disc packs are portable, so not only can data be moved from one computer to another but libraries of data can also be kept.

Data is no longer represented using READ/DATA statements in a program. Such statements would only be used to represent constants within a program.

Data stored on magnetic tape or disc can be duplicated for security.

Changes to data held on peripheral media (magnetic tape or disc) will not involve changes to the program. In fact a program can and will bring about changes to the data, and not the reverse.

16.2 Elements of a Computer File

A computer file is a collection of information stored on magnetic tape or magnetic disc.

The reader has already come across the concept of a file when storing a computer program. A *program file* was composed of a line by line collection of BASIC statements stored under a name given to the program.

Data files are similar in concept. Each line of data is known as a *logical* record and is subdivided into smaller areas of discrete information known as **fields.** Each **field** is composed of a series of **characters.**

The number of characters grouped into a field can vary from field to field in a record.

The records of a file can be of either **fixed** length or **variable** length. For example figure 16.1 illustrates the format of a fixed length record used to store the details of a factory employee.

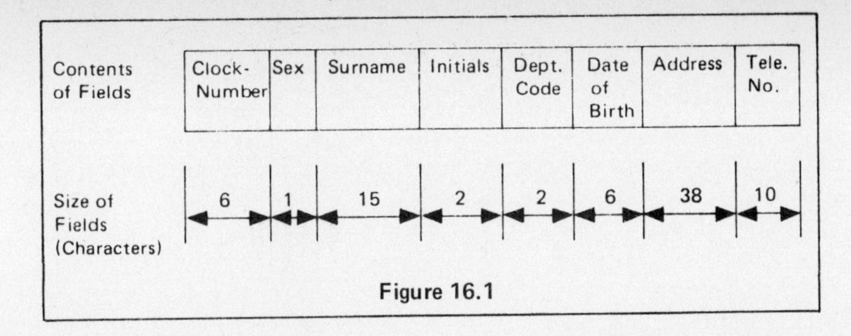

Figure 16.1

Each record in this example has a fixed length of 80 characters, however, although such fields as SURNAME, INITIALS and ADDRESS have fixed lengths of 15, 2 and 38 characters respectively, their contents will not always fill the size of the fields. Each field that is not completely filled will be *padded* with space characters. The result will be an accumulated waste of space between the records of the file. For this reason the fields of a record can be allowed to vary according to the size of the data contained in them. This in turn will bring about records of varying length throughout the file. The records of such a file are said to be of variable length.

Notice from figure 16.1 that the information contained in the file is related to a specific application, in this example personnel in a factory. Different files are used for different applications, for example, stock records, airline flight reservations, customer details, etc.

One field of a record is specified as the *primary* key to that record. For example in figure 16.1 CLOCK-NUMBER is a **unique** value for an employee in the factory and could be used as the key to a record. Thus if one required information relating to an employee whose clock number was known in advance, the file would be searched comparing the clock number of each record with the known clock number. When a match was found the information for that record could be extracted.

A *physical* record is defined as one or more logical records read into or written from main memory as a *unit* of information. Records are not usually transferred to and from main memory as single *logical* records but grouped together and stored in an area of memory known as a *buffer*. When information is transferred to the buffer it is transferred as a *block* of logical records; and again when information is transferred from the buffer to the storage medium it is transferred as a *block* of logical records.

16.3 File Organisation

16.3.1 Serial

The records of a file are positioned one after another and stored on an appropriate medium (magnetic tape or disc).

However, the records of a file are **not** ordered on a key, and the position of adjacent records has no predefined meaning. To access information from the file a serial record by record search, comparing the key of every record is necessary before a key match is possibly found. Figure 16.2 illustrates the organisation of logical records in a serial file.

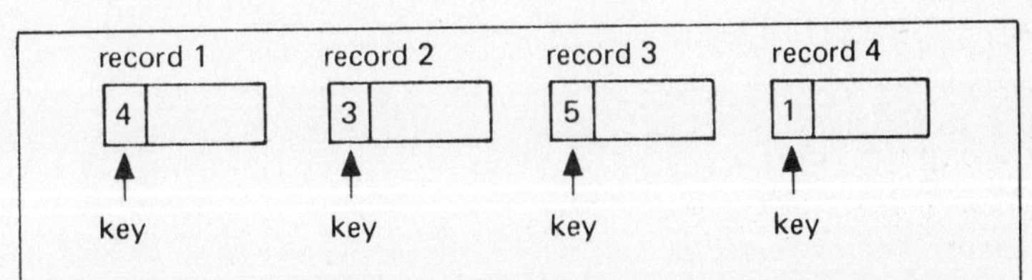

Figure 16.2 A series of records **not** placed in an ascending or descending order by the key. Records organised in this manner form a serial file.

16.3.2 Sequential

The records of a file are stored in similar manner to a serial file with **one** exception. The positions of records are ordered on a specific key and, therefore, the position of adjacent records has a meaning. For example in figure 16.1 if the employee records are ordered by CLOCK-NUMBER the positions of adjacent records must be such that the records are placed in numerical sequence by CLOCK-NUMBER. If the *primary* key for the file had been SURNAME then the records of the file would be positioned into alphabetical sequence by SURNAME.

Access to an individual record is still based on a record-by-record search through the file until a key match is possibly found, but in this case it will not be necessary to search the whole file if the required record is not present. Figure 16.3 illustrates the organisation of logical records in a sequential file.

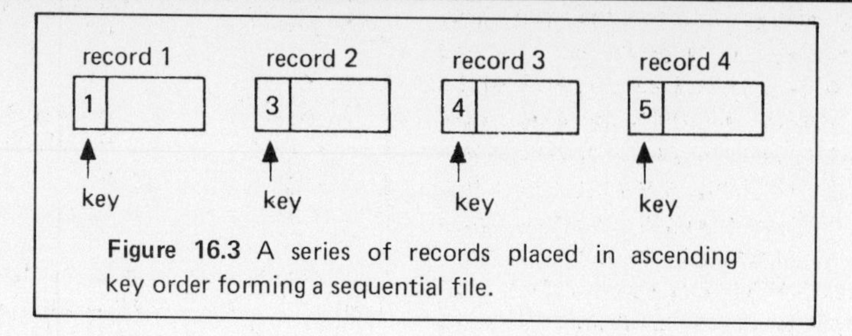

Figure 16.3 A series of records placed in ascending key order forming a sequential file.

16.4 File Processing Activities

16.4.1 Opening a file

In some dialects of BASIC the action of opening a file will cause buffer areas to be created within the main memory and allocated to respective files. However, other dialects of BASIC use pre-defined buffers for all file input/output. Many dialects of BASIC require the mode under which a file is opened to be specified. A file is opened for *INPUT* if records are to be read, *OUTPUT* if records are to be written to the file or *APPEND* if records are to be written at the end of an existing file.

Before a file can be used it must be opened. There are many functions associated with *OPEN* which may include:

ensuring that the device (disc or tape unit) is ready for use;
checking labels on an existing file;
creating labels on a new file;
filling the input buffer with a physical record for a file that is about to be read.

16.4.2 Reading a file

This is a similar process to reading from a **DATA** statement. However, a file replaces a series of **DATA** statements and fields of a record represent respective items of data. The first execution of a *READ* statement will cause the *input* buffer to be filled with a physical record. The first logical record in the buffer is then accessed. The execution of subsequent *READ* statements will cause successive records to be accessed in sequence from the buffer. When all the logical records from the buffer have been accessed, the buffer will be refilled by a physical record upon the execution of the next *READ* statement. Figure 16.4 is used to illustrate the relationship between records in the buffer area and the *READ* statement.

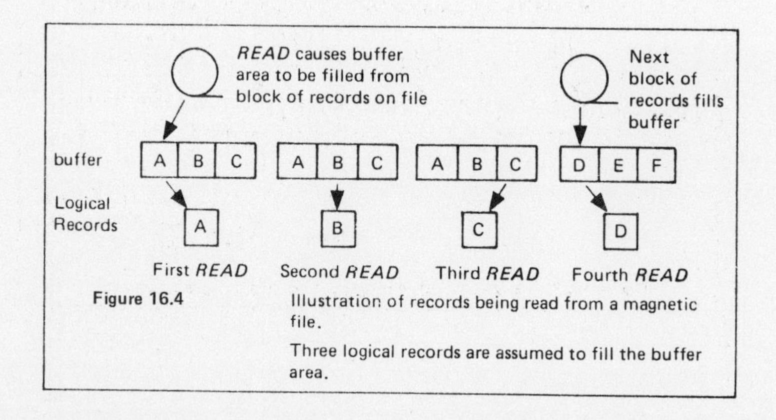

Figure 16.4 Illustration of records being read from a magnetic file.
Three logical records are assumed to fill the buffer area.

16.4.3 Testing for end of file

The repeated execution of a *READ* file statement will eventually cause all the records in the file to have been read. For this reason it is important that a method for detecting the end of a file is incorporated into the file processing statements of the BASIC language. In the absence of a method a run-time error will occur when an attempt is made to read beyond the end of the file.

There are three methods available for testing when the end of a file has been reached. The first is independent of the dialect of BASIC being used, while the last two methods are dependent upon the dialect of BASIC and computer being used. The methods are:

Ensuring that the last record of the file contains a *rogue* value, and testing for this value after every *READ*. A similar technique was used earlier in the book with READ/DATA statements.

Using a BASIC statement to *trap* when the end of file has been reached, and executing this statement when such a condition is true. This method requires that the *trap* statement is placed before a *READ* statement, yet **cannot** be executed until **after** a *READ* statement has read **beyond** the end of the file.

Common statements used to trap the end of file in BASIC are:

ON END#1 GOTO 200

or *ON ERR GOTO 200*

Both statements require an error condition to arise (e.g. attempt to read beyond end of file) before they are executed.

The flowchart representation for this method of testing for the end of a file is shown in figure 16.5 with the appropriate BASIC code.

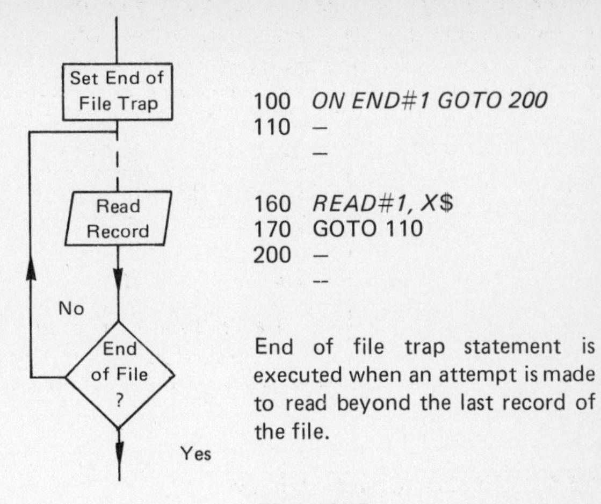

Figure 16.5

In the third method an end of file BASIC function is used in conjunction with a conditional statement. The function returns a value equivalent to true if the end of file is reached or false if not at the end of the file.

16.4.4 Writing to a file

This is the activity of storing a record on a file. The format of a logical record would be specified in a program, and the fields used to represent that format would be assigned values before writing a record. The use of successive *WRITE* statements will cause the *output* buffer to be filled, having one logical record placed after the next in sequence. When the buffer is full the computer system will store the contents of the buffer on the magnetic file. The buffer is then empty, and ready to receive more logical records. Figure 16.6 illustrates writing records to a file.

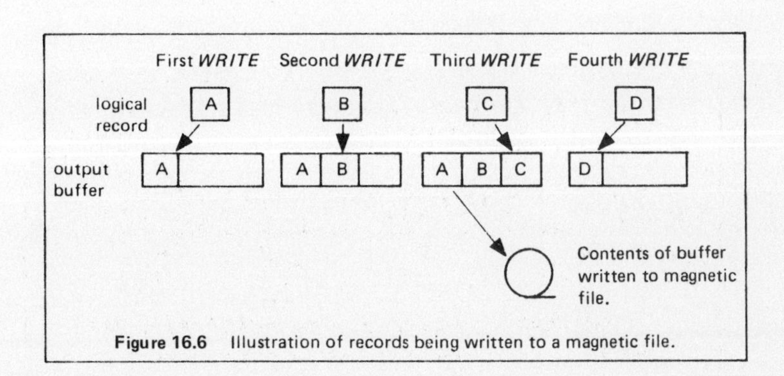

Figure 16.6 Illustration of records being written to a magnetic file.

16.4.5 Appending records to a file

Often it is desirable to attach records to the end of an existing file. The activity of appending allows records to be written to a file starting at a position after the last record of the file. Some BASIC dialects cater for this activity. However, the same result can be obtained if the file containing the additional records is *merged* with the existing file.

16.4.6 Closing a file

When all processing activities are completed on a file it must be closed. The activity of closing a file serves the following purposes.

The contents of a buffer (may be partially full) is written to the file if the mode is set to *OUTPUT*.

To allow the file to be re-opened for a different mode of processing. For example a file that is opened for *OUTPUT* could be closed, and re-opened in the *INPUT* mode ready for reading.

16.5 Dialect Differences

16.5.1 Open file

Microsoft.

Format:

```
OPEN filename FOR { OUTPUT } AS #channel
                  { INPUT  }
                  { APPEND }
```

Examples.

```
OPEN "TELEFILE" FOR INPUT AS #1
OPEN "SORTDATA" FOR OUTPUT AS #2
OPEN "TELEFILE" FOR APPEND AS #3
```

Channel is represented by an integer in the range 1–4 for tape units and 1–3 for disc units. The channel number is used in the other file processing statements to identify the file to be processed. The APPEND option can only be used on disc files.

BBC/Electron.

Format: channel = OPENIN(filename)
channel = OPENOUT(filename)

Examples. X = OPENIN("TELEFILE")
Y = OPENOUT("REPORT")
Z = OPENOUT(X$)

Files may only be opened for input or output. The *append* mode is not used in this dialect. The channel, any suitable numeric variable name, is used in other file processing statements to identify the file to be processed.

16.5.2 Read file

Both dialects use a similar format for reading records from a serial or sequential data file.

Format: INPUT channel, variable [,variable] .....

Example. INPUT#3, X$,Y$,Z$

16.5.3 End of file

Microsoft and **BBC/Electron** support a function that returns a specific value if the end of a file is reached.

Format: EOF channel

Examples.		
	EOF#3	(Microsoft)
	EOF#X	(BBC/Electron)
	EOF(#7)	(SuperBASIC)

The Microsoft and BBC/Electron dialects return a value of −1 to EOF when the end of file is reached.

16.5.4 Write record

Both dialects use a similar format for writing records to a serial or sequential data file.

Format: PRINT #channel, variable [,variable] .....

Example. PRINT # 2, X$,Y$,Z$

Microsoft

PRINT # does not compress data on a file. An image of the data is written to a file just as it would be displayed on a screen with a PRINT statement. If semi-colons are used as separators between variables then extra blanks are not inserted between the fields of a record.

Example. A$ = "12, TOWER HILL"
B$ = "WANTAGE"

PRINT#1,A$;B$ would write:–

12, TOWER HILLWANTAGE to the file. By using INPUT#1,A$,B$ to read the file A$ = 12 and B$ = TOWER HILLWANTAGE

To separate these fields correctly double quote string delimiters would have to be written.

PRINT #1,CHR$(34);A$;CHR$(34);CHR$(34);B$;
CHR$(34) would write

"12, TOWER HILL""WANTAGE" to the file. Therefore, using INPUT#1,A$,B$ would cause A$ = 12, TOWER HILL and B$ = WANTAGE

BBC/Electron.

Despite the use of comma separators between variables in the PRINT# statement all values are stored in a special internal format.

16.5.5 Append record

Microsoft incorporate an APPEND option in the OPEN statement. This allows records to be written to a file starting at the end of the file. Other dialects do not have this facility. In the absence of a file being opened in an *append* mode records can be appended in one of two ways. These are to write the records of the old file to a second new file, and at the end of the transfer continue writing to the second file with the extra records to be appended. Alternatively, appending records to a file can under certain circumstances take place through merging the two files.

16.5.6 Close file

Microsoft, and **BBC/Electron** both use a close statement of the format.

CLOSE#channel

Examples.	CLOSE#1	(Microsoft and SuperBASIC)
	CLOSE#X	(BBC/Electron)

Using your computer

Type, SAVE, LOAD and RUN all the example programs that follow this section. Where file processing statements differ on your computer to those printed, substitute the correct statements.

Specimen results are listed after each program.

16.6 Worked Examples
16.6.1 Problem

A college administrator requires a file of academic staff names, their departments and extension telephone numbers. Design and write a program to create such a serial file having variable length records.

16.6.2 Design

open file for writing (output)
REPEAT
  input name
  input department
  input extension number
  write record
UNTIL no more data
close file
stop

16.6.3 Program

All programs coded in this chapter will use the BBC/Electron dialect of BASIC. Conversion to the other dialects can be made by consulting the version of BASIC for your machine.

```
 10  X = OPENOUT ("TELEXT")
 20  REPEAT
 30    INPUT "NAME:",NAME$
 40    INPUT "DEPARTMENT:", DEPT$
 50    INPUT "TEL EXT:", TEL$
 60    PRINT#X, NAME$, DEPT$, TEL$
 70    INPUT "MORE DATA ANSWER Y OR N:", REPLY$
 80  UNTIL REPLY$ = "N"
 90  CLOSE#X
100  STOP
```

Specimen results

```
>LOAD "CREATE"
>RUN
NAME:?SMITH P
DEPARTMENT:?MATHEMATICS
TEL EXT:?126
MORE DATE ANSWER Y OR N:?Y
NAME:?JONES F
DEPARTMENT:?SCIENCE
TEL EXT:?894
MORE DATE ANSWER Y OR N:?Y
NAME:?KING L
DEPARTMENT:?CATERING
TEL EXT:?138
MORE DATE ANSWER Y OR N:?Y
NAME:?MURPHY T
DEPARTMENT:?GEN. STUDIES
TEL EXT:?216
MORE DATE ANSWER Y OR N:?Y
NAME:?PALMER S
DEPARTMENT:?SCIENCE
TEL EXT:?514
MORE DATE ANSWER Y OR N:?Y
NAME:?HARPER W
DEPARTMENT:?GEN. STUDIES
TEL EXT:?216
MORE DATE ANSWER Y OR N:?Y
NAME:?FOWLER A
DEPARTMENT:?MATHEMATICS
TEL EXT:?126
MORE DATE ANSWER Y OR N:?Y
NAME:?MORAN T
DEPARTMENT:?LANGUAGES
TEL EXT:?328
MORE DATE ANSWER Y OR N:?N

STOP at line 100
>
```

16.6.4 Problem

The college administrator wishes to extend the contents of the file to include all the administrative staff. Design and write a program to append these extra records to the end of the file.

16.6.5 Design

open original file for reading (input)
open new file for writing (output)
WHILE not end of original file **DO**
  read original file
  write record to new file
END WHILE
REPEAT
  input name
  input department
  input extension number
UNTIL no more data
close files
stop

16.6.6 Program

```
 10  X = OPENIN ("TELEXT")
 20  Y = OPENOUT ("NEWFILE")
 30  IF EOF#X THEN 70
 40    INPUT#X,NAME$,DEPT$,TEL$
 50    PRINT#Y,NAME$,DEPT$,TEL$
 60  GOTO 30
 70  CLOSE#X
 80  REPEAT
 90    INPUT "NAME:",NAME$
100    INPUT "DEPARTMENT:",DEPT$
110    INPUT "TEL EXT:",TEL$
120    PRINT#Y,NAME$,DEPT$,TEL$
130    INPUT "MORE DATA ANSWER Y OR N:",REPLY$
140  UNTIL REPLY$ = "N"
150  CLOSE#Y
160  STOP
```

Specimen results

```
>LOAD "APPEND"
>RUN
NAME:?CARTER B
DEPARTMENT:?ADMIN
TEL EXT:?416
MORE DATA ANSWER Y OR N:?Y
NAME:?BRUCE W
DEPARTMENT:?ADMIN
TEL EXT:?413
MORE DATA ANSWER Y OR N:?Y
NAME:?WILLIAMS R
DEPARTMENT:?ADMIN
TEL EXT:?418
MORE DATA ANSWER Y OR N:?N

STOP at line 160
>
```

16.6.7 Problem

The college administrator having created a file of staff records requires a computer print-out of the contents of the file. Design and write a program to print such a report.

16.6.8 Design

```
input name of file
open file for reading (input)
print headings
WHILE not end of file
  read file
  print fields of record
END WHILE
close file
stop
```

16.6.9 Program

```
 5  INPUT "NAME OF FILE:",N$
10  X = OPENIN (N$)
20  PRINT "NAME"; TAB(12): "DEPARTMENT"; TAB(30); "EXTENSION"
30  IF EOF#X <> 0 THEN 70
40    INPUT#X,NAME$,DEPT$,TEL$
50    PRINT NAME$; TAB(12); DEPT$; TAB(30); TEL$
60  GOTO 30
70  CLOSE#X
80  STOP
```

Specimen results

```
>LOAD "OUTPUT"
>RUN
NAME OF FILE:?TELEXT
NAME          DEPARTMENT          EXTENSION
SMITH P       MATHEMATICS         126
JONES F       SCIENCE             894
KING L        CATERING            138
MURPHY T      GEN. STUDIES        216
PALMER S      SCIENCE             514
HARPER W      GEN. STUDIES        216
FOWLER A      MATHEMATICS         126
MORAN T       LANGUAGES           328

STOP at line 80
>


>RUN
NAME OF FILE:?NEWFILE
NAME          DEPARTMENT          EXTENSION
SMITH P       MATHEMATICS         126
JONES F       SCIENCE             894
KING L        CATERING            138
MURPHY T      GEN. STUDIES        216
PALMER S      SCIENCE             514
HARPER W      GEN. STUDIES        216
FOWLER A      MATHEMATICS         126
MORAN T       LANGUAGES           328
CARTER B      ADMIN               416
BRUCE W       ADMIN               413
WILLIAMS R    ADMIN               418

STOP at line 80
>
```

16.7 Sequential files

If the reader looks back at the specimen report produced by the last program it is clear to see that the information is of little use. To obtain the department and extension number of a member of staff would require inspecting each record. However, if the file was sorted into alphabetical order on surname and initial as a primary key the information would be listed in the report in alphabetical sequence and the location of a particular record would be much easier. The file of staff records needs to be sorted to produce a sequential file.

16.7.1 Sorting files

Internal Sorting. If the number of records on a file is small enough to occupy the main memory of a computer then the file can be read and the records stored in a table. The records in the table can then be sorted by key; and when the sort is completed they can be stored as a sorted file. If the number of records is too large to store in an internal table, the file can be divided into several smaller files, each file in turn being sorted internally, and finally the individually sorted files can be *merged* to produce one sorted file.

External Sorting. The following method can be used to sort records of large files, and is known as a *Merge-Sort.* Figure 16.7 illustrates the Merge-Sort using only a small number of record keys.

a. This method is based on the fact that every unsequenced file will have sequences of keys which are in order (even if the sequence is of length one) scattered throughout the file. The sequences or strings of keys are merged to form longer strings of ordered keys. This process continues until eventually only one merged string is output. Note a string here refers to a sequence of keys.

b. The method requires five serial files to be used, one input file and four work files. The four work files should be as long as the input file, in which case there will be no worry about successive strings being too long for a file.

c. The input file is read and written to one of the four work files (A initially) as long as each succeeding key is greater than the previous one. This provides a sequenced string on file A(S1).
This same procedure is used to produce a sorted string on the second file B(S2). The first file (A) is written to again, after the first string, producing two strings (S1) (S3). Alternate files will be used for the output of strings until all the keys of the input file have been written onto these two files.

d. Next, the two files (A and B) are used as input files, and the first string in each (S1 and S2) is **merged** and output to the third file (C). The second two strings (S3 and S4) are merged and output to the fourth file (D). The next two strings (S5 and S6) are output to the third file (C) again; and in a sort involving many more keys the files will be alternated until all the strings have been merged onto files C and D.

e. Files C and D are then used as input files and merged strings are written to files A and B. When all the strings from C and D have been merged the procedures described in d and e are continued alternately until there is only one string remaining, in which case the file has been sorted.

Note, the main memory is only used to compare two keys and store two records belonging to the keys being compared.

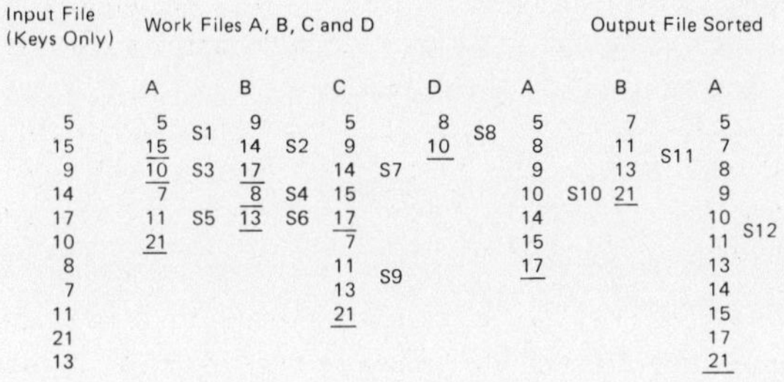

Input File (Keys Only)	Work Files A, B, C and D												Output File Sorted	
	A		B		C		D		A		B		A	
5	5	S1	9		5		8	S8	5		7		5	
15	15		14	S2	9		10		8		11	S11	7	
9	10	S3	17		14	S7			9		13		8	
14	7		8	S4	15				10	S10	21		9	
17	11	S5	13	S6	17				14				10	S12
10	21				7				15				11	
8					11	S9			17				13	
7					13								14	
11					21								15	
21													17	
13													21	

Figure 16.7

16.7.2 Problem

Store the contents of the staff data file used in the last problem (16.6.7) in a two-dimensional table. Each column of the table is used to store a field of a record and each row of the table a record. Modify the Quicksort described in chapter 14 section 14.3.3 to sort the records in the table using the name field as the primary key. When the table is sorted write its contents to a new sequential file. Re-run the program given in 16.6.9 to output a new report giving an alphabetical listing of the names of the staff.

16.7.3 Program

```
10  X = OPENIN ("NEWFILE")
20  Y = OPENOUT ("SORTEXT")
30  DIM FIELD$ (100,3), W$ (3)
40  I = 0
50  IF EOF#X <> 0 THEN 90
60    I = I + 1
70    INPUT#X, FIELD$ (I,1), FIELD$ (I,2), FIELD$ (I, 3)
80  GOTO 50
90  L = 1: R = I
100 PROCSORT (L,R,FIELD$)
110 FOR I = 1 TO R
120   PRINT#Y, FIELD$ (I,1), FIELD$ (I,2), FIELD$ (I, 3)
130 NEXT I
140 CLOSE#X
150 CLOSE#Y
160 STOP
1000 DEF PROCSORT (L,R,FIELD$)
1010 LOCAL I, J, A, W$
1020 I = L: J = R: X$ = FIELD$ (INT (L + R) / 2,1)
1030 IF I > J THEN 1180
1040   IF FIELD$ (I, 1) >= X$ THEN 1070
1050     I = I + 1
1060   GOTO 1040
1070   IF X$ >= FIELD$ (J, 1) THEN 1100
1080     J = J - 1
1090   GOTO 1070
1100   IF I > J THEN 1170
1110     FOR A = 1 TO 3
1120       W$ (A) = FIELD$ (I, A)
1130       FIELD$ (I, A) = FIELD$ (J, A)
1140       FIELD$ (J, A) = W$ (A)
1150     NEXT A
1160   I = I + 1: J = J - 1
1170 GOTO 1030
1180 IF L < J THEN PROCSORT (L, J, FIELD$)
1190 IF I < R THEN PROCSORT (I, R, FIELD$)
1200 ENDPROC
```

Specimen results

```
>LOAD "FSORT"
>RUN

STOP at line 160
>LOAD "OUTPUT"
>RUN
NAME OF FILE:?SORTEXT
NAME          DEPARTMENT         EXTENSION
BRUCE W       ADMIN              413
CARTER B      ADMIN              416
FOWLER A      MATHEMATICS        126
HARPER W      GEN. STUDIES       216
JONES F       SCIENCE            894
KING L        CATERING           138
MORAN T       LANGUAGES          328
MURPHY T      GEN. STUDIES       216
PALMER S      SCIENCE            514
SMITH P       MATHEMATICS        126
WILLIAMS R    ADMIN              418

STOP at line 80
>
```

16.8 Worked Example

16.8.1 Problem

A sequential file is used to store details of a home-video collection. The records on the file are of fixed length and contain the following information.

Type of video (1 character) D – drama
E – educational
N – natural history
S – science fiction

Title of video (maximum of 20 characters)
Duration in minutes (3 digits)

An example of a fixed length record from this file is:

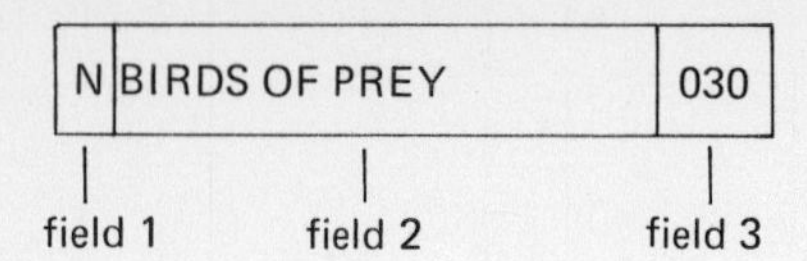

The record can be divided up into fields by using the string functions LEFT$, MID$ and RIGHT$

FIELD1$ = LEFT$ (RECORD$,1)
FIELD2$ = MID$ (RECORD$, 2,20)
FIELD3$ = RIGHT$ (RECORD$, 3)

Design and write a program to read the sequential file and produce the following report.

```
VIDEO COLLECTION

CATEGORY:DRAMA

TITLE                     DURATION (MINS)

GONE WITH THE WIND        060
THE TEMPEST               080
THE KITCHEN SINK          050

TOTAL NUMBER OF TAPES IN CATEGORY IS 3

CATEGORY:EDUCATIONAL
  .
  .
```

16.8.2 Design

For the purpose of this design assume that the sequential file contains a sentinel record to mark the end of the file. This record will only be read and not processed in order to set the end of file function to (−1).

```
open file for reading (input)
print heading
read record
REPEAT
  store type of video
  print category
  CASE type OF
  WHEN D
    print drama
  WHEN E
    print educational
  WHEN N
    print natural history
  OTHERWISE
    print science fiction
  END CASE
  print sub-heading
  initialise total
  REPEAT
    print title and duration
    increase total by 1
    read record
  UNTIL change of category
  print total
UNTIL end of file
close file
stop
```

16.8.3 Program

```
 10 X = OPENIN ("VIDEO")
 20 PRINT "VIDEO COLLECTION":PRINT
 30 INPUT#X,RECORD$
 40 REPEAT
 50    TYPE$ = LEFT$(RECORD$,1)
 60    PRINT "CATEGORY:";
 70    IF TYPE$ <> "D" THEN 100
 80      PRINT "DRAMA"
 90    GOTO 170
100    IF TYPE$ <> "E" THEN 130
110      PRINT "EDUCATIONAL"
120    GOTO 170
130    IF TYPE$ <> "N" THEN 160
140      PRINT "NATURAL HISTORY"
150    GOTO 170
160      PRINT "SCIENCE FICTION"
170   PRINT "TITLE"; TAB(22); "DURATION (MINS)"
180   PRINT
190   VIDTOTAL = 0
200   REPEAT
210    PRINT MID$ (RECORD$,2,20); TAB(22); RIGHT$ (RECORD$, 3)
220    VIDTOTAL = VIDTOTAL + 1
230    INPUT#X, RECORD$
240   UNTIL TYPE$ <> LEFT$ (RECORD$,1)
250   PRINT
260   PRINT "TOTAL NUMBER OF TAPES IN CATEGORY IS ";VIDTOTAL
270   PRINT: PRINT
280 UNTIL EOF#X <> 0
290 CLOSE#X
300 STOP
```

Specimen results

```
>LOAD "VIDREP"
>RUN
VIDEO COLLECTION

CATEGORY:DRAMA
TITLE                 DURATION (MINS)

GONE WITH THE WIND    060
THE TEMPEST           080
THE KITCHEN SINK      050

TOTAL NUMBER OF TAPES IN CATEGORY IS 3


CATEGORY:EDUCATIONAL
TITLE                 DURATION (MINS)

SPLITTING THE ATOM    030
MATHS FOR ADULTS      025
ART IN ATHENS         060
THE TROJAN WARS       055

TOTAL NUMBER OF TAPES IN CATEGORY IS 4


CATEGORY:NATURAL HISTORY
TITLE                 DURATION (MINS)

UNDER THE OCEANS      045
BIRDS OF PREY         030
THE OTTER             060
DOWN ON THE FARM      025
EAGLES IN SCOTLAND    045

TOTAL NUMBER OF TAPES IN CATEGORY IS 5


CATEGORY:SCIENCE FICTION
TITLE                 DURATION (MINS)

THE VAMPIRE BAT       120
RAIDERS OF PLANET X   110
THE INVISIBLE MAN     100

TOTAL NUMBER OF TAPES IN CATEGORY IS 3



STOP at line 300
>

>LOAD "INSP"
>LIST
   10 INPUT "NAME OF FILE",X$
   20 X=OPENIN(X$)
   30 IF EOF£X THEN 60
   40    INPUT£X,N$
   50    PRINT N$
   55 GOTO 30
   60 CLOSE£X
   70 STOP
>RUN
NAME OF FILE?VIDEO
DGONE WITH THE WIND  060
DTHE TEMPEST         080
DTHE KITCHEN SINK    050
ESPLITTING THE ATOM  030
EMATHS FOR ADULTS    025
EART IN ATHENS       060
ETHE TROJAN WARS     055
NUNDER THE OCEANS    045
NBIRDS OF PREY       030
NTHE OTTER           060
NDOWN ON THE FARM    025
NEAGLES IN SCOTLAND  045
STHE VAMPIRE BAT     120
SRAIDERS OF PLANET X 110
STHE INVISIBLE MAN   100
X

STOP at line 70
>
```

16.9 Keywords

File, records, fields, fixed-length, variable-length;
serial file, sequential file;
OPEN for input, output, append;
channel, buffer;
READ (INPUT#), WRITE (PRINT#), end of file (EOF#);
CLOSE
Internal sorting, external sorting – Merge Sort.

16.10 Questions

1 Create a serial file that contains the details of items of stock in a brewery. Records are of variable length and contain the following details.

Stock number
Description
Stock quantity
Unit price.

Assume that the records are not in stock number order when they are input into the computer. Limit the number of test data records to twenty in this question. Design and write a program to input and store the test data on a serial file. Sort the contents of the serial file and store the sorted records on a new sequential file. The records should be sorted on the stock number as primary key using one of the sorting algorithms described in chapter 14.

2 Using the sequential file created in the last question, design and write a program to print the following report.

STOCK REPORT

STOCK NO.	DESCRIPTION	UNIT COST	QUANTITY	STOCK VALUE
91189	BEST BITTER BRLS	25.50	100	2,550.00
92258	MASTER BREW MILD BRLS	20.00	200	4,000.00
9238X	STOCK ALE BRLS	15.00	100	1,500.00
.	.	.	.	.
.	.	.	.	.
			TOTAL VALUE	12,450.00

3 A serial file is to be created containing the details of telephone subscribers. Records are of variable length and contain the following details.

Surname and initials
Address
Telephone number
Previous meter reading
Present meter reading

Invent a minimum of twenty test data records containing the fields described. Design and write a program to input and store the records in a serial file. Sort the records on surname and initials as primary key and store the sorted records on a new sequential file.

---

4 Using the sequential file created in the last question, design and write a program to print the following report.

SUBSCRIBERS

NAME	TELEPHONE NUMBER	UNITS USED
ALLEN P	ABINGDON 41937	2,719
BROWN J	OXFORD 2245643	645
CARTER F	BANBURY 212	1,768
.	.	.
.	.	.

5 A small building society keeps on file details of all its customers holding ordinary share accounts. Records are of fixed length and contain the following fields.

Branch code (5 characters)
Account number (6 characters)
Number of £1 shares 5 digits with no decimal places.

Assume that the file is already sorted on branch code as primary key (in ascending order) and account number as secondary key (in ascending order). Design and write a program to read the file and print the following report. This question assumes that you have already created a test data file in the format given.

THE HAPPY HOMES BUILDING SOCIETY.
DETAILS OF ORDINARY SHARE ACCOUNT CUSTOMERS.
BRANCH CODE:BRAD2

ACCOUNT NUMBER	£1 SHARES
112345	1,000
121456	550
.	.
.	.
TOTAL	£23,456

BRANCH CODE:HAL17

ACCOUNT NUMBER	£1 SHARES
101456	2,578
101577	1,234
.	.
.	.

6 An estate agent wants to keep on file the following details about properties.

Vendor's name (20 characters)
Address of property (40 characters)
Price of property (6 digits with no decimal places)
Type of dwelling (1 character A – detached
B – semi-detached
C – terraced
D – bungalow
E – maisonette or flat)
Number of bedrooms (2 digits)
Tenure (1 character F – freehold
L – leasehold)

The file contains fixed length records already sorted on type of dwelling as primary key (in ascending order) and price of property as secondary key (in decending order). Design and write a program to read the file and print the following report.

This question assumes that you have already created a test data file in the format given.

```
HOLMES & HOLMES ESTATE AGENTS
PROPERTY TYPE:DETACHED
VENDOR      ADDRESS            PRICE     BEDS    TENURE
SMITH C     2 LIBERAL WALK     44,675    4       FREEHOLD
BOWYER F    69 CHURCH VIEW     44,350    4       FREEHOLD
SUMNER S    3 HOPE STREET      43,000    4       FREEHOLD
  .
  .
TOTAL NUMBER OF PROPERTIES: 23

PROPERTY TYPE:SEMI–DETACHED
VENDOR      ADDRESS            PRICE     BEDS    TENURE
JONES M     145 RIVER WALK     36,750    4       FREEHOLD
EVANS M     27 RIDGE BANK      35,500    3       FREEHOLD
  .
  .
```

17 Advanced File Processing

17.1 Introduction

This chapter can broadly be divided into two halves. In the first half merging and the maintenance of sequential files is explained. The second half introduces the reader to relative file organisation and the use of address generation techniques.

17.2 Merging

The technique of merging sequential files involves the interleaving of records from both files to form a new sequential file. In chapter 14 figure 14.4 illustrated a two-way merge between keys stored in two tables. The principle of merging two files is very similar. The keys of the two files to be merged are compared, if the keys are in ascending order, the record with the lower key value is written to the new file. The file that supplied the record is then read again and processing continues until the end of both files is encountered.

17.2.1 Problem

Two sequential files, file A and file B, exist containing the name, department and extension telephone number of staff based on two sites of a college. Design and write a program to merge the two files into one new sequential file, file C.

17.2.2 Design

```
open files A and B for input, file C for output
read file A, read file B
WHILE not end of both files DO
  IF key file A < key file B THEN
    write file A record to file C
    read file A at end set Key A high
  ELSE
    write file B record to file C
    read file B at end set Key B high
  END IF
END WHILE
close files
stop
```

When reading a file the following points should be kept in mind.

In the last chapter it was implied that there are three methods for testing whether the end of a file has been reached. When an end of file function (EOF) is used in a dialect of BASIC it is set when the last record in the file has been read. In the algorithms that follow it is assumed that there exists a sentinel record at the end of each file. The purpose of such record is to mark the end of the file, such a record will not be processed. However, in some dialects of BASIC it is necessary to read **beyond** the last record in order to either set the EOF function or ON EOF trap. In such circumstances the sentinel record should be removed prior to processing the files.

In the algorithm used to merge the two files it is necessary to compare the key of file A with the key of file B, however, when the end of either file is reached it is necessary to set the key field of the file that has ended to a value higher than all the other keys in the two files. The purpose of this practice is to force the remainder of the records in the remaining file to be copied to file C. A high value that would never be used in a record key would be CHR$(127) which represents the DEL character, therefore, in all the examples that require the key to be set at a *high-value* CHR$(127) will be used.

The action of reading a record must be followed by testing for the end of file and if this condition is true, then setting the key field to a *high-value*. Since the action of reading a record from the same file will be coded twice in the algorithm given, it makes sense to use a subroutine for this action. Such a subroutine would appear as:

```
500 REM··SUBROUTINE TO READ A RECORD
510 INPUT#X, NAME$, DEPT$, TEL$
520 IF EOF#X THEN NAME$ = CHR$(127)
530 RETURN
```

or alternatively as a procedure:

```
500 REM··PROCEDURE TO READ A RECORD
510 DEF PROCFLREAD(X)
520 INPUT#X,NAME$, DEPT$, TEL$
530 IF EOF#X THEN NAME$ = CHR$(127)
540 ENDPROC
```

Using your computer

Type, SAVE, LOAD and RUN all the example programs that follow this section, substituting the appropriate file processing statements for your computer where necessary.

Specimen results are listed after each program as before.

17.2.3 Program

In this example the BBC/Electron dialect will be used. Readers with other computers should substitute the appropriate file statements for their machines.

```
 10 A = OPENIN ("FLA"): B = OPENIN ("FLB"): C = OPENOUT ("FLC")
 20 PROCFLREAD (A): PROCFIELDA
 30 PROCFLREAD (B): PROCFIELDB
 40 IF EOF#A AND EOF#B THEN 120
 50   IF NAME A$ >= NAMEB$ THEN 90
 60     PRINT#C, NAMEA$, DEPTA$, TELA$
 70     PROCFLREAD (A): PROCFIELDA
 80   GOTO 110
 90     PRINT#C, NAMEB$, DEPTB$, TELB$
100     PROCFLREAD (B): PROCFIELDB
110 GOTO 40
120 CLOSE#A: CLOSE#B: CLOSE#C
130 STOP
140 DEF PROCFLREAD (X)
150 INPUT#X, NAME$, DEPT$, TEL$
160 IF EOF#X THEN NAME$ = CHR$(127)
170 ENDPROC
180 DEF PROCFIELDA
190 NAMEA$ = NAME$: DEPTA$ = DEPT$: TELA$ = TEL$
200 ENDPROC
210 DEF PROCFIELDB
220 NAMEB$ = NAME$: DEPTB$ = DEPT$: TELB$ = TEL$
230 ENDPROC
```

Specimen results

```
 LOAD "FMERGE"
>RUN

STOP at line 130
>LOAD "INSPECT"
>LIST
   10 INPUT "NAME OF FILE",X$
   20 X=OPENIN(X$)
   30 IF EOF£X THEN 60
   40     INPUT£X,N$,D$,T$
   50     PRINT N$;TAB(20);D$;TAB(35);T$
   55 GOTO 30
   60 CLOSE£X
   70 STOP
>RUN
NAME OF FILE?FLA
APPLETON J N        CPS           446
BAINBRIDGE R        EDUC          210
BEAUMONT J E        CATR          415
BUTLER N J          COMP          422
DAINDRIDGE J        LIB           552
DUNFORD C           ARCI          512
x                   x             x

STOP at line 70
>RUN
NAME OF FILE?FLB
AXFORD B            LPE           397
AYERS C A           COMP          305
BARRETT D A         CONS          579
ELLIOT M J          GPS           447
x                   x             x

STOP at line 70
>RUN
NAME OF FILE?FLC
APPLETON J N        CPS           446
AXFORD B            LPE           397
AYERS C A           COMP          305
BAINBRIDGE R        EDUC          210
BARRETT D A         CONS          579
BEAUMONT J E        CATR          415
BUTLER N J          COMP          422
DAINDRIDGE J        LIB           552
DUNFORD C           ARCI          512
ELLIOT M J          GPS           447

STOP at line 70
>
```

17.3 File Maintenance

Information that is contained in data files is not always static, it can be subject to changes. Such changes to the information will come about through the insertion, amendment and deletion of records. The process of changing the information held on data files is known as updating.

The most common types of files used in an updating situation are the *master* file and the *transaction* file.

Master files are files of a fairly permanent nature. For example a stock file, a personnel file, a customer file. A feature to note is the regular updating of these files to show a current position. For example when orders are processed the amount of stock should be decreased in the stock file. It is seen, therefore, that master records will contain both data of a static nature, for example, a stock number, description of stock and a minimum re-order level, and data which by its nature will change each time a transaction occurs, for example the depletion of a stock level.

A transaction file is made up from the various transactions created from source documents, e.g. sales invoices. In a stock control application the file will contain a list of stock items that have been sold. This file will be used to update the master file. As soon as it has been used for this purpose it is no longer required. It will, therefore, have a very short life because it will be replaced by another transaction file containing the next list of stock items that have been sold.

17.3.1 Problem

In the last problem file C can be regarded as a master file, created from merging the two files A and B together. This master file will eventually require updating. New staff may enter the college (insertions), staff may change either their department, telephone extension number or both (amendments), and staff may leave the college (deletions).

The transaction file could have the following specimen records.

File T:			
	AXFORD B		
	BAILEY S.K.	SOC	832
	BESWICK K.P.	MEDI	654
	BUTLER N.J.	MATH	342
	DUNFORD C		
	ELLIOT M.J.	COMP	422
	HARRIS P.T.	CATR	416

From this file new members of staff to be inserted into the master file are BAILEY S.K, BESWICK K.P and HARRIS P.T. Those members of staff who already exist on the master file yet require to have their records amended because they have changed departments are BUTLER N.J and ELLIOT M.J. The records of AXFORD B and DUNFORD C are to be deleted since they have left the college.

To distinguish between those records that are to be deleted and those that are to be amended, records that contain only the key field (name) will be deleted in this example.

If the transaction file, file T, is processed against the master file, file C from the previous example, then the following updated master file, file U, will be the outcome.

File U:	APPLETON J.N	CPS	446
	AYERS C.A	COMP	305
	BAILEY S.K	SOC	832
	BAINBRIDGE R	EDUC	210
	BARRETT D.A	CONS	579
	BEAUMONT J.E	CATR	415
	BESWICK K.P	MEDI	654
	BUTLER N.J	MATH	342
	DAINBRIDGE J	LIB	552
	ELLIOT M.J.	COMP	422
	HARRIS P.T	CATR	416

Design and write a program to process the transaction file, file T, against the master file, file C, and create an updated master file, file U.

17.3.2 Design

```
open transaction and master files for input
open updated master file for output
read transaction file
read master file
WHILE not end of both files DO
  IF key transaction < key master THEN
    write transaction record to updated file
    read transaction file
  ELSE
    IF key transaction = key master THEN
      IF department and telenumber fields not blank THEN
        write transaction record to updated file
      END IF
      read transaction file
      read master file
    ELSE
      write master record to updated file
      read master file
    END IF
  END IF
END WHILE
close files
stop
```

17.3.3 Program

```
 10 T = OPENIN ("FLT"): C = OPENIN ("FLC")
 20 U = OPENOUT ("FLU")
 30 PROCFLREAD (T): PROCFIELDT
 40 PROCFLREAD (C): PROCFIELDC
 50 IF EOF#T AND EOF#C THEN 190
 60   IF NAMET$ >= NAMEC$ THEN 100
 70     PRINT#U, NAMET$, DEPTT$, TELT$
 80     PROCFLREAD (T): PROCFIELDT
 90   GOTO 180
100     IF NAMET$ <> NAMEC$ THEN 160
110       IF DEPTT$ = "    " AND TELT$ = "    " THEN 130
120         PRINT#U, NAMET$, DEPTT$, TELT$
130         PROCFLREAD (T): PROCFIELDT
140         PROCFLREAD (C): PROCFIELDC
150       GOTO 180
160         PRINT#U, NAMEC$, DEPTC$, TELC$
170         PROCFLREAD (C): PROCFIELDC
180 GOTO 50
190 CLOSE#T: CLOSE#C: CLOSE#U
200 STOP
210 DEF PROCFLREAD (X)
220 INPUT#X, NAME$, DEPT$, TEL$
230 IF EOF#X THEN NAME$ = CHR$ (127)
240 ENDPROC
250 DEF PROCFIELDT
260 NAMET$ = NAME$: DEPTT$ = DEPT$: TELT$ = TEL$
270 ENDPROC
280 DEF PROCFIELDC
290 NAMEC$ = NAME$: DEPTC$ = DEPT$: TELC$ = TEL$
300 ENDPROC
```

Specimen results

```
>LOAD "MAINT"
>RUN

STOP at line 200
>LOAD "INSPECT"
>RUN
NAME OF FILE?FLT
AXFORD B
BAILEY S K              SOC              832
BESWICK K P             MEDI             654
BUTLER N J              MATH             342
DUNFORD C
ELLIOT M J              COMP             422
HARRIS P T              CATR             416
X                       X                X

STOP at line 70
>RUN
NAME OF FILE?FLC
APPLETON J N            CPS              446
AXFORD B                LPE              397
AYERS C A               COMP             305
BAINBRIDGE R            EDUC             210
BARRETT D A             CONS             579
BEAUMONT J E            CATR             415
BUTLER N J              COMP             422
DAINDRIDGE J            LIB              552
DUNFORD C               ARCI             512
ELLIOT M J              GPS              447
X                       X                X
STOP at line 70
>RUN
NAME OF FILE?FLU
APPLETON J N            CPS              446
AYERS C A               COMP             305
BAILEY S K              SOC              832
BAINBRIDGE R            EDUC             210
BARRETT D A             CONS             579
BEAUMONT J E            CATR             415
BESWICK K P             MEDI             654
BUTLER N J              MATH             342
DAINDRIDGE J            LIB              552
ELLIOT M J              COMP             422
HARRIS P T              CATR             416

STOP at line 70
>
```

17.3.4 Problem

The video-tape collection file described in the last chapter, section 16.8.1 will periodically require maintaining as the collector will want to buy or record new tapes (insertion), record over existing tapes with new material (amendment), sell or have accidently damaged a tape (deletion). In this example the records on the video-tape file are reorganised by including an extra field for the tape number. The format of a fixed length record on the master file is:

tape number – 3 digits (key)
category – 1 character, D-drama, E-educational, N-natural history, S-science fiction.
title – 20 characters
duration – 3 digits

The master file is sorted on tape number as primary key in ascending order.

Over the period of a month all changes to the collection are stored on a transaction file, the format of which is:

tape number – 3 digits (key)
maintenance code – 1 digit, 1-amend, 2-delete, 3-insert.
remaining fields
- category – 1 character
- title – 20 characters
- duration – 3 digits

The remaining fields contain spaces if the maintenance code is 2 to delete a record.

In the solution to this problem it will be necessary to check that a record can only be amended or deleted if it is present on the master file. Similarly a record can only be inserted if it is not already present on the master file. Any deviation from these conditions must be reported to the user as an error.

Design and write a program to process the transaction file TRANS, against the master file MAST to create a new sequential file called UPDATE. Display on the screen any errors that occur when processing the two files. Assume that both files have already had their respective fields validated.

17.3.5 Design

```
open transaction and master files for input
open updated master file for output
read transaction file
read master file
WHILE not end of both files DO
 IF key transaction < key master AND code = 3 THEN
  write transaction record to updated file
  read transaction file
 ELSE
  IF key transaction = key master AND code <> 3 THEN
   IF code = 1 THEN
    write transaction record to updated file
   END IF
   read transaction file
   read master file
  ELSE
   IF transaction key > master key THEN
    write master record to updated file
    read master file
   ELSE
    print error – transaction record
   END IF
  END IF
 END IF
END WHILE
close files
stop
```

17.3.6 Program

```
 10 T = OPENIN ("TRANS"): M = OPENIN ("MAST")
 20 U = OPENOUT ("UPDATE")
 30 GOSUB 500: GOSUB 600
 40 IF EOF#T AND EOF#M THEN 190
 50   IF KEYT$ >= KEYM$ OR CODE$ <> "3" THEN 90
 60     PRINT#U, RECT$
 70     GOSUB 500
 80   GOTO 180
 90     IF KEYT$ <> KEYM$ OR CODE$ = "3" THEN 130
100       IF CODE$ = "1" THEN PRINT#U, RECT$
110       GOSUB 500: GOSUB 600
120     GOTO 180
130       IF KEYT$ < = KEYM$ THEN 170
140         PRINT#U, RECORDM$
150         GOSUB 600
160       GOTO 180
170         PRINT "ERROR TRANSACTION RECORD "; RECORDT$
180 GOTO 40
190 CLOSE#T: CLOSE#M: CLOSE#U
200 STOP

500 REM . . SUBROUTINE TO READ TRANSACTION FILE
510 INPUT#T, RECORDT$
520 KEYT$ = LEFT$ (RECORDT$,3)
530 CODE$ = MID$ (RECORDT$,4,1)
540 RECT$ = KEYT$ + RIGHT$ (RECORDT$,23)
550 IF EOF#T THEN KEYT$ = CHR$(127)
560 RETURN

600 REM . . SUBROUTINE TO READ MASTER FILE
610 INPUT#M, RECORDM$
620 KEYM$ = LEFT$ (RECORDM$,3)
630 IF EOF#M THEN KEYM$ = CHR$(127)
640 RETURN
```

Specimen results

```
>LOAD "SMAINT"
>RUN

STOP at line 200
>LOAD "INSP"
>RUN
NAME OF FILE?TRANS
0031NSPIDERS                 090
0052
0063DTHE TEMPEST             100
0093DANTHONY & CLEOPATRA     150
X

STOP at line 70
>RUN
NAME OF FILE?MAST
001SVOYAGE INTO SPACE     100
002NTHE BAT               030
003DPRIDE AND PREJUDICE   090
004SSPACESHIP MARS        120
005EHISTORY OF MAN        240
007EAFRICA 1920-1969      135
008STHE ROBOT             105
010NBIRD OF PREY          045
X

STOP at line 70
>RUN
NAME OF FILE?UPDATE
001SVOYAGE INTO SPACE     100
002NTHE BAT               030
003NSPIDERS               090
004SSPACESHIP MARS        120
006DTHE TEMPEST           100
007EAFRICA 1920-1969      135
008STHE ROBOT             105
009DANTHONY & CLEOPATRA   150
010NBIRD OF PREY          045

STOP at line 70
>
```

17.4 Random File Processing

With sequential file processing a key to a record does **not** give the position of that record in relation to the other records.

It is impossible given a key to access a record directly, without having first, to inspect each key of each record before the record that is required can be found.

With random files the key to each record is translated by the computer system into a position on the disc surface where the record is stored. Thus knowing the key to a record means that access to that record is direct without having to search through the keys of other records on the file.

The processing activities (insertion, deletion and amendment) that were described for sequential files also apply to random files. However, it is common practice to overwrite records on a master file and not produce a separate master file as was indicated in sequential file processing. However, it is essential that a copy of the master file is made before overwriting records on the master file. If the master file became corrupted during a computer run it would then be possible to restore the master file to its original state from the copy that had been taken prior to processing the master file.

The only new activity associated with random file processing is to **position** the record pointer against the record to be processed having first specified the key to the record. Many dialects of BASIC that use a disc operating system will implement **Relative** files.

Files organised in this manner are stored on magnetic disc and will allow either sequential or random access to records. A relative record key is a positive numeric integer that represents the relative position of a logical record with respect to the beginning of a file. For example a record with a key value of 10 represents the record occupying the tenth logical record area in the file, irrespective of whether the relative record areas 1 through to 9 have been filled. Potentially, Relative files are efficient because records are in sequence, access is fast, and there are no problems with overflow. However, with record deletions or the fact that the keys are numerically spaced far apart, gaps of wasted space can soon occur in such a file organisation.

17.5 Dialect Differences

Unlike serial/sequential file processing statements, those BASIC statements used for relative file processing vary considerably between dialects. For this reason the program statements, together with supporting examples, will be considered separately for each dialect in this section.

17.5.1 Microsoft

The OPEN statement allocates a buffer for input/output to the file and determines the mode of access that will be used with the buffer. The format of the OPEN statement is:

OPEN filename AS# channel [LEN = record length]

In omitting the mode OUTPUT, INPUT or APPEND the mode is assumed to be RANDOM access for input and output.

Example. OPEN "STOCKFL" AS#1 LEN = 24

Reading and writing to a relative file both involve the use of a relative record key to position a record pointer prior to either operation. A file is read by using:

GET#channel, relative key

and written to by:

PUT#channel, relative key

Example.
```
GET#1,N   GET#2,3
PUT#1,N   PUT#2,3
```

Notice that in each of these statements the format of a record in the file is not given. A separate FIELD statement is used for this purpose. The format of this statement being:

FIELD#channel, width AS dataname–1
[,width AS dataname–2] . . . . .

where width is the size of a record field in bytes.

Example. FIELD#2, 20 AS STOCK$, 4 AS PRICE$

indicates that the format of a record in the buffer has two fields STOCK$ and PRICE$, the width of each field being 20 and 4 bytes respectively.

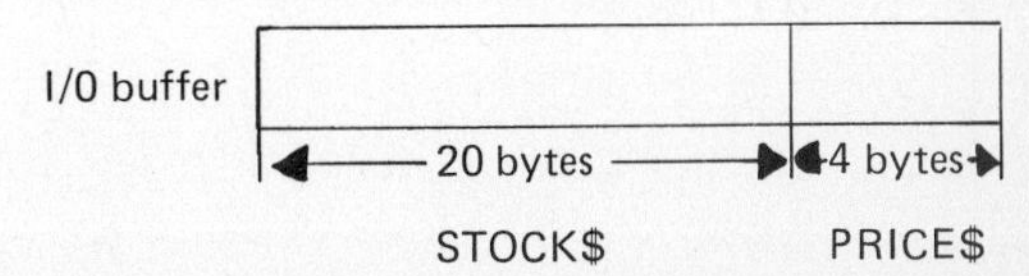

Data can be moved into these fields and justified either left or right by using the statements LSET and RSET respectively. The format of such statements is:

{ LSET / RSET } dataname–1 = dataname–2

Both statements move data into the buffer in preparation for writing. If the data is too large to fit into the buffer it is truncated to the right. LSET left justifies a datum and space fills to the right if necessary. RSET right justifies a datum and space fills to the left if necessary.

Example. If S$ = "CHAIN" and P$ = "645" then LSET STOCK$ = S$ and RSET PRICE$ = P$ would have the following effect on the contents of the buffer.

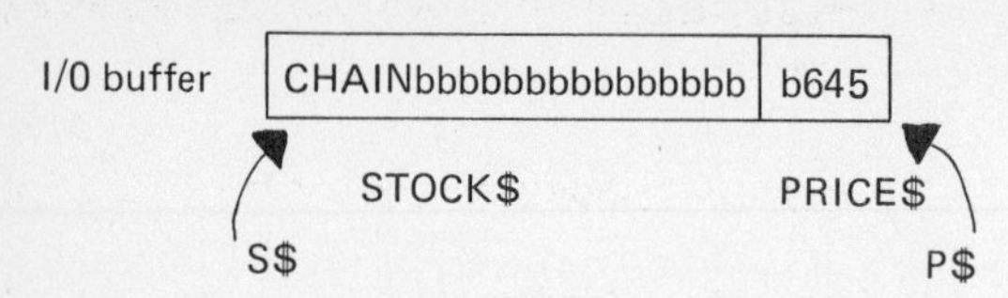

Relative files are closed by using CLOSE#channel e.g CLOSE#2

Example. The following programs illustrate how to create and read a relative file containing the stock name and price of bicycle components. The relative key is the stock number.

stock number (key)	stock name	price (pence)
1	CHAIN	645
2	HANDLEBARS	750
3	FRAME	1930
4	SADDLE	500
•		
•		

```
 10  REM · · PROGRAM TO CREATE STOCK FILE
 20  OPEN "STOCKFL" AS#1  LEN = 24
 30  FIELD#1, 20 AS STOCK$, 4 AS PRICE$
 40  INPUT "STOCK NUMBER", STOCKNUMB%
 50  WHILE STOCKNUMB% > 0
 60    INPUT "STOCK NAME", S$
 70    INPUT "PRICE", P$
 80    LSET STOCK$ = S$
 90    RSET PRICE$ = P$
100    PUT#1, STOCKNUMB%
110    INPUT "STOCK NUMBER", STOCKNUMB%
120  WEND
130  CLOSE#1
140  STOP
```

```
 10  REM · · PROGRAM TO READ STOCK FILE
 20  OPEN "STOCKFL" AS#1  LEN = 24
 30  FIELD#1, 20 AS STOCK$, 4 AS PRICE$
 40  INPUT "STOCK NUMBER", STOCKNUMB%
 50  WHILE STOCKNUMB% > 0
 60    GET#1, STOCKNUMB%
 70    PRINT STOCK$, PRICE$
 80    INPUT "STOCK NUMBER", STOCKNUMB%
 90  WEND
100  CLOSE#1
110  STOP
```

17.5.2 BBC/Electron

The only new statement in this dialect to allow random access to a file is PTR#X. The statement points to the next record in a file to be read or position of a record to be written. The programmer must keep an account of the size of each record so that the pointer may be positioned accurately at the beginning of a record area. Stored record sizes are calculated on the following basis.

Integer	5 bytes
Real	6 bytes
String	number of characters in string + 2 bytes

In the last problem each stock record would require 22 bytes (stock name) + 5 bytes (price if treated as an integer and not a string). Total record size 27 bytes. This can be illustrated as a serial collection of data.

0	1	2	3	4
	CHAIN 645	HANDLEBARS 750	FRAME 1930	
	← 27 →	← 27 →	← 27 →	

The file can be created using the following program.

```
10  X = OPENOUT ("STOCKFL")
20  INPUT "KEY", K
30  IF K < 1 THEN CLOSE#X:STOP
40    INPUT "STOCK NAME",STOCK$
50    INPUT "PRICE",PRICE
60    PTR#X = 27*K
70    PRINT#X,STOCK$,PRICE
80    INPUT "KEY",K
90  GOTO 30
```

The file can be read by using the following program.

```
10  X = OPENIN ("STOCKFL")
20  INPUT "KEY",K
30  IF K < 1 THEN CLOSE#X:STOP
40    PTR#X - 27*K
50    INPUT#X,STOCK$,PRICE
60    PRINT STOCK$,PRICE
70    INPUT "KEY",K
80  GOTO 30
```

17.6 Address Generation (Hashing)

17.6.1 Self-Addressing

In the last example about a stock file for recording information on bicycle parts each part had a stock number 1,2,3,4 . . . . . . and this stock number was a pointer to the relative position of a stock record. If the number of different stock items was, say, 100 then a file of 100 records would be needed to store the data. All the keys and hence record positions in the file are used, therefore, as well as being a simple method of access the method is also efficient in storage space.

Such an example does not illustrate the nature of a real-life problem! What if the stock file held information on motor-car spares and each stock number was a 7 digit number (excluding the check-digit). Would a relative file of 10 million record areas be necessary to store the information? If the key range was 0000001 to 9999999 in an unbroken sequence then, yes, 10 million records would be necessary. However, in practice 10 million different keys do not exist, and the stock numbers do not form a continuous range of key values. The key values form a sparse set of the possible key values, therefore, an addressing function (hashing function) must be chosen to map the key values onto some dense set of values 1,2,3,4 . . . . . N where the total number of record areas N in the file will be very much less than the theoretical number of keys, but greater than the number of key values actually allocated. The following examples illustrate four other methods (there are more but not included here) of generating addresses for a 7 digit key where only 1000 record areas are available.

17.6.2 Prime Division

The key value is divided by the nearest prime number below the number of record areas in the file and the remainder after this division plus 1 gives the relative record number.

Example.
key 2028277 → 2028277mod997 + 1 → relative key 380

17.6.3 Mid-square

The key value is squared and the middle digits (which will be the most random) are used to obtain the relative record number.

Example.
key 2028277 → 41139(075)88729 → 075 + 1 relative key 76

17.6.4 Folding algorithm

The key value is split into a number of parts which are added together and the result mod 1000 (+1) is taken as the relative record number.

Example.
2028277 → (202+282+277)mod1000 + 1 → relative key 762

17.6.5 Radix transformation

The key value is considered to be expressed in a radix (base) greater than 10 (11) and then converted to radix 10.

Example.
2028277_{11} → 3583378_{10} mod 1000 + 1 → relative key 379

If keys are non-numeric they must first be transformed to corresponding numeric values before these algorithms can be applied; A = 1, B = 2, C = 3 . . . . Remember, if an algorithm other than self indexing is used it is no longer possible to access the records in key value sequence.

17.6.6 Collisions

Before leaving the topic of address generation it is worth mentioning that the last four algorithms do not guarantee that each key will map onto a unique relative key value. A *collision* occurs when keys map onto the same relative address. A good address generation function is one which produces a low number of collisions.

There are two methods of finding an alternative address for keys that collide. The first is to re-hash the key and generate another address. The second is to allow more than one record to be stored in one record area and when this becomes full provide an overflow area for storing records with the same relative address.

These methods are mentioned to inform the reader that address generation can be a complex issue. This section serves as an introduction to the topic only, and further work on this subject is beyond the scope of this book.

17.7 Worked Example
17.7.1 Problem

An international computer company has agencies throughout the world. A random access computer file is used to store the addresses of the agencies. Access to an address is through the name of a country as key. Design and write a program to store the addresses using hashed key values, and retrieve the addresses on demand by using the country as the key.

17.7.2 Design

In the design it is assumed that the keys when hashed do not collide.

```
open file for output
FOR counter = 1 TO number of agencies
  read name of country and address of agency
  calculate hash address using country as key
  position pointer at hash address
  write record
NEXT counter
close file

open file for input
input name of country
WHILE country not = "STOP" DO
  calculate hash address using country as key
  position pointer at hash address
  read file
  print address of agency
  input name of country
ENDWHILE
close file
stop
```

17.7.3 Program

```
 10 X = OPENOUT ("AGENCY")
 20 FOR C = 1 TO 7
 30   READ COUNTRY$, ADDRESS$
 40   DATA "JAPAN"    , "CPO 896 TOKYO 200-93                              "
 50   DATA "BELGIUM"  , "WEIVELDLAAN 6-8, 1940 ZAVENTEM ZUID-6             "
 60   DATA "GERMANY"  , "3000 hamburg 82 (LOKSTEDT), GRANDWEG 64           "
 70   DATA "USA"      , "147 INVERNESS DRIVE EAST, ENGLEWOOD, COLARADO 8112"
 80   DATA "CANADA"   , "1940 WEST 3RD AVE, VANCOUVER, B.C. V6j 2K3        "
 90   DATA "UK"       , "NORTH AVE, HARROW, MIDDLESEX HA2 0LT              "
100   DATA "BRASIL"   , "RUA ESTADOS UNIDOS, 1530 SAO PAULO-SP             "
110   PTR#X = FNHASH (COUNTRY$)*52
120   PRINT#X,ADDRESS$
130 NEXT C
140 CLOSE#X
150 X = OPENIN ("AGENCY")
160 INPUT "NAME OF COUNTRY ",COUNTRY$
170 IF COUNTRY$ = "STOP" THEN CLOSE#X:STOP
180   PTR#X = FNHASH(COUNTRY$)*52
190   INPUT#X,ADDRESS$
200   PRINT "ADDRESS: ",ADDRESS$
210   INPUT "NAME OF COUNTRY ",COUNTRY$
220 GOTO 170

500 DEF FNHASH(X$)
510 LOCAL S, I
520 FOR I = 1 TO LEN(X$)
530   S = S + (ASC(MID$(X$,I,1)) – 64)
540 NEXT I
550 = S MOD 13
```

Specimen results

```
>LOAD "HASH"
>RUN

NAME OF COUNTRY ?CANADA
ADDRESS   1940 WEST 3RD AVE, VANCOUVER, B.C. V6J 2K3
NAME OF COUNTRY ?JAPAN
ADDRESS   CPO 896 TOKYO 200-93
NAME OF COUNTRY ?UK
ADDRESS   NORTH AVE, HARROW, MIDDLESEX HA2 0LT
NAME OF COUNTRY ?GERMANY
ADDRESS   3000 HAMBURG 82(LOKSTEDT),GRANDWEG 64
NAME OF COUNTRY ?BELGIUM
ADDRESS   WEIVELDLAAN 6-8, 1940 ZAVENTEM ZUID-6
NAME OF COUNTRY ?USA
ADDRESS   147 INVERNESS DRIVE EAST, ENGLEWOOD, COLARADO 8112
NAME OF COUNTRY ?STOP

STOP at line 170
>
```

17.8 Keywords

Merge, transaction, master, update, maintenance;
random access, relative files;
hashing, self-addressing, prime division, mid-square, folding, radix;
collisions, re-hashing, overflow.

17.9 Questions

1 Three files contain lists of English words and their meanings in alphabetical sequence. Each word (key) and its meaning occupies one fixed length record. Design and write a program to merge the three files into one file and output the contents of the new file as a dictionary. Assume the format of a record is:

word (key) 10 characters.
meaning 70 characters.

2 In a simplified weekly wage system, factory employees are allocated one fixed length record per employee on a wages master file. The format of a record on this file is:

Employee number – 10 characters.
Hourly rate of pay – 4 digits inc 2 dec.pl.
Fixed allowances against pay – 5 digits inc 2 dec.pl.
Total gross income to date – 7 digits inc 2 dec.pl.
Total tax paid to date – 7 digits inc 2 dec.pl.
Total pension contribution to date – 6 digits inc 2 dec.pl.
Total National Insurance contributions to date – 6 digits inc 2 dec.pl.

For every employee the pension contribution is 6% of the gross income, the National Insurance is £10.50 and income tax is levied at 30% of taxable income.

Taxable income is calculated as the difference between gross income and pension contributions and fixed allowances.

A transaction file contains fixed length records with the format:

Employee number – 10 characters
Hours worked in week (including overtime) – 3 digits.

Design and write a program to process the transaction file against the employee master file and produce both an updated master file and pay-slips for each employee on the transaction file.

Assume that both files are sequential and ordered on employee number. The number of employees on the transaction file is less than those on the master file and only amendments to the master file are required (no deletions or insertions).

The format of a pay-slip is:

```
Employee number:X342567SMI
Gross wage: £307.69
                          Pension:  £18.46
                          NatIns:   £10.50
                          Tax:      £77.77
Nett wage:£200.96
```

3 A small college keeps on file a description of the use of all its rooms. The format of a record on the master room file is:–

room number (key)	2 digits
description of use	20 alphanumeric characters.

The records on the master room file are stored in ascending key order.

Over the period of a year the use each room is put to may change. The records on the master room file will, therefore, have to be updated. Such changes that exist will be:–

change of use of room (amendment to the description)
room demolished (deletion)
new room built (insertion)

These changes are described in a transaction file the format of which is:–

room number (key)	2 digits	
transaction code	1 digit	1 amend 2 delete 3 insert
description of use	20 alphanumeric characters	

(this field is absent when a record on the master file is to be deleted).

The records on the transaction file are stored in ascending key order, and each record has a unique key.

Design and write a program to update the master file from the transaction file. Incorporate into your design error conditions that might exist between the keys on the two files.

4 Write subroutines for each of the hashing algorithms described in 17.6. Invent 20 alphanumeric keys and test the algorithms changing the number of relative record areas available from 30 to 60. Note the number of collisions that each algorithm produces and see how the collisions diminish as the number of record areas available increase.

5 A doctor requires a computerised appointments system for use in his surgery. He holds a two hour surgery in the morning (10.00 – 12.00) and a two hour surgery in the evening (17.00 – 19.00) each day from Monday to Friday. Write a program to allow his patients to make and cancel appointments throughout the week. The appointments file is a relative file having a key coded as a 3 digit integer. The coding of this key is as follows:

First digit (0–9) day and session e.g. 0–Monday A.M. 1–Monday P.M. 2–Tuesday A.M. 3–Tuesday P.M. etc.

Next two digits is the time of the appointment e.g. 01 – first time slot 02 – second time slot 03 – third time slot etc. Assume every appointment is allocated a 10 minute time slot.

An appointment record consists of the name (25 characters) and address (30 characters) of the patient.

6 Using the file created in the last question write a program to output a list of the vacant appointment slots for each day and list of the names and addresses of the patients the doctor can expect to see.

18 Process Control

18.1 Introduction

Within the context of this book it would appear that data is input to a program through either a keyboard or files, processed by the C.P.U. and the results displayed on a screen or printer. The use of computers in this manner is only half the story. Computers are commonly used for controlling and monitoring devices, for example traffic lights, washing machines, robots, missiles, etc. The list of applications is, in reality, very extensive. These applications have several features in common.

The input of data is through *sensors* and not through a keyboard or files. For example, in the control of traffic lights the input of data is via traffic sensors in the road or pedestrian controlled buttons.

The output of results or information is used to *control* a device within its environment and not to produce printed output. In the traffic light application this involves lighting the appropriate red, amber and green lights to control the flow of traffic and pedestrians.

A device must respond fast enough in order to be able to control events within its environment. A device will operate in a *real-time* mode. With traffic lights the time taken to monitor the volume of traffic and control the traffic lights must be compatible with the changing traffic patterns throughout a day.

The purpose of this chapter is to demonstrate how the BASIC language can be used to control devices. Two applications will be considered. The first uses a *simulation* board to control traffic lights and a pedestrian crossing at a cross-roads. The second steers a small vehicle, connected via an umbilical cable to a computer, around a pre-defined path.

It must be emphasised that BASIC is **not** a suitable language for *real-time* applications, since it is often an interpreted language and is, therefore, slow in responding to many real-time environments. The language in its present state also lacks many of the features required in *real-time* programming. However, there are developments to the language in the form of *Industrial Real-time BASIC* that will help overcome many of its present deficiencies.

18.2 Interface

An interface provides a means of connecting peripheral devices to the CPU. Visual display units, floppy disc units and printers all require interfaces to connect them to a computer. In using a computer to control devices it is necessary to connect a device to a computer via an interface. Interfaces should allow a two-way communication between a device and a computer.

The input and output of data and information to and from the interface is normally via input and output *ports* respectively.

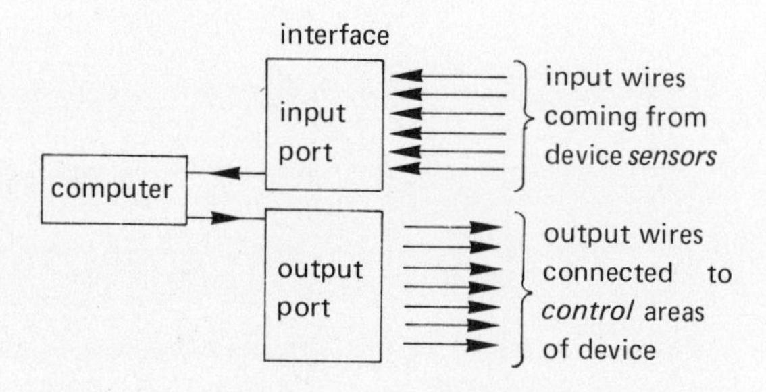

The wires connecting an interface with a device operate at low voltages. A voltage greater than 2.0 volts can represent the binary digit (1); a voltage less than 0.8 volts can represent the binary digit (0). Similar voltage levels will exist between the interface and computer. By inspecting the binary pattern stored in the input port, it is possible to detect which sensors have be activated. This assumes that each sensor is attached to individual wires connected to the input port. If the contents of the output port is set to a particular binary pattern, each bit can be used to control the appropriate part of the device. The BASIC language has the facility to inspect and change the contents of input and output ports respectively, using PEEK and POKE.

18.3 Peek and Poke

The function PEEK(X), where X represents the address of a memory location, enables the contents of X to be read and stored in a user defined variable name.

For example, if location X contained the bit pattern 00010110, Y = PEEK(X) would store the value (22) in location Y.

Note. In translating a binary digit (bit) pattern into a decimal value, each bit represents a power of 2.

2^7 2^6 2^5 2^4 2^3 2^2 2^1 2^0

0 0 0 1 0 1 1 0 $= (1 \times 2^4) + (1 \times 2^2) + (1 \times 2^1) = 22$

The statement POKE X,Y, where X represents the address of a memory location, and Y the data to be written to that location, enables the contents of location X to be changed to the value Y. For example, if location X contained the bit pattern 01100110, and Y contained the decimal value 12, POKE X,Y would change the bit pattern at X to 00001100.

18.4 Dialect Differences

Both dialects considered in this book all support the concept of PEEK and POKE. The format of the two statements is identical to that described for microsoft, however, BBC/Electron use a different symbolism. In this dialect Y = ?X is the same as Y = PEEK(X) and ?X = Y is the same as POKE X,Y.

Warning. BASIC does not do any checking on addresses. DO NOT go POKEing around memory at random, since you could, very easily, corrupt your program and data.

18.5 Traffic Light Control
18.5.1 Configuration

Figure 18.1 shows a *traffic signal control board* available from Feedback Instruments Limited, Crowborough, Sussex. This board can be connected to a wide range of microcomputers using the appropriate interface. The board requires a separate 5V power supply.

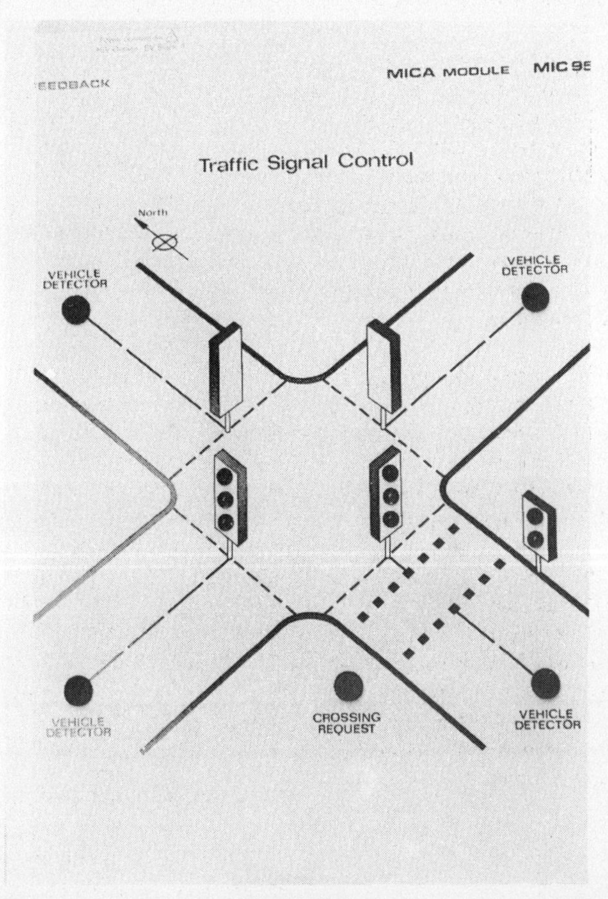

Figure 18.1

18.5.2 Interface

The connections between the interface and traffic signal control board are as follows.

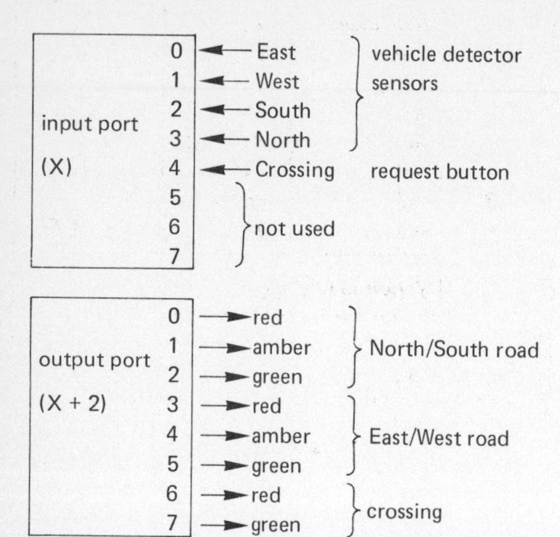

The numbers 0-7 indicate the appropriate bit position. For example, the pedestrian crossing request button is wired to bit 4 on the input port, and the pedestrian crossing lights are wired to bit 6 (red) and bit 7 (green) on the output port.

The input and output ports are labelled as address X and address X + 2 respectively. The value of X will vary between microcomputers. Before each port can be used it must be initialised by including the following segment of code at the beginning of the control program.

```
Input Port.     POKE X + 1,0
                POKE X,0
                POKE X + 1,4

Output Port.    POKE X + 3,0
                POKE X + 2,255
                POKE X + 3,4
```

18.5.3 Control

To set each of the lights to ON the appropriate bit must be set to (1) on the output port. For example, if all the lights are to be set to red the output port must contain the following information.

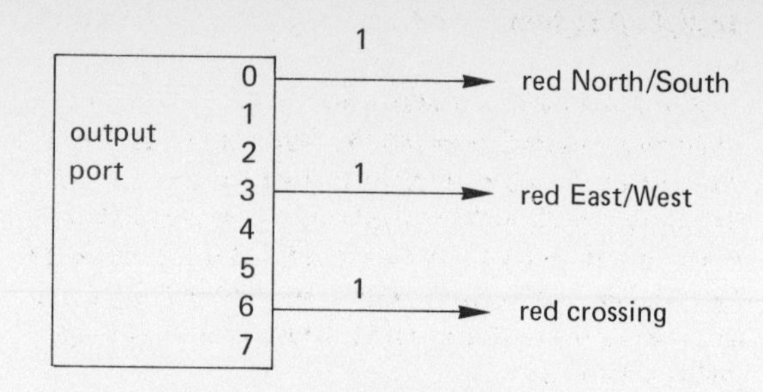

Lines 1, 2, 4, 5 and 7 are all set to (0).

The bit pattern is 01001001 which equates to decimal value 73. Therefore, POKE X + 2,73 would be used to set all the lights to red.

The input port operates in a *reverse* manner to the output port. When a sensor or pedestrian crossing request button is pressed the appropriate wire is reset to (0). All input wires remain at (1) unless activiated. To detect a request to use the crossing the following configuration would be true.

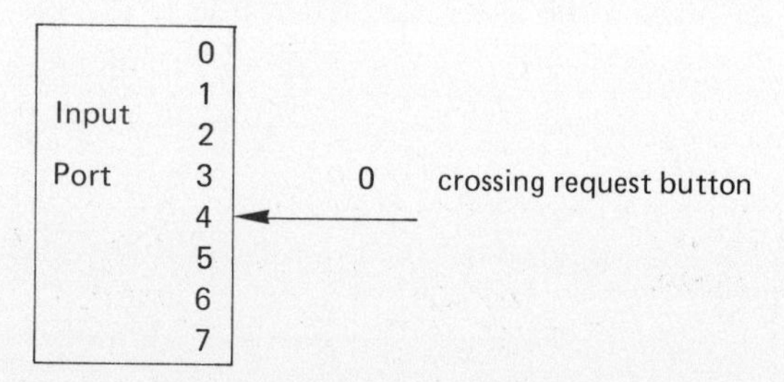

Only wire 4 is reset to (0), the remaining wires are set at (1). The bit pattern is 11101111 = 239. If PEEK(X) = 239 then the pedestrian crossing request button was pressed. Upon releasing the button the wire will be set to (1) by the board. This fact reveals that continous sampling of the input port is necessary if requests are not to be lost.

It may be more convenient to think of the request bit as being set to (1) and not (0) when the button is pressed, although in reality this is not true. In which case the complement of the original bit pattern 11101111 becomes 00010000 and the code can be modified to, if 255 − PEEK(X) = 16 then the pedestrian crossing request button was pressed.

18.5.4 Problem

Write a program to allow the lights to cycle over a fixed time interval between the North/South and East/West roads. If the pedestrian request button is pressed the current cycle will terminate naturally, the pedestrian crossing light will go to green for a fixed time, then back to red, and the traffic lights will continue to cycle. Otherwise, without a crossing request, the traffic lights will cycle normally.

Table 18.1 shows the sequence of lights for both roads and the pedestrian crossing. The time interval indicates the proportion of time the lights are set to a particular colour.

Table 18.2 shows the decimal values required to change the colour of the lights.

Sequence number	North/South	East/West	Time interval (secs)
1	red	red	0.5
2	red/amber	red	1
3	green	red	10
4	amber	red	1
5	red	red	1
6	red	red/amber	1
7	red	green	10
8	red	amber	1
9	red	red	0.5
	Pedestrian Crossing		
10	green		5
11	red		0

Table 18.1

Sequence number	Output Port (X + 2)								Decimal Value Y
	Crossing		East/West			North/South			
	7	6	5	4	3	2	1	0	
	green	red	green	amber	red	green	amber	red	
1	0	1	0	0	1	0	0	1	73
2	0	1	0	0	1	0	1	1	75
3	0	1	0	0	1	1	0	0	76
4	0	1	0	0	1	0	1	0	74
5	0	1	0	0	1	0	0	1	73
6	0	1	0	1	1	0	0	1	89
7	0	1	1	0	0	0	0	1	97
8	0	1	0	1	0	0	0	1	81
9	0	1	0	0	1	0	0	1	73
10	1	0	0	0	1	0	0	1	137
11	0	1	0	0	1	0	0	1	73

Table 18.2

18.5.5 Design

```
input address of port
input delay factor
read and store time intervals
read and store values to control lights
initialise ports
initialise pedestrian request flag to zero
REPEAT
  FOR sequence number = 1 TO 9
    change lights according to sequence number
    call PROC delay
  NEXT sequence number
  IF request flag set THEN
    call PROC service
  END IF
UNTIL escape button pressed on computer

PROC delay
  FOR delay = 1 TO time interval for sequence
    IF crossing request THEN
      set pedestrian request flag to (1)
    END IF
  NEXT delay
END PROC

PROC service crossing
  reset pedestrian request flag to (0)
  FOR sequence number = 10 TO 11
    change lights according to sequence number
    FOR delay = 1 TO time interval for sequence
    NEXT delay
  NEXT sequence number
END PROC
```

18.5.6 Program

Glossary

Delay factor	F
Table to store time intervals	D
Table to store light sequence	S
Port address	X
Sequence number	I
Pedestrian crossing request flag	R
Loop variable	J

```
10   DIM D(11),S(11)
20   INPUT "ADDRESS OF PORT ",X
30   INPUT "DELAY FACTOR ",F
40   REM · · STORE TIME INTERVALS
50   FOR I = 1 TO 11
60     READ D(I)
70   NEXT I
80   DATA 0.5,1,10,1,1,1,10,1,0.5,5,0
90   REM · · STORE CONTROL VALUES
100  FOR I = 1 TO 11
110    READ S(I)
120  NEXT I
130  DATA 73,75,76,74,73,89,97,81,73,137,73
140  REM · · INITIALISE PORTS
150  POKE X + 1,0
160  POKE X,0
170  POKE X + 1,4
180  POKE X + 3,0
190  POKE X + 2,255
200  POKE X + 3,4
210  REM · · INITIALISE CROSSING REQUEST FLAG
220  LET R = 0
230  REM · · CYCLE THROUGH LIGHT SEQUENCE
240  FOR I = 1 TO 9
250    POKE X + 2, S(I)
260    GOSUB 1000
270  NEXT I
280  REM · · CHECK FOR CROSSING REQUEST
290  IF R = 1 THEN GOSUB 2000
300  GOTO 240

1000 REM · · SUBROUTINE DELAY
1010 FOR J = 1 TO F*D(I)
1020   IF 255–PEEK(X) = 16 THEN R = 1
1030 NEXT J
1040 RETURN

2000 REM · · SUBROUTINE SERVICE CROSSING
2010 LET R = 0
2020 FOR I = 10 TO 11
2030   POKE X + 2,S(I)
2040   FOR J = 1 TO F*D(I): NEXT J
2050 NEXT I
2060 RETURN
```

18.6 Vehicle Control
18.6.1 Configuration

Figure 18.2 shows a vehicle called a *BBC Buggy,* available from Economatics Limited, Sheffield, Yorkshire, and can be connected via an umbilical cable to a BBC microcomputer. The Buggy is moved and steered by two independently controllable stepper motors, which drive the left and right wheels. There are four sensors on the Buggy, which can send information to the BBC microcomputer. These sensors are the left and right bumpers, a light dependent resistor and a bar-code reader.

Figure 18.2

18.6.2 Interface

The user port has sixteen memory locations from address 65120 to 65135. Each memory location can represent eight bits. The user port has eight data wires which can send signals to and from the BBC microcomputer, via address 65120. These wires are used to drive the Buggy as follows.

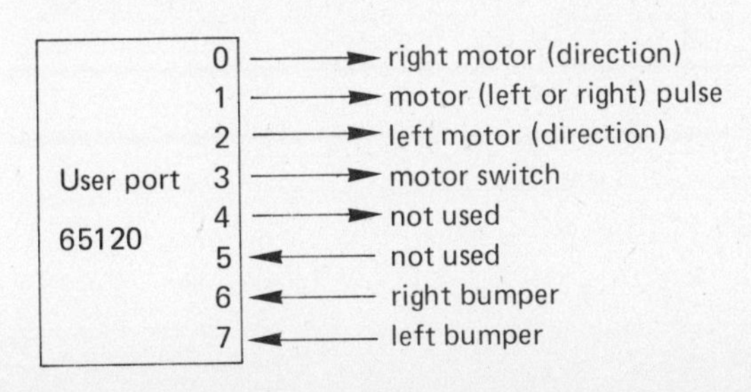

The direction of the motors is governed by the setting of a bit (1) backwards, (0) forwards. The motors are switched off by bit (1) and switched on by bit (0). A pulse is sent to the motors by bit (1) and no pulse by bit (0). Each of the bumpers being hit registers a (1) on lines 6 and 7, otherwise, these lines remain at (0).

The Buggy has the ability to detect a light source using a light dependent resistor, and detect reflected light levels using a bar-code reader which is an infra red transmitter and receiver. Both sensors are connected to a separate analogue input port.

18.6.3 Control

Initialisation of the port involves storing at memory address 65122 the positions of those lines used for input and output. Input is coded as (0), output is coded as (1). From the last diagram of the user port it is clear that the bit pattern 00011111 i.e. (31) defines the position of the input and output lines. The data wires are, however, connected to address 65120. Thus PORT = 65120, ?(PORT + 2) = 31 will define the input and output lines of the port.

Table 18.3 shows the necessary values required to control the left and right motors in order to steer the Buggy.

Direction value	Action	Direction of movement
0	motors on; left/right forward; no pulse	↑ forwards no pulse
1	motors on; right backwards/ left forwards; no pulse	↱ turn right no pulse
2	motors on; left/right forward; pulse on	↑ forwards pulse
3	motors on; left forward/ right backwards; pulse on	↱ turn right pulse
4	motors on; left backwards/ right forwards; no pulse	↰ turn left no pulse
5	motors on; left/right backwards; no pulse	↓ backwards no pulse
6	motors on; left backwards/ right forwards; pulse on	↰ turn left pulse
7	motors on; left/right backwards; pulse on	↓ backwards pulse

Table 18.3

The following program segment illustrates how the Buggy can be controlled to move to the right through 10 steps.

```
100  For I = 1 TO 10
110    ?PORT = 1
120    PROCWAIT(10)
130    ?PORT = 3
140    PROCWAIT(2)
150  NEXT I

500  DEF PROCWAIT(DELAY)
510  FOR J = 1 TO DELAY:NEXT J
520  ENDPROC
```

The ADVAL function (analogue to digital converter value) in BBC/Electron BASIC will convert either the level of brightness or level of reflected infra red light from both sensors to a digital value.

For the light dependent resistor use ADVAL(1), and for the bar-code reader use ADVAL(2).

In a series of tests the bar-code reader gave the following approximate values for different shades of card.

shade	reading
white	5200
grey	6100
black	58000

18.6.4 Problem

Write a program to steer the Buggy along a black line painted on a white card. The line is not straight and contains many turns. For example, a typical line path might look like this.

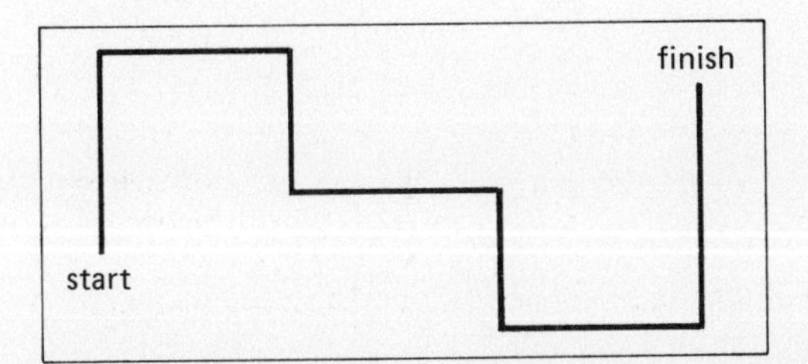

The Buggy must detect the end of the line (finish) and stop moving.

18.6.5 Design

```
initialise port
set reflected threshold limit
set number of attempts required to find black line
set direction of last turn to left
REPEAT
  IF reflected value >= threshold THEN
    set direction to move forward (along black line)
    call PROC move
  ELSE
    call PROC sample (to find black line)
  END IF
UNTIL end of black line
stop

PROC move
  set port to direction (no pulse)
  wait
  set port to direction (with pulse)
  wait
ENDPROC

PROC sample
  IF last turn was left THEN
    call PROC turn left
  ELSE
    call PROC turn right
  END IF
  IF black line found THEN exit procedure
  IF last turn was right THEN
    call PROC turn left (through twice angle of previous turn)
  ELSE
    call PROC turn right (through twice angle of previous turn)
  END IF
ENDPROC

PROC turn left
  move backwards 2 steps
  REPEAT
    turn left
  UNTIL black line found or
      number of attempts at finding black line = maximum attempts
  set direction of last turn to left
END PROC

PROC turn right
  move backwards 2 steps
  REPEAT
    turn right
  UNTIL black line found or
      number of attempts at finding black line = maximum attempts
  set direction of last turn to right
ENDPROC
```

Glossary

address of user port	PORT
infra red value for non-white background	THRESHOLD
maximum number of attempts at finding black line	ATTEMPTS
direction of last turn	LASTTURN$
flag showing whether black line found (1-found, 0-not found)	BLACKLINE
direction code showing which way Buggy moves	DIRECTION
ratio of amount of turn (x1 or x2)	TURNFACTOR
number of attempts at finding black line	COUNTER

18.6.6 Program

```
 10 REM · · INITIALISATION
 20 PORT = 65120
 30 ? (PORT + 2) = 31
 40 THRESHOLD = 10000
 50 ATTEMPTS = 50
 60 LASTTURN$ = "LEFT"
 70 BLACKLINE = 1
 80 REM · ·
 90 REM · ·
100 REM · · SAMPLE REFLECTED INFRARED
110 REPEAT
120   IF ADVAL (2) >= THRESHOLD THEN DIRECTION = 0: PROCMOVE ELSE PROCSAMPLE
130 UNTIL BLACKLINE = 0
140 STOP
150 REM · ·
160 REM · ·
170 DEF PROCMOVE
180 ?PORT = DIRECTION
190 PROCWAIT (10)
200 ?PORT = DIRECTION + 2
210 PROCWAIT (2)
220 ENDPROC
230 REM · ·
240 REM · ·
250 DEF PROCSAMPLE
260 REM · · CONTINUE TO TURN IN THE SAME DIRECTION
270 TURNFACTOR = 1
280 IF LASTTURN$ = "LEFT" THEN PROCTURNLEFT ELSE PROCTURNRIGHT
290 REM · · TEST FOR BLACK LINE
300 IF BLACKLINE = 1 THEN 340
310 REM · · BLACKLINE NOT FOUND THEREFORE TURN IN OPPOSITE DIRECTION
320 TURNFACTOR = 2
330 IF LASTTURN$ = "RIGHT" THEN PROCTURNLEFT ELSE PROCTURNRIGHT
340 ENDPROC
350 REM · ·
```

```
360  REM ··
370  DEF PROCTURNLEFT
380  REM ·· MOVE BACK 2 STEPS
390  FOR I = 1 TO 2: DIRECTION = 5: PROCMOVE: NEXT I
400  REM ·· TURN LEFT
410  COUNTER = 0
420  REPEAT
430    DIRECTION = 4: PROCMOVE: COUNTER = COUNTER + 1
440  UNTIL COUNTER = ATTEMPTS*TURNFACTOR OR ADVAL (2) > THRESHOLD
450  REM ·· WAS BLACK LINE FOUND?
460  IF ADVAL (2) > THRESHOLD THEN BLACKLINE = 1 ELSE BLACKLINE = 0
470  LASTTURN$ = "LEFT"
480  ENDPROC
490  REM ··
500  REM ··
510  DEF PROCTURNRIGHT
520  REM ·· MOVE BACK 2 STEPS
530  FOR I = 1 TO 2: DIRECTION = 5 PROCMOVE: NEXT I
540  REM ·· TURN RIGHT
550  COUNTER = 0
560  REPEAT
570    DIRECTION = 1: PROCMOVE: COUNTER = COUNTER + 1
580  UNTIL COUNTER = ATTEMPTS*TURNFACTOR OR ADVAL (2) > THRESHOLD
590  REM ·· WAS BLACK LINE FOUND?
600  IF ADVAL (2) > THRESHOLD THEN BLACKLINE = 1 ELSE BLACKLINE = 0
610  LASTTURN$ = "RIGHT"
620  ENDPROC
630  REM ··
640  REM ··
650  DEF PROCWAIT(D)
660  FOR I = 1 TO D: NEXT I
670  ENDPROC
```

18.7 Keywords

sensors, control, real-time;
interface, user port;
PEEK, POKE.

19 Computer Graphics

19.1 Introduction

The study of computer graphics is a specialised area of computing. The purpose of this chapter is to explain how the BASIC language supports many of the requirements of graphics. By the end of the chapter the reader should understand some of the terminology used and be able to write computer programs to generate point and line diagrams, the animation of shapes and the use of colour. Computer graphics is dialect dependent. Each BASIC dialect has a unique set of graphics statements. Many of these statements will not be considered in this chapter since they do little towards the reader's understanding of the subject. Such material is best studied from a manufacturer's BASIC language manual after having first been introduced to the subject through reading this chapter.

19.2 Terminology

19.2.1 Pixel

Up to now the screens of monitors, visual display units and televisions have been used as output units to display computer programs, data and information. Such output has been confined to, say, a maximum of 25 lines on a screen, where each line was capable of displaying either 40 or 80 characters. Thus output was limited to either a 25 x 40 or 25 x 80 character matrix. When a screen is used for computer graphics it must be divided up into a much larger matrix for the same screen area in order to represent graphical detail more clearly. Since a character on a screen is normally formed from an 8 x 8 dot matrix, each dot can be used as a picture element or graphics point known as a *pixel*. Therefore, a 25 x 80 character matrix now becomes a 200 x 640 pixel matrix, where each pixel can be accessed separately.

19.2.2 Resolution

The number of pixels in a picture or screen depends upon the *resolution* selected. A low number of pixels to a screen will give a coarse appearance to pictures, whereas a high number of pixels to a screen will allow much more detail to be clearly defined in a picture. For a typical screen size used with microcomputers (25 lines x 80 characters) a matrix of 200 x 640 pixels will give a high resolution picture and a matrix of 200 x 320 pixels will give a medium resolution picture. These figures will vary with the type of microcomputer being used.

19.2.3 Windows

Windows are areas of a screen that behave as though each individual window was a screen in its own right. A window can contain either graphical output or text.

19.2.4 Colour

The BASIC language offers the facility to change the colours of pictures on a screen. The colour of the pixels forming a picture and the colour of the pixels forming the background can be changed. An amount of computer memory is used to store the characteristics (position, intensity, colour, etc) of each pixel. Therefore, when constrained by a fixed amount of memory, the higher the resolution used, the less memory can be used to represent different pixel colours. High resolution graphics normally restricts the user to less colours than medium or low resolution graphics.

19.3 Graphical Output

19.3.1 Coordinates

The position of a point on a screen can be thought of in relation to a matrix or grid covering the area of the screen. A point will be given *coordinates* in order to fix its position in relation to the matrix or grid. The position of the origin, coordinate (0,0), will be either in the top left-hand or bottom left-hand corner of a screen depending upon the dialect of BASIC being used.

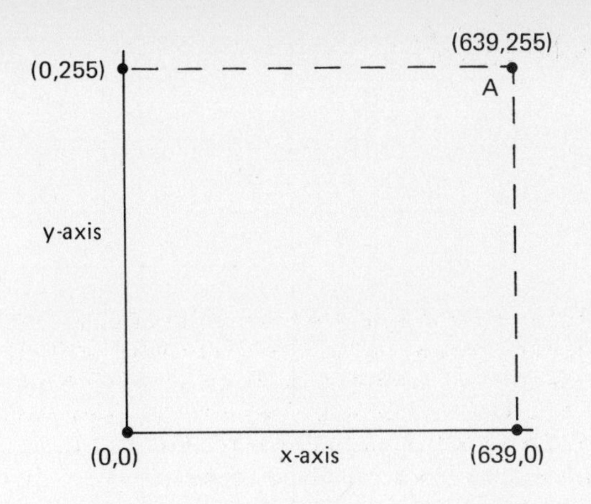

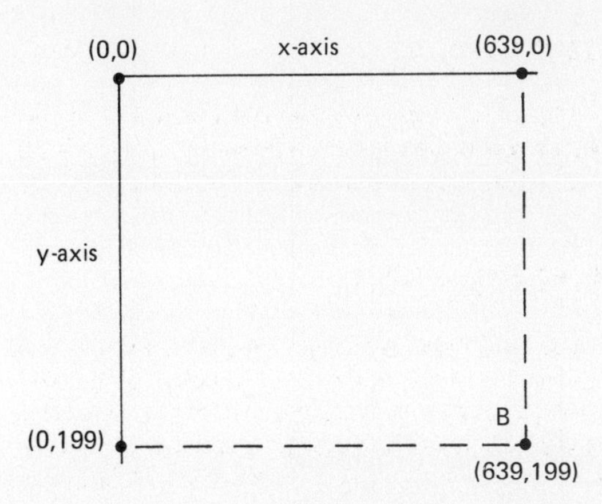

Reference to a point on the screen is made by specifying the x and y coordinate of the point. For example, (639,255) is point A and (639,199) is point B.

19.3.2 Plotting Points

In computer graphics there is a requirement to plot points on a screen. The BASIC language must, therefore, contain a statement to locate a specific point on a screen, given the coordinates of the point, and illuminate the pixel at that point.

PLOT X, Y could be used to plot many different points on a screen.

PLOT 100,50 would plot a point at A.
PLOT 200,75 would plot a point at B.
PLOT 50,100 would plot a point at C.

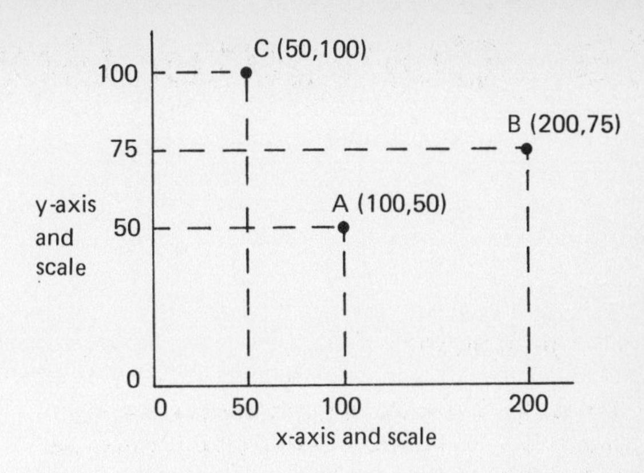

Note. The axes X and Y and scales DO NOT appear on the screen. If you want such a refinement you must program them into the output.

19.3.3 Drawing Lines

Having plotted points on a screen there may be a requirement to join these points using straight lines. BASIC must also provide a statement for line drawing between two points.

LINE $X_1 Y_1$ TO $X_2 Y_2$ could be used to draw a straight line between the points whose coordinates are ($X_1 Y_1$) and ($X_2 Y_2$).

LINE 100,50 TO 200,75 would draw a straight line between points A and B.

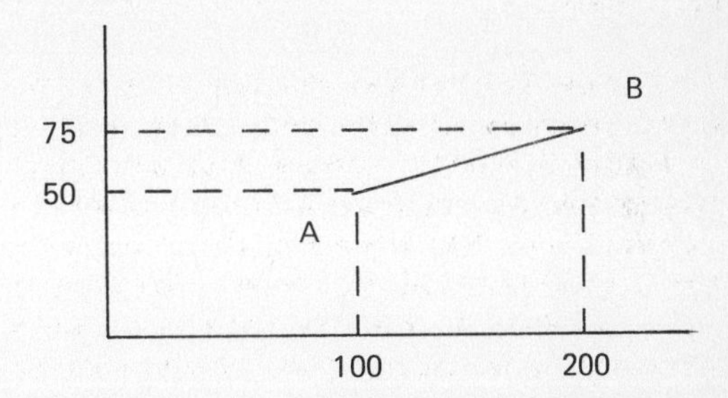

Similarly, LINE 100,50 TO 50,100 would join A and C, and LINE 200,75 TO 50,100 would join B and C, thus forming a triangle ABC.

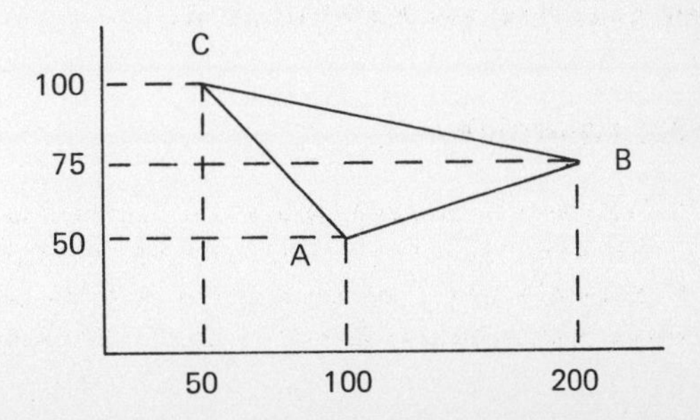

The language should also allow for an abbreviated form of the LINE statement for joining many pairs of points by straight lines.

LINE 100,50 TO 200,75 TO 50,100 TO 100,50 would have the same effect as the three LINE statements used to draw the triangle ABC.

19.3.4 Drawing Curves

Drawing curves can be accomplished by two different methods. The first involves plotting points from given coordinates knowing the equation of the curve, i.e. y = f(x). The second method uses statements in the language for drawing specific shapes (e.g. circles and ellipses).

In the first method either cartesian or polar coordinates can be used. For example, if a circle of radius 25 units is to be drawn; the equation for a circle $x^2 + y^2 = r^2$ can be re-arranged to $y = \pm\sqrt{r^2 - x^2}$. For a range of values of x, 25 to −25 in steps of −1, say, and r = 25, y can be calculated and plotted on the screen against the respective values for x.

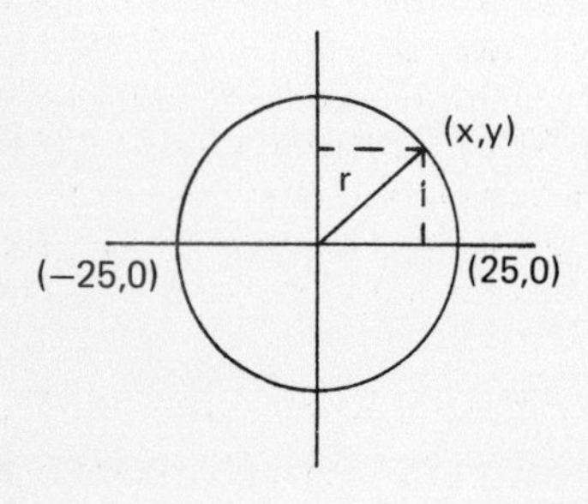

A BASIC program to plot a circle using this method can be reduced to the following lines of code.

```
10  FOR X = 25 TO −25 STEP −1
20    LET Y = SQR(625 − X*X)
30    PLOT 100 + X, 100 + Y
40    PLOT 100 + X, 100 − Y
50  NEXT X
60  STOP
```

Note. The coordinates X,Y have each been increased by 100 so that every point plotted will lie on the screen.

The same circle can be plotted using the following relationship for x and y and the radius of the circle and angle of the arc.

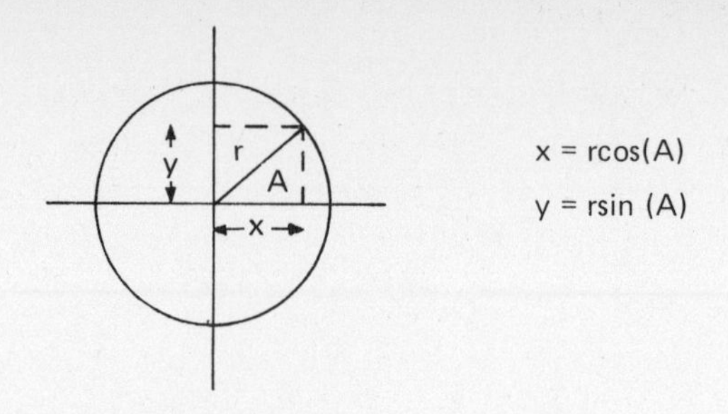

The program code becomes:

```
10  FOR A = 0 TO 360
20    LET X = 25 * COS(A*3.14159/180)
30    LET Y = 25 * SIN(A*3.14159/180)
40    PLOT 100 + X, 100 + Y
50  NEXT A
60  STOP
```

19.3.5 Filling Shapes

Having created a shape it might be necessary to colour or shade the interior of the shape. A further requirement, therefore, of the BASIC language is a statement to FILL or PAINT the inside of the shape on the screen, having first specified the colours of the shape and the background.

19.4 Dialect Differences

19.4.1 Setting the resolution

Microsoft. Format: SCREEN mode
where mode is an integer 0,1 or 2.

0 — sets the text mode, the width of the screen is either 40 or 80 characters depending on the use of the WIDTH statement.
1 — sets medium resolution 200 (depth) x 320 (width) pixels.
2 — sets high resolution 200x640 pixels.

BBC/Electron. Format: MODE integer
where integer is in the range 0 to 7 inclusive.

0 — sets very high resolution 640x256 rectangles.
1 — sets high resolution 320x256 rectangles.
2 — sets medium resolution 160x256 rectangles.
3 — text only.
4 — high resolution (restriction on colours).
5 — medium resolution (restriction on colours).
6 — text only.
7 — teletext only.

In very high resolution a rectangle is 2x4 pixels giving a 1280x1024 pixel matrix.

19.4.2 Colour

Microsoft. Format: COLOR [background] [,[palette]]

where background is a numeric expression specifying the background colour and palette is a numeric expression that selects a palette of colours.

Background colour numbers range from 0 (black), 1 (blue), 2 (green) . . . . 15 (high-intensity white).

If the palette number is **even** then the colour numbers are 1 (green), 2 (red) and 3 (brown) on the *paint* palette, however, if the palette number is **odd** then the colour numbers are 1 (cyan), 2 (magenta) and 3 (white) on the *paint* palette.

Background colour and palette colours may be the same.

BBC/Electron. Format: GCOL A,B

where A is an integer in the range 0 to 4 inclusive and specifies a mode of action as follows.

0 – plot the colour specified.
1 – OR the specified colour with that already there.
2 – AND the specified colour with that already there.
3 – Exclusive OR the specified colour with that already there.
4 – invert the colour already there.

The parameter B defines the logical colour to be used in the future.

If B > 127 then it defines the background colour, otherwise B defines the foreground colour. There are 16 different colour codes: 0 (black), 1 (red), 2 (green), 3 (yellow) . . . . 15 (flashing white-black). Remember the mode of resolution chosen will dictate how many of these colours can be used. Modes 0, 3, 4 and 6 allow 2 colours, modes 1 and 5 allow 4 colours, and mode 2 only allows 16 colours.

In mode 2 GCOL 0, 3 would define a yellow foreground and GCOL 0,129 would define a red background.

19.4.3 Windows

Microsoft. Format: VIEW [SCREEN] $(X_1,Y_1) - (X_2,Y_2)$ [,colour [,boundary]]

where (X_1,Y_1) and (X_2,Y_2) are the upper-left and lower-right coordinates of the defined viewing area. Colour will fill the area with colour and boundary will draw a line around the viewing area. Both colour and boundary are integers in the range 0 to 3 inclusive, defining a colour code.

The purpose of VIEW is to allow subsets of the viewing surface to be defined. Although multiple viewing areas can be defined, only one viewing area may be active at a time.

Examples. VIEW (50,50)–(150,100) will define the following viewing area in medium resolution. A point whose coordinates are (30,20) would be plotted at the point (80,70) within the viewing area defined.

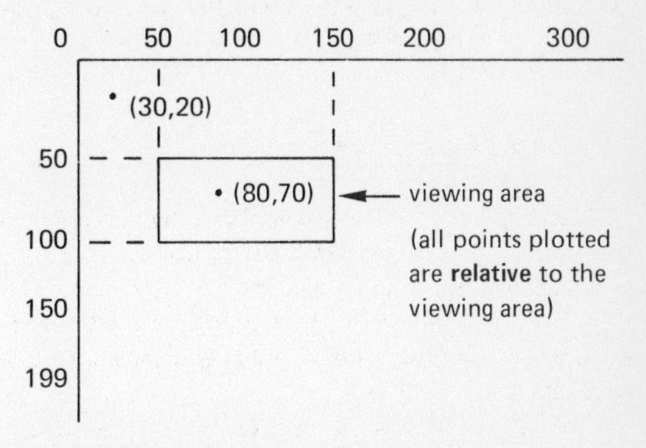

If the VIEW statement was changed to include the SCREEN option:

VIEW SCREEN (50,50)–(150,100)

then the point (30,20) would not appear on the screen since it lies outside of the viewing area. Only those coordinates that lie within the viewing area will be displayed on the screen if plotted.

The use of VIEW will allow the scaling of graphics on the screen. Using VIEW without the SCREEN option (relative coordinates) will cause the expansion of a picture when plotted in a large viewing area, and a contraction of a picture when plotted in a small viewing area.

Format: WINDOW [SCREEN] $(X_1,Y_1)-(X_2,Y_2)$

where (X_1,Y_1) and (X_2,Y_2) are coordinates used to define the size of a window. The purpose of the WINDOW statement is to redefine the coordinates of the screen.

Examples. WINDOW SCREEN (–10,–10)–(40,40) would define a screen such that (–10,–10) was in the top left-hand corner and (40,40) was in the bottom right-hand corner.

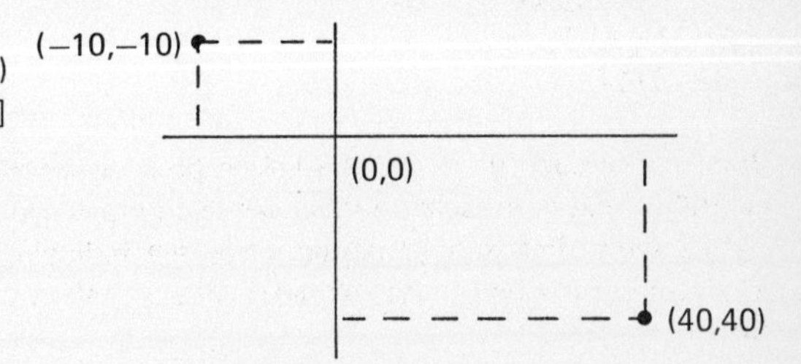

If the SCREEN option is omitted then the coordinates of the screen conform to true cartesian coordinates.

WINDOW (−10,−10)−(40,40) would define a screen such that (−10,−10) was in the bottom left-hand corner, and (40,40) was in the top right-hand corner.

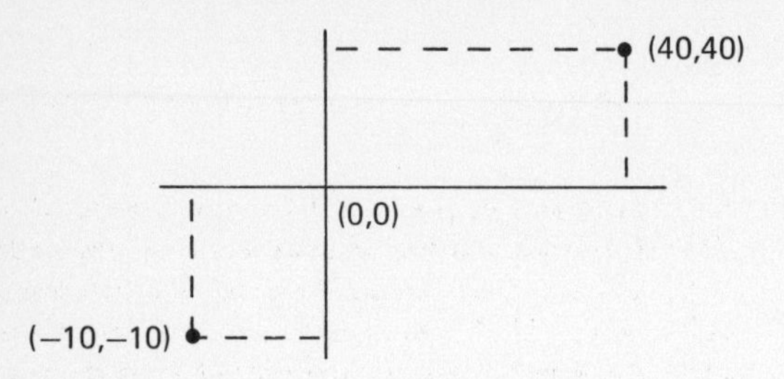

The WINDOW statement will only display those points whose coordinates lie within the window. Therefore, if the WINDOW coordinates are chosen to be smaller than the picture, only part of the picture will be displayed and give a sense of magnification. However, if the WINDOW coordinates are chosen to be larger than the picture then the entire picture will be displayed as a diminished image. WINDOW coordinates that get progressively smaller than the picture coordinates will give the effect of zooming into a picture and WINDOW coordinates that get progressively larger will give the effect of zooming out of a picture.

BBC/Electron. Format: VDU24, X_1;Y_1;X_2;Y_2;

where (X_1,Y_1) and (X_2, Y_2) are the bottom left-hand corner and top right-hand corner coordinates of the graphics window.

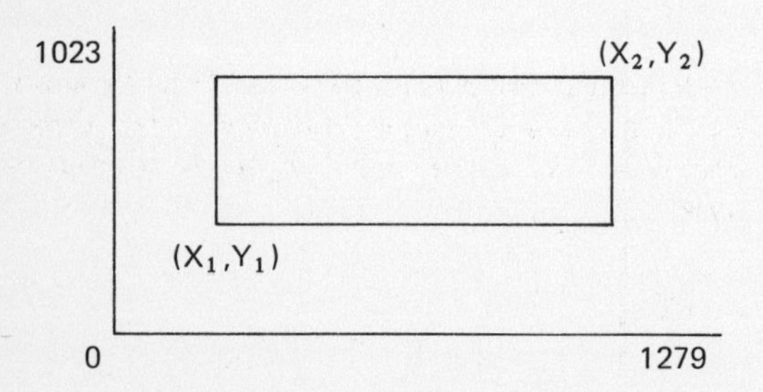

The position of the origin can also be moved by using the statement

VDU 29, X;Y;

where X,Y is the coordinate of the new origin.

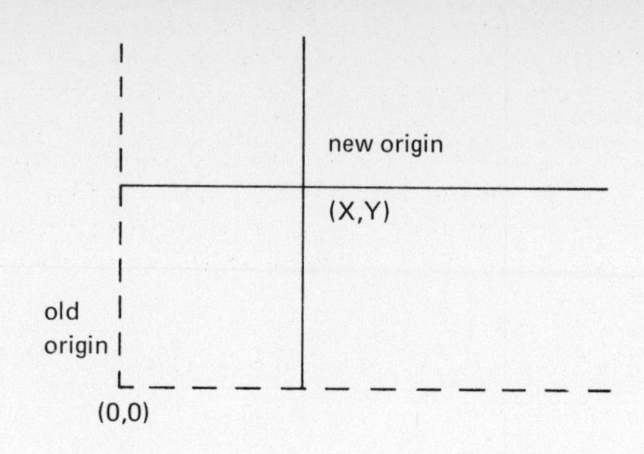

The graphic window and origin can be returned to their initial values by using the statement VDU 26.

19.4.4 Plotting Points

Microsoft. Format: PSET (x,y) [,colour]

where x,y are the coordinates of the point on a screen and colour is an integer in the range 0 to 3 (previously described).

BBC/Electron. Format: PLOT 69,X,Y

19.4.5 Drawing Lines

Microsoft. Format: LINE [(X_1,Y_1)]−(X_2,Y_2)[,colour]

The statement draws a line between (X_1,Y_1) and (X_2,Y_2) in the colour specified.

BBC/Electron. Format: DRAW X,Y

will draw a straight line between the last pair of coordinates stated in the program and the coordinate (X,Y). To initialise line drawing the graphics cursor should be moved using the statement MOVE X,Y. Therefore, to draw a straight line between the coordinates (100,50) and (500,250) the following statements would be used.

```
MOVE 100,50
DRAW 500,250
```

19.4.6 Shape Statements

Microsoft.

Format: CIRCLE (x,y),r [,colour [,start, end [,aspect]]]

where (x,y) are the coordinates of the centre of the circle, r is the radius of the circle. Colour is an integer in the range 0 to 3 defining the colour the circle is drawn.

Start and end are angles in radians that range from -2π to 2π, and indicate the angles at which drawing starts and finishes. Aspect is a numeric expression that changes the shape of the circle. The default value for the aspect is 5/6 in medium resolution and 5/12 in high resolution. An aspect less than 1 (i.e 5/18) will produce an ellipse with major axis parallel with the x-axis; an aspect greater than 1 will produce an ellipse with minor axis parallel to the x-axis.

BBC/Electron. This dialect does not support any shape statements.

19.4.7 Colouring Shapes

Microsoft. Format: PAINT (x,y) [[,paint] [,boundary]]

where (x,y) are the coordinates of a point within the area to be coloured, and both paint and boundary are integer values in the range 0 to 3 describing the colour of the interior and boundary of the shape respectively.

BBC/Electron. Format: PLOT 85, X,Y

where (X,Y) represents the coordinates of one corner of a triangle; the remaining two points being the last two pairs of coordinates stated in the program. The statement draws the triangle from the last two points plotted to the point defined by X,Y and fills in the triangle with the current foreground graphics colour.

19.5 Worked Examples

The following examples have all been written for the BBC model B microcomputer. The programs can easily be translated to the other computer dialects considered in this book.

The graphics mode of the BBC dialect uses a system of coordinates with the origin (0,0) in the bottom left-hand corner and the largest coordinates (1279,1023) in the top right-hand corner.

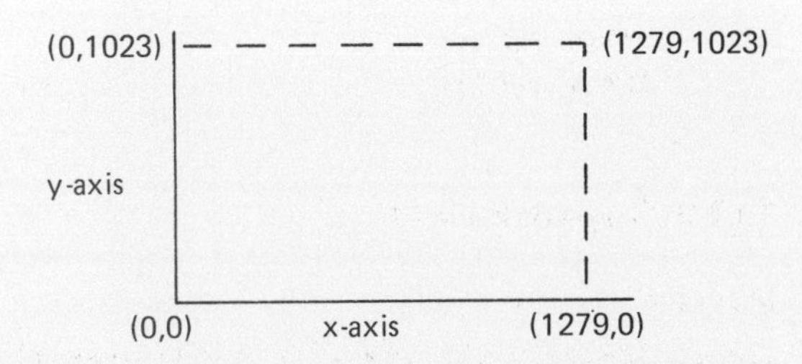

The text mode in the BBC dialect uses a different system of coordinates to the graphics mode. The origin is in the top left-hand corner and the largest coordinates (79,31) are in the bottom right-hand corner.

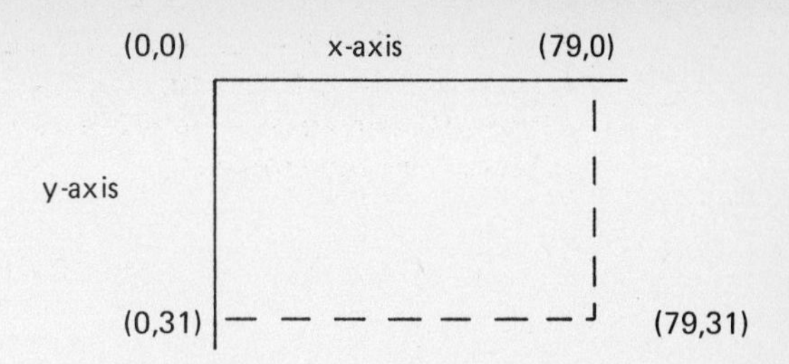

All the examples given in this section use MODE 0, with the exception of the first example that uses modes 0, 1 and 2 separately. Mode 0 will allow a two colour display only, black and white, and high resolution graphics and text to be displayed together on the same screen. Setting the graphics mode automatically clears the screen and assigns the foreground colour to be white and the background colour black.

19.5.1 Circle

Write a program to draw a circle using the relationship x = rcosA, y = rsinA.

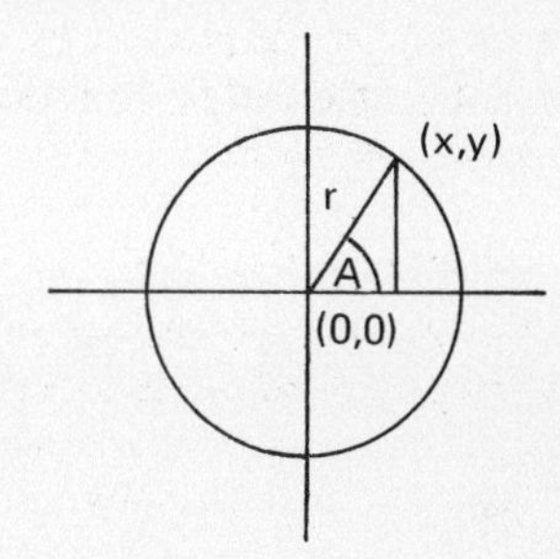

Before the program can be written it is advisable to sketch the expected output in relation to the graphics coordinates so that the correct degree of scaling can be achieved.

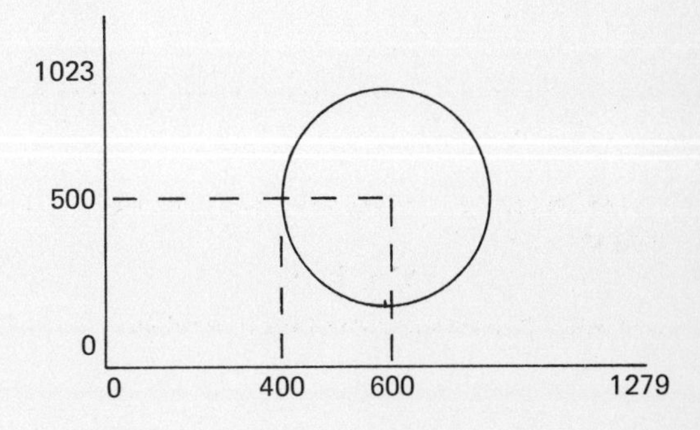

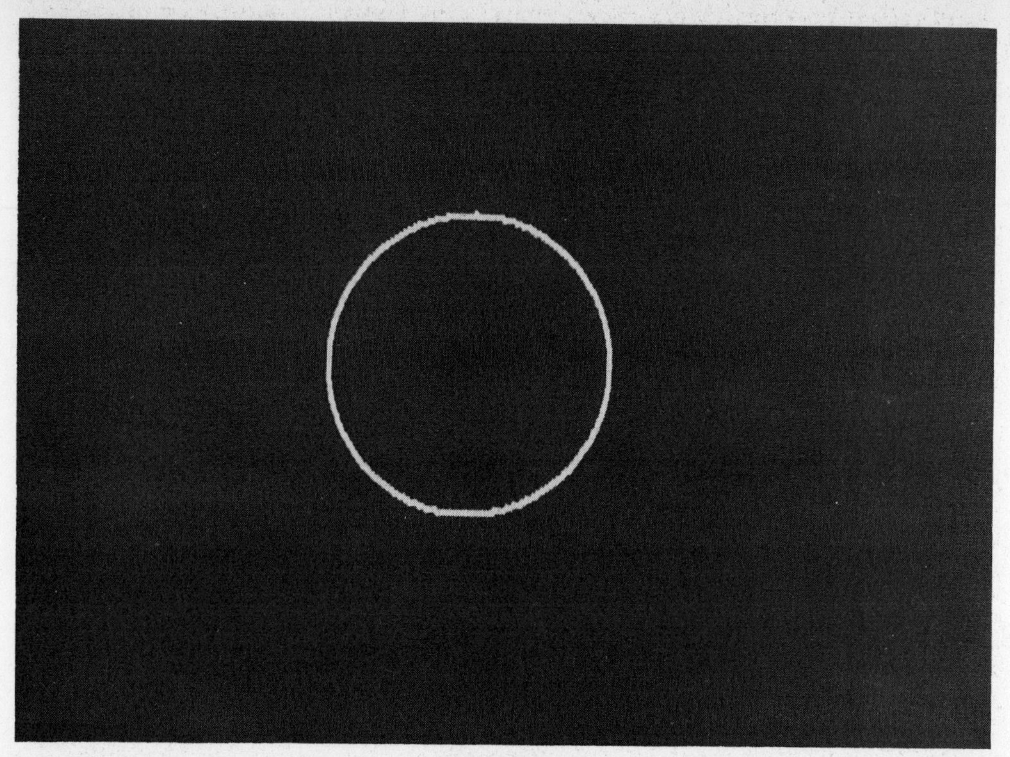

Figure 19.1

Figure 19.2

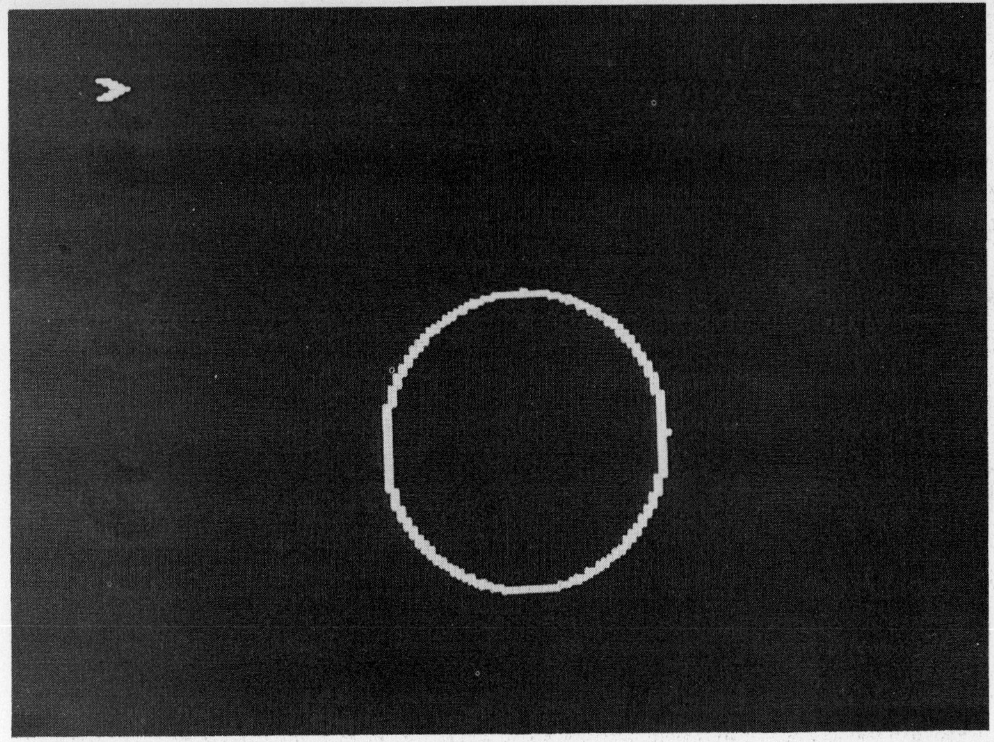

Figure 19.3

From the diagram a centre of (600,500) and a radius of 200 should give a reasonable output for a circle on the screen. The coordinates x = rcosA and y = rsinA are derived with respect to a centre at (0,0). The coordinates will require modifying with respect to the new centre of the circle. The coordinates must be plotted as (600 + x, 500 + y).

Program

```
10  INPUT "MODE",M
20  MODE M
30  FOR ANGLE=0 TO 360
40    LET ANG=ANGLE*PI/180
50    LET X=200*COS(ANG)
60    LET Y=200*SIN(ANG)
70    PLOT 69,X+600,Y+500
80  NEXT ANGLE
```

This program has been run three times using modes 0,1 and 2 respectively. The results are given in figures 19.1, 19.2 and 19.3. Notice how the shape of the circle degenerates as the resolution decreases.

19.5.2 Ellipse

Write a program to draw an ellipse using the following equation:

$$y = \pm b\sqrt{(1 - (x^2/a^2))}$$

where a is the length of the semi-major axis, and b is the length of the semi-minor axis.

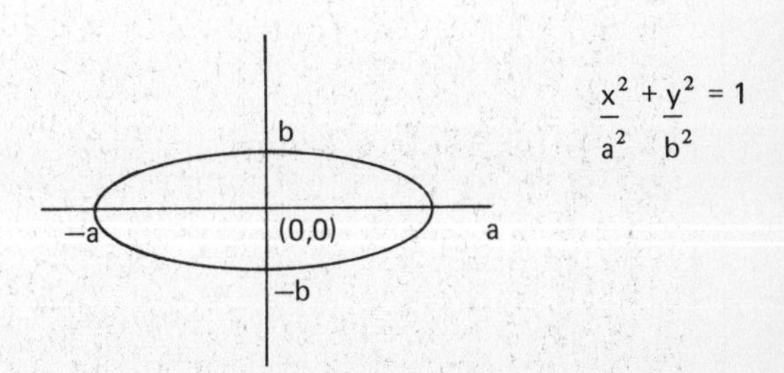

$$\frac{x^2}{a^2} + \frac{y^2}{b^2} = 1$$

Sketch the expected output in relation to the graphics coordinates in order to obtain approximate values for a, b and the centre of the ellipse.

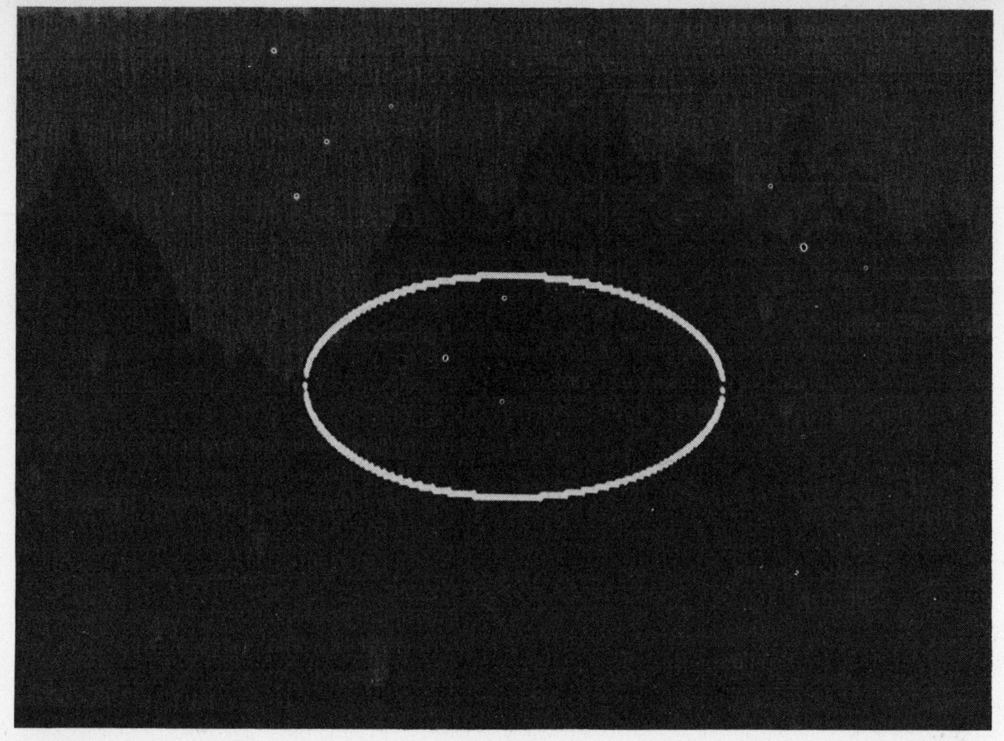

Figure 19.4

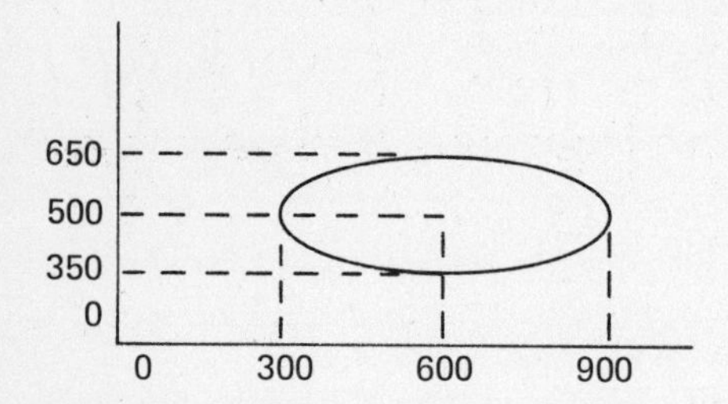

From the diagram a = 300, b = 150 and the centre of the ellipse has been moved from the point (0,0) to the point (600,500), hence, the plotted coordinates become (600 + x, 500 ± y). Values of y are calculated using the equation from values of x taken along the length of the major axis –300 to +300.

Program

```
10  MODE 0
20  FOR X = –300 TO 300
30    Y = 150*SQR(1–(X*X)/90000)
40    PLOT 69,600+X,500+Y
50    PLOT 69,600+X,500–Y
60  NEXT X
```

The results of this program being run are given in figure 19.4.

19.5.3 Rose Curve

Write a program to plot the polar equation r = acos2t for t=0 to $2\pi^c$. Use the relationship that x=rsint and y=rcost, the value of a=300 and the centre of the figure at the point (600,500).

There is no need to draw a preliminary sketch of the curve and graphics axes since all the data about the size of the figure and its position on the screen has been provided in the question.

Program

```
10  MODE 0
20  FOR ANGLE=0 TO 360
30    LET ANG=ANGLE*PI/180
40    LET R =300*COS(2*ANG)
50    LET X=R*SIN(ANG)
60    LET Y=R*COS(ANG)
70    PLOT 69,X+600,Y+500
80  NEXT ANGLE
```

The results of this program being run are given in figure 19.5.

Figure 19.5

19.5.4 Sine Curve

Write a program to plot four cycles (0 to 8π) of a sine wave. Include the axes and scales in the output.

Sketch of the axes and the sine wave using graphical coordinates.

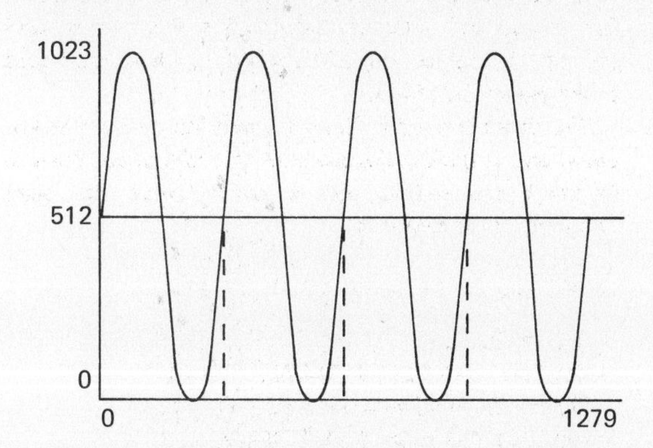

Four cycles would require the scale to range from 0° to 1440°. Since the largest graphics coordinate is (1279,1023) the value of x will be scaled by a factor of $7/8$. As the value of y ranges from -1 to 1 this must also be scaled by a factor of 511, and shifted in relation to the new origin (0,512).

Sketch of the axes, scales and sine wave using text coordinates.

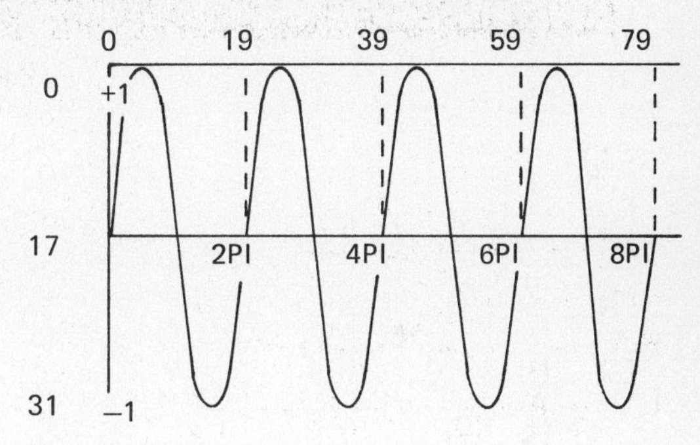

Program

```
 10  MODE 0
 20  MOVE 0,0
 30  DRAW 0,1023
 40  MOVE 0,511
 50  PRINT TAB(0,1);"+1"
 60  PRINT TAB(0,31);"–1"
 70  DRAW 1279,511
 80  PRINT TAB(16,17);"2PI"
 90  PRINT TAB(36,17);"4PI"
100  PRINT TAB(56,17);"6PI"
110  PRINT TAB(76,17);"8PI"
120  VDU 30
130  FOR X=0 TO 4*360
140    Y=SIN(X*PI/180)
150    PLOT 69,7*X/8,512+Y*511
160  NEXT X
```

The results of this program being run are given in figure 19.6

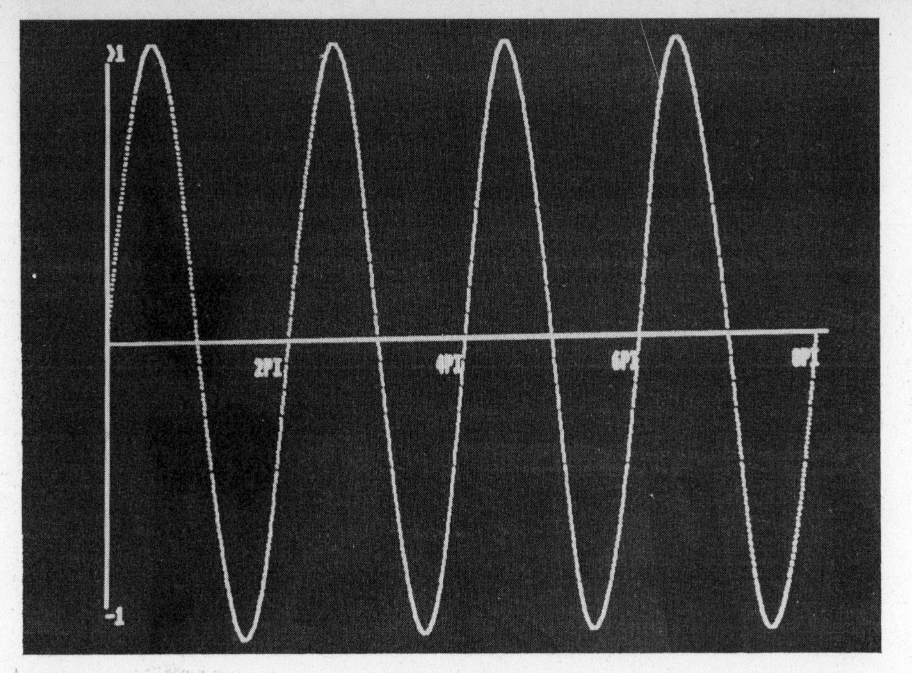

Figure 19.6

19.5.5 Pie Chart

An analysis of examination results in a school gave the following distribution of grades for all subjects taken in one year.

grade	%
A	10
B	25
C	45
F	20

Write a program to represent the distribution of each grade in a pie chart. In the solution to this problem the percentage distribution must be converted into part of a complete revolution of a circle. For example 10% would be represented by a sector (slice of pie) having an angle of 36°, 25% would represent 90°, etc. The program should draw a set of continuous sectors forming a circle, corresponding to the percentage for each grade.

Sketch of pie chart using graphics coordinates

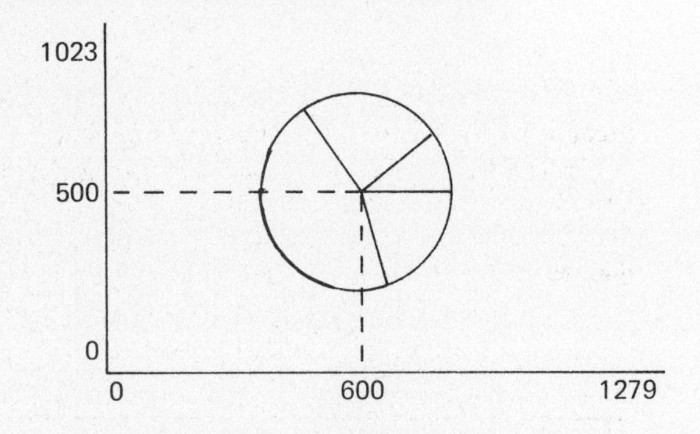

Sketch of pie chart using text coordinates in order to approximately locate the position of each grade.

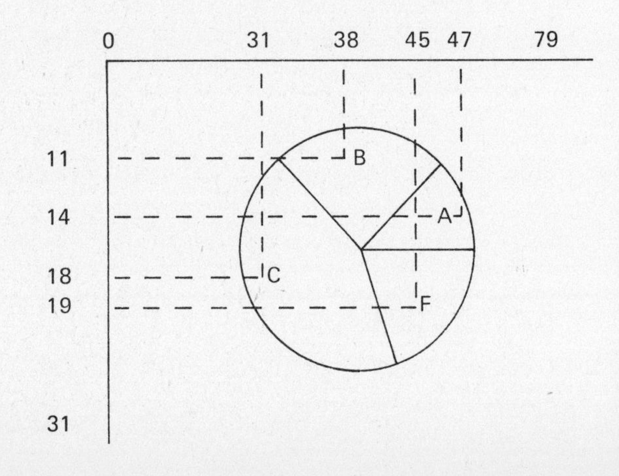

Program

```
 10 MODE 0
 20 A=0
 30 FOR I=1 TO 4
 40   READ P
 50   LET L=A+(P*360)
 60   FOR ANGLE=A TO L
 70     LET ANG=ANGLE*PI/180
 80     LET X=200*COS(ANG)
 90     LET Y=200*SIN(ANG)
100     PLOT 69,X+600,Y+500
110   NEXT ANGLE
120   PLOT 5,600,500
130   LET A=A+(P*360)
140 NEXT I
150 DATA .1,.25,.45,.2
160 PRINT TAB(47,14);"A"
170 PRINT TAB(38,11);"B"
180 PRINT TAB(31,18);"C"
190 PRINT TAB(45,19);"F"
```

The results of this program being run are given in figure 19.7

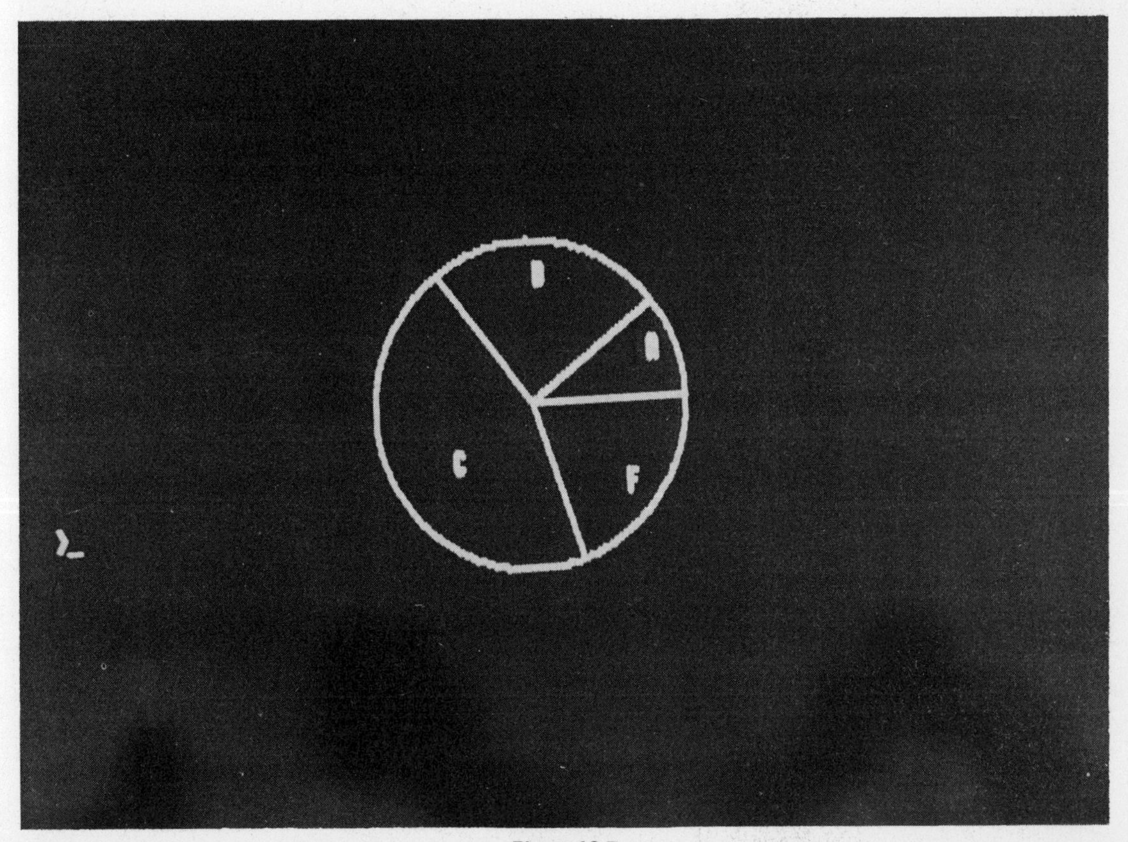

Figure 19.7

19.5.6 Histogram

The monthly sales figures (units sold) for a computer manufacturing company are as follows.

Jan	Feb	Mar	Apr	May	Jun	Jul	Aug	Sept	Oct	Nov	Dec
20	25	37	27	19	25	34	40	50	60	55	42

Write a computer program to plot a histogram of the sales. For a histogram made up from strips of equal width, the respective monthly sales figures will be proportional to the height of each strip.

Sketch of histogram using graphical coordinates.

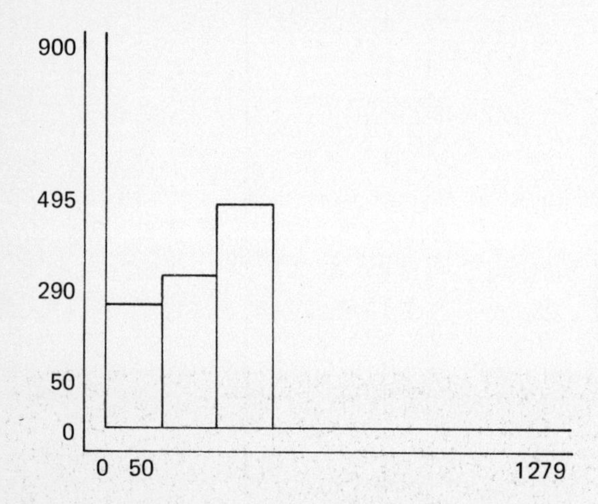

The first strip represents a sales figure of 20. In the sketch this has been drawn to a length of (290–50) 240 units on the screen. Each sales figure should, therefore, be scaled by a factor of 12 (240/20) to give a histogram of a reasonable size.

Sketch of histogram using text coordinates.

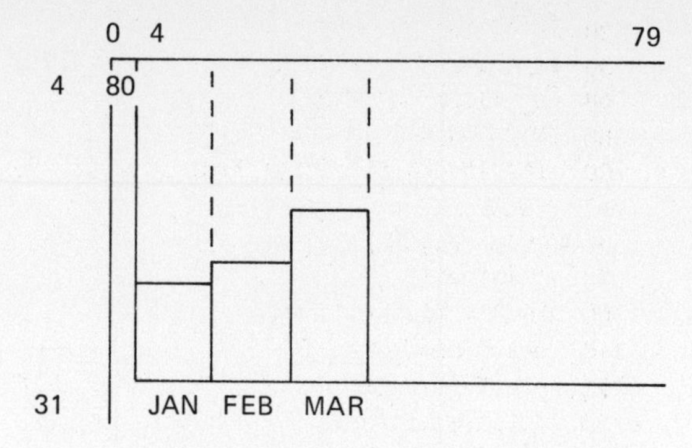

The information printed along the bottom of the x-axis must partly determine the width of each strip. Since the width of each strip will correspond to three characters (month) and two spaces, giving a total of five characters, the width of a strip will be 80 units on the screen.

In this example, the axes that form part of the histogram have an origin of (50,50), therefore, instead of adding an offset value to (x,y) before the points are plotted the origin has been moved instead. All the values of (x,y) used in plotting the positions of the strips are relative to the new origin (50,50) and not (0,0).

Program

```
 10  CLG
 20  DIM S(13)
 30  FOR MONTH = 1 TO 13
 40    READ S (MONTH)
 50  NEXT MONTH
 60  DATA 20,25,37,27,19,25,34,40,50,60,55,42,0
 70  MODE 0
 80  MOVE 50,900
 90  DRAW 50,50
100  DRAW 1000,50
110  PRINT TAB(0,4);"80"
120  PRINT TAB(4,31);"JAN  FEB  MAR  APR  MAY  JUN  JUL  AUG  SEP  OCT  NOV  DEC"
130  VDU 29,50;50;
140  MOVE 0, 12*S(1)
150  FOR MONTH = 1 TO 12
160    DRAW 80*MONTH, 12*S(MONTH)
170    IF S(MONTH) >= S(MONTH+1) THEN 190
180      MOVE 80*MONTH, 12*S(MONTH+1)
190    DRAW 80*MONTH, 50:MOVE 80*MONTH, 12*S(MONTH+1)
200  NEXT MONTH
```

The results of this program being run are given in figure 19.8

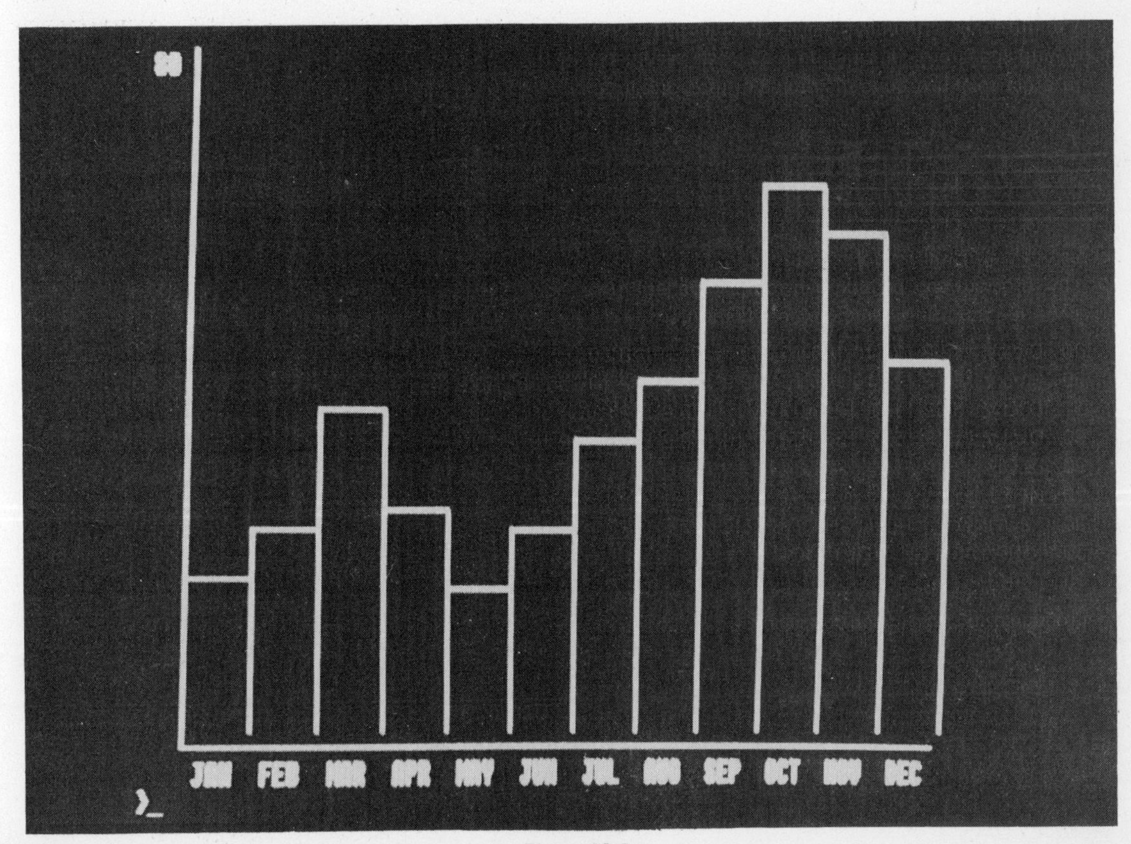

Figure 19.8

The next program demonstrates a general algorithm for plotting any histogram with up to twenty frequencies, however, it can be modified to cater for any number of frequencies. The origin is not shifted and remains at (0,0) throughout the program. The following stages were regarded as being necessary in the design of the program.

Invite the user to input the number of frequencies (N) and the corresponding frequencies from 1 . . .N. The frequencies are stored in a one-dimensional table F.

Calculate the value of the largest frequency (MAXFREQ) since this will be used in the calculation of the vertical scaling factor and the upper limit of the scale on the y-axis.

Calculate the vertical scaling factor: length of vertical axis (y-axis) divided by the largest frequency.

Calculate the horizontal scaling factor: length of horizontal axis divided by the number of frequencies.

Plot the axes and scales where necessary.

Plot the histogram using the same technique as in the previous example.

19.5.6 (cont.)

Program

```
 10 CLG
 20 DIM F(21)
 30 REM · · INPUT AND STORE DATA
 40 INPUT "NUMBER OF CLASS INTERVALS (MAX 20)",N
 50 FOR I=1 TO N
 60   PRINT "FOR INTERVAL ";I;" INPUT FREQUENCY "
 70   INPUT F(I)
 80 NEXT I
 90 F(N+1)=0
100 REM · · FIND THE LARGEST FREQUENCY
110 MAXFREQ=F(1)
120 FOR I=2 TO N
130   IF MAXFREQ<F(I) THEN MAXFREQ = F(I)
140 NEXT I
150 REM · · CALCULATE THE VERTICAL AND HORIZONTAL SCALING FACTORS
160 LET VS=INT (900/MAXFREQ)
170 LET HS=INT(1250/N)
180 REM · · PLOT AXES
190 MODE 0
200 MOVE 0, 900
210 DRAW 0,0
220 DRAW 1250,0
230 PRINT TAB(0,2); MAXFREQ
240 VDU 30
250 REM · · PLOT HISTOGRAM
260 MOVE 0,VS*F(1)
270 FOR I=1 TO N
280   DRAW HS*I,VS*F(I)
290   IF F(I)>=F(I+1) THEN 310
300     MOVE HS*I,VS*F(I+1)
310   DRAW HS*I,0:MOVE HS*I,VS*F(I+1)
320 NEXT I
```

The results of this program being run are given in figure 19.9 using the following test data.

(N) 15

(frequencies):

30 40 45 55 75 90 125 135 140 120 130 80 60 25 10

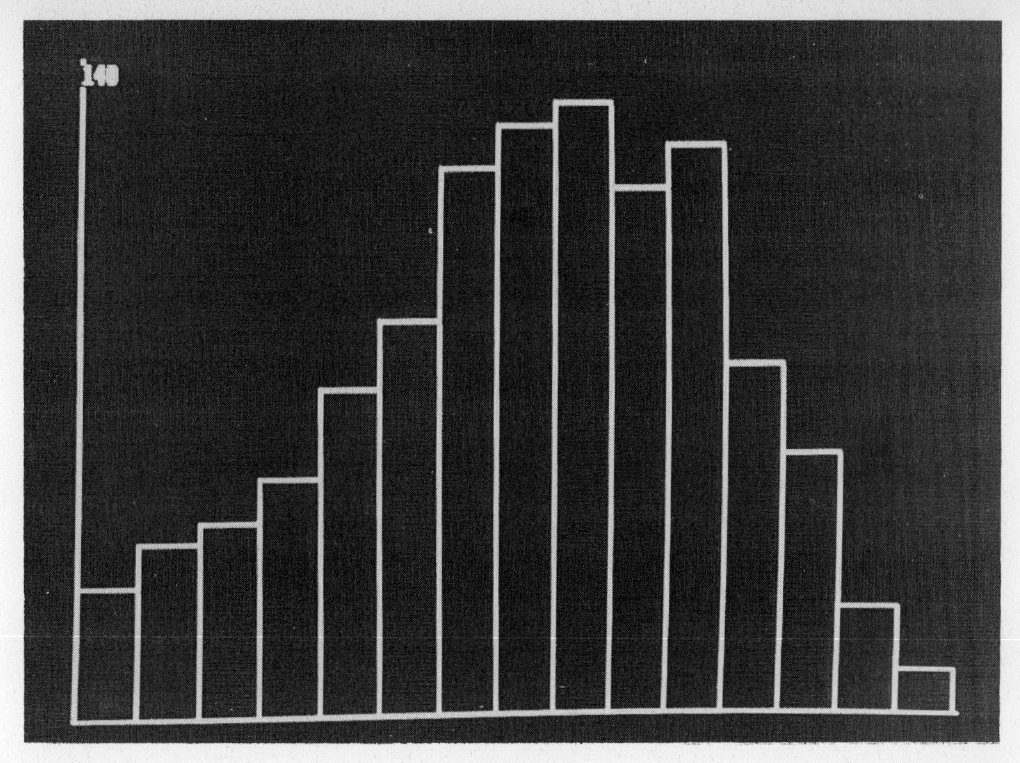

Figure 19.9

19.5.7 Concentric Circles

The purpose of this example is to define a window on the screen and draw a border around the window. Concentric circles are then plotted within the window. Points that lie outside the window will not appear on the screen.

Program

```
 10  MODE 0
 20  VDU 24,150;300;1100;700;
 30  MOVE 150,300
 40  DRAW 150, 700:DRAW 1100,700:DRAW 1100,300:DRAW 150,300
 50  FOR R=100 TO 500 STEP 100
 60    FOR ANGLE=0 TO 360
 70      ANG=ANGLE*PI/180
 80      X=R*COS(ANG)
 90      Y=R*SIN(ANG)
100      PLOT 69,X+620,Y+500
110    NEXT ANGLE
120  NEXT R
```

The results of this program being run are given in figure 19.10

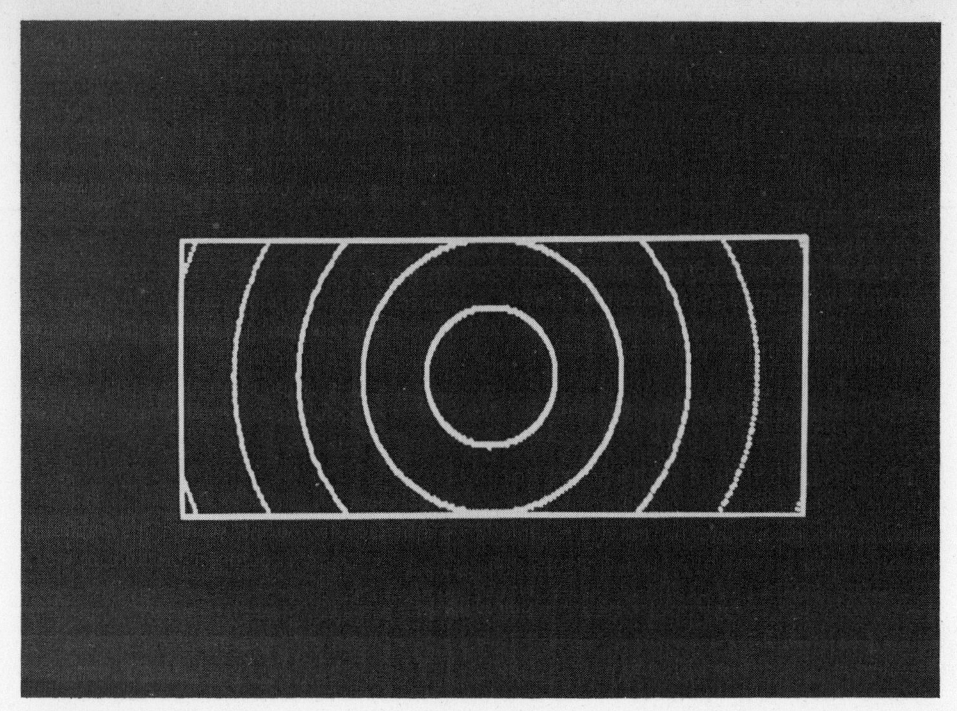

Figure 19.10

19.6 Animation
19.6.1 Storing Shapes

Shapes that are to be used many times in a computer program should first be drawn on squared paper, and the coordinates of the points forming the shape stored in a table. In the following example the shape of an aeroplane is drawn and its coordinates stored in table V. Using the graphics mode of a computer the shape can be reproduced on the screen by drawing straight lines between the points.

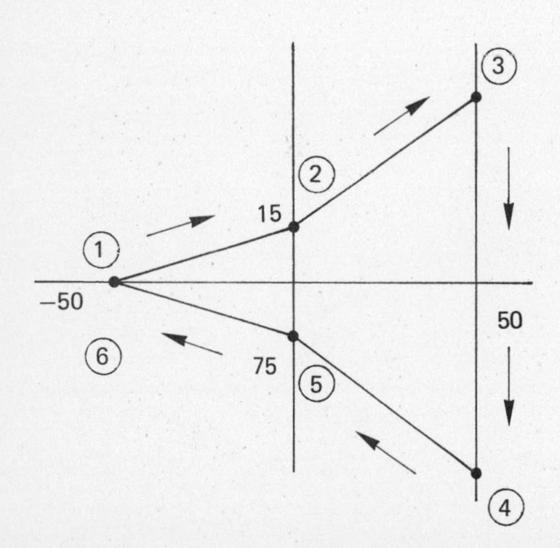

Table V.

	x	y
1	–50	0
2	0	15
3	50	50
4	50	–50
5	0	–15
6	–50	0

19.6.2 Movement

The outline of the aeroplane can be moved across the screen using the following technique.

Draw the figure on the far right, half-way up the screen.
Wait for a specified time.
Change the colour of the foreground to the same colour as the background.
Re-draw the figure. (This has the effect of erasing the first figure, since the colour of the foreground is now the same as the background).
Change the colour of the foreground back to its original colour.
Decrease the value of the x coordinate by a fixed amount.
Repeat these steps until the figure has reached the left-hand edge of the screen.

Program

```
 10 DIM V(6,2)
 20 REM · · STORE COORDINATES OF SHAPE
 30 FOR I = 1 TO 6
 40   READ V (I,1),V(I,2)
 50 NEXT I
 60 DATA –50,0,0,15,50,50,50,–50,0,–15,–50,0
 70 MODE 0
 80 LET Y = 500
 90 INPUT "SPEED FACTOR  ",T
100 REM · · CHANGE VALUE OF X COORDINATE
110 FOR X = 1200 TO 50 STEP –T
120   MOVE X + V (1,1), Y+V(1,2)
130   REM · · DRAW SHAPE
140   FOR I = 1 TO 5
150     DRAW X + V(I + 1,1), Y+V(I + 1,2)
160   NEXT I
170   REM . . DELAY
180   FOR D = 1 TO 50: NEXT D
190   REM · · CHANGE FOREGROUND COLOUR
200   GCOL 0,0
210   MOVE X + V(1,1), Y + V(1,2)
220   REM · · RE-DRAW SHAPE
230   FOR I = 1 TO 5
240     DRAW X + V(I + 1,1), Y + V(I + 1,2)
250   NEXT I
260   REM · · CHANGE FOREGROUND COLOUR BACK TO ORIGINAL COLOUR
270   GCOL 0,1
280 NEXT X
```

This program has been run three times for different values of (T), the amount the x coordinate is decreased after each drawing of the plane. The smaller the value of (T) the slower the aeroplane appears to be in moving across the screen. The results are given in figures 19.11, 19.12 and 19.13.

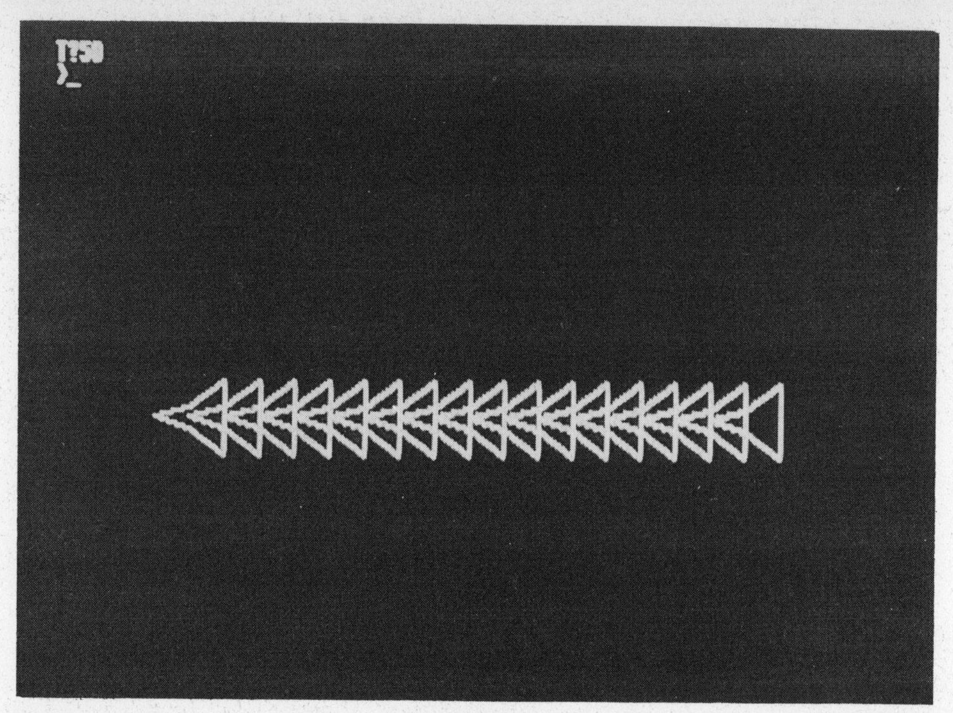

Figure 19.11

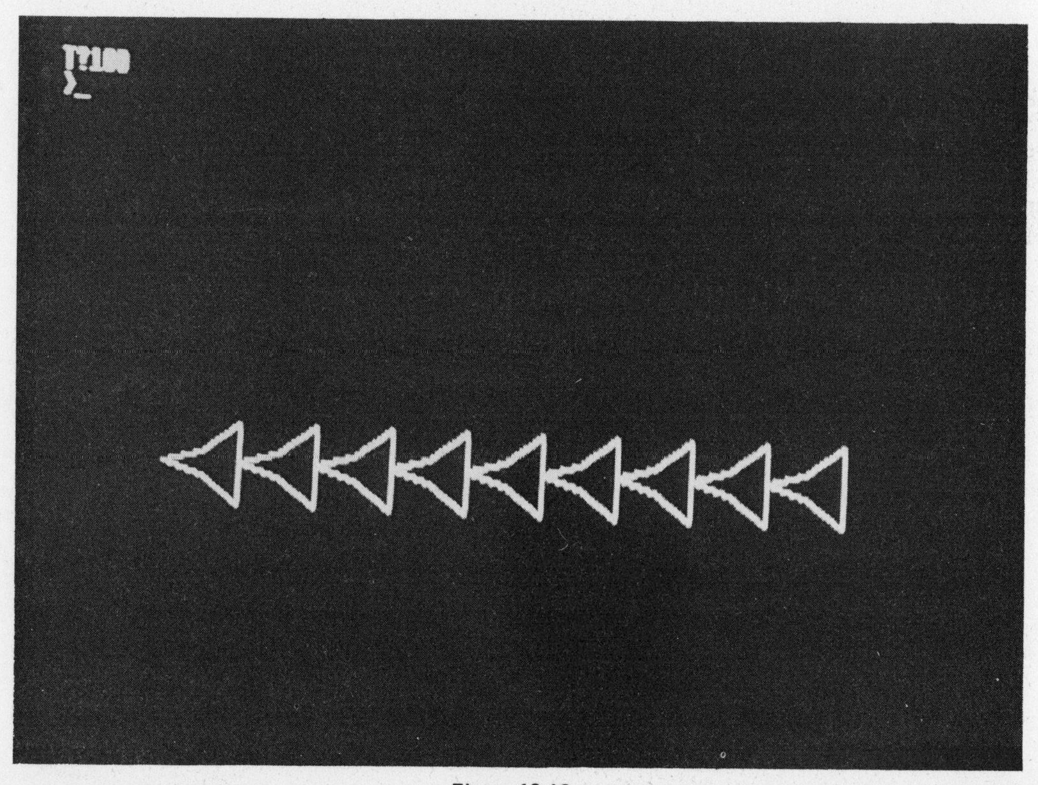

Figure 19.12

Figure 19.13

If the reader transfers the last program to their computer, and runs the program it becomes clear that this technique of animation suffers from several disadvantages.

The figure does not appear on the screen instantly, its construction at every stage can be detected. Depending upon the computer being used the formation of this figure can appear to be fairly slow.

The movement of the figure across the screen tends to be jerky.

If the screen has contained other information, a green coloured grid, say, then part of the grid would be erased when re-drawing the figure in the same colour as the background.

If the figure was to be rotated or changed in size, trigonometric functions would be used to manipulate the coordinates. These transformations are very slow and make fast-action animation impossible.

19.6.3 Miscellaneous Techniques

Several of the dialects have facilities that improve on the last technique for moving shapes.

Microsoft.

The graphics statement GET stores the colours of the points within a specified rectangle in a table.

Format: GET (x1,y1)–(x2,y2),table

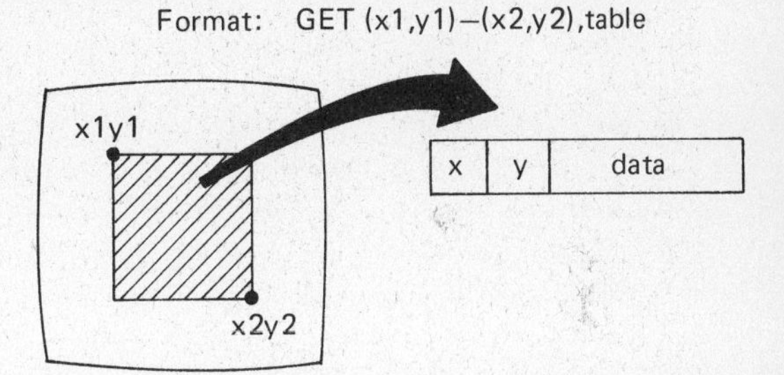

The graphics statement PUT is the opposite of GET, and will read the data stored in the table and display the coloured points on the screen.

Format: PUT (x,y),table [,action]

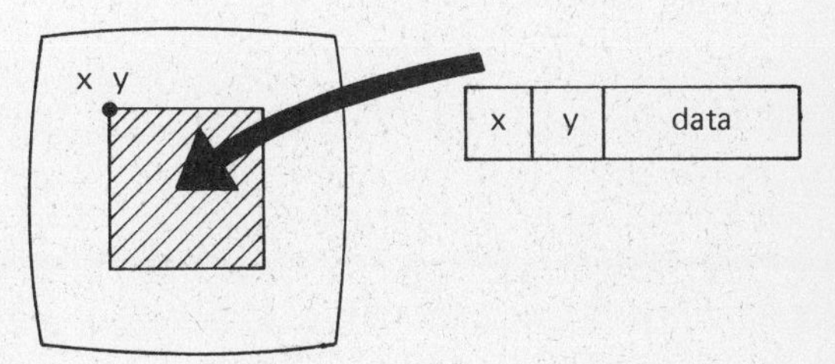

The table that is used must be numeric, and the size of the table is calculated from the expression 4 + INT((x*bitsperpixel + 7)/8)*y where x and y are the lengths of the horizontal and vertical sides of the rectangle. The number of bits per pixel is 2 in medium resolution and 1 in high resolution. For example if a picture was contained in a rectangle 50x20 pixels in high resolution then the number of bytes necessary for storing the table would be: 4 + INT ((50 + 7)/8)*20, or 144 bytes. If the table is declared for single precision numbers then a single element within the table uses 4 bytes, hence, the dimension of the table is defined as DIM T(36). The data is stored in the table as first two bytes (x dimension), next two bytes (y dimension), remainder of table (colour codes for points).

In animation the action specified in the PUT statement is either XOR or PSET. XOR causes the colours of the points on the screen to be inverted where a point exists in the table image. When an image is PUT against a background twice, the background is restored unchanged. An image can be moved around the screen without the background being destroyed.

Having first created a shape on the screen and stored the details of the shape in a table using GET, the animation of the shape can be performed as follows.

PUT the shape on the screen using XOR.
PUT the shape on the screen for a second time using XOR. This has the effect of removing the original foreground shape, but leaves the background unchanged.
Re-calculate the new position of the shape (change the values of x,y in the PUT statement).
Repeat the procedure until the shape is meant to stop moving.

PUT and GET will operate faster if the rectangle boundary falls on the byte boundary i.e. in high resolution X_1 MOD8 is zero and in medium resolution X_1 MOD4 is zero.

Flicker can be reduced by introducing a delay between drawing and removing the image, and ensuring a minimum delay in drawing the shape with modified coordinates.

If it is not necessary to preserve the background then PSET should be used for the action in the PUT statement. The function of PSET is to draw points at specified positions on the screen. The use of PSET should be faster than XOR since only one PUT is required to move the shape. This technique requires two images to be displayed on the screen, one before movement and one after movement. The after movement image has the effect of erasing the before image.

BBC/Electron.

When a character is displayed on a screen the ASCII code for that character is used to look-up the composition of the character. All characters are formed from an 8x8 dot matrix. ASCII codes 224 to 255 inclusive have been set aside for user defined dot matrix patterns when using the VDU 23 command.

Each row of the 8x8 dot matrix corresponds to 8 binary digits (bits). The value of each bit position is shown in the following diagram.

single row of matrix	128	64	32	16	8	4	2	1

A binary number (00110101) can be evaluated as:
(0x128)+(0x64)+(1x32)+(1x16)+(0x8)+(1x4)+(0x2)+(1x1) = 53

If bit (0) represents the absence of a dot and bit (1) the presence of a dot, then each row of the 8x8 matrix used to define a character will correspond to a number. The following diagram illustrates a picture of a fighter plane used in a very popular science fiction film. The value of each row of the matrix has been included.

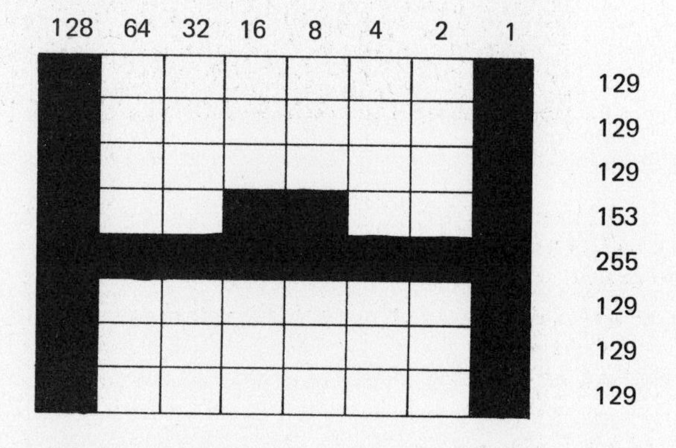

To store the character as code 224 the VDU command is coded as:

```
VDU  23,224,129,129,129,153,255,129,129,129
```

Since code 224 is a character it can be moved in relation to the text coordinates using the PRINT and TAB statements.

The following program will move the fighter plane across the screen.

```
10  MODE 4
20  VDU 23,224,129,129,129,153,255,129,129,129
30  FOR X=0 TO 39
40    PRINT TAB(X,15);CHR$(224)
50      FOR D=1 TO 100:NEXT D
60    PRINT TAB(X,15);"  "
70  NEXT X
```

The results of this program are given in figure 19.14.

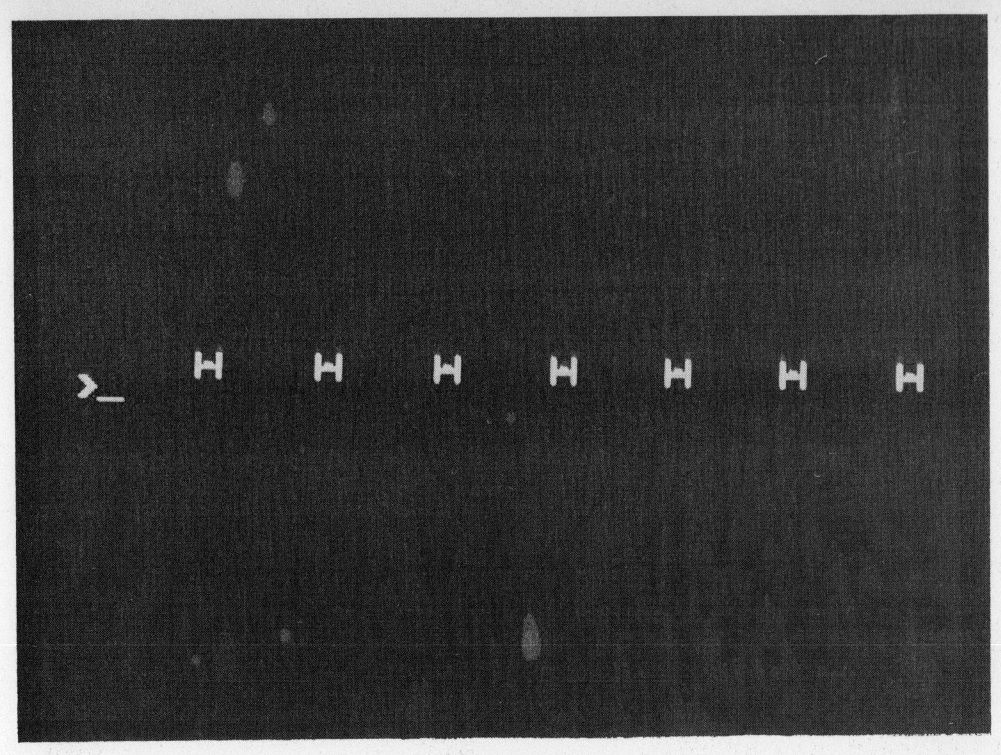

Figure 19.14

If figures larger than the size of a single character are required, they should be defined by using a combination of characters. Each character, and hence the entire figure, can be displayed on a screen using repeated VDU 23 commands.

19.7 Keywords

Pixel, resolution (high, medium, low), windows, colour; coordinate systems, plotting points, drawing lines, drawing curves, filling shapes;
storing shapes, animation.

19.8 Questions

1 Write computer programs to plot the following shapes.

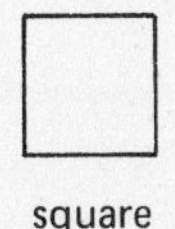
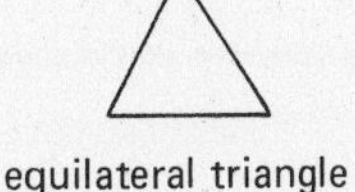
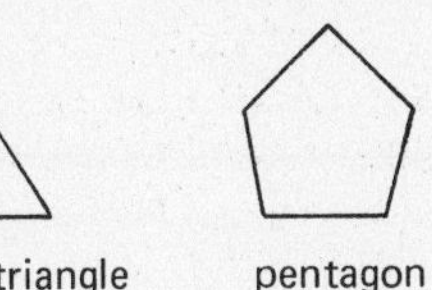

square   equilateral triangle   pentagon

2 Write a computer program to plot the path of a small circle moving around the circumference of a larger circle.

3 Using the polar equation $r = a(1 + e\cos\theta)$ where $0 \leqslant \theta \leqslant 2\pi$ and the relations $x = r\sin\theta$, $y = r\cos\theta$. Write a program to plot graphs for e = 0.5, 1 and 2. Select a value for a so that the graphs are large enough to fill the screen of your monitor. Hint: try values of a between 20 and 100.

4 Write a program to play *noughts and crosses* against the computer. Use a board that fills a large window on the screen. The nought and cross should be constructed from points within a 1" (2.5 cm) square. Use different colours for the lines, noughts, crosses and background. Hint: use medium resolution graphics.

5 Write a program to use the screen as an analogue clock (i.e. with face and hands). Use the computer's clock to update the position of both hands every minute.

20 Sound

20.1 Introduction

A computer users first contact with sound coming from their machine is either through an audible signal when their machine is switched on, or through playing computer games or by using the BEL character in the ASCII character set. However, several dialects of BASIC have taken the use of sound much further than this. Such dialects offer the facility to mimic many different sounds, reproduce notes and chords and hence play synthesised music. The sound statements are specific to different makes of computer. For example within the two dialects of BASIC studied in this book, microsoft use the statements PLAY and SOUND; BBC/Electron use ENVELOPE and SOUND.

This chapter explores the use of sound on a computer through two areas, musical sounds and sound patterns.

20.2 Musical Sounds

20.2.1 Notes

Both the dialects of Microsoft and BBC/Electron BASIC have SOUND statements.

Microsoft.

Format: SOUND frequency, duration

frequency — numeric expression in the range 37 to 32767 Hertz

duration — numeric expression in the range 0 to 65535 clock ticks (there are 18.2 clock ticks in 1 second).

Musical notes can only be obtained from certain frequencies, for example the following table illustrates the frequencies of the notes in the octave from middle C.

Note	Frequency
C	261.63
D	293.66
E	329.63
F	349.23
G	392.00
A	440.00
B	493.88
C	523.25

If the statement SOUND 261.63, 36.4 is typed on an IBM PC then the musical note middle C will be generated for 2 seconds.

The following program will generate the notes of the natural diatonic scale in the key of C major, ascending from middle C.

```
10 FOR I = 1 TO 8
20   READ FREQ
30   DATA 261.63, 293.66, 329.63, 349.23
40   DATA 392, 440, 493.88, 523.25
50   SOUND FREQ, 18.2
60 NEXT I
70 STOP
```

BBC/Electron.

Format: SOUND C,A,P,D

C — channel number 0,1,2,3
channel 0 produces noises, channels 1, 2 and 3 produce notes.

A — amplitude or loudness in a scale −15 to 0, where, −15 is the loudest and 0 is silence.

P — pitch 0 to 255, where, an increment of 1 corresponds to a ¼ of a semi-tone.

D — duration 1 to 255, where, each unit represents 1/20th of a second.

The following table illustrates the pitch values and corresponding notes for two octaves starting at middle C. Since semi-tones correspond to an increase or decrease of 4 on each of these values it is possible to calculate the flats and sharps for the relevant notes.

NOTE	PITCH (octave 3)	NOTE	PITCH (octave 4)
C (middle)	53	C	101
D	61	D	109
E	69	E	117
F	73	F	121
G	81	G	129
A	89	A	137
B	97	B	145

If in the last program lines 30, 40 and 50 were replaced with

```
30 DATA 53,61,69,73,81,89,97,101
40 SOUND 1,−15,FREQ,20
50 —
```

then the natural diatonic scale would again be generated.

Since the SOUND statement uses three channels for generating notes it is possible to generate up to three notes simultaneously and form a chord. For example the chord of C major consists of the notes C,E and G. Therefore, the statements

```
10  SOUND 1,–15,101,40
20  SOUND 2,–15,117,40
30  SOUND 3,–15,129,40
```

would generate C major for a duration of 2 seconds.

20.2.2 Music

In both the Microsoft and BBC/Electron dialects it is possible to generate synthesised music on the computer.

Example. The following music is the tune of *Clementine.*

If the music is played at a moderate tempo (Moderato) then the musical notes on the stave will take on the following values for the parameter *duration.*

Quaver ♪ 5   Crotchet ♩ 10   Minim 𝅗𝅥 20

A table can now be drawn up of the value of the notes, their pitch and duration.

Value	Pitch	Duration	Value	Pitch	Duration
G	129	5	A	137	20
G	129	5	A	137	5
G	129	10	B	145	5
D	109	10	C	149	10
B	145	5	C	149	10
B	145	5	B	145	5
B	145	10	A	137	5
G	129	10	B	145	10
G	129	5	G	129	10
B	145	5	G	129	5
D	157	10	B	145	5
D	157	10	A	137	10
C	149	5	D	109	10
B	145	5	F#	125	5
			A	137	5
			G	129	20

Program using BBC/Electron dialect.

```
10  FOR I = 1 TO 30
20    READ PITCH, DURATION
30    SOUND 1,–15,PITCH,DURATION
40  NEXT I
50  STOP
60  DATA 129,5,129,5,129,10,109,10,145,5,145,5,145,10,129,10
70  DATA 129,5,145,5,157,10,157,10,149,5,145,5,137,20,137,5
80  DATA 145,5,149,10,149,10,145,5,137,5,145,10,129,10,129,5
90  DATA 145,5,137,10,109,10,125,5,137,5,129,20
```

Type and run this program on your computer.

This program can be modified to play the last three notes of *Clementine* as chords, thus:

In order to synchronise the timing of the notes in the loop with the chords outside the loop it has been necessary to introduce a dummy SOUND statement that plays *silent* notes.

```
 10  FOR I = 1 TO 27
 20    READ PITCH, DURATION
 30    SOUND 1,–15, PITCH,DURATION
 40    SOUND 2,0,PITCH,DURATION
 50  NEXT I
 60  SOUND 1,–15,125,5
 70  SOUND 2,–15,109,5
 80  SOUND 1,–15,137,5
 90  SOUND 2,–15,101,5
100  SOUND 1,–15,129,20
110  SOUND 2,–15,109,20
120  DATA 129,5,129,5,129,10,109,10,145,5,145,5,145,10,129,10
130  DATA 129,5,145,5,157,10,157,10,149,5,145,5,137,20,137,5
140  DATA 145,5,149,10,149,10,145,5,137,5,145,10,129,10,129,5
150  DATA 145,5,137,10,109,10
```

After typing in this program and running it try removing line 40 and hear what happens to the music.

A similar program for *Clementine* without chords could be written to run on the IBM PC, the only changes would be to line 30 SOUND FREQUENCY, DURATION and the DATA statements would contain the frequency of the notes and not the pitch. The duration would remain the same.

Using Microsoft BASIC there is a different method of producing a synthesised tune that does not require a knowledge of the frequencies. Such a method uses the PLAY statement.

Format: PLAY string

where string consists of single character music commands. The single character commands are:

a) The notes A to G followed by either a + indicating a sharp or a – indicating a flat corresponding to the black keys on a piano.

b) O n sets the current octave. There are seven octaves numbered 0 to 6. Each octave spans the notes C to B. Octave 3 starts with middle C. Octave 4 is taken as the default.

c) > n increases the pitch by 1 octave and plays note n; < n decreases the pitch by 1 octave and plays the note n.

d) L n sets the length of the note (1/n) where n is in the range 1 to 64.

e) P n sets a rest where n is in the range 1 to 64.

f) T n sets the tempo (number of quarter notes in a minute) where n is in the range 32 to 255, the default is 255.

g) MF sets the mode to music foreground – each subsequent note will not start until the previous note or sound is finished. This is the default mode.

h) MB sets the mode to music background – each note or sound is placed in a buffer allowing the program to continue executing while music plays in the background. The maximum size of the buffer is 32 characters.

i) X is used to execute a specific string.

The tune *Clementine* can be recoded to run on the IBM PC using the PLAY statement.

20.2.2 (cont.)

```
10 REM ·· CLEMENTINE
20 LINE1$ = "L8 GG L4 GD L8 BB L4 BG L8 GB 05 L4 DD L8 C 04 B"
30 LINE2$ = "L2 A L8 AB 05 L4 CC 04 L8 BA L4 BG L8 GB L4 AD L8 F+A L2 G"
40 PLAY "T100;XLINE1$;XLINE2$;P1"
50 STOP
```

20.3 Sound Patterns

The BBC/Electron dialect contains an ENVELOPE statement that allows the loudness and the pitch of a sound to vary. The format of this statement can be simplified to:

ENVELOPE envelope number, length of step,pitch control, loudness control

The following two graphs represent the design of the sound from an alarm system.

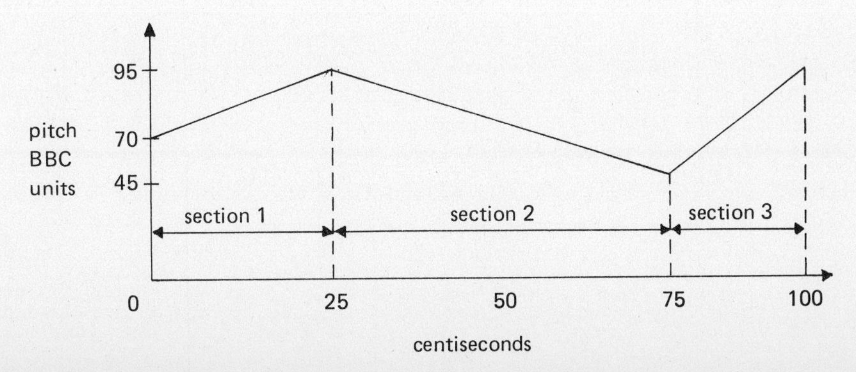

The pitch control is divided into six parameters:

- a change of pitch per step in section 1 25 pitch / 25 time = 1
- b change of pitch per step in section 2 −50 pitch / 50 time = −1
- c change of pitch per step in section 3 50 pitch / 25 time = 2
- d number of steps in section 1 (time) = 25
- e number of steps in section 2 (time) = 50
- f number of steps in section 3 (time) = 25

The pitch control is a,b,c,d,e,f = 1,−1,2,25,50,25

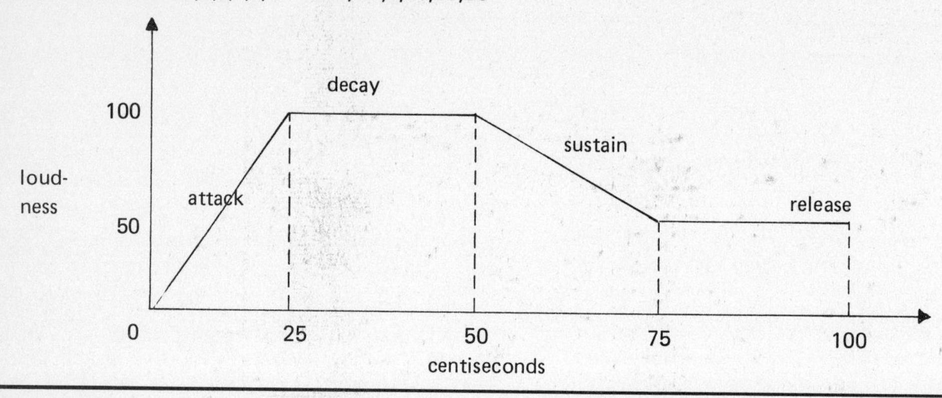

20.3 (cont.)

The loudness control is divided into six parameters:

- g change of loudness per step during attack
  100 / 25 = 4
- h change of loudness per step during decay
  0 / 25 = 0
- i change of loudness per step during sustain
  50 / 25 = 2
- j change of loudness per step during release
  0 / 25 = 0
- k target level at end of attack = 100
- l target level at end of decay = 100

The loudness control is g,h,i,j,k,l = 4,0,2,0,100,100

If the envelope number is an integer in the range 1 to 4 that replaces the loudness parameter in the SOUND statement, and the length of step in each graph is 1 centisecond then the alarm system sound is defined by the BASIC statements.

```
10 ENVELOPE 1,1,1,-1,2,25,50,25,4,0,2,0,100,100
20 SOUND 1,1,70,100
```

Try this sound on your computer. When you have had enough press *escape* to silence the machine.

If the length of each step was to change to 5 centiseconds then the parameters in the envelope would change to:

```
10 ENVELOPE 1,5,5,-5,10,5,10,5,20,0,10,0,100,100
```

How has the sound changed using a new envelope?

20.4 Keywords

Pitch (frequency), duration, octave, notes, flat, sharp; synthesised music, SOUND, PLAY; sound patterns, ENVELOPE.

20.5 Questions

1 Write a program to generate a random number in the range 1 to 9 and output in *beeps* the size of the number.

2 Write a program to store the notes C, D, E, F, G, A, and B together with their respective pitches (frequencies), from an octave of your choice, in a one-dimensional table. Input a note (including a flat or sharp) and generate the sound of that note for two seconds.

3 Write a program to play the following tune. The names of the notes have been written in to help you. Can you recognise the tune?

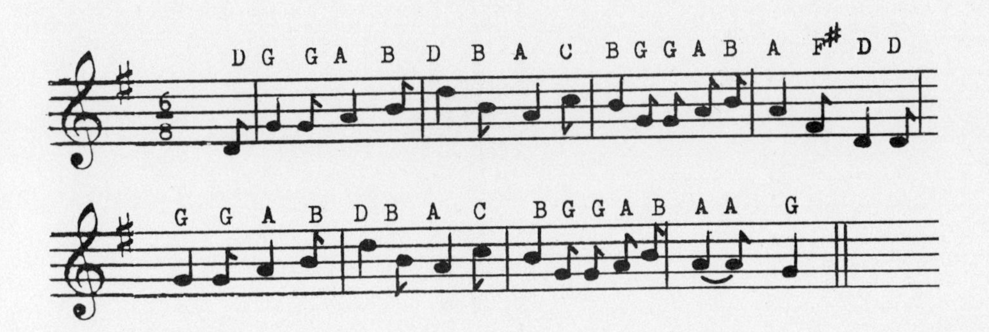

4 Write a program to generate the sound of a police car's siren, moving in relation to an observer. The police car approaches and passes the observer causing the sound of the siren to generate a *doppler effect.*

Appendix I
Answers to questions

Chapter 2

1 Input devices: bar-code reader (supermarket)
magnetic stripe reader (bank cards/credit cards)
joystick (computer games)

Output devices: synthesised speech unit (automobile warning system)
printer (bills, statements, invoices – through the post)
devices controlled by computers (traffic lights, some car braking systems)

2 Data: name(s)
destination
number of nights
airport departure
number in party

Information: price
availability of holiday
hotel name
surcharges
times of flights
dates of departure and return

3 From left to right:

integer, real, real, character string, character string, character string, integer.

4

– 128.21	embedded spaces between sign and first digit could cause an error
"AVERAGE	no closing delimiter (")
0.0147–	in most dialects the presence of a trailing sign will cause an error
9,328	no commas allowed within real or integer numbers
£761.54	currency sign is not allowed as part of a real or integer number

5

B=36, C=36, D=36
D=89
C=122
Y=–15
X=–87
B=13
Z=54
B=7

6 From left to right:

65, 77, 42, 97, 109, 47, 63, 7, 0

Chapter 3

The program designs for questions 1 to 5 inclusive, are given as questions 1 to 5 respectively, at the end of chapter 4.

6
input length
input width
input shallow depth
input deep depth
calculate volume (½ length × width (shallow + deep))
print volume
stop

7
input length
input width
input height
calculate wall space 2 × height × (length + width) – 4.5
calculate number of rolls (wall space/4.8)
calculate cost (2.5 × number of rolls)
print wall space
print number of rolls
print cost
stop

The modification required is to input values for window and door areas, wallpaper dimensions and costs, and replace the following constants in the program by:

4.5 window + door areas
4.8 paper length × paper width
2.5 cost of paper

Chapter 4

1

```
10  INPUT "NAME OF DAY",N$
20  INPUT "STARTER",S$
30  INPUT "MAIN COURSE",M$
40  INPUT "DESSERT",D$
50  PRINT "RESTAURANT MENU FOR",N$
60  PRINT
70  PRINT "STARTER:",S$
80  PRINT "MAIN COURSE:",M$
90  PRINT "DESSERT:",D$
100 PRINT
110 PRINT "THANK YOU FOR YOUR CUSTOM"
120 STOP
```

2

```
10  INPUT "NAME",N$
20  INPUT "HEIGHT",H
30  INPUT "WEIGHT",W
40  LET H1 = H*2.54
50  LET W1 = W*14*0.454
60  PRINT "PERSONAL DETAILS"
70  PRINT "NAME:",N$
80  PRINT "HEIGHT (cm):",H1
90  PRINT "WEIGHT (Kg):",W1
100 STOP
```

3

```
10 INPUT "FAHRENHEIT TEMPERATURE",F
20 LET C=(F–32)*(5/9)
30 PRINT "CENTIGRADE TEMPERATURE",C
40 STOP
```

4

```
10 INPUT "LENGTH",L
20 INPUT "WIDTH",W
30 LET A = L*W
40 LET T = 0.5*A
50 PRINT "AREA OF LAWN",A
60 PRINT "COST OF TURF",T
70 STOP
```

5

```
10 INPUT "RADIUS",R
20 LET C = 2*3.14159*R
30 LET A = 3.14159*R*R
40 PRINT "CIRCUMFERENCE",C
50 PRINT "AREA",A
60 STOP
```

6

```
10 INPUT "LENGTH",L
20 INPUT "WIDTH",W
30 INPUT "SHALLOW END",D1
40 INPUT "DEEP END",D2
50 LET V=0.5*L*W*(D1+D2)
60 PRINT "VOLUME",V
70 STOP
```

7

```
10 INPUT "LENGTH",L
20 INPUT "WIDTH",W
30 INPUT "HEIGHT",H
40 INPUT "DOOR AREA",A1
50 INPUT "WINDOW AREA",A2
60 INPUT "PAPER LENGTH",P1
70 INPUT "PAPER WIDTH",P2
80 INPUT "COST PER ROLL",C
90 LET A=2*H*(L+W)-(A1+A2)
100 LET N=A/(P1*P2)
110 LET T=N*C
120 PRINT "AREA OF PAPER",A
130 PRINT "NUMBER OF ROLLS",N
140 PRINT "COST OF PAPER",T
150 STOP
```

Chapter 5

Using your computer enter your answers to the questions given in chapter 4. LIST and RUN each program separately.

The computer will inform you of any typing errors you might have made. Correct those lines that are in error by re-typing the line (including the line number).

When each program runs correctly SAVE or FILE (depending upon your dialect of BASIC) the program using an appropriate filename. Be sure that you have a secondary storage device connected to your computer before you issue the command to SAVE or FILE your programs.

Chapter 6

1 From left to right:

false, true, true, false
true, true, false
true

2

```
X = Y
X<>Y
A>=B
Q<=T
X>=Y
(X<=Y) AND ( A<>B)
A>18 AND H>68 AND W>75
G<100 AND G>50
H<50 OR H>100
```

3

a) No statement after THEN and no END IF. The pseudocode could be re-written as:

```
IF A<=B THEN
  X = Y
END IF
```

b) The pseudocode contains an extra **ELSE** or alternatively, the lines **END IF** / **ELSE** should be coded as **ELSE** / Z = X / **END IF**

The pseudocode can be re-written in two ways.

```
IF A>B THEN
  X = Y
  IF C>D THEN
    P = Q
  END IF
  Z = X
ELSE
  A = B
END IF
```

```
IF A>B THEN
  X = Y
  IF C>D THEN
    P = Q
  ELSE
    Z = X
  END IF
ELSE
  A = B
END IF
```

4

A	B	C	output	
16	16	32	Y	Z
16	–18	32	X	Z
–2	–4	16	(none)	

5

```
 10 INPUT "MATERIAL OF TROPHY",M$
 20 IF M$ <> "gold" THEN 50
 30   PRINT "£5000"
 40 GOTO 150
 50 IF M$ <> "silver" THEN 80
 60   PRINT "£2100"
 70 GOTO 150
 80 IF M$ <> "stainless steel" THEN 110
 90   PRINT "£1000"
100 GOTO 150
110 IF M$ <> "bronze" THEN 140
120   PRINT "£300"
130 GOTO 150
140   PRINT "£200"
150 STOP
```

Note. This program assumes that the correct spelling for any metal is typed into the computer, otherwise, the cost will always be £200. The program can be improved by the following modification.

```
140 IF M$ <> "pewter" THEN 149
145   PRINT "£200"
146 GOTO 150
149 PRINT "TROPHY NOT MADE OF  ",M$
```

6

```
10 INPUT "SALES",S
20 IF S>0 AND S<1000 THEN P = .01
30 IF S>999 AND S<10000 THEN P = .05
40 IF S>9999 AND S<100000 THEN P = .1
50 LET C = S*P
60 PRINT "COMMISSION",C
70 STOP
```

7

```
 10 INPUT "PRODUCT CODE",P
 20 INPUT "VALUE OF SALE",S
 30 ON P GOTO 40,60,80,100,120
 40   LET C=0.005*S
 50 GOTO 130
 60   LET C=0.01*S
 70 GOTO 130
 80   LET C=0.02*S
 90 GOTO 130
100   LET C=0.025*S
110 GOTO 130
120   LET C=0.035*S
130 PRINT "COMMISSION ON PRODUCT",C
140 STOP
```

8

```
10 INPUT "FIRST READING",Q1
20 INPUT "SECOND READING",Q2
30 LET T=1.04*(Q2-Q1)
40 IF T>50 THEN 70
50   LET C=24*T
60 GOTO 80
70   LET C=21*(T-50)+1200
80 PRINT "COST OF GAS",C
90 STOP
```

9

```
 10 INPUT "HOURS WORKED",H
 20 IF H>60 THEN 80
 30   IF H>35 THEN 60
 40     LET W=8*H
 50   GOTO 90
 60     LET W=12*(H-35)+280
 70   GOTO 90
 80   LET W=16*(H-60)+580
 90 PRINT "GROSS WAGE",W
100 STOP
```

10

```
 10 INPUT "COURSEWORK MARK",C
 20 INPUT "EXAMINATION MARK",E
 30 LET S=C+E
 40 IF S<39 THEN 120
 50   IF C<15 THEN 110
 60     IF E<15 THEN 90
 70       IF S=39 THEN LET S=40
 80       GOTO 120
 90     LET S=39
100     GOTO 120
110   LET S=39
120 PRINT "TOTAL MARK",S
130 STOP
```

Chapter 7

1

a) No negative step value if the intention is to decrease I between the limits of 10 and 1.
No variable (I) after NEXT.

b) In line 10 and 20 the (,) is illegal it should be replaced by TO.
The I and the J loops cross.

c) I is used as a loop variable, however, this is changed in value within the loop (line 20).

2

a) I = 1 TO 4 is not a condition.

b) Syntax incorrect. REPEAT marks the entry point into the loop, and UNTIL J > 3 marks the end point of the loop **not** END REPEAT.

c) The condition I < = 0 is used to exit from the loop, however, I will remain positive until it becomes too large for the computer to store. A loop has been set up with no control over the number of iterations.

3

```
10 FOR I = 1 TO 10
20   INPUT "HOURS WORKED",H
30   LET P = 12*(H–40)
40   IF P > 0 THEN PRINT "OVERTIME PAY",P
50 NEXT I
60 STOP
```

4

a)

```
10 FOR I = 1 TO 49 STEP 2
20   PRINT I
30 NEXT I
40 STOP
```

b)

```
10 FOR I = 2 TO 50 STEP 2
20   LET S = I*I
30   PRINT I,S
40 NEXT I
50 STOP
```

c)

```
10 LET S=0
20 FOR I = 11 TO 19 STEP 2
30   LET S = S + I ↑ 3
40 NEXT I
50 PRINT "SUM OF CUBES",S
60 STOP
```

5

```
 10 REM..GLOSSARY
 20 REM..N1 FIRST NUMBER
 30 REM..N2 SECOND NUMBER
 40 REM..C COUNTER
 50 N1=1
 60 N2=1
 70 C=2
 80 IF C>20 THEN STOP
 90   PRINT N1
100   PRINT N2
110   N1=N1+N2
120   N2=N2+N1
130   C=C+2
140 GOTO 80
```

6

```
 10 REM..GLOSSARY
 20 REM..T TOTAL
 30 REM..N NUMBER OF NUMBERS
 40 REM..X CURRENT NUMBER
 50 REM..M ARITHMETIC MEAN
 60 T=0
 70 N=0
 80 INPUT "NUMBER",X
 90 IF X=0 THEN 140
100    T=T+X
110    N=N+1
120    INPUT "NUMBER",X
130 GOTO 90
140 M=T/N
150 PRINT "MEAN",M
160 STOP
```

7

```
 10 REM..GLOSSARY
 20 REM..N NUMBER
 30 REM..L LARGEST NUMBER
 40 REM..C COUNTER
 50 INPUT "NUMBER",N
 60 C=1
 70 L=N
 80 IF C=10 THEN 130
 90    INPUT "NUMBER",N
100    C=C+1
110    IF N>L THEN L=N
120 GOTO 80
130 PRINT "LARGEST",L
140 STOP
```

8

```
 10 REM..GLOSSARY
 20 REM..P NUMBER OF POUNDS STERLING
 30 REM..T TEN POUND NOTES
 40 REM..F FIVE POUND NOTES
 50 INPUT "NUMBER OF POUNDS",P
 60 T=0
 70 F=0
 80 IF P<10 THEN 120
 90   P=P-10
100   T=T+1
110 GOTO 80
120 IF P<5 THEN 150
130   P=P-5
140   F=1
150 PRINT "TENS",T
160 PRINT "FIVES",F
170 PRINT "ONES",P
180 STOP
```

This answer may be re-written using mathematical functions described in Chapter 13 section 13.8.2.

```
10 INPUT "NUMBER OF POUNDS",P
20 T=P DIV 10
30 P=P MOD 10
40 F=P DIV 5
50 P=P MOD 5
60 PRINT "TENS",T
70 PRINT "FIVES",F
80 PRINT "ONES",P
90 STOP
```

Chapter 8

1

```
 10 REM..SET WEIGHTS IN EACH CLASS TO ZERO
 20 A=0:B=0:C=0:D=0
 30 REPEAT
 40   INPUT "WEIGHT",W
 50   REM..ANALYSE WEIGHTS
 60   IF W<=4 THEN 90
 70      D=D+1
 80   GOTO 160
 90   IF W<=2 THEN 120
100     C=C+1
110  GOTO 160
120  IF W<=1 THEN 150
130    B=B+1
140  GOTO 160
150    A=A+1
160  INPUT "MORE JOINTS Y/N",A$
170 UNTIL A$="N"
180 PRINT "CLASS A",A
190 PRINT "CLASS B",B
200 PRINT "CLASS C",C
210 PRINT "CLASS D",D
220 STOP
```

2

```
 10 REM..INITIALISE TOTALS TO ZERO
 20 FS=0:FD=0:FP=0:SS=0:SD=0:SP=0
 30 P=0
 40 REPEAT
 50   INPUT "FIRST F OR SECOND S",T$
 60   INPUT "SINGLE S, DAY D OR PERIOD P",D
 70   IF T$="S" THEN 120
 80     IF D$="S" THEN FS=FS+1:GOTO 150
 90     IF D$="D" THEN FD=FD+1:GOTO 150
100     FP=FP+1:GOTO 150
120    IF D$="S" THEN SS=SS+1:GOTO 150
130    IF D$="D" THEN SD=SD+1:GOTO 150
140    SP=SP+1
150 P=P+1
160 INPUT "MORE PASSENGERS Y/N",A$
170 UNTIL A$="N"
180 PRINT "FIRST SINGLE",FS
190 PRINT "      DAY   ",FD
200 PRINT "      PERIOD",FP
210 PRINT "SECOND SINGLE",SS
220 PRINT "       DAY   ",SD
230 PRINT "       PERIOD",SP
240 PRINT "TOTAL NUMBER OF PASSENGERS",P
250 STOP
```

3

```
  5 REPEAT
 10 INPUT "AGE",A
 20 INPUT "UK OR F",M$
 30 INPUT "TIME OF LAST ACCIDENT",Y
 40 INPUT "VALUE OF CAR",V
 50 IF A<25 THEN 110
 60   IF M$="F" THEN 90
 70      IF Y>=3 THEN P=0.06*V:T$="COMP" ELSE P=0.07*V:T$="COMP+$10 EXCESS"
 80   GOTO 160
 90      IF Y>=3 THEN P=0.06*V:T$="COMP+$10 EXCESS" ELSE P=0.07*V:T$="THIRD PARTY"
100 GOTO 160
110 IF M$="F" THEN 140
120   IF Y>=3 THEN P=0.06*V:T$="COMP+$10 EXCESS" ELSE P=0: T$="DECLINE RISK"
130   GOTO 160
140   IF Y>=3 THEN P=0.08*V:T$="COMP+$10 EXCESS" ELSE P=0: T$="DECLINE RISK"
160 PRINT "TYPE OF POLICY",T$
170 PRINT "PREMIUM",P
180 INPUT "ANOTHER CLIENT Y/N",A$
190 UNTIL A$="N"
200 STOP
```

4

```
  5 REPEAT
 10 INPUT "GROSS SALARY",G
 20 INPUT "PERSONAL STATUS M/S",P$
 30 INPUT "NUMBER OF CHILDREN",C
 40 REM..CALCULATE TAXABLE INCOME
 50 IF P$="S" THEN 80
 60   T=G-2300-(100*C)
 70 GOTO 90
 80   T=G-1200
 90 REM..CALCULATE INCOME TAX
100 IF T>4000 THEN 160
110   IF T>2000 THEN 150
120      IF T>1000 THEN 140
130         X=0:GOTO 170
140         X=0.2*T:GOTO 170
150         X=0.3*(T-2000)+200:GOTO 170
160         X=0.4*(T-4000)+800
170 PRINT "TAX PAID",X
180 INPUT "ANOTHER EMPLOYEE Y/N",A$
190 UNTIL A$="N"
200 STOP
```

5

```
 10 S=0
 20 INPUT "LIMITS A,B",A,B
 30 INPUT "INCREMENT",H
 40 FOR X=A TO B STEP H
 50    Y0=X^2:Y1=(X+H/2)^2:Y2=(X+H)^2
 60    S=S+(1/6*H*(Y0+4*Y1+Y2))
 70 NEXT X
 80 PRINT "AREA",S
 90 STOP
```

6

```
 10 F=0:T=0:W=0
 20 INPUT "LENGTH OF MOULDING",L
 30 IF L=0 THEN 110
 40   IF L<0.5 THEN 60
 50     L=L-0.5:F=F+1:GOTO 40
 60   IF L<0.2 THEN 80
 70     L=L-0.2:T=T+1:GOTO 60
 80   IF L>0 THEN W=W+1
 90   INPUT "LENGTH OF MOULDING",L
100 GOTO 30
110 PRINT "0.5M",F
120 PRINT "0.2M",T
130 PRINT "WASTED LENGTHS",W
140 STOP
```

7

```
 10 FOR T=600 TO 659
 20  IF T=600 THEN PRINT "CH ON",T:GOTO 50
 30  IF T=645 THEN PRINT "TEAMAKER ON",T:GOTO 50
 40  IF T=655 THEN PRINT "TEAMAKER OFF",T:GOTO 50
 50 FOR D=1 TO 1000:NEXT D
 55 NEXT T
 60 FOR T=700 TO 759
 70  IF T=700 THEN PRINT "RADIO ON",T:GOTO 160
 80  IF T=701 THEN PRINT "BED LIGHT ON",T:GOTO 160
 90  IF T=705 THEN PRINT "BATH TAPS ON",T:GOTO 160
100  IF T=707 THEN PRINT "BATH TAPS OFF",T:GOTO 160
110  IF T=708 THEN PRINT "BATH & LANDING LIGHTS ON",T:GOTO 160
120  IF T=730 THEN PRINT "HALL LIGHTS ON",T:GOTO 160
130  IF T=745 THEN PRINT "CH OFF",T:GOTO 160
140  IF T=755 THEN PRINT "RADIO OFF",T:GOTO 160
150  IF T=759 THEN PRINT "ALL LIGHTS OFF",T
160 FOR D=1 TO 1000:NEXT D
165 NEXT T
170 STOP
```

8

```
 10 REPEAT
 20 INPUT "TYPE OF CAR",T$
 30 INPUT "NUMBER OF DOORS",D
 40 IF T$<>"HATCHBACK" THEN 90
 50   ON D-2 GOTO 60,80,70
 60   P=4000:E=1400:M$="A":GOTO 80
 70   P=4500:E=1400:M$="B"
 80 GOTO 150
 90 IF T$<>"SALOON" THEN 140
100   ON D-1 GOTO 110,130,120
110   P=8000:E=2100:M$="C":GOTO 130
120   P=8750:E=2100:M$="D"
130 GOTO 150
140   P=9950:E=2300:M$="E"
150 PRINT "PRICE",P
160 PRINT "ENGINE SIZE CC",E
170 PRINT "MODEL",M$
180 INPUT "ANOTHER CUSTOMER Y/N",A$
190 UNTIL A$="N"
200 STOP
```

Chapter 9

1

a) Variable names should not be separated by semi-colons. INPUT A, B, C is legal.

b) Exclamation mark at end of statement illegal.

c) Semi-colon is not a legal separator in a READ statement READ X, Y, Z is legal.

d) Colon and semi-colon are not legal separators in a DATA statement DATA – 6, 14, 32 is legal.

e) The BASIC statement should be RESTORE.

f) String delimiter missing.

g) Semi-colon or comma separator missing between string literal and variable.

h) This is not a syntax error but back tabulation is not common to many BASIC dialects.

i) Multiple PRINT must appear on separate lines, or use colon separators.

j) / and; are illegal separators.

2

Line Number	A	B	C	D$	E$	F$	X	Y	Z
10	8	16	32						
30				EIGHT	SIXTEEN	THIRTY-TWO			
50							8	16	32

3

Line Number	A	B	X$	Y$	Z$
10	Error data type mismatch				
40			SALARY	TAX	out of data

4

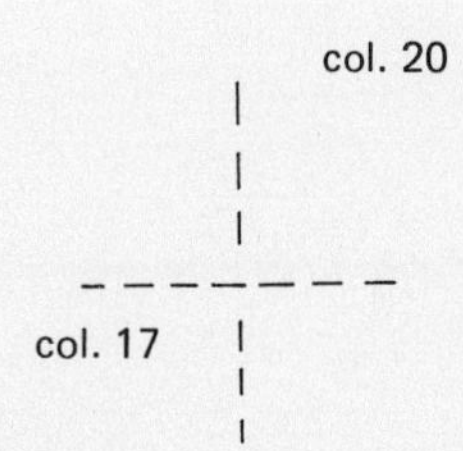

5

Glossary		
Pounds Sterling		P
French Francs		F
German Marks		M
Italian Lire		L
Exchange rate	Francs	R1
	Marks	R2
	Lire	R3

```
 10 REM · · INPUT EXCHANGE RATES
 20 PRINT "INPUT RATES FOR FRANCS, MARKS AND LIRE"
 30 INPUT R1, R2, R3
 40 PRINT
 50 REM · · OUTPUT HEADINGS
 60 PRINT TAB (25); "CURRENCY CONVERSION TABLE"
 70 PRINT
 80 PRINT "POUNDS", "FRANCS", "MARKS", "LIRE"
 90 PRINT
100 REM · · SET POUNDS TO INITIAL VALUE
110 LET P = 5
120 REM · · COMPUTE CURRENCIES
130   LET F = P * R1
140   LET M = P * R2
150   LET L = P * R3
160   REM · · OUTPUT CONVERSIONS
170   PRINT P, F, M, L
180   REM · · INCREASE POUNDS
190   LET P = P + 5
200   REM · · TEST FOR UPPER LIMIT OF TABLE
210 IF P <= 50 THEN 130
220 STOP
```

6

```
10 INPUT "PRICE PER UNIT",U
20 INPUT "RENTAL CHARGE",R
30 INPUT "VAT RATE",V1
40 INPUT "NAME OF SUBSCRIBER",N$
50 INPUT "ADDRESS - STREET",S$
60 INPUT "         - TOWN",T$
70 INPUT "         - POSTCODE",P$
80 INPUT "TELEPHONE NUMBER",D$
90 INPUT "PREVIOUS METER READING",P1
100 INPUT "PRESENT METER READING",P2
110 N=P2-P1:C=U*N:T=C+R:V2=V1*T:A=T+V2
120 PRINT TAB(20);"TELEPHONE BILL"
130 PRINT TAB(20);"--------------"
140 PRINT
150 PRINT "NAME:";N$;TAB(33);"ADDRESS:",S$
160 PRINT TAB(42);T$
170 PRINT "TELEPHONE NUMBER:"D$;TAB(42);P$
180 PRINT
190 PRINT "PREVIOUS METER READING:";P1
200 PRINT "CURRENT METER READING:";P2
210 PRINT
220 PRINT "CHARGES"
230 PRINT "-------"
240 PRINT "CALLS @ "U;"P PER UNIT ON ";N;" UNITS";TAB(47);C
250 PRINT "RENTAL";TAB(46);R
260 PRINT
270 PRINT "SUB-TOTAL";TAB(46);T
280 PRINT "VAT @ ";V1;"%";TAB(47);V2
290 PRINT
300 PRINT "TOTAL AMOUNT DUE";TAB(46);A
310 STOP
```

Chapter 10

1

a) Subroutine starts at line 100 not 1000.
RTN is an illegal statement, the end of a subroutine should contain RETURN.

b) The program ALPHA would continue to load itself and execute line 60.

c) Procedures are **not** called using GOSUB.
Procedures are usually defined by DEF PROC .....
Procedures are not ended with RETURN but END PROC.

d) After returning from the subroutine the computer will re-enter the subroutine since there is no STOP statement after line 60.

e) If X and Y are defined as being LOCAL to the procedure then they cannot be used as parameters in DEF PROC CALC(X,Y). X and Y can, however, exist as separate variables in the main program as well as local variables in the procedure.

2

a) GOTO 70 does not allow for the subroutines (2000) and (1000) to return naturally. (Technically — the return link addresses have not been popped from the system stack).

b) Since entry into subroutine 1 and subroutine 2 was through GOTO statements, the return addresses will not have been stored by the system. The statement RETURN cannot be executed correctly since the computer has no stored return link addresses.

3 The following results were obtained using a BBC model B computer.
When X = −3, 0 and 4 an ON RANGE error message was displayed. However, when X = 2.5 then the statement X = 2 was displayed (X was truncated to the nearest integer).

4

	main program	ALPHA
a	A=1 B=2 C=3	A=15 B=30 C=45
b	A=6 B=7 C=8	A=15 B=14 C=13
c	A=2 B=7 C=12	A=9 B=−5 C=4
	A=2 B=7 C=4	

5

x = 2	Y	I
entry to BETA		
1	4	2
2	16	4
3	256	16
	32	16
2	8	4
1	4	2

The effect of deleting LOCAL I is as follows.

X = 2	Y	I
entry to BETA		
1	4	2
2	16	4
3	256	16
	32	16
2	32	16
1	32	16

Chapter 11

1

a) The declaration of the size of the table A is too small, should be DIM A (50).

b) The intentional error is missing parenthesis around the subscripts for X1, X2 and X3. The use of a variable to declare the size of a table is dialect dependent.

c) If M > 15 and N > 10 then B (I + N, J + M) will be outside the range of the declared table DIM B (20, 30).

d) Line 10 should be DIM V(10).
If N > 10 then the declaration for the size of the table is too small.
However, if N > 5 then the program will be out of data. There exists a type mismatch between V(I) and the data.

e) Line 40 there exists a type mismatch between T(I, J) and the first five items of data.

2

```
10 DIM T (6, 9)
20 FOR I = 1 TO 6
30   FOR J = 1 TO 9
40     LET T (I,J) = 100
50   NEXT J
60 NEXT I
```

3

```
10 DIM X(8), Y(8)
20 FOR I = 1 TO 8
30   LET J = 9 – I
40   LET Y(J) = X(I)
50 NEXT I
```

4

```
 10  DIM A(10), B(10)
 20  REM · · PROCEDURE TO INPUT NUMBERS
 30  FOR I = 1 TO 10
 40    INPUT A(I), B(I)
 50  NEXT I
 60  REM · · TO OUTPUT THOSE NUMBERS THAT ARE COMMON (a)
 70  FOR I = 1 TO 10
 80    FOR J = 1 TO 10
 90      IF A(I) <> B(J) THEN 120
100        PRINT A(I)
110      GOTO 130
120    NEXT J
130  NEXT I
140  REM · · FIND SUMS OF CORRESPONDING ELEMENTS (b)
150  FOR I = 1 TO 10
160    LET S = A(I) + B(I)
170    PRINT S
180  NEXT I
190  REM · · FIND SMALLEST OF CORRESPONDING ELEMENTS (c)
200  FOR I = 1 TO 10
210    IF A(I) < B(I) THEN 240
220      PRINT B(I)
230    GOTO 250
240    PRINT A(I)
250  NEXT I
260  STOP
```

5

Glossary	
One dimensional table to hold word	A$
One dimensional table to hold vowels	V$
One dimensional table to hold number of vowels	S
Letters of word	X$
Subscripts	I,J,K

Assume the end of a word is terminated by a space, and a word contains no more than twenty letters.

```
10  DIM A$(20), V$(5), S(5)
20  REM · · STORE VOWELS IN TABLE V
30  FOR I = 1 TO 5
40    READ V$(I)
50    DATA "A", "E", "I", "O", "U"
60  NEXT I
70  REM · · INITIALISE TABLE S
80  FOR I = 1 TO 5
90    LET S(I) = 0
100 NEXT I
110 REM · · INPUT AND STORE LETTERS OF WORD
120 REM · · TERMINATE WORD WITH A SPACE
130 LET I = 1
140   INPUT X$
150   IF X$ = " " THEN 200
160   LET A$(I) = X$
170   LET I = I + 1
180 GOTO 140
190 REM · · COUNT NUMBER OF VOWELS IN WORD
200 FOR J = 1 TO I - 1
210   FOR K = 1 TO 5
220     IF A$(J) <> V$(K) THEN 250
230       LET S(K) = S(K) + 1
240     GOTO 260
250   NEXT K
260 NEXT J
270 REM · · OUTPUT CLASSIFIED VOWEL COUNT
280 FOR I = 1 TO 5
290   PRINT V$(I); TAB(10); S(I)
300 NEXT I
310 STOP
```

6a

```
 10 DIM V(50),A(49),B(49)
 20 INPUT "NUMBER OF ENTRIES IN LIST",N
 30 FOR I=1 TO N
 40   INPUT "ENTRY",V(I)
 50 NEXT I
 60 P=1
 70 FOR I=1 TO N
 80   IF V(I)>V(P) THEN A(P)=A(P)+1
 90 NEXT I
100 B(P)=N-A(P)-1
110 P=P+1
120 IF P<N+1 THEN 70
130 FOR I=1 TO N
140    IF A(I)=B(I) THEN 160
150 NEXT I
160 PRINT "MEDIAN IS";V(I)
170 STOP
```

6b

```
 10 DIM V(50),A(49),B(49)
 20 INPUT "NUMBER OF ENTRIES IN LIST",N
 30 FOR I=1 TO N
 40   INPUT "ENTRY",V(I)
 50 NEXT I
 60 P=1
 70 FOR I=1 TO N
 80   IF V(I)>V(P) THEN A(P)=A(P)+1
 90 NEXT I
100 B(P)=N-A(P)-1
110 P=P+1
120 IF P<N+1 THEN 70
130 FOR I=1 TO N
140    IF A(I)=B(I)+1 THEN M1=V(I)
150    IF B(I)=A(I)+1 THEN M2=V(I)
160 NEXT I
170 M=(M1+M2)/2
180 PRINT "MEDIAN IS ";M
190 STOP
```

7

```
 10 DIM M(4,5)
 20 FOR I=1 TO 4
 30    FOR J=1 TO 5
 40      INPUT "ENTRY",M(I,J)
 50    NEXT J
 60 NEXT I
 70 REM..SEARCH ROWS FOR HIGHEST AND LOWEST VALUES
 80 FOR I=1 TO 4
 90   B=M(I,1):S=M(I,1)
100    FOR J=2 TO 5
110      IF B<M(I,J) THEN B=M(I,J)
120      IF S>M(I,J) THEN S=M(I,J)
130    NEXT J
140    PRINT "ROW";I;"MAX ";B;" MIN ";S
150 NEXT I
160 REM..SEARCH COLUMNS FOR HIGHEST AND LOWEST VALUES
170 FOR J=1 TO 5
180   B=M(1,J):S=M(1,J)
190   FOR I=2 TO 4
200    IF B<M(I,J) THEN B=M(I,J)
210    IF S>M(I,J) THEN S=M(I,J)
220   NEXT I
230   PRINT "COLUMN";J;" MAX ";B;" MIN ";S
240 NEXT J
250 STOP
```

8/9

```
 10 GOSUB 110:GOSUB 300:GOSUB 400
 20 STOP
110 DIM C$(3),T$(3,3),P(3,3)
120 C$(1)="CORNWALL":C$(2)="DORSET":C$(3)="HAMPSHIRE"
130 FOR I=1 TO 3
140    READ T$(I,1),T$(I,2),T$(I,3)
150 NEXT I
160 DATA PENZANCE,TRURO,NEWQUAY
170 DATA POOLE,DORCHESTER,SHAFTESBURY
180 DATA SOUTHAMPTON,BASINGSTOKE,WINCHESTER
190 FOR I=1 TO 3
200    READ P(I,1),P(I,2),P(I,3)
210 NEXT I
220 DATA 19360,15690,13890
230 DATA 118922,13880,4180
240 DATA 204406,60910,31620
250 RETURN
300 INPUT "COUNTY",X$
310 INPUT "TOWN",Y$
320 FOR I=1 TO 3
330   IF X$=C$(I) THEN X=I
340 NEXT I
350 FOR J=1 TO 3
360   IF Y$=T$(X,J) THEN Y=J
370 NEXT J
380 PRINT "POPULATION OF ";Y$;" IS ";P(X,Y)
390 RETURN
400 INPUT "COUNTY",X$
410 FOR I=1 TO 3
420    IF X$=C$(I) THEN X=I
430 NEXT I
440 T=P(X,1)+P(X,2)+P(X,3)
450 PRINT "POPULATION OF TOWNS IN ";X$;" IS ";T
460 T1=0
470 FOR I=1 TO 3
480   FOR J=1 TO 3
490     T1=T1+P(I,J)
500   NEXT J
510 NEXT I
520 PRINT "THIS REPRESENTS ";T/T1*100;"% OF ALL TOWNS LISTED"
530 RETURN
```

10

```
10 DIM M$(16,4)
20 FOR I=1 TO 16
30   READ M$(I,1),M$(I,2),M$(I,3),M$(I,4)
40 NEXT I
50 DATA SUNBURY,1,A308," "
60 DATA KINGSTON,1,A308,5
70 DATA CENTRAL LONDON,1,A316,14
80 DATA THE NORTH (M1),2,M25," "
90 DATA HEATHROW (M4),2,M25,10
100 DATA STAINES (A30),2,M25,4
110 DATA CHERTSEY (A320),2,M25,4
120 DATA GUILDFORD,3,A322,11
130 DATA BRACKNELL,3,A322,6
140 DATA FARNBOROUGH,4,A325,3
150 DATA FARNHAM,4,A325,8
160 DATA CAMBERLEY,4,A321,3
170 DATA ALTON,5,A32,10
180 DATA READING,5,A32,14
190 DATA BASINGSTOKE,6,A339,2
200 DATA NEWBURY,6,A339,21
210 INPUT "NAME OF TOWN",T$
220 FOR I=1 TO 16
230   IF T$=M$(I,1) THEN 260
240 NEXT I
250 PRINT "NAME NOT FOUND":GOTO 210
260 PRINT "JUNCTION ";M$(I,2);" ROAD ";M$(I,3);" DISTANCE ";M$(I,4)
270 STOP
```

Chapter 12

1

a) The function ASC returns a numeric value, hence K$ causes a mismatch of data types.

b) The function CHR$ requires a numeric argument **not** a string argument. The function returns a single character, hence K causes a mismatch of data types.

c) The function RIGHT only requires two arguments.

d) A string **literal** has been used as an argument that only contains two characters X$. Yet the second argument 3 suggests the third character of X$ should be printed.

e) The function VAL requires a string argument. The function returns a numeric value, hence Y$ will cause a mismatch of data types.

f) The argument of VAL should be a string consisting of or at least beginning with digits.

g) The function is LEN not LEN$.

h) The GET verb requires a string variable name.

i) The CHANGE statement must contain one string variable and one numeric variable.

j) The minus sign is **not** defined in string manipulation.

2

```
 10  READ A$
 20  DATA "ABCDEFGHIJKLMNOPQRSTUVWXYZ"
 30  REM · · PRINT ALPHABET
 40  PRINT A$
 50  REM · · PRINT FIRST SIX CHARACTERS
 60  PRINT LEFT$ (A$,6)
 70  REM · · PRINT LAST TEN CHARACTERS
 80  PRINT RIGHT$ (A$,10)
 90  REM · · PRINT TENTH CHARACTER
100  PRINT MID$ (A$, 10, 1)
110  STOP
```

3

```
  5  LET X$ = " "
 10  READ A$
 20  DATA "ABCDEFGHIJKLMNOPQRSTUVWXYZ"
 30  FOR I = 1 TO 25 STEP 2
 40    LET X$ = X$ + MID$ (A$, I, 1)
 50  NEXT I
 60  REM · · PRINT LENGTH OF STRING X$
 70  PRINT LEN(X$)
 80  REM · · SEARCH FOR POSITION OF SUBSTRING QSU
 90  FOR I = 1 TO 13
100    IF MID$ (X$, I, 1) = "Q" THEN 120
110  NEXT I
120  PRINT "SUBSTRING STARTS AT POSITION";I
130  STOP
```

4

```
 10  DIM V(26)
 20  READ A$
 30  DATA "ABCDEFGHIJKLMNOPQRSTUVWXYZ"
 40  REM · · INITIALISE V TO ZERO
 50  FOR I = 1 TO 26
 60    LET V(I) = 0
 70  NEXT I
 80  REM · · INPUT POEM CHARACTER BY CHARACTER, TERMINATED
 90  REM · · BY A FULL STOP
100  REM · · THE POEM IS NOT STORED
110    GET C$
120    IF C$ = "." THEN 200
130    REM · · INCREASE FREQUENCY COUNT
140    FOR I = 1 TO 26
150      IF C$ = MID$(A$,I,1) THEN 180
160    NEXT I
170    GOTO 190
180    LET V(I) = V(I) + 1
190  GOTO 110
195  REM · · OUTPUT FREQUENCY OF LETTERS
200  PRINT "LETTER", "FREQUENCY"
210  FOR I = 1 TO 26
220    PRINT MID$(A$,I,1), V(I)
230  NEXT I
240  STOP
```

5

```
 10 DIM X$(9,3),Y(9)
 20 FOR J=1 TO 3
 30   FOR I=1 TO 9
 40   READ X$(I,J)
 50   NEXT I
 60 NEXT J
 70 DATA ONE,TWO,THREE,FOUR,FIVE,SIX
 80 DATA SEVEN,EIGHT,NINE
 90 DATA ELEVEN,TWELVE,THIRTEEN,FOURTEEN
100 DATA FIFTEEN,SIXTEEN,SEVENTEEN,EIGHTEEN
110 DATA NINETEEN
120 DATA TEN,TWENTY,THIRTY,FORTY,FIFTY
130 DATA SIXTY,SEVENTY,EIGHTY,NINETY
140 FOR I=1 TO 9
150   LET Y(I)=0
160 NEXT I
170 INPUT "NUMBER ",N$
180 REM..SPLIT NUMBER INTO TWO PARTS
190 REM..INTEGER M$, FRACTION D$
200 M$="":D$=""
210 FOR I=1 TO LEN(N$)
220   Z$=MID$(N$,I,1)
230   IF Z$="." THEN 260
240     M$=M$+Z$
250 NEXT I
260 FOR J=I+1 TO LEN(N$)
270   D$=D$+MID$(N$,J,1)
280 NEXT J
290 N$=M$
300 LET J=9
310 FOR I=LEN(N$) TO 1 STEP -1
320   LET Y(J)=VAL(MID$(N$,I,1))
330   LET J=J-1
340 NEXT I
350 IF LEN(N$)>6 THEN 410
360   IF LEN(N$)>3 THEN 390
370     LET G=1
380   GOTO 420
390     LET G=2
400   GOTO 420
410     LET G=3
420 LET T$=""
430 GOSUB 610
440 REM..PROCESS DECIMAL FRACTION
450 T$=T$+" POINT "
460 REM..SCAN FRACTION AND REPLACE EACH
470 REM..DIGIT BY A FIGURATIVE CONSTANT
480 FOR I=1 TO LEN(D$)
490   Z$=MID$(D$,I,1)
500   IF Z$="0" THEN 530
510     T$=T$+" "+X$(VAL(Z$),1)+" "
520   GOTO 540
530     T$=T$+" ZERO "
540 NEXT I
550 PRINT T$
560 PRINT
570 PRINT "MORE DATA ENTER Y(YES) N(NO)"
580 INPUT A$
590 IF A$="Y" THEN 140
600 STOP
610 IF G<>3 THEN 650
620 LET I=1
630 GOSUB 740
640 LET T$=T$+" MILLION, "
650 IF MID$(N$,4,3)="000" THEN 700
660 IF G=1 THEN 700
670 LET I=4
680 GOSUB 740
690 LET T$=T$+" THOUSAND, "
700 IF RIGHT$(N$,3)="000" THEN 730
710 LET I=7
720 GOSUB 740
730 RETURN
```

```
740 IF Y(I)=0 THEN 760
750 LET T$=T$+X$(Y(I),1)+" HUNDRED "
760 IF Y(I+1)<>1 THEN 820
770 IF Y(I+2)<>0 THEN 800
780 LET T$=T$+X$(Y(I+1),3)
790 GOTO 840
800 LET T$=T$+X$(Y(I+2),2)+" "
810 GOTO 840
820 IF Y(I+1)<>0 THEN LET T$=T$+X$(Y(I+1),3)+" "
830 LET T$=T$+X$(Y(I+2),1)
840 RETURN
```

6

```
10 T=0
20 REPEAT
30    C$=INKEY$(0):PRINT C$;
40    IF C$=" " THEN T=T+1
50 UNTIL C$="."
60 T=T+1
70 PRINT
80 PRINT "NUMBER OF WORDS ";T
90 STOP
```

7

```
10 DIM X(20),Y(20),Z(20)
20 INPUT "FIRST NUMBER - 20 DIGITS",N$
30 INPUT "SECOND NUMBER - 20DIGITS",M$
40 FOR I=1 TO 20
50    X(I)=VAL(MID$(N$,I,1))
60    Y(I)=VAL(MID$(M$,I,1))
70 NEXT I
80 C=0
90 FOR I=20 TO 1 STEP -1
100    S=X(I)+Y(I)+C
110    IF S>9 THEN Z(I)=S-10:C=1 ELSE Z(I)=S:C=0
120 NEXT I
130 N$=""
140 FOR I=1 TO 20
150    N$=N$+STR$(Z(I))
160 NEXT I
170 PRINT "SUM=";N$
180 C=0
190 FOR I=20 TO 1 STEP -1
200    D=X(I)-Y(I)-C
210    IF D<0 THEN Z(I)=10-ABS(D):C=1 ELSE Z(I)=D:C=0
220 NEXT I
230 M$=""
240 FOR I=1 TO 20
250    M$=M$+STR$(Z(I))
260 NEXT I
270 PRINT "DIFFERENCE=";M$
280 STOP
```

8

```
 10 DIM M$(26,2)
 20 FOR I=1 TO 26
 30   READ M$(I,1),M$(I,2)
 40 NEXT I
 50 DATA A,.-,B,-...,C,-.-.,D,-..,E,.,F,..-.
 60 DATA G,--.,H,....,I,..,J,.---,K,-.-,L,.-..
 70 DATA M,--,N,-.,O,---,P,.--.,Q,--.-,R,.-.
 80 DATA S,...,T,-,U,..-,V,...-,W,.--,X,-..-
 90 DATA Y,-.--,Z,--..
 95 GOSUB 100:GOSUB 200:STOP
100 INPUT "SENTENCE",N$
110 FOR I=1 TO LEN(N$)
120   C$=MID$(N$,I,1)
130   FOR J=1 TO 26
140     IF C$=M$(J,1) THEN PRINT M$(J,2);" ";:GOTO 155
150   NEXT J
155 NEXT I
156 PRINT
160 RETURN
200 I=1:INPUT "MORSE CODE",Z$
210 REPEAT
220 C$=""
230   REPEAT
231     X$=MID$(Z$,I,1)
240     IF X$<>" " THEN C$=C$+X$
250     I=I+1
260   UNTIL X$=" "
270   FOR J=1 TO 26
280     IF C$=M$(J,2) THEN 300
290   NEXT J
300   PRINT M$(J,1);" ";
310 UNTIL I=LEN(Z$)+1
320 RETURN
```

Chapter 13

1

a)	4817.395	b)	−0.0001942
c)	0.1784318E + 38	d)	129.74
e)	183796219	f)	−0.2684715E − 06
g)	0.1493786E − 14	h)	0.274647941E + 35
i)	overflow	j)	0.7927194E − 36

2

a)	4.29	b)	−5	c)	−1
d)	1.3090	e)	0.5774	f)	1.6094
g)	7.3891	h)	error negative argument.		
i)	+1.0	j)	+1		

3

```
 10 DEF FNL(A) = LOG(A) / LOG(B)
 20 PRINT "NUMBERS", "BASES"
 30 PRINT TAB(10); "2"; TAB(25); "4"; TAB(40); "6"; TAB(55);
 40 PRINT "8"; TAB(70); "10"
 50 FOR A = 2 TO 10 STEP 0.5
 60   PRINT A;
 70   FOR B = 2 TO 10 STEP 2
 80     PRINT TAB(10 + 15 * (B – 2) / 2); FNL(A);
 90   NEXT B
100   PRINT
110 NEXT A
120 STOP
```

4

```
10 INPUT "COEFFICIENTS A,B,C",A,B,C
20 IF A=0 THEN STOP
30   D=B*B-4*A*C
40   IF D>0 THEN PRINT "REAL DISTINCT ROOTS ";(-B+SQR(D))/(2*A);"  ";(-B-SQR(D))/(2*A):GOTO 70
50   IF D<0 THEN PRINT "IMAGINARY ROOTS ";-B/(2*A);"+";SQR(ABS(D))/(2*A);"I";"  ";-B/(2*A);"-";SQR(ABS(D))/(2*A);"I":GOTO 70
60    PRINT "CO-INCIDENT ROOTS ";-B/(2*A)
70 INPUT "COEFFICIENTS A,B,C",A,B,C
80 GOTO 20
```

5

The method of solution to these questions is similar to the worked example given in the text, and will not be included here to avoid repetition. However, the reader should remember the following points before attempting a solution.

1. Draw a sketch of the function.
2. Pay particular attention to the behaviour of the function when X tends towards infinity (both + and –), and when X = 0.
3. Devise a suitable scale for printing the graph. From the scale chosen, the dimension of the table used to plot the points can be determined.
4. When computing the value of the function avoid values of X that are likely to cause the program to be terminated (eg LOG(O))

The reader is recommended to study Chapter 19 for further work on plotting functions.

6

a)
```
10  FOR X = 0 TO 1 STEP 0.05
20   LET Y = (SQR (X)) ↑2 – X
30   PRINT X, Y
40  NEXT X
50  STOP
```

b)
```
10  FOR X = 1 TO 10
20   LET Y = EXP(LOG(X)) – X
30   PRINT X,Y
40  NEXT X
50  STOP
```

c)
```
10  FOR X = –100 TO 100 STEP 10
20   LET Y = TAN (ATN(X)) – X
30   PRINT X,Y
40  NEXT X
50  STOP
```

7

```
 10 PRINT "KILOMETRES";TAB(15);"MILES";TAB(25);"YARDS";TAB(35);"FEET";TAB(45);"INCH
 20 PRINT
 30 FOR K=1 TO 51 STEP 5
 40    M=K*0.6214:M1=INT(M)
 50    Y=1760*(M-M1):Y1=INT(Y)
 60    F=3*(Y-Y1):F1=INT(F)
 70   I=INT(12*(F-F1))
 80   PRINT K;TAB(15);M1;TAB(25);Y1;TAB(35);F1;TAB(45);I
 90 NEXT K
100 STOP
```

8

```
 10  INPUT X,Y
 20  REM · · CALCULATE ORDINATE OF Y = 2X + 3
 30  LET Y1 = 2 * X + 3
 40  REM · · FIND POSITION OF POINT RELATIVE TO LINE
 50  LET D = Y – Y1
 60  PRINT "CO-ORDINATES";X;"  ";Y;
 70  IF D < 0 THEN PRINT "BELOW LINE"
 80  IF D = 0 THEN PRINT "ON LINE"
 90  IF D > 0 THEN PRINT "ABOVE LINE"
100  STOP
```

9

```
 10 DIM D(6)
 20 FOR S=1 TO 3
 30   READ M
 40   DATA 10,100,1000
 50   FOR J=1 TO 6
 60     D(J)=0
 70   NEXT J
 80  FOR R=1 TO M
 90    X=INT(6*RND(1)+1)
100    Y=INT(6*RND(1)+1)
110    IF X=Y THEN D(X)=D(X)+1
120  NEXT R
130  PRINT "FOR ";M;" ROLLS OF DICE, DOUBLES ARE:"
140  PRINT
150  PRINT "NUMBER","FREQUENCY"
160  FOR J=1 TO 6
170    PRINT J,D(J)
180  NEXT J
190 NEXT S
200 STOP
```

10

```
 10 DIM S(2)
 20 REM · · SET SCORES TO ZERO
 30 LET S(1) = 0
 40 LET S(2) = 0
 50 REM · · SELECT FIRST PLAYER
 60 LET N = 1
 70 IF S(N) = 51 THEN 290
 80   LET D1 = INT (6 * RND(0) + 1)
 90   LET D2 = INT (6 * RND(0) + 1)
100   REM · · TEST EITHER DIE FOR 6
110   IF D1 = 6 THEN 130
120     IF D2 <> 6 THEN 150
130     LET S(N) = S(N) + 3
140   REM · · TEST FOR BOTH DICE SAME
150   IF D1 = D2 THEN 190
160     REM · · TEST FOR TOTAL = 9
170     IF D1 + D2 = 9 THEN LET S(N) = S(N) + 3
180   GOTO 210
190   LET S(N) = S(N) + 3
200   REM · · TEST SCORE FOR END OF GAME
210   IF S(N) = 51 THEN 290
220     IF S(N) > 51 THEN S(N) = S(N) – 6
230   REM · · CHANGE PLAYER
240   IF N = 1 THEN 270
250     LET N = 1
260   GOTO 280
270     LET N = 2
280 GOTO 70
290 PRINT "PLAYER";N;"WINS"
300 STOP
```

11

```
500 DEF PROCMATREAD
510 DIM M(9,9)
520 INPUT "NUMBER OF ROWS",R
530 INPUT "             COLUMNS",C
540 FOR I=1 TO R
550   FOR J=1 TO C
560     READ M(I,J)
570   NEXT J
580 NEXT I
590 ENDPROC
600 DEF PROCMATPRINT
610 FOR I=1 TO R
620   FOR J=1 TO C
630     PRINT M(I,J);
640   NEXT J
650   PRINT
660 NEXT I
670 ENDPROC
```

12

```
100 DEF PROCZER(N)
110 FOR I=1 TO N
120   FOR J=1 TO N
130     M(I,J)=0
140   NEXT J
150 NEXT I
160 ENDPROC
200 DEF PROCCON(N)
210 FOR I=1 TO N
220   FOR J=1 TO N
230     M(I,J)=1
240   NEXT J
250 NEXT I
260 ENDPROC
300 DEF PROCIDN(N)
310 PROCZER(N)
320 FOR I=1 TO N
330   M(I,I)=1
340 NEXT I
350 ENDPROC
400 DEF PROCDET(N)
410 FOR K=1 TO N-1
420   FOR I=K+1 TO N
430     ZM=-M(I,K)/M(K,K)
440     FOR J=K+1 TO N
450       M(I,J)=M(I,J)+ZM*M(K,J)
460     NEXT J
470   NEXT I
480 NEXT K
490 S=1
500 FOR J=1 TO N
510   S=S*M(J,J)
520 NEXT J
530 ENDPROC
600 DEF PROCTRN(N)
610 FOR I=1 TO N
620   FOR J=1 TO N
630     M(I,J)=T(J,I)
640   NEXT J
650 NEXT I
660 ENDPROC
```

13

```
100 DEF PROCADD(N)
110 FOR I=1 TO N
120   FOR J=1 TO N
130     C(I,J)=A(I,J)+B(I,J)
140   NEXT J
150 NEXT I
160 ENDPROC
200 DEF PROCSUB(N)
210 FOR I=1 TO N
220   FOR J=1 TO N
230     C(I,J)=A(I,J)-B(I,J)
240   NEXT J
250 NEXT I
260 ENDPROC
300 DEF PROCMLT(N)
310 FOR R=1 TO N
320   FOR C=1 TO N
330   T=0
340     FOR P=1 TO N
350       T=T+A(R,P)*B(P,C)
360     NEXT P
370     C(R,C)=T
380   NEXT C
390 NEXT R
400 ENDPROC
```

14

```
 10 DIM DW(3,3),DX(3,3),DY(3,3),DZ(3,3),M(3,3)
 20 FOR I=1 TO 3
 30   FOR J=1 TO 3
 40     READ DW(I,J),DX(I,J),DY(I,J),DZ(I,J)
 50   NEXT J
 60 NEXT I
 70 DATA 1,20,1,1,2,2,20,2,5,5,5,20
 80 DATA 2,7,2,2,1,1,7,1,1,1,1,7
 90 DATA 5,5,5,5,-3,-3,5,-3,2,2,2,5
100 N=3
110 FOR I=1 TO N:FOR J=1 TO N:M(I,J)=DW(I,J):NEXT J:NEXT I
120 PROCDET(N,M)
130 T=S
140 FOR I=1 TO N:FOR J=1 TO N:M(I,J)=DX(I,J):NEXT J:NEXT I
150 PROCDET(N,M)
160 X=S/T
170 FOR I=1 TO N:FOR J=1 TO N:M(I,J)=DY(I,J):NEXT J:NEXT I
180 PROCDET(N,M)
190 Y=S/T
200 FOR I=1 TO N:FOR J=1 TO N:M(I,J)=DZ(I,J):NEXT J:NEXT I
210 PROCDET(N,M)
220 Z=S/T
230 PRINT "X=";X,"Y=";Y,"Z=";Z
240 STOP
250 DEF PROCDET(N,M)
260 FOR K=1 TO N-1
270   FOR I=K+1 TO N
280      ZM=-M(I,K)/M(K,K)
290      FOR J=K+1 TO N
300        M(I,J)=M(I,J)+ZM*M(K,J)
310      NEXT J
320   NEXT I
330 NEXT K
340 S=1
350 FOR J=1 TO N
360   S=S*M(J,J)
370 NEXT J
380 ENDPROC
```

Chapter 14

1

```
 10 DIM T(20)
 20 FOR I = 1 TO 20
 30   READ X
 40   LET T(X) = X
 50 NEXT I
 60 DATA 16,18,1,3,20,7,5,2,10,19,17,13,4,6,9,11,8,14,12,15
 70 FOR I = 1 TO 20
 80   PRINT T(I)
 90 NEXT I
100 STOP
```

Note. The output from this program will be the twenty integers sorted into ascending order.

2

```
 10  DIM V$(10)
 20  FOR I = 1 TO 10
 30    INPUT V$(I)
 40  NEXT I
 50  N = 10
 60  GOSUB 999
 70  FOR I = 1 TO 10
 80    PRINT V$(I)
 90  NEXT I
100  STOP
```

Note. Necessary changes to the Shell sort are all references to table X being changed to table V$, and temporary store T to T$ in lines 1070,1500,1510,1520,1590,1610, 1620,1630.

3

```
10  DIM A$(20,2)
20  FOR I = 1 TO 20
30    INPUT "NAME",A$(I,1)
40    INPUT "ADDRESS",A$(I,2)
50  NEXT I
60  INPUT "NAME OF PERSON",K$
70  N = 20: GOSUB 1000
80  IF F = 2 THEN PRINT A$(P3,2)
90  STOP
```

Note. Necessary changes to the binary search are all references to table V being changed to table A$(X,1) where X is either P1, P2 or P3 as defined in the program. The key K must also be changed to K$. The lines that must be modified are 1040,1070,1100,2010,2020,2030.

4

```
 10 REM..GLOSSARY
 20 REM..A$ 2D TABLE, T$ 1D TABLE
 30 REM..M NUMBER OF ENTRIES
 40 REM..N NUMBER OF ENTRIES TO BE SORTED
 50 REM..X POSITION OF FIRST ENTRY
 60 REM..K KEY 1-PRIMARY, 2-SECONDARY
 70 REM..S DIRECTION OF SORT 0-ASCENDING, 1-DESCENDING
 80 REM..I,J,P,C SUBSCRIPTS
 90 DIM A$(20,3),T$(3)
100 INPUT "NUMBER OF ENTRIES",M
110 REM..INPUT DATA TO TABLE
120 FOR I=1 TO M
130   INPUT "SEX",A$(I,1)
140   INPUT "YOB",A$(I,2)
150   INPUT "NAME",A$(I,3)
160 NEXT I
170 GOSUB 290
180 REM..SORT TABLE ON PRIMARY KEY - SEX
190 N=M:X=1:K=1:S=1:GOSUB 340
200 REM..SORT MALES ON SECONDARY KEY - YOB
210 FOR I=1 TO M-1
220   IF A$(I,1)<>A$(I+1,1) THEN 240
230 NEXT I
240 N=I:X=1:K=2:S=0:GOSUB 340
250 REM..SORT FEMALES ON SECONDARY KEY - YOB
260 N=M:X=I+1:K=2:S=0:GOSUB 340
270 GOSUB 290
280 STOP
290 REM..CONTENTS OF TABLE A$
300 FOR I=1 TO M
310   PRINT A$(I,1),A$(I,2),A$(I,3)
320 NEXT I
330 RETURN
340 REM..SUBROUTINE TO SORT DATA
350 FOR P=X TO N-1
360    FOR C=X TO N-1
370       IF S=1 THEN 410
380          IF A$(C,K)<=A$(C+1,K) THEN 400
390             GOSUB 460
400          GOTO 430
410          IF A$(C,K)>=A$(C+1,K) THEN 430
420             GOSUB 460
430    NEXT C
440 NEXT P
450 RETURN
460 REM..SWAP KEYS
470 FOR J=1 TO 3
480   T$(J)=A$(C,J):A$(C,J)=A$(C+1,J)
490 NEXT J
500 FOR J=1 TO 3
510   A$(C+1,J)=T$(J)
520 NEXT J
530 RETURN
```

5 The procedures required to solve this problem are set out in diagramatic form below.

Procedure 1. Store extension numbers and names in tables X and Y$ respectively, and their positions (subscripts) in tables X2 and Y1.

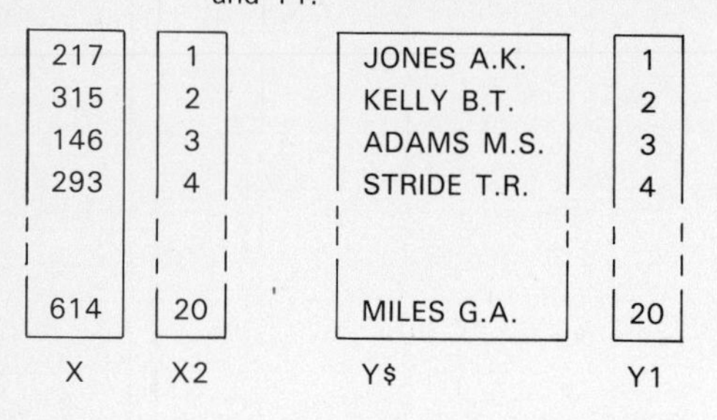

Procedure 2. Sort extension numbers and names, moving their original positions as stored in X2 and Y1.

X	X2	Y$	Y1
146	3	ADAMS M.S.	3
217	1	JONES A.K.	1
293	4	KELLY B.T.	2
315	2	MILES G.A.	20
614	20	STRIDE T.R.	4

Procedure 3. For the contents of each cell of X2 search Y1 for the same value, create a new table X1 containing the subscripts of Y1 where the pointers match. The contents of X2 and Y1 are known as pointers.

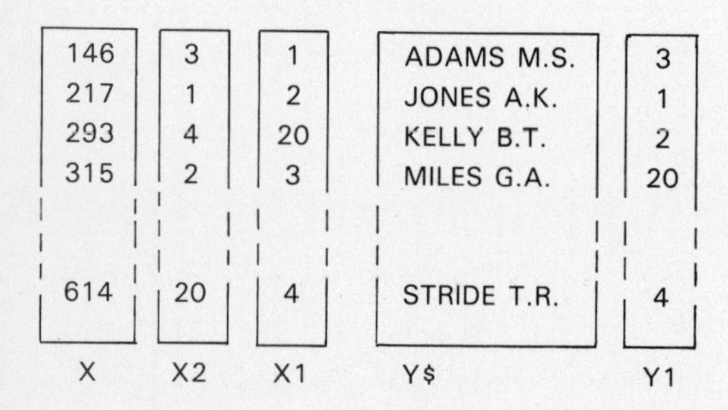

Procedure 4. Repeat procedure 3 only this time for the contents of each cell of Y1 search X2 for the same value and overwrite Y1 with the subscript of X2 where the pointers match. Table X2 is of no further use after this procedure is complete.

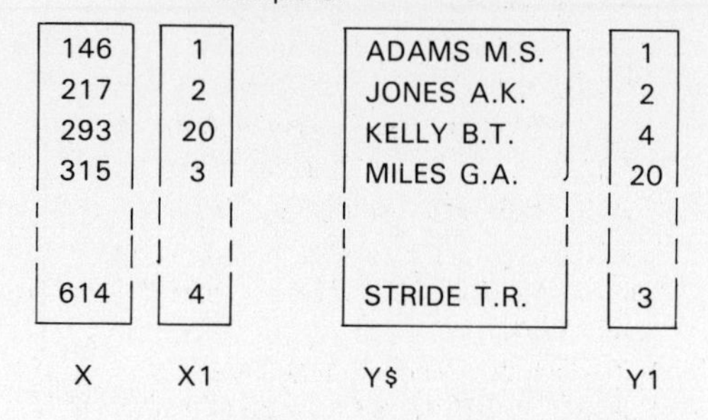

Procedure 5. If an extension number is known (e.g. 315) table X is searched using the binary search, and a match is found at X(4), the name being located at Y$(X1(4)).
Alternatively, if a name is known (e.g. STRIDE T.R.) table Y1 is searched using the binary search and a match is found at Y$(20) and the extension number is located at X(Y1(20)).

Comment. Since it was necessary to perform linear searches through tables Y1 and X2 in order to set up a system of pointers, the reader may wonder why a linear search was not used in the original unsorted data? In practice once the pointers have been allocated the search time for extension numbers or names is greatly reduced using the binary search method. If this method was to be incorporated into a telephone directory system, procedures 1 through 4 would only be run once as part of the system initialisation.

Chapter 15

1

```
10   INPUT "ENTER TIME AS FOUR DIGITS e.g. 1436",T$
20   GOSUB 1000
30   IF F = 1 THEN PRINT "ERROR": GOTO 10
40   STOP

1000 F = 0
1010 REM · · test for length of string
1020 IF LEN (T$) <> 4 THEN F = 1: RETURN
1030 REM · · test for digits
1040 FOR I = 1 TO 4
1050   IF MID$(T$,I,1) < "0" OR MID$(T$,I,1) > "9" THEN F = 1: RETURN
1060 NEXT I
1070 REM · · test for range
1080 IF LEFT$(T$,2) > "23" OR RIGHT$(T$,2) > "59" THEN F = 1
1090 RETURN
```

2

```
 10 DIM M$(12),D(12)
 20 FOR I=1 TO 12
 30   READ M$(I),D(I)
 40 NEXT I
 50 DATA JAN,31,FEB,28,MAR,31,APR,30,MAY,31,JUN,30
 60 DATA JUL,31,AUG,31,SEP,30,OCT,31,NOV,30,DEC,31
 70 GOSUB 150
 80 GOSUB 200
 90 IF F=1 THEN 70
100 GOSUB 270
110 IF F=1 THEN 70
120 PRINT MONTH$,DAY$
130 STOP
140 REM..
150 REM..INPUT DATE
160 INPUT "DATE IN FORMAT MMMDD eg MAR18",D$
170 IF LEN(D$)>5 THEN 150
180 RETURN
190 REM..
200 REM..VALIDATE MONTH
210 F=0:MONTH$=LEFT$(D$,3)
220 FOR I=1 TO 12
230   IF MONTH$=M$(I) THEN RETURN
240 NEXT I
250 F=1:PRINT "ERROR-RE ENTER DATE":RETURN
260 REM..
270 REM..VALIDATE DAY
280 F=0:DAY$=RIGHT$(D$,2)
290 IF LEN(D$)=4 OR MID$(D$,4,1)=" " THEN DAY$="0"+RIGHT$(D$,1)
300 FOR J=1 TO 2
310   T$=MID$(DAY$,J,1)
320   IF T$<"0" OR T$>"9" THEN F=1:PRINT "ERROR-RE ENTER DATE":RETURN
330 NEXT J
340 IF VAL(DAY$)<=D(I) THEN RETURN
350 F=1:PRINT "ERROR-RE ENTER DATE":RETURN
```

```
10 REM..GLOSSARY
20 REM..U$ TABLE OF VALID USERS-ACCOUNT NO., PASSWORD, LAST LOGIN
30 REM..TIME CURRENT TIME -24 HR CLOCK
40 REM..A$ ACCOUNT NO., P$ PASSWORD
50 REM..X$,Y$,T$ SUBSTRINGS OF A$ OR P$
60 REM..F ERROR FLAG, I SUBSCRIPT
70 REM..H CURRENT HOUR, M CURRENT MINUTE
80 REM..H1, M1 HOUR AND MINUTE OF LAST LOGIN
90 REM..LAPSE   TIME SINCE LAST LOGIN IN MINUTES
100 DIM U$(10,3)
110 FOR I=1 TO 10
120   READ U$(I,1),U$(I,2),U$(I,3)
130 NEXT I
140 DATA TP000101,ALPHA00001,101500
150 DATA PS001234,BETA000025,093000
160 DATA PS003456,BETA111111,175000
170 DATA PS010101,ALPHA10101,113000
180 DATA TP112233,OMEGA77777,114500
190 DATA TP001007,OMEGA00001,120000
200 DATA PS000011,BETA234543,114500
210 DATA PS987654,OMEGA19203,120100
220 DATA PS000234,EPSILON001,115500
230 DATA TP155555,OMEGA55555,135000
240 INPUT "HOUR",HOUR
250 INPUT "MINUTE",MIN
260 TIME=((HOUR*60+MIN)*60)*100
270 GOSUB 410
280 GOSUB 470
290 IF F=1 THEN PRINT "ERROR":GOTO 270
300 GOSUB 560
310 GOSUB 610
320 IF F=1 THEN PRINT "ERROR":GOTO 300
330 GOSUB 710
340 IF F=1 THEN PRINT "ILLEGAL USER":GOTO 270
350 GOSUB 780
360 IF F=1 THEN PRINT "TIME OF LAST LOGIN WITHIN LAST 30 MIN":GOTO 270
370 PRINT "SECURITY CHECK O.K."
380 STOP
390 REM..
400 REM..INPUT ACCOUNT NO
410 INPUT "ACCOUNT NO.",A$
420 IF LEN(A$)<>8 THEN PRINT "ERROR":GOTO 410
430 X$=LEFT$(A$,2):Y$=RIGHT$(A$,6)
440 RETURN
450 REM..
460 REM..VALIDATE SYNTAX OF ACCOUNT NO
470 F=0
480 IF X$<>"TP" AND X$<>"PS" THEN F=1:RETURN
490 FOR I=1 TO 6
500   T$=MID$(Y$,I,1)
510   IF T$<"0" OR T$>"9" THEN F=1:RETURN
520 NEXT I
530 RETURN
540 REM..
550 REM..INPUT PASSWORD
560 INPUT "PASSWORD",P$
570 IF LEN(P$)<>10 OR (LEFT$(P$,1)<"A" OR LEFT$(P$,1)>"Z") THEN PRINT "ERROR":GOTO 56
580 RETURN
590 REM..
600 REM..VALIDATE SYNTAX OF PASSWORD
610 F=0
620 FOR I=2 TO 10
630    T$=MID$(P$,I,1)
640    IF (T$>="0" AND T$<="9") THEN 670
650 IF (T$>="A" AND T$<="Z") THEN 670
660      F=1
670 NEXT I
680 RETURN
```

```
690 REM
700 REM..CHECK ON VALIDITY OF USER
710 F=0
720 FOR I=1 TO 10
730   IF (X$+Y$=U$(I,1)) AND P$=U$(I,2) THEN RETURN
740 NEXT I
750 F=1:RETURN
760 REM
770 REM..CHECK ON TIME OF LAST LOGIN
780 F=0
790 H=(TIME DIV 360000)MOD 24
800 M=(TIME DIV 6000)MOD 60
810 H1=VAL(LEFT$(U$(I,3),2))
820 M1=VAL(MID$(U$(I,3),3,2))
830 LAPSE=60*(H-H1)+(M-M1)
840 IF LAPSE >30 THEN RETURN
850 F=1:RETURN
```

Chapter 16

The answers to the questions given at the end of this chapter will be written in pseudocode to allow a flexibility in the use of BASIC dialects.

1

```
open stock file for output
FOR record counter = 1 TO 20
    input stock number
    input description
    input stock quantity
    input unit price
    format record
    write record
NEXT record counter
close stock file
stop
```

Note. The text adequately covers the sorting of computer files – one of the suggested methods should be used.

2

```
open stock file for input
print first line (STOCK REPORT)
print second line (STOCK NO. DESCRIPTION.......)
initialise total stock value to zero
read record
WHILE not end of file DO
    calculate stock value
    increase total stock value
    format record fields
    print record line
    read record
ENDWHILE
print total value
close file
stop
```

3 The design of this program is very similar to the design given in the first answer and will not be repeated here.

4

```
open subscribers file for input
print first line (SUBSCRIBERS)
print second line (NAME TELEPHONE.........)
read record
WHILE not end of file DO
    calculate units used
    format record fields
    print record line
    read record
ENDWHILE
close file
stop
```

5

```
open building society file for input
print first line (THE HAPPY HOMES.......)
print second line (DETAILS OF.......)
read record
WHILE not end of file DO
    store branch code
    initialise shares to zero
    print third line (BRANCH CODE.....)
    print fourth line (ACCOUNT NUMBER.....)
    WHILE same branch code and not end of file DO
      format record fields
      print record line
      increase shares total
      read record
    ENDWHILE
    print shares total
ENDWHILE
close file
stop
```

6

```
open estate agent file for input
print first line (HOLMES & HOLMES........)
read record
WHILE not end of file DO
    print second line (PROPERTY TYPE:)
    CASE property type OF
    WHEN "A"
      print detached
    WHEN "B"
      print semi-detached
    WHEN "C"
      print terraced
    WHEN "D"
      print "bungalow"
    OTHERWISE
      print maisonette/flat
    ENDCASE
    print third line (VENDOR ADDRESS.........)
    initialise property counter to zero
    store property code
    WHILE same property and not end of file DO
      format record
      print record line
      IF tenure = "F" THEN
        print freehold
      ELSE
        print leasehold
      ENDIF
      increase property counter by 1
      read record
    ENDWHILE
    print total number of properties
ENDWHILE
close file
stop
```

Chapter 17

With the exception of the answer to question 4, solutions to the questions at the end of this chapter will be written in pseudocode.

1

```
open three files (A,B,C) for input
open merge file D for output
read file A
read file B
read file C
WHILE not end of three files DO
    IF key A < key B and key A < key C THEN
      write record A to file D
      read file A
    ELSE
      IF key B < key A and key B < key C THEN
        write record B to file D
        read file B
      ELSE
        write record C to file D
        read file C
      ENDIF
    ENDIF
ENDWHILE
close files
stop
```

2

```
open transaction file for input
open master file for input
open update master file for output
open payslip file for output
read transaction file
read master file
WHILE not end of both files DO
    IF key A < key B THEN
        print error message
        read transaction file
    ELSE
        IF key A = key B THEN
            calculate gross income
            calculate pension
            calculate income tax
            format new master record
            write update master record
            format fields of pay-slip
            write lines to pay-slip file
            read transaction file
            read master file
        ELSE
            write update from master record
            read master file
        ENDIF
    ENDIF
ENDWHILE
close files
stop
```

3

```
open transaction file A for input
open master file B for input
open updated master file C for output
read transaction file
read master file
WHILE not end of both files DO
    IF key A < key B THEN
        IF transaction code = 3 THEN
            format new master record
            write updated master record
            read transaction file
        ELSE
            print error
            read transaction file
        ENDIF
    ELSE
        IF key A = key B THEN
            IF transaction code = 1 THEN
                format new master record
                write updated new master record
                read master file
                read transaction file
            ELSE
                IF transaction code = 2 THEN
                    read master file
                    read transaction file
                ELSE
                    print error
                    read transaction file
                ENDIF
            ENDIF
        ELSE
            write updated master record from master
            read master file
        ENDIF
    ENDIF
ENDWHILE
close files
stop
```

```
 10 REM..GLOSSARY
 20 REM..P,M,F,R TABLES CONTAINING NUMBER OF COLLISIONS
 30 REM..I LOOP COUNTER
 40 REM..R AVAILABLE RECORD AREA 30 OR 60
 50 REM..X NUMERIC KEY X$ ALPHANUMERIC KEY
 60 REM..K$ AND K USED TO HASH KEY X
 70 REM..E HASHED KEY VALUE
 80 REM..CP,CM,CF,CR NUMBER OF COLLISIONS USING RESPECTIVE ALGORITHMS
 90 REM..
100 DIM P(60),M(60),F(60),R(60)
110 R=30:PROCINITIALISE
120 PROCREADHASH
130 PROCPRINTCOLLISIONS
140 RESTORE:R=60:PROCINITIALISE
150 R=60:PROCREADHASH
160 PROCPRINTCOLLISIONS
170 STOP
180 REM..
190 DEF FNPRIME(X,R)
200 =X MOD (R-1)+1
210 REM..
220 DEF FNMID(X,R)
230 LOCAL K$,K
240 K$=STR$(X*X)
250 K=VAL(MID$(K$,4,2))
260 =K MOD (R-1)+1
270 REM..
280 DEF FNFOLD(X,R)
290 LOCAL K$,K
300 K$=STR$(X)
310 K=VAL(LEFT$(K$,3))+VAL(MID$(K$,4,3))+VAL(RIGHT$(K$,3))
320 =K MOD R +1
330 REM..
340 DEF FNRADIX(X,R)
350 LOCAL K$,K,I
360 K$=STR$(X)
370 K=0
380 FOR I=LEN(K$) TO 1 STEP -1
390     K=K+VAL(MID$(K$,I,1))*(11^(LEN(K$)-I))
400 NEXT I
410 =K MOD R +1
420 REM..
430 DEF FNCONVERT(X$)
440 LOCAL K,I
450 K=0
460 FOR I=1 TO LEN(X$)
470      K=K+(9^I)*ASC(MID$(X$,I,1))
480 NEXT I
490 =K
500 REM..
510 DEF PROCINITIALISE
520 FOR I=1 TO 60:P(I)=-1:M(I)=-1:F(I)=-1:R(I)=-1:NEXT I
530 ENDPROC
540 REM..
550 DEF PROCREADHASH
560 FOR I=1 TO 20
570    READ X$:X=FNCONVERT(X$)
580    E=FNPRIME(X,R):P(E)=P(E)+1
590    E=FNMID(X,R):M(E)=M(E)+1
600    E=FNFOLD(X,R):F(E)=F(E)+1
610    E=FNRADIX(X,R):R(E)=R(E)+1
620 NEXT I
630 ENDPROC
```

```
640 REM..
650 DEF PROCPRINTCOLLISIONS
660 CP=0:CM=0:CF=0:CR=0
670 FOR I=1 TO R
680   IF P(I)>0 THEN CP=CP+P(I)
690   IF M(I)>0 THEN CM=CM+M(I)
700   IF F(I)>0 THEN CF=CF+F(I)
710   IF R(I)>0 THEN CR=CR+R(I)
720 NEXT I
730 PRINT "NUMBER OF COLLISIONS WITH ";R;" RECORD AREAS"
740 PRINT
750 PRINT "PRIME",CP
760 PRINT "MID-SQUARE",CM
770 PRINT "FOLDING",CF
780 PRINT "RADIX",CR
790 PRINT:PRINT
800 ENDPROC
810 REM..
820 DATA BEEVERS,HERN,KINDER,MORAN,HOLMES
830 DATA SOPERS,MCKENNA,CLARKE,HARPER,OWENS
840 DATA GRUNDY,STOTT,SCURRY,HICKS,TOPLEY
850 DATA OLDHAM,MORTON,WALSH,SMITH,WHELDON
```

5/6 In this answer a two-dimensional table is used to store information about which time slots throughout the week are free and which are already booked. A free slot is designated by storing 0, and a booked slot by storing 1. This table is used in conjunction with the relative file in order to gain access to the relative file. When the user wants to exit from the system the contents of this table is written to serial file so that the table may be restored to its current state when the system is used again.

The system is menu driven as follows:

DO YOU REQUIRE:

1. AN APPOINTMENT
2. TO CANCEL
3. INFORMATION FROM THE FILE
4. EXIT SYSTEM

The system contains the following procedures.

procedure initialise
procedure book an appointment
procedure cancel an appointment
procedure list information from the file
procedure finish

```
main program

call procedure initialise
print menu
input menu code (1,2,3,4)
WHILE menu-code not = 4 DO
    IF menu-code = 1 THEN
        call procedure book appointment
    ELSE
        IF menu-code = 2 THEN
            call procedure cancel an appointment
        ELSE
            call procedure list information from file
        ENDIF
    ENDIF
    print menu
    input menu-code (1,2,3,4)
ENDWHILE
call procedure finish
stop

PROC initialise
  open relative file
  open serial file
  read serial file record
  move record to table
  WHILE not end of serial file DO
      read serial file record
      move record to table
  ENDWHILE
  close serial file
ENDPROC

PROC book appointment
  input day and session
  convert day and session to code
  set error flag to 1
  WHILE slot not > 12 or error flag not = 0 DO
      IF appointment slot in table = 0 THEN
          set error flag to 0
          set appointment slot in table to 1
      ELSE
          set error flag to 1
      ENDIF
  ENDWHILE
  IF error flag = 0 THEN
      input details of patient
      write patient's details to relative file
  ELSE
      print appointments fully booked
  ENDIF
ENDPROC

PROC cancel an appointment
  input day and session
  input slot number
  delete record in relative file
  set appointment slot in table to 0
ENDPROC

PROC list information in file
  WHILE session not > 10 DO
      print heading
      WHILE slot not > 12 DO
          IF appointment slot = 0 THEN
              print slot number free
          ELSE
              print slot number
              read record from relative file
              print name of patient
          ENDIF
      ENDWHILE
  ENDWHILE
ENDPROC

PROC finish
  open serial file for output
  WHILE session not > 10 DO
      move row of table to output record
      write record to serial file
  ENDWHILE
  close files
ENDPROC
```

Chapter 19

1

```
 10 INPUT "LENGTH OF SIDE",L
 20 INPUT "NUMBER OF SIDES",N
 30 X=180-(90*(2*N-4)/N)
 40 CLS:MODE 0
 50 X1=600:Y1=500
 60 MOVE X1+L,Y1
 70 FOR A=X TO 360 STEP X
 80   D1=COS(PI/180*A):D2=SIN(PI/180*A)
 90   DRAW X1+L*D1,Y1+L*D2
100 NEXT A
110 STOP
```

2

```
 10 MODE 0
 20 R=200:X1=600:Y1=500
 30 GOSUB 100
 40 R=50
 50 FOR A=0 TO 360 STEP 20
 55    X1=600+250*COS(A*PI/180):Y1=500+250*SIN(A*PI/180)
 60    GOSUB 100
 70 NEXT A
 80 STOP
100 FOR ANGLE=0 TO 360
110       LET ANG=ANGLE*PI/180
120       LET X=R*COS(ANG)
130       LET Y=R*SIN(ANG)
140       PLOT 69,X+X1,Y+Y1
150 NEXT ANGLE
160 RETURN
```

3

```
10 MODE 0
20 INPUT "A",A
30 INPUT "E",E
40 CLS
50 FOR ANGLE =0 TO 360
60    ANG=ANGLE*PI/180
70    LET R=A*(1+E*COS(ANG))
80    PLOT 69,600+R*SIN(ANG),500+R*COS(ANG)
90 NEXT ANGLE
```

4

```
 10 REM..GLOSSARY
 20 REM..B$ 3X3 TABLE REPRESENTING BOARD
 30 REM..R,C ROW AND COLUMN
 40 REM..CX,CY POSITION OF CENTRE FOR EACH SQUARE OF BOARD ON SCREEN
 50 REM..P$ PLAYER X OR 0
 60 REM..W FLAG - 0 GAME IN PLAY,1 WINNER,2 STALE MATE
 70 REM..ANGLE, ANG, X1, X2 USED INPLOTTING 0 - SEE TEXT
 80 DIM B$(3,3)
 90 VDU 28,0,31,19,28
100 MODE 5
110 GCOL 0,2
120 REM..
130 REM..DRAW BOARD ON SCREEN
140 MOVE 250,250
150 DRAW 250,1000:DRAW 1000,1000:DRAW 1000,250:DRAW 250,250
160 MOVE 500,250:DRAW 500,1000
170 MOVE 750,250:DRAW 750,1000
180 MOVE 250,500:DRAW 1000,500
190 MOVE 250,750:DRAW 1000,750
200 FOR R=1 TO 3:FOR C=1 TO 3
210   B$(R,C)=" "
220 NEXT C:NEXT R
230 REM..
240 REM..PLAY GAME
```

```
250 REPEAT
260     PRINT TAB(0,29);"YOUR MOVE":INPUT R,C
270     IF R<1 OR R>3 THEN 260
280     IF C<1 OR C>3 THEN 260
290     IF B$(R,C)<>" " THEN 260
300     CX=250*C+125:CY=1250-(250*R+125)
310     B$(R,C)="X":GOSUB 610
320     P$="X":GOSUB 470
330     IF W=1 THEN 420
340     PRINT TAB(0,29);"                        "
350     PRINT TAB(0,30);"                  "
360     GOSUB 780
370     CX=250*C+125:CY=1250-(250*R+125)
380     IF W=2 THEN 420
390     GOSUB 680
400     IF W=1 THEN 420
410     P$="O":GOSUB 470
420 UNTIL W=1 OR W=2
430 PRINT TAB(0,30);"            "
440 END
450 REM..
460 REM..CHECK FOR WINNING LINE
470 W=0
480 FOR R=1 TO 3
490   IF B$(R,1)+B$(R,2)+B$(R,3)=P$+P$+P$ THEN 570
500 NEXT R
510 FOR C=1 TO 3
520   IF B$(1,C)+B$(2,C)+B$(3,C)=P$+P$+P$ THEN 570
530 NEXT C
540 IF B$(1,1)+B$(2,2)+B$(3,3)=P$+P$+P$ THEN 570
550 IF B$(1,3)+B$(2,2)+B$(3,1)=P$+P$+P$ THEN 570
560 RETURN
570 W=1:PRINT TAB(0,29);"PLAYER ";P$;" WINS"
580 RETURN
590 REM..
600 REM..DRAW X
610 MOVE CX+53,CY+53
620 DRAW CX-53,CY-53
630 MOVE CX-53,CY+53
640 DRAW CX+53,CY-53
650 RETURN
660 REM..
670 REM..DRAW O
680 FOR ANGLE=0 TO 360 STEP 20
690   ANG=ANGLE*PI/180
700   X1=75*COS(ANG)
710   Y1=75*SIN(ANG)
720   PLOT 69,X1+CX,Y1+CY
730 NEXT ANGLE
740 RETURN
750 REM..
760 REM..COMPUTER TO MAKE MOVE FOR O
770 REM..CHECK EACH ROW TO BLOCK 2 X'S
780 FOR R=1 TO 3:S$="":FOR C=1 TO 3
790   IF B$(R,C)="X" THEN S$=S$+"X"
800 NEXT C
810 IF S$<>"XX" THEN 850
820 IF B$(R,1)=" " THEN B$(R,1)="O":C=1:RETURN
830 IF B$(R,2)=" " THEN B$(R,2)="O":C=2:RETURN
840 IF B$(R,3)=" " THEN B$(R,3)="O":C=3:RETURN
850 NEXT R
860 REM..
870 REM..CHECK EACH COLUMN TO BLOCK 2 X'S
880 FOR C=1 TO 3:S$="":FOR R=1 TO 3
890  IF B$(R,C)="X" THEN S$=S$+"X"
900 NEXT R
910 IF S$<>"XX" THEN 980
920 IF B$(1,C)=" " THEN B$(1,C)="O":R=1:RETURN
930 IF B$(2,C)=" " THEN B$(2,C)="O":R=2:RETURN
940 IF B$(3,C)=" " THEN B$(3,C)="O":R=3:RETURN
950 NEXT C
```

```
960 REM..
970 REM..CHECK EACH DIAGONAL TO BLOCK 2 X'S
980 S$=""
990 FOR R=1 TO 3
1000   IF B$(R,R)="X" THEN S$=S$+"X"
1010 NEXT R
1020 IF S$<>"XX" THEN 1060
1030 IF B$(1,1)=" " THEN B$(1,1)="O":R=1:C=1:RETURN
1040 IF B$(2,2)=" " THEN B$(2,2)="O":R=2:C=2:RETURN
1050 IF B$(3,3)=" " THEN B$(3,3)="O":R=3:C=3:RETURN
1060 S$=""
1070 FOR R=1 TO 3
1080   IF B$(R,4-R)="X" THEN S$=S$+"X"
1090 NEXT R
1100 IF S$<>"XX" THEN 1160
1110 IF B$(1,3)=" " THEN B$(1,3)="O":R=1:C=3:RETURN
1120 IF B$(2,2)=" " THEN B$(2,2)="O":R=2:C=2:RETURN
1130 IF B$(3,1)=" " THEN B$(3,1)="O":R=3:C=1:RETURN
1140 REM..
1150 REM..CHECK FOR NEXT VACANT SQUARE TO PLACE O
1160 FOR R=1 TO 3:FOR C=1 TO 3
1170   IF B$(R,C)=" " THEN B$(R,C)="O":RETURN
1180 NEXT C:NEXT R
1190 W=2:PRINT TAB(0,29);"STALE MATE"
1200 RETURN
```

5

```
10 MODE 0
20 GOSUB 170
30 GOSUB 250
40 GOSUB 400
50 GOSUB 470
60 MINTEMP=M
70 REPEAT
80   M=(TIME DIV 6000) MOD 60
90 UNTIL MINTEMP<>M
100 GCOL 0,0
110 MINANG=6*MINTEMP:HOURANG=30*H+(0.5*MINTEMP)
120 GOSUB 470
130 GCOL 0,1
140 GOSUB 400:GOTO 50
150 REM..
160 REM..INPUT TIME OF DAY
170 INPUT "HOUR",HOUR
180 INPUT "MINUTE",MIN
190 TIME=((HOUR*60+MIN)*60)*100
200 CLS
210 RETURN
220 REM..
230 REM..PLOT CIRCULAR CLOCK FACE
240 REM..DRAW 1/4 HOUR MARKS ON FACE
250 FOR ANGLE=0 TO 360
260    LET ANG=ANGLE*PI/180
270    X=350*COS(ANG)
280    Y=350*SIN(ANG)
290    PLOT 69,X+600,Y+500
300 NEXT ANGLE
310 MOVE 250,500:DRAW 300,500
320 MOVE 900,500:DRAW 950,500
330 MOVE 600,150:DRAW 600,200
340 MOVE 590,800:DRAW 590,850
350 MOVE 610,800:DRAW 610,850
360 RETURN
370 REM..
380 REM..CALCULATE CORRECT TIME
390 REM..CONVERT TIME INTO ANGLE
400 M=(TIME DIV 6000)MOD 60
410 H=(TIME DIV 360000)MOD 24
420 IF H>12 THEN H=H-12
430 MINANG=6*M:HOURANG=30*H+(0.5*M)
440 RETURN
```

```
450 REM..
460 REM..DRAW POSITION OF HANDS
470 MOVE 600,500
480 DRAW 600+200*SIN(HOURANG*PI/180),500+200*COS(HOURANG*PI/180)
490 MOVE 600,500
500 DRAW 600+250*SIN(MINANG*PI/180),500+250*COS(MINANG*PI/180)
510 RETURN
```

Chapter 20

1

```
 10 N=INT(9*RND(1)+1)
 20 PRINT N
 30 FOR I=1 TO N
 40    PRINT CHR$(7)
 50    FOR J=1 TO 1000:NEXT J
 60 NEXT I
 70 FOR J=1 TO 2000:NEXT J
 80 GOTO 10
```

2

```
 10 DIM P$(7)
 20 FOR I=1 TO 7
 30  READ P$(I)
 40 NEXT I
 50 DATA C53,D61,E69,F73,G81,A89,B97
 60 CLS
 70 INPUT "NAME OF NOTE",N$
 80 FOR I=1 TO 7
 90  IF LEFT$(N$,1)=LEFT$(P$(I),1) THEN P=VAL(RIGHT$(P$(I),2)):GOTO 120
100 NEXT I
110 PRINT "NOTE UNKNOWN":GOTO 70
120 IF LEN(N$)=1 THEN 140
130   IF RIGHT$(N$,1)="£" THEN P=P+4 ELSE P=P-4
140   SOUND 1,-15,P,40
150 STOP
```

3

```
 10 FOR I=1 TO 34
 20    READ PITCH,DURATION
 30    SOUND 1,-15,PITCH,DURATION
 40 NEXT I
 50 STOP
 60 DATA 109,5,129,10,129,5,137,10,145,5
 70 DATA 157,10,145,5,137,10,149,5,145,10
 80 DATA 129,5,129,5,137,5,145,5,137,10,125,5
 90 DATA 109,10,109,5,129,10,129,5,137,10,145,5
100 DATA 157,10,145,5,137,10,149,5,145,10
110 DATA 129,5,129,5,137,5,145,5,137,10,137,5,129,10
```

4

```
 10 ENVELOPE 2,1,2,-2,2,10,20,10,1,0,0,-1,100,100
 20 SOUND 1,2,100,100
```

Appendix II
Suggested programming projects

Suggested Programming Projects

The following questions can form the basis of examination project work. The level of suitability is given after each question.

1. Write a program to represent a *Currency Exchange Bureau* that converts up to ten foreign currencies into sterling.

A commission is charged on each transaction according to the following scale of charges.

Amount customer receives in Sterling	Commission
<£10	fixed charge 50p
£10 to <£100	fixed charge £1
£100 to <£1000	½% of exchange
£1000 to <£10000	1% of exchange
£10000 or above	1¼% of exchange

The system developed should allow for

a. New exchange rates to be input each day (obtainable from a bank or newspaper).

b. A *menu* driven system to allow the user to select a currency and input an amount to be exchanged.

c. The total transactions for each currency to be output at the close of trading.

d. The total commission to be output at the close of trading.

e. The amount to be exchanged, exchange rate, Sterling equivalent, commission and nett Sterling amount (Sterling equivalent less commission) to be output for each transaction.

2. Write a program to plot the trajectory of a missile fired at an angle θ to the horizontal ground, with an initial velocity of u ms^{-1}.

The equation of the trajectory is:

$$y = x\tan\theta - \frac{gx^2}{2u^2\cos^2\theta}$$

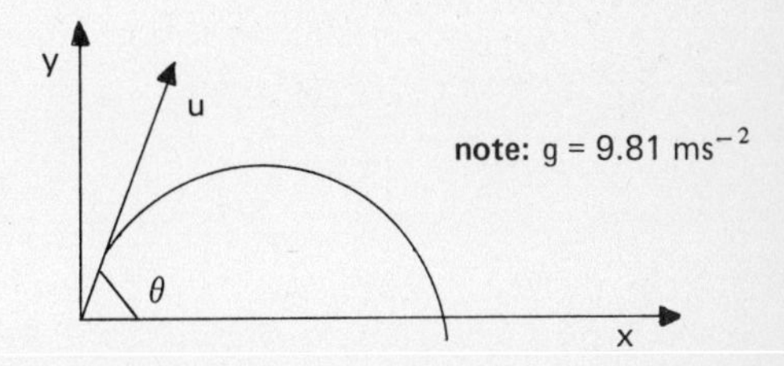

note: $g = 9.81\ ms^{-2}$

Different plots should be made for θ varying from 20° to 70° in steps of 5°.

A value of u should be chosen to give a convenient scale to the graph.

3. A minefield has been divided into a lattice having 5 rows facing North/South and 5 rows facing East/West.

A mine is buried at random at each of three squares of the lattice.

A remote controlled tank has to cross the minefield from North to South, moving one square at a time in either a North/South, South/North, East/West or West/East direction.

The result of moving to a square containing a buried mine is the total destruction of the tank.

Write a computer program to simulate the situation.

The computer should be used to generate the random position of the mines.

A remote operator instructs the computer where he wants the tank to move by specifying the co-ordinates of the square he wants it to move into.

The lattice of the minefield and the tanks route should be displayed before each new move.

NORTH

	1	2	3	4	5
1		*			
2	*	*			
3	*				
4	*	*	*	*	
5				*	

SOUTH

Note: The positions of the mines are **not** shown on the lattice, the * indicates the path the tank has taken. The tank can start from **any** square in the North.

4. Write a program that will allow:

a. the lengths of two sides and one internal angle

or

b. the lengths of three sides

or

c. the length of one side and the two internal angles at the extremities of a line

to be input as the minimum information to construct a triangle.

Calculate the sizes of the remaining angles and/or sides, the area of the triangle and the radius of both the inscribed circle and the circumcircle. Draw the triangle.

The reader may wish to make reference to the following information.

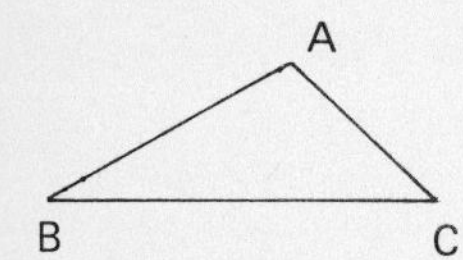

A,B,C – sizes of internal angles.
a,b,c – lengths of the three sides.
s – semi perimenter = $\frac{a + b + c}{2}$

$$\frac{a}{\text{SinA}} = \frac{b}{\text{SinB}} = \frac{c}{\text{SinC}} = 2R$$

$$a^2 = b^2 + c^2 - 2\,b\,c\cos A$$

Area of triangle $\Delta = \sqrt{s\,(s-a)\,(s-b)\,(s-c)}$

Radius of circumcircle $R = \frac{a\,b\,c}{4\Delta}$

Radius of inscribed circle $r = \frac{\Delta}{s}$

(standard: 'O/A' level or equivalent)

5. A builders merchants sells ballast at a flat rate of £2 per cubic metre. Two forms of discount are allowed:

a. A discount on bulk purchases according to the following table.

Ballast m^3	Discount %
<5	0
5 to <10	5
10 to <20	10
20 to <50	15
50 to <100	20
100 and over	25

b. A discount for prompt payment.

7% if payment is within one month.
3% if payment is within three months.

Design and write a program which will accept dated orders and produce invoices showing the discounts illustrated above.

Charge VAT at the current rate.

6. A teaching machine is used to test a student's ability at arithmetic – addition, subtraction, multiplication and division. However, the machine is to cater for a student's level of development in this subject by introducing levels of difficulty.

Level 1 (simple) uses integers in the range 1 – 10, except for division when the division is an integer in the range 1 – 5.

Level 2 (harder) uses integers in the range 10 – 19 except for divisors which are integers in the range 1 – 10.

Level 3 (difficult) uses integers in the range 20,99 and divisors in the range 10,19.

A random number generator should be used to generate numbers for different arithmetic problems.

Design and write a program to implement the teaching machine.

7. A small airline that operates flights to **one** destination uses a computer system to:

a. Provide an enquiry system regarding the number and type of seats available for a flight on a specified day.

b. Issue a single ticket to a passenger containing the following information.

i. Name of destination.
ii. Type of seat booked ie. first class or tourist class.

iii. Departure, arrival times and date.
iv. Cost of ticket.
v. Name of the passenger.

c. Output a passenger list for each flight.

Assume the following:

a. There is only **one** flight per day at different times over a period of five days. The airline operates from Monday to Friday only. The duration of the flight is 2 hours.

b. Every aeroplane used has a maximum of fifty seats, the distribution of first class seats to tourist class seats being 10 to 40 respectively.

c. A seat is bookable up to one week in advance but **not** on the day of the flight.

d. The cost of a first class seat is £50, whilst that of a tourist class seat is £30.

Write a computer program to implement the airline reservation system.

8. Store a passage of text in a serial file such that each line of text represents a record. Records will be of variable length since words will **not** be split between two lines.

Analyse the text line by line such that each **new** word on a line is stored in a table and the frequency of occurences of each word in the passage is also stored. For example:

Word	Frequency
TO	2
BE	2
OR	1
NOT	1
THAT	1
IS	1
THE	1
QUESTION	1

At the end of the passage the table should be sorted into descending order of usage of the words, and then the contents of the two-tables output.

Repeat the procedure for different passages of text.

9. Write a program to implement the Merge Sort described in Chapter 16 section 16.7.1.

10. A sequential file is used to store the details of library books. The format of a record on the file is:

book title	(30 characters)
catalogue index	(8 digits)
author(s)	(40 characters)
publisher	(20 characters)
status code	(1 character)
price	(4 digits)

where status code is

A for active
L for lost
D for damaged
E for external loan.

Design and write a program which will enable a librarian to up-date the file through amendment, deletion and insertion of records. The librarian should be able to obtain complete lists of old and new master files.

11. A college lecturer wants to hold on file the following details about his students.

Student number	(3 digits)
Surname	(20 characters)
Initial	(1 character)
Date of Birth	(6 digits)

Percentage examination marks for:

English language
Mathematics
Computer Studies
General Science
Geography
History.

The organisation of the file is relative, using student number as the key.

The college lecturer wants to be able to manipulate the contents of the file to:

a. Enrol students (enter surname, initial and date of birth), the student number should be generated by the system as the next available relative key.

b. Enter individual examination marks by subject.

c. Print out a list of all the students on the file together with their performance in each subject area.

d. Display records.

e. Amend and delete records.

Design and write a program to implement the system required by the college lecturer.

12. A popular restaurant will take table reservations one day in advance only, for lunches and evening meals.

There are twenty tables in the restaurant with a distribution of seating as follows.

Table Number	Seats per table
1,2,7,14,20	2
3,4,5,6,10,11,12,13	4
8,15,17,18,19	6
9,16	8

The restaurant proprietor has purchased a cheap microcomputer that includes a teleprinter for input of data and for the output of information. The machine has no secondary storage devices (ie. no backing store).

The proprietor wishes to use the micro computer for a table reservation system. He plans to use the computer between 9.00 a.m. to 12.00 midnight to take table reservations for the next day. At midnight he will obtain from the computer a complete listing of all the tables that have been reserved, and then switch the machine off.

The proprietor is not worried if the computer breaks down or is accidently switched off during the day since the system prints the details of every transaction as it occurs. In the event of the computer breaking down he would resort to a manual system for table reservations; alternatively if only the power had been switched off, he would switch the power back on and re-build the contents of memory from the print out of transactions prior to the failure.

The computer system should cater for the following features.

i. Allow an enquiry whether a table is vacant and reserve that table.
ii. Cancel a reservation.
iii. Obtain a printed listing of table reservations and vacant tables.

The proprietor wishes to impose certain restrictions on the computer reservations system, as follows.

iv. The restaurant will not cater for parties that exceed fourteen persons.
v. The computer system, in order to cater for parties of different numbers, will combine two **adjacent** tables when necessary.
vi. If as the result of combining tables more than one seat will not be occupied then the proprietor will refuse the reservation.

Design and write a program for this system.

BASIC Reserved Words Index

General Index